CHASING INNOVATION

PRINCETON STUDIES IN
CULTURE AND TECHNOLOGY

Tom Boellstorff and Bill Maurer, Series Editors

This series presents innovative work that extends classic ethnographic methods and questions into areas of pressing interest in technology and economics. It explores the varied ways new technologies combine with older technologies and cultural understandings to shape novel forms of subjectivity, embodiment, knowledge, place, and community. By doing so, the series demonstrates the relevance of anthropological inquiry to emerging forms of digital culture in the broadest sense.

Chasing Innovation

MAKING ENTREPRENEURIAL
CITIZENS IN MODERN INDIA

LILLY IRANI

PRINCETON UNIVERSITY PRESS

PRINCETON & OXFORD

Copyright © 2019 by Princeton University Press

Published by Princeton University Press
41 William Street, Princeton, New Jersey 08540
6 Oxford Street, Woodstock, Oxfordshire OX20 1TR

press.princeton.edu

Library of Congress Control Number 2018949928
Cloth ISBN 978-0-691-17513-3
Paperback ISBN 978-0-691-17514-0

British Library Cataloging-in-Publication Data is available

Editorial: Fred Appel and Thalia Leaf
Production Editorial: Jill Harris
Cover Design: Layla Mac Rory
Cover Credit: Design for a lota, based on original art by Avnish Mehta
Production: Erin Suydam
Publicity: Tayler Lord
Copyeditor: Anita O'Brien

This book has been composed in Arno Pro.

Printed on acid-free paper. ∞

Printed in the United States of America

10 9 8 7 6 5 4 3 2 1

Of course, no one man could have possibly designed the Lota. The number of combinations of factors to be considered gets to be astronomical—no one man designed the Lota, but many men over many generations.

The hope for and the reason for such an institute as we describe is that it will hasten the production of the "Lotas" of our time.

—RAY AND CHARLES EAMES, *THE INDIA REPORT* (1958)

A lota and water bottle re-engineered as cooling vessels in rural Andhra Pradesh.

FIGURE 1. Red Hat Linux, Delhi launch event,
December 22, 2010. (Photograph by author)

If the subject does not dream of controlling the agency of capital, capital does not move.

—GAYATRI SPIVAK, "MEGACITY" (2000)

CONTENTS

FIGURES

ACKNOWLEDGMENTS

THIS BOOK owes its development to so many places, people, and institutions.

Paul Dourish was the first to brave the whole manuscript draft, cover to cover. He models intellectual fearlessness, having tread paths from computer science to social theory long before I did. He gives his students a long rope, even to critique, historicize, and challenge the values and assumptions of human-computer interaction and information studies. Kavita Philip and Keith Murphy have been generous and rigorous interdisciplinarians. From Keith by way of Garfinkel, I learned that cultural imaginaries do not simply have agency; people are not cultural dopes. From Kavita Philip, I learned to see capitalism, socialism, gender, race, and sexuality as analytics for understanding the workings of contemporary technology, its subjects, and our methodologies for representing and intervening. Gillian Hayes, Judith Gregory, Melissa Mazmanian, and Bonnie Nardi generously offered mentorship and support. I am grateful to UCI's rich interdisciplinary programs in critical theory, women's studies, and arts, computation, and engineering for creating radically interdisciplinary space for reworking research practice as worldly intervention.

Geof Bowker, Susan Leigh Star, Lucy Suchman, Fred Turner, and Erica Robles-Anderson were particularly influential throughout the development of this work. Leigh Star passed suddenly and far too soon, but, through her writing and friends, her energy and critical generosity stay with many of us still.

Laura Portwood-Stacer was an ideal development editor and reader. She helped translate my arguments and data into stories with momentum. Tom Boellstorff, Bill Maurer, and Fred Appel offered encouragement and thoughtful questions as series and acquisition editors at Princeton. I thank Anita O'Brien for editing the copy. Librarians at UC Irvine and UC San Diego, especially Gayatri Singh, provided invaluable assistance locating historical documents.

At UC San Diego, Chandra Mukerji, Fernando Dominguez Rubio, Christo Sims, Angela Booker, Kelly Gates, and Shawna Kidman contributed ongoing support and comments. Chandra deserves special appreciation for creating the writing circle that kept us developing our work in collaboration. Saiba Varma and Kalindi Vora offered extended conversations on labor, development, and

South Asia. Peter Gourevitch and Latha Varadarjan put forward key provocations on political science questions. Vijayendra Rao deserves special thanks for reading the whole manuscript and pointing me to rich policy work on participation and democracy. The Science Studies Colloquium audience, especially David Pedersen and Kamala Visweswaran, posed challenging questions that forced me to draw my claims into higher relief.

Networked collectives also offered intellectual energy and input on the manuscript along the way. Labor-tech, sustained by Winifred Poster, offered fertile video-mediated collaboration with Itty Abraham, Sareeta Amrute, Aneesh Aneesh, Tom Boellstorff, Megan Finn, Ellie Harmon, Ilana Gershon, Karl Mendonca, Anil Menon, Geeta Patel, Sreela Sarkar, Luke Stark, and Stephanie Steinhardt and so many others. The Clouds and Crowds Working Group, supported by the University of California, reinforced my interest in questions of subjects, objects, and collective kinds. I am especially indebted to comments and framings by Tim Choy, Cori Hayden, Chris Kelty, and Lawrence Cohen. Advice and commiseration through my online writing community—coaches and comrades include Nicholas D'Avella, Lisbeth Fuisz, Laura Forlano, Alan Klima, and Sarah McCullough, and others thanked below—were essential in developing a healthy relationship to writing.

At the Spaces of Technoscience Workshop organized by Itty Abraham at National University of Singapore, Priti Ramamurthy and Amit Prasad made particularly helpful comments. The Digital South Asia workshop at the University of Michigan, especially Matt Hull, Purnima Mankekar, Aswin Punatambekar, gave helpful comments on an early sketch of the book argument. At the Digital Cultures Research Lab, comments by Armin van Beverungen and Wendy Chun encouraged my emphasis on infrastructure and time. At the Society for Advanced Research in Santa Fe, Lily Chumley dissected with me the ways political economy and political desire condition creative future making. Tom Rodden, in a fleeting comment at the SIGCHI Doctoral Consortium in 2010, asked me to pay attention to ethnomethods of drawing others close or keeping them far; this influenced my analysis of consultancy, labor infrastructure, and film. Steven Jackson raised the persistent question of hope.

Many of the insights of research emerge in kitchens, coffee shops, and carpools. I appreciate the supportive copresence of my writing circles; at UC San Diego, this included Amy Cimini, Paloma Checo-Gismero, Ben Cowan, Claire Edington, Ari Heinrich, Roshy Kheshti, Simeon Man, Dan Navon, Saiba Varma, Nir Shafir, and Matt Vitz. In New York, Anand Vaidya and Nishita Trisal raised crucial questions about politics and the specificities of Delhi. Morgan Ames, Lilly Nguyen, Daniela Rosner, and Shinjoung Yeo offered writing fellowship and critical dialogue on technology. Fellow students (at the time) Marisa Brandt, Marisa Cohn, Ellie Harmon, Martha Kenney,

Silvia Lindtner, Lilly Nguyen (again!), Raphaelle Rabanes, Six Silberman, and Amanda Williams have forged paths through critical theory, feminist science and technology studies, and activism. Anand Vaidya, Jyothi Nataranjan, Jane Lynch, Raghu Karnad, and Shruti Ravindran worked through Delhi's political histories and social networks. Colleagues at the Laboratory for Ubiquitous Computing and Interaction, especially Eric Baumer, Jed Brubaker, Lynn Dombrowski, and Sen Hirano, gave support and critical dialogues on design. Postdocs Charlotte Lee, Katie Pine, Irina Shklovski, and Janet Vertesi stepped up as mentors time and time again. Marc da Costa, Nalika Gajaweera, Padma Govindan, Paul Morgan, Beth Reddy, and Nick Seaver generated insights across anthropology, sociology, and informatics in the study of contemporary culture, value, and technology.

A great many people made my fieldwork rich, energetic, and intense. The late MP Ranjan at the National Institute of Design offered time and globe-spanning histories of design from his vantage point. Dhruv Raina at Jawaharlal Nehru University paved my official path to Delhi. Yodakin Bookstore in Hauz Khas Village offered a meeting place around books; even as it closed its doors, memories of it will inspire intellectual experiments. A number of designers, development workers, and researchers—at studios, at schools, and at large—gave me time, meals, and reflective commentary on design's changing roles in their work. I retain their anonymity, but some have already discussed these pages with me. Most generously of all, the staff of DevDesign let me into their lives over the past decade, housing me, feeding me, putting me to work, and reflecting on design practice with me. As I worried about the awkwardness of writing about life with DevDesign, Tara reminded me that our relations are more than just the book. It is true. The contradictions of innovation are part of an ongoing discussion already happening in India. Here, I hope this book offers useful fodder—a long-term sensing—to inform those late-night rant sessions about the felt alienations of work.

I thank longtime friends who reminded me I am more than my work. Mariam Pessian, family in the Iranian sense, has seen me through this before; she proofed my undergrad thesis twenty years ago. Davie Yoon, my favorite neuroscientist, shared advice on academic life and fun but easy bike routes. Dave Akers helped me communicate early iterations of this work to funders. Many friends kept in touch, sharing ideas, laughter, snark, and care: Mary Anne Brennan, Kirstin Cummings, Ryan Germick, Nathan Naze, Patrick Perry, Kim Samek, Megan Wachspress. Roma Jhaveri, formerly of Kiva.org, read the manuscript and offered encouragement stemming from her own alienations in the practice of development. Prabhakar and Beverly Vaidya offered interdisciplinary curiosity and intellectual encouragement.

My family, especially Guity and Reza Irani, has been my first source of lessons in globalization, modernity, and making a life when marked as other. A steady stream of home-cooked food sustained this project. I also thank my cousins, aunts, uncles, and my sister, Nina Irani, for patience with me for the decade that the book was "still not done."

The following institutions sustained my work: the Fulbright-Nehru Scholarship, the National Science Foundation through awards 0712890, 083860, 0838499, 0917401, and the Graduate Research Fellowship. Intel, through a UCI program, provided seed funding for pilot fieldwork. At UC San Diego, the Faculty Career Development Program offered course relief that allowed me to finish the draft of the manuscript. Leuphana University's Digital Cultures Research Lab in Germany gave me three months of office space and intellectual companionship as I wrote. I thank Rolex Awards for Enterprise for permission to use their image.

Not least, to Twiggs and its morning shift residents Alessia, Anna, Brandon, Cassidy, Catherine, Jim, Matty, Anthony, and Norma, thank you for providing a space where I could be with this project and with my neighbors at the same time.

CHASING INNOVATION

1

Introduction

INNOVATORS AND THEIR OTHERS

BEFORE THE TWENTIETH CENTURY, the entrepreneur was someone who managed an enterprise, undertaking projects financed by others and seeing them through (see Sarkar 1917). This once managerial figure has in the early twenty-first century become mythic, symbolically bound to social progress through invention, production, and experiment. Globally circulating digital media—TED (Technology, Entertainment, Design) videos and *Harvard Business Review* articles, for instance—popularize the entrepreneur as a normative model of social life. The ethos of innovation and entrepreneurship, honed in high-technology firms, has colonized philanthropy, development projects, government policies, and even thinking about international diplomacy. Innovation competitions, hackathons, and corporate mythologies around figures such as Bill Gates and Steve Jobs proliferate optimism that passionate dreamers can change the world. Austerity is no barrier; in myth, entrepreneurs are fueled by nothing more than perseverance, empathy, and resourcefulness in the face of adversity or injustice.

The entrepreneur, no longer just a manager, has become an "agent of change," an ideal worker, an instrument of development, and an optimistic and speculative *citizen*. This citizen cultivates and draws what resources they can—their community ties, their capacity to labor, even their political hope—into the pursuit of entrepreneurial experiments in development, understood as economic growth and uplift of the poor. Most important, entrepreneurial citizens promise value with social surplus; as they pursue their passions, they produce benefits for an amorphous but putatively extensive social body. The entrepreneurial citizen belongs to an imagined community of consumers, beneficiaries, and fellow entrepreneurs. If this imaginary of the entrepreneurial citizen sounds grandiose and vague, this is no coincidence; vagueness has been core to the global promise and portability of the entrepreneurial ethos. State and corporate elites point to entrepreneurs as those who can make opportunity out of the innumerable shortcomings of development.

I call this economic and political regime *entrepreneurial citizenship*. Entrepreneurial citizenship promises that citizens can construct markets, produce value, and do nation building all at the same time. This book shows how people adopt and champion this ethos in India in the early twenty-first century, articulating entrepreneurship with long-standing hierarchies and systems of meaning. Entrepreneurial citizenship attempts to hail people's diverse visions for development in India—desires citizens could channel toward oppositional politics—and directs them toward the production of enterprise. Elites, political and industrial, produce this ideology. It makes the most sense for India's middle classes—those with access to institutional, capitalist, and philanthropic patronage and investment. Entrepreneurial citizenship's language and social forms discipline political hope. As people—privately or through nongovernmental organizations (NGOs)—pitch to funders, to innovation competitions, or to corporate partners, they have to articulate dissatisfaction and demands as "opportunities" in patrons' interests. They monitor themselves, their relations, and their environments as terrains of potential. On these terrains, they look for opportunities to take on projects and redirect their lives to add value. These practices bend away from the slow, threatening work of building social movements; rather, people articulate desires to work for change as demos and deliverables. Calls to entrepreneurial citizenship promise national belonging for those who subsume their hopes, ideals, particular knowledges, and relationships into experiments in projects that promise value.

Proponents of this form—often technocrats and capital investors—promise that everyone is potentially an entrepreneur, from the least to the most privileged. Prominent business school faculty Anil Gupta (2006) and C. K. Prahalad (2004), for example, have celebrated the entrepreneurial capacities of rural inventors and informal producers. A report by the Planning Commission of the Government of India (2012d) featured a woman selling colored powder dyes on its cover, but its pages were filled with policy recommendations targeted at developing high-tech ventures. In casting street hawkers and elite technologists alike as entrepreneurs in potentia, proponents collapse the vast gaps in money, formal knowledge, and authority that separate these two. Entrepreneurial citizenship becomes one attempt at hegemony, a common sense that casts the interests of ruling classes as everyone's interests.

But this entrepreneurialism is not only a project of the self but also a project that posits relations between selves and those they govern, guide, and employ: leaders and led, benefactors and beneficiaries, the avant-garde and the laggards, innovators and their others. Champions of innovation and entrepreneurship often leave this hierarchy implicit or deny its existence, leaving the problems it raises unaddressed. So who becomes an innovator and who becomes the innovator's other? Who conceptualizes and valorizes, and who does the work? Who modernizes whom, and toward what horizon?

Advocates of entrepreneurial citizenship argue that society must invest in innovators, as innovators promise a better future for all. This book depicts the practices by which institutions, organizations, and individuals selectively invest only in some people, some aspirations, and some projects in the name of development. As powerful institutions actively cultivate "the capacity to aspire" (Appadurai 2004) through entrepreneurial citizenship, this book illustrates the seductions, limits, and contradictions of entrepreneurial citizenship's promise of inclusion through the generation of economic and social possibility.

The politics of entrepreneurial citizenship play out diffusely, in sometimes hazy, sometimes passionate, and sometimes convenient decisions people make about who to work with, who to work for, who to invest in, and what spaces to inhabit. Schools, training programs, venture capitalists, NGOs, and entrepreneurial individuals cultivate and cull futures as they invest in some projects and people and not others. As these actors decide whom to fund, whom to have coffee with, and whose feedback to take, they select and culti-vate relationships that produce emergent forms of hierarchy. These decisions play out moment to moment in studios, NGOs, and social innovation spaces, shaped by assumptions about caste, class, region, and cosmopolitanism. These judgments are often glossed ones of "like-mindedness," "authenticity," and "fit."

Value orients entrepreneurial citizens and those who invest in them. But it is not tangible productivity, but what anthropologist Kaushik Sunder Rajan characterizes as "the felt possibility of future productivity or profit" (2006, 18). They produce and respond to vision, hope, and hype as they pursue speculative capital investments; they promise not only financial value but also social value and legitimation for socially responsible funders and inves-tors (Friedner 2015). With this book, I render these social forces visible so that those working toward horizons of justice might channel their hopes and labor in ways less easily appropriated and disciplined by capital investments, and the demand for financial value. I assess entrepreneurial citizenship in light of the still lively legacies of enlightenment and colonial projects that position some people as India's past and fewer people—the educated, the modern-ized, and now the innovators—as India's future, deserving of investment in the name of the nation.

This book offers an ethnography of entrepreneurial citizenship. I pay close attention to why entrepreneurial citizenship makes sense to people—what his-tories, mediations, and ideologies make it compelling for those who respond

to its call. I link affects and practices to institutional, political, and political economic structures that necessitate them. I begin by analyzing various visions in
India of how state and society ought to relate to one another and what kinds
of subjects have emerged in such arrangements. Entrepreneurial citizenship
is one such arrangement that emerged as the Indian state attempted to privatize the functions of development to private industry and civil society while
managing surplus populations (Sanyal 2007). I draw on studies of South Asia's
history, political economy, and culture to show why these arrangements began
to make sense to elites and to many in the middle classes in the decades following liberalization in 1991. I address questions about the organization of
neoliberal hegemonic projects and how they shape class, caste, and gender
relations (e.g., Bhatt, Murty, and Ramamurthy 2010). To understand what is
new about this arrangement, I turn to development studies' examinations of
rule of experts and civil society NGOs and introduce the concept of "rendering entrepreneurial" to explain how the state goes beyond the management of
poverty to the proliferation of enterprise around poverty. I draw on science
and technology studies, economic sociology, and economic anthropology to
show the kinds of infrastructures, social relations, media forms, and epistemologies that make such enterprises seem tractable in practice and in promise.
From literature on human computer interaction (HCI) and design, I take the
insight that interfaces and materialities of mediation condition interactions
and intersubjectivities up close and at a distance (see, e.g., Lave and Wenger
1991; Dourish 2004). Drawing from feminist analyses of labor, I analyze these
resulting subject formations and divisions of labor as regimes of invisibility
and hierarchies of value. Debates about power and values in design processes
(e.g., Friedman 1996; Nissenbaum 2001; Muller 2003) must reckon with the
colonial, postcolonial, and capitalist processes that lend design and innovation
their social promise in the first place.[1] And I turn to postcolonial and feminist
studies to pose the question of how the social promise of innovation responds
to anxieties about difference and disorder in the national community. Policy
elites, for example, saw in India's youthful population a productivity boon
or fodder for political fire; all depended on whether entrepreneurship and
industrialization could absorb and direct their energies (see Nilekani 2009,
52; Gupta 2016, 297, 341).

I use citizenship here as both an emic and an analytic term. Many whom
I met in the course of fieldwork positioned entrepreneurship not just as an
economic activity but as a nation-building one. They built on long-standing
understandings of development as a collective national project demanding
contributions from all citizens. As they spoke of their vocations and biographies, many spoke explicitly of problems of "civic sense" and what the government ought to expect from them. People did not speak of "citizenship" per se

but of the civic, of India, and of "doing one's bit." I also use citizenship as an analytic category to draw into sharper relief the implications of people's own ideologies of belonging and specific state policies to recognize membership in the nation. In chapter 2 I show how the state redefined citizenship policies specifically to include the technical expertise and wealth of diaspora in the nation, elevating upper castes and classes with access to education over laborers abroad. Within South Asian studies, sociologists and anthropologists have primarily discussed citizenship in terms of rights demanded from the state, whether as consumers of services or as groups demanding affirmative action, land rights, or recognition; this book puts in the foreground the responsibilities the state attempts to place on citizens as well. I bring this study of citizenship into dialogue with the perspectives of science and technology studies, which I argue ought to attend not only to the practices and histories surrounding technology but also to the ways in which states hierarchize people in terms of their capacities to offer expertise recognized as high value at particular historical moments.

Innovation as the Rearticulation of Development

People champion a variety of cultural imaginaries under the seemingly global banner of innovation. A challenge of this analysis is to locate the stabilities among entrepreneurial and innovation projects while recognizing contestations and variations among them. Here, I begin by contrasting three different prescriptions for development from three elite policy actors. Their visions are varyingly capitalist, socialist, and Gandhian, yet they share a belief in entrepreneurial innovators as a vehicle for national growth and distribution. They share a vision that draws distinctions between valorized innovators and their beneficiary others. Differences among them signal the varied historical strands of development that still animate Indian politics today.

Arvind Subramanian, a former International Monetary Fund economist, served as chief economic advisor to Prime Minister Narendra Modi from 2014 through 2018. Sam Pitroda headed the National Knowledge Commission in the early 2000s after decades leading technology infrastructure projects for the Congress Party. Anil Gupta, a Gandhian Indian Institute of Management (IIM) professor, served the Modi government as second-in-command of the National Innovation Foundation. The three men vary in their political affiliations, but all envision entrepreneurship and innovation as engines of development.

Addressing the University of Pennsylvania's India Innovation Conference in November 2013, Subramanian speculated about India's future, painting the country as a temporal contradiction. "Despite being very poor, it is still cutting edge. . . . [India] does things which a country at its level of development is not supposed to do"—Subramanian called this "the precocious model of development." He envisioned an India that exported information services like programming and tech support; it trained skilled entrepreneurs and managers; its wealthy invested their capital not only in India but in other countries. But this precocious India had not yet arrived. "India contains all ten centuries within it," he explained, pointing to the low-skill workers and low-caste Indians still mired in "backwards traditions" and without jobs. For Subramanian, innovation was key to growth, but it was the province of capitalists and highly educated managers and engineers who could invent it and organize it. He prescribed policies to empower these elites through easing restrictions on land, labor, trade, and foreign direct investment.

Pitroda is, like Subramanian, a nonresident Indian deeply involved in central government policy. He headed the National Knowledge Commission during Congress rule from 2005 through 2014. During a televised panel on innovation and the Indian Institutes of Technology (IITs) staged by parliament, Pitroda spoke about the poorest Indians at "the bottom of the pyramid" not as potential workers to be stabilized by incorporation in low-skill jobs but as village Indians in need of technical solutions, innovation, and uplift. The market alone—and finance capital in particular—simply "extracts value" through exchange, Pitroda argued in a swipe at commercial capital. By contrast, engineers have the capacity to innovate by going to people, identifying their problems, and "creating value" by solving them. Pitroda is himself an icon of this form; he had led the central government mission to bring telephone service to rural India in the 1980s (Chakravartty 2004). This was a vision not of inventing for export but rather of dedicating professional Indian inventiveness to domestic consumers' and citizens' needs.

A business professor with a starkly different ethos, Gupta (2009) posited rural India as the true "hotbed of innovation." He taught for decades at India's premier management institute, IIM-Ahmedabad, and led annual *yatras*, or walking pilgrimages, through rural India on a search for "indigenous innovation." He mobilized audiences through TED Talk videos, a trade book (2016), and Indian national television. A global voice, but always donning Indian *kurta* and *salwar*, he made the case that rural Indians have appropriate technologies and traditional knowledge ripe for capitalization. These rural innovators, he argued, made affordable, repairable, and clever technologies driven by their impatience to make life easier. Gupta and his team documented these inventions and aided in diffusing them through patenting and licensing support, as well as a decades-old newsletter translated into a variety of regional languages.

In some ways, the three men could not seem more different. For Subramanian, innovation emanated from the gleaming towers of urban India to the networked globe. For Pitroda, it moved from urban offices into rural villages. And for Gupta, it could, with proper state support, circulate within and beyond rural India itself.

Yet across this spectrum of sensibilities and politics, all three agreed that India's development hinged on its capacity to innovate. "Innovation" blurred distinctions between social development and economic development, promising solutions to human needs and the production of new wealth. In this vision of development, progress came from individual innovators or small communities who developed novel systems that could be replicated and distributed—through others' labor—to multiply use value through conversion into exchange value. Subramanian, Pitroda, and Gupta only quibbled over which people or groups had that capacity and what policy measures would best locate and nurture them.

Innovation brings to mind for many high technology: Mars missions, Apple computers, or new smartphone apps. In India, it also signaled the possibility of technological progress not mimetic of the West—a problem central to postcolonial nationalisms writ large (Lu 2010; Chatterjee 1993) but now a question of valorization in patent culture as well.[2] Gupta and others argued that a pedal-powered washing machine could also be a site of less recognized but no less profound forms of innovation. Even as these men negotiated what ought to count as innovation, they agreed on the basic vision of the inventions of the few replicated for the benefit of the masses—innovators' others. Modernization theorist Everett Rogers (2003, 42) championed this model of innovation, which he called diffusionism. Like modernization theory, this theory positioned inventors and early adopters of innovations as closest to modernity; others became adopters, laggards, and backward refusers.[3]

The promise of entrepreneurship, then, is not only that one makes one's own future but that one can generate progressive futures *for others* through organization, know-how, and resourcefulness. Subramanian, Pitroda, and Gupta all saw entrepreneurs as the source of invention, innovation, and cultural creativity that could also transform communities and societies. This was the vision of the entrepreneur put forth by economist Joseph Schumpeter in the mid-twentieth century but deemphasized in many Foucauldian readings of entrepreneurial production that emphasize the market appreciation of the self (W. Brown 2015; Feher 2009).[4] Schumpeter (1947) theorized the entrepreneur as the driver of economic history—a creative agent that escaped falling rates of profit by generating novel sources of profit within an economy. The entrepreneur found new arrangements of existing resources, relationships, and techniques to organize novel forms of production. For Schumpeter, however, the entrepreneur was just one functional role in the economy, distinct from inventors, capitalists, and managers. Fifty years later, a wide range of state, NGO, and corporate actors began to cultivate entrepreneurialism as a silver bullet, a highly flexible answer to the contradictions between human development and accumulation. Through myriad practices—conclaves, hackathons, and design research, for example—entrepreneurial citizens were to reimagine everyday life as a latent opportunity and the masses not as an exploited or disadvantaged class to feed but as potential "users"—customers who could be managed and mined for value at the same time.

Projects to cultivate innovators and, implicitly, their others reproduced long-standing divisions between those who develop and those who must be developed. After 1947 Indian nationalists formed a postindependence state where administrators in the public sector made up a class, disproportionately dominated by upper castes (Subramanian 2015; Desai and Dubey 2012), with access to higher education and tasked with calculating, planning, and administering development for what Jawaharlal Nehru called the "needy masses" (S. Roy 2007). These masses voted to legitimate the planning state, but the planning state saw these citizens as ill-equipped to exercise proper democratic reason. The state saw them as mired in local politics, religion, superstition, and hunger. The practices of planning tasked administrators with rising above the "squabbles and conflicts of politics" to express the *rational* will and consciousness of the nation (Chatterjee 1993, 202–3). During this period, planners directed the economy while the state figured producers—farmers (Philip 2016) and factory workers (S. Roy 2007)—as ideal citizens. Through the process of liberalization, state and proliberalization elites pushed for a different figure of productivity: the entrepreneur.

With liberalization, in 1991, the Indian government withdrew from its monopoly on planning India's future (Mazzarella 2005; Chatterjee 1993). The state asked entrepreneurs armed with expertise from business- and NGO-sector worlds to step into the void left by the withdrawal of state-led planning and implementation. This was true of central government policies and rhetoric across the political spectrum, under both the conservative Bharatiya Janata Party (BJP) and the centrist Congress leadership. Political parties, media, and business lobbies promoted the Silicon Valley diaspora as symbols of what Indians could achieve in the right institutional environment. The central government promoted nonprofit business incubators, called Startup Villages, across India (Upadhyaya 2014). The National Science Center in Delhi—a museum designed to cultivate appreciation for scientific knowledge among Indians—added an innovation lab focused on tinkering, invention, and promoting "patent culture" (see Kumar 2003, 217; Ganguli 1999, 286). The lab was meant to teach visitors that the entrepreneurial innovator tinkered not as a means of extending the life of scarce commodities but as a practice of experiment to invent (and patent) new ones.

The state backed this figuration with concrete transformations to law and institutions. The Citizenship Act of 2003 reconfigured belonging in the nation by endowing Indians in the Silicon Valley diaspora (and in fourteen other wealthy countries more broadly) with rights to invest capital in India.[5] In the 1950s moment of anticolonial nationalism, Nehru had shunned the diaspora, instructing its members to become good citizens in the sovereign nations where they lived (Varadarajan 2010, 76). Through the process of liberalization, the state, under both Congress and BJP, tapped these wealthier Indians as investors and entrepreneurs of economic development, for-profit and nonprofit alike (Varadarajan 2010; High Level Committee 2001). Although "unskilled and semiskilled" diasporic workers in the Middle East sent more money back to India, the Citizenship Act initially left them out of this extension of national belonging, focusing instead on highly educated, often upper-caste professionals in wealthy countries (Varadarajan 2010, 91).

Parliament also dramatically revised the Companies Act, on the books since 1956, to formalize entrepreneurs as agents of development. The act made it possible for individuals to incorporate as "one-person companies" so the state could recognize the proverbial coders in the garage and offer them the liability protections of companies (Dash 2016). The act also called on large companies to become "socially responsible," mandating that large Indian firms contribute a portion of their profits to Corporate Social Responsibility efforts; an update to the act in 2016 counted technology incubation in elite universities as a fundable area of social responsibility, alongside health, women's empowerment, and education (Bahl 2014). Together, these aspects of the act figured the for-profit corporation as a site of potential and the bearer of responsibility to the nation. The private citizen, in turn, could become a corporation, both socially responsible and shielded from private liabilities. Entrepreneurial citizenship translated for capitalism older socialist figurations of the citizen as an engine of development, the bearer not only of rights but of responsibility for nation building.

Entrepreneurship even displaced older understandings of how government agencies plan and coordinate. India's Planning Commission had been central to Nehruvian nationalism; the Delhi-based institution housed economists, statisticians, and other experts who optimized development inputs and outputs to balance economic growth and social welfare (M. Sengupta 2015). By 2015 the Planning Commission was gone. In its place, the Narendra Modi government installed NITI Aayog, a "think tank" and "knowledge, innovation and entrepreneurial support system." NITI Aayog would coordinate the devolution of development to state-level and local public-private partnerships. The devolution had been in progress for decades (M. Sengupta 2015); the central government after liberalization treated state-level and municipal governments as entrepreneurs, tasked with finding their own investors and generating revenue for the central government (Bear 2016; J. Cross 2014; see also Sunder Rajan 2006). With NITI Aayog, the state narrated this shift as a move to support diffuse entrepreneurship over centralized planning as the engine and steering mechanism of development.

Entrepreneurial citizens carried forward older ideologies of planning rationality and state-citizen relations into their personal, civic experiments in development. Instead of a Planning Commission in Delhi, people worked out of design studios, personal offices, and NGO offices. Entrepreneurial citizens, like the Planning Commission, had to address national fragments— women and children, the Northeast, the informal sector, Muslims, or other groups defined through governmental expertise—but they did so through experimental offerings that generated communities of consumption. They researched and reasoned, but instead of attempting to model the nation as a statistical object, they collected stories, quasi-ethnographic observations, and the occasional statistic that inspired design ideas to test and informed them of cultural risks and constraints. If Nehru eschewed politics as tarnishing objectivity, designers and entrepreneurs could welcome politics to the point that they generated innovation: inspiration, creativity, and new ways to make development into an opportunity (see also Elyachar 2012a). State planners and their populations had given way to myriad innovators and consuming others.

Innovators' Others

While Indian celebrations of entrepreneurship posit everyone as a potential entrepreneur, they do not posit everyone as currently entrepreneurial or capable of innovating. Just as some justified late colonialism on the grounds that backward masses required preparation to govern themselves, the logic and practices of entrepreneurial citizenship differentiate innovators who find the edges of the future from those who are posed as beneficiaries of this avant-garde. This relationship between innovators and their others builds on long-standing accounts of India being not one nation but two. Anthropologist Ravinder Kaur (2012) calls this "the nation's two bodies": one is the new India that can attract investment and produce a recognizably modern standard of living; the other is cast as the "old India" that protests, strikes, and blocks this vision of development. These two Indias haunt the everyday work of development at social enterprise conferences, at design studios, in advertisements, and in policy debates. Sometimes they are called India 1 and India 2. Sometimes they are called India—referring to the modern nation—and *Bharat*—the Sanskrit term for nation as ancient soil but also referring to the masses of "real India" as both locus of cultural difference and developmental problem (Jodhka 2002). These two Indias are cast as temporally disjointed but interdependent.

Their interdependence erupts into visibility whenever rural Indians resist selling their land or vacating their villages to make room for factories, mines, and dams; subsistence and home sometimes threaten the promise of economic value. The interdependence of the two Indias weighs on urbanites—especially in Delhi—as middle classes worry about the density of cities when poorer Indians come to seek jobs they cannot find (see Sanyal 2007).[6] Their interdependence weighs on India's brand image abroad as well. India's presentations in forums like Davos have attempted to present its population as a face of diversity and burgeoning reform and as a canvas blank of institutional and social blockages to implementing enterprising initiatives.[7]

State and business elites transformed what they expected and promised of the entrepreneurial citizen in response to these tensions. In the decade after liberalization, as I elaborate in chapter 2, technocrats and politicians envisioned the entrepreneur as the "global Indian"—the highly educated, wealthy visionary who could innovate industries and value for India. As the polity rejected this vision through voting and through protest, policy makers both in India and in multinational institutions like the World Bank responded to these tensions by calling for "inclusive growth" (Roy Chowdhury 2013; C. Rao 2009; Kannan 2007). Inclusive growth casts a progressive glow around a diverse swath of projects to generate economic value while addressing poverty. Projects include incorporating the poor into financial capital through microfinance (A. Roy 2010; L. Karim 2011; Moodie 2014), addressing them as consumers through social enterprise, and even treating them as repositories of cultural resources to fuel innovation, as I will show in chapter 7. Inclusive growth called on the beneficiaries of Indian capitalism to make the benefits of development felt by the masses, whether through monetary payments, food rations, or improvements to material life (see also Bhatt, Murty, and Ramamurthy 2010; Ray and Quyum 2009). In doing so, inclusive growth celebrated the incorporation of diversity and difference among Indians into projects of value creation while eliding the specific destinations to which the wealth generated in these encounters flowed.

These experiments attempted to inch toward development, experimenting with ways that civil society, both domestic and transnational, could work with the state to develop novel forms of "sustainable" governance—projects that manage social order, generate profits, or, at best, both (Chatterjee 2004).[8] Political economist Kalyan Sanyal (2007, 235) argues that the problem of inclusive growth is part of a much larger problem in postcolonial capitalist development. The majority of Indians, according to Sanyal, live as surplus populations to formal capitalist concerns—not as a reserve army of workers, not outside of capitalism, but dispossessed by processes like land acquisition, mineral extraction, or the importation of mass consumer goods. These poor, he asserts, live in "the need economy"—an economy of informality, subsistence, and scraping by locked out of the organized sector. This sector is not a vestige of precapitalist relations but rather emerges through the workings of postcolonial capitalism. For Sanyal, the work of the postcolonial development state is not only to produce economic development but also to maintain state legitimacy in the face of such mass marginalization. Before the 1970s, Sanyal argues, the Nehruvian state attempted to incorporate the multitudes into industrialized development as workers. Failing this, it shifted to a policy of addressing the needs of the poor through a complex of programs, funded by the World Bank, aid agencies, NGOs, philanthropies, and microloan institutions, to manage poverty through entitlements—of food, of education, and of rural employment guarantees in recent years (Sanyal 2007, 208–52; Jayal 2013, 178). To Sanyal, the management of poverty through this state-NGO assemblage is central to how the state retains legitimacy among the poor dispossessed by capitalist processes (218). In making this argument, he resists moves in several strands of scholarship to see the poor as representatives of difference: as representatives of precapitalist relations in Marxist political economy, of essential cultural difference between, say, West and non-West in postcolonial and some decolonial approaches, or as alternative economies in feminist studies of the economy (92–97).[9] Instead, he insists that capitalist processes also produce people who live on its margins and develop diverse ways of organizing and making meaning out of their survival.

Practices of entrepreneurial citizenship offer elites a way of making this diversity productive of value while also legitimizing India's highly unequal economic order. Sanyal (2007, 224–25) identifies microcredit as one way that capital incorporates and generates value out of highly heterogeneous ways of surviving while keeping the poor at a distance. Geographer Ananya Roy (2010) calls the rush to invest and extract profit from loaning to and selling to the poor "poverty capital." Anthropologist Julia Elyachar (2012a) has documented the range of ways the development sector has worked to map practices and social networks of the poor, overturning development's traditional-modern distinctions by casting poor people's practices as "next practices" for corporate innovation (see also Gajjala and Tetteh 2016). As poor people's practices become latent sources of value, the mediators who can mine those practices are participatory designers, social entrepreneurs, and even activists who weave between the worlds of firms, NGOs, philanthropies, and start-ups. It is precisely this weaving between worlds and its relation to value that this book shows at work. Entrepreneurial citizenship promises those on the margins that they too can achieve social mobility; it also asks entrepreneurs to find the opportunities for value amid the diversity and marginality of India's poor.

I met hundreds of Indians, mostly middle class, who answered the call to become entrepreneurial citizens. I conducted fieldwork primarily between

2009 and 2012, with follow-up visits each year up to 2017. I worked at a design studio I will call DevDesign. The studio employed engineers, business school graduates, filmmakers, and designers, many of whom had left corporate jobs in marketing, consulting, video production, and even oil drilling. They shared a desire to find personally meaningful work that engaged their interests while contributing to nation building. They moved through a world of similarly charged citizens—optimistic, curious about others, prolific generators of projects, and avoidant of formal politics, protest, or open critique. In the chapters that follow, I will show the ways they connected to the worlds of the poor and brought those worlds into design studios, coworking spaces, conferences, and expert meetings. These were the spaces of production, times of experimentation, and infrastructures of circulation by which entrepreneurial citizens engaged those they sought to develop. They could do the work of uplift with intimate familiarity but at a comfortable distance.

Rendering Development Entrepreneurial

Entrepreneurial citizenship rearticulates old distinctions between those who can govern others and those who must be governed, cared for, and drawn into modernity.[10] Yet the shift from managerial professionalism and planning to design, entrepreneurship, and innovation accompanied a shift in images of nation building. Growth through planned industrial production and the village *charkha*, or spinning wheel, gave way to promises of India as a nation of a "billion entrepreneurs." Citizens, nationalists had once imagined, ought to produce while the state deliberated, calculated, and planned development for the masses. Now citizens answered the call to plan, to feel out opportunity, and to experiment in the nation's future. What was once the province of economists, urban planners, and sociologists expanded to include innovators more likely to be generalists than experts.

More than a set of methods, principles, or epistemologies, what entrepreneurial citizens share is an ethos of collaboration, experimental life, empathic civic interest, and the monitoring of possibility. Designers, entrepreneurs, and pedagogues often used "design thinking" to describe and train others in this ethos (Irani 2018; Kimbell 2011). Beyond design, these skills of collaboration, empathy, and experiment are now formalized in education at many levels, from elite business and design schools to job-training programs (Friedner 2015; Thrift 1997).

With the concept of ethos, I indicate the attitudes and styles of interaction by which entrepreneurial citizens explored their passions, knowledge, relations, and surrounds for opportunities—those possible futures occupying the overlap among the interests of those with the power to fund and act as gatekeepers. School reformers taught children to empathize, act, and lead their peers (chapter 3). Studio members interacted playfully, quickly, and intensely with one another; in brainstorms and data analyses, they worked together to probe for potential value in their fieldwork stories about people's lives (chapters 4 and 6). Michel Foucault elaborated ethos as "a mode of relating to contemporary reality; a voluntary choice made by certain people; in the end, a way of thinking and feeling; a way, too, of acting and behaving that at one and the same time marks a relation of belonging and presents itself as a task" (1984, 39). I use ethos here as it tracks how Indians taught and practiced entrepreneurialism—as a style of interacting, seeing, and experimenting to add value. "Design thinking" was one professional practice that accommodated middle-class citizens' pursuit of "authentic" selfhood, professionalism, and expressive cultural experimentation—a sensibility routinely contrasted with crushing competition for civil service or corporate jobs that offered little scope for personal expression. Ethos also marks shifts in nation-building discourse from collectivist to individualist registers. Rather than take this turn toward individualism as natural, then, I denaturalize the ethos by describing the social processes by which actors are ethicalized, through everyday talk and through the mediated forms of action, storytelling, and system building by which their ethics became the enterprise of innovating a nation.

The ethos of entrepreneurial citizenship is not the sort of standardizing discipline that requires people to bring their bodies and emotions in line with a norm (Foucault 1995). Rather, it thrives on people who can bring their differences into productive interaction—in brainstorming, in workshops, in the wandering chats that can become projects and partnerships. Difference—as long as it is embodied within an ethos that seeks to add value—is not something to be smoothed away. Studios, workshops, and conferences welcomed filmmakers, artists, chefs, economists, and literature buffs as long as they enjoyed hanging out, creating, and speculating about probable futures. Other kinds of workers—tailors, chai sellers, accountants—were essential to projects but offered orders rather than invitation into productively playful circles. In her ethnography of stock trading, Caitlin Zaloom (2006, 72) also notes a futures trading firm that sought value in human difference; the firm actively worked to diversify the gender, race, and ethnic composition of the trading room to "generate diverse points of view on the market." Diverse forms of knowledge, in the trading room and in the studio, allow finance capital to intensify the detection of opportunity where competitors may not. Difference becomes a repository of potential to mine for value (see also Tsing 2009).

The ethos of entrepreneurial citizenship differs from assessments offered by existing sociologies of India's postliberalization middle classes. Sociologists and political scientists argue that India's middle classes are "consumer citizens" who orient toward the state as a provider of commodities and services (Lukose 2009; Fernandes and Heller 2006). In such accounts, these consumer citizens want cars. They want faster roads for those cars. They want to accumulate wealth (Nigam 2011). And they want poorer Indians off the sidewalk, off the land, and out of the way (Rajagopal 2001; Gidwani and Reddy 2011; Kaur 2012). In some ways, the entrepreneurial citizens I met fit this profile. They saw consumer goods as vehicles for the good life; as designers and entrepreneurs, they wanted to design nice things for others.

But they also differed starkly from sociological diagnoses of consumer citizenship. They did not only see themselves as bearers of rights with respect to the nation-state. They also saw themselves as responsible to the nation-state. They spoke of design as a way of talking about improving the material culture and systems of the nation, reorganizing and reforming everyday life. Kritika, one friend, could not stop herself from critiquing the design of an ATM as she pulled money; "occupational hazard," she commented wryly.[11] Vivek, a social entrepreneur, griped that the state should design better water pump systems for the poor by accounting for installation, maintenance, and cultural practices. The scope of their hopes varied widely; they imagined new projects for themselves, their families, their friends, and the nation. Though they were happy to do this for companies or for the state, entrepreneurship also allowed them to initiate projects that expressed their own ideas of the good.

Festivals, design research presentations, crowdfunding, and Skype meetings with clients and partners were ways entrepreneurial citizens imagined hearing from and acting on the nation. This was a form of nationhood studio members imagined as cohering through products and services—an imagined community not of generalized citizens (Anderson 1991) but of innovators and their consuming and laboring others. These events invited people to imagine how their critiques and dissatisfaction might be turned into projects to transform those realities. These spaces seemed, on their face, compatible with political debate, dissent, and solidarity building through collaboration. DevDesign members often discussed politics. They made films about rural India and debated government policies; they looked up to activists in the Right to Information movement and even the occasional Maoist. They debated their own and others' labor conditions. They talked a lot about values on cigarette breaks; during project time, they drew energy from their own values when they aligned with the project, but the desires of funders and investors always took precedence. These criticisms and values beyond the economic became, themselves, fodder for creativity rendered entrepreneurial. Entrepreneurial citizenship subsumed frustration and idealism, rendering it productive of new enterprise. Innovation was the promise that the nation's varied use values, sensibilities, and lifeways could be realized as improvement, as modernization, and as economic growth. This book chronicles the hope and waste of problematization and dreaming rendered productive.

This mode of experimenting in development, I argue, is more than searching for the technical fix (Morozov 2013) or rendering political and structural problems into technical ones. To render developmental technical, anthropologists convincingly argue, is to frame a situation as a problem to be solved through interventions at hand—markets, water filters, or fertilizers, for example (Li 2007; Ferguson 1994). Technical, in this sense, means expertise and seemingly objective knowledge rather than machines and computational systems. Interventions that "render technical," anthropologists argue, dehistoricize social life, erasing politics and political economy in favor of fixes by experts: development economists, health officials, or agricultural scientists. Even grassroots participation, Tania Li (2007) argues, has been rendered technical by World Bank practices that fix the meaning of community and communication. Messy realities usually overrun development expertise, though even in failure the projects have sustained effects. James Ferguson (1994) shows how failed agricultural projects in Lesotho still bring state offices—tax collectors, overseers—closer to peasants. Li (2007) shows how failed expert interventions provoke political resistance among small farmers in Indonesia.

The practices of entrepreneurial citizens fit this image only loosely. Consultants, entrepreneurs, and engineers did render the social and behavioral into a problem of technique through expert interventions such as product design, "nudging" techniques, or development communication. These projects often, though not always, employed experts working to engineer impact. Entrepreneurial citizenship, however, was an engine for proliferating projects—experiments in what intervention had the right timing, the right investors, and the right partners, and the cultural resonance to stick. Entrepreneurial citizens were often involved in multiple projects at once, keeping many options as an uncertain world roiled around them. Failures were not endpoints but rather chances to learn, modify the attempt, and try again. Silicon Valley companies, influential in global governance, made such celebrations of failure iconic as precursors to progress. Google management advised engineers to launch early, launch often, and learn from mistakes. Facebook instructed engineers to "move fast and break things" (Fattal 2012, 940). Silicon Valley produced high-tech elites nursed on complexity theory—they fully expected models to fail and even celebrated failure as a chance to learn; what anthropologists of development called the act of "rendering technical" was, to entrepreneurial subjects, a provisional attempt to know and intervene just enough to learn something and try again. This was not an epistemology of certainty but of uncertain attempts and feedback loops (see Maurer 1995). The failures of attempts to render technical *could* open up contingent forms of politics, as Li (2007) argues. But more often, entrepreneurs took failure as a source of data about the messy worlds and relations they worked to transform. Even the Gates Foundation, known for its global health and education experts, suspended expertise sometimes. Addressing a team redesigning toilets, a program officer told them to "err on the side of innovation" (chapter 6). Design thinking pedagogies celebrated this suspension, advising those who intervene to "see through the eyes of a beginner" and learn through experiment. These projects made life itself a site of enterprising experiment; I call this the process of rendering entrepreneurial.

Global philanthropies—the Gates Foundation, Rockefeller Foundation, and CitiFoundation, for example—disseminated these practices of rendering entrepreneurial globally. Human-centered design appeared both in development and in education projects as a pedagogy of caring entrepreneurialism; it taught citizens how to muster a will to improve, experimentally intervene, learn from failures, and try again. The Gates Foundation funded Palo Alto design firm IDEO (2009) to publish three guides on how "innovate and design for people living on under \$2/day." CitiFoundation funded Grameen Bank to train NGOs across several countries, including India, in innovation and design as well. These pedagogies were meant to infuse NGOs with optimism, experimental spirit, and customer focus so they could help develop financial products for the poor (Grameen Foundation 2013). UK charity Nesta similarly partnered with a celebrity list of development organizations—the United Nations Development Programme, USAID, OxFam, and social entrepreneurship NGO Ashoka— to produce social innovation and design pedagogies for development and aid workers (http://diytoolkit.org). As institutions trained people to see like entrepreneurs, they found citizens to take up their agendas, distancing themselves from direct responsibility for failed projects. They distributed the costs and risks of research and development throughout society. Rather than censoring dissatisfaction, institutions redirected it toward the pursuit of value. Those with capital could selectively invest only in those people and projects most aligned with their own interests, disciplining progress without disciplining people.

The middle-class Indians I met readily stepped into the role of entrepreneur and agent of development, even if they had qualms about entrepreneurship. Through their education and upbringing, they learned to see themselves as trustees—the name Tania Li (2007) gives to those elites who claim the right to speak for the well-being of the population. They understood their projects not just as the implementation of technical programs of improvement but as syntheses of and compromises between their own and poor potential users' visions of what interventions ought to look like. As middle classes, they saw the creativity of the poor as beautiful, inspirational, and chaotic—a source of "next practices" (Elyachar 2012) to organize under the putatively rational, systematic, and deliberative practices of management, design, and innovation.

Development rendered entrepreneurial generated complex tangles of partners across NGOs, corporations, and government. The work of the Tata Group
offers an illustration. The family-run group operates over one hundred companies, as well as the philanthropic Tata Trusts. While the trusts historically funded
education, academic research, and NGOs serving the poor, they have lately
turned toward venture capital to fund social innovation ventures—water filters,
education platforms, and toilets are just some of the funded projects. Tata's long-
standing networks of NGOs become logistical organizations that help funded
innovators intervene in the lives of the poor. Development rendered entrepreneurial lives in the alignments among these interests, infrastructures, labors, and
passions, rather than in the strictures of technical, expert prescriptions.

Sites and Methods

The core of this book's empirical material is drawn from fourteen months
of daily, immersive fieldwork at a product design and research studio I call
DevDesign located in Delhi, India. I inhabited varying positions: early on, I
was a participant-observer oscillating between recording observations and
assisting with studio tasks; over time, I participated intensely and accountably,
organizing events, analyzing research, and teaching. I did this in the studio, in
homes, in the field, and at workshops. I followed the studio's work to Ahmedabad, Auroville, Bangalore, Hyderabad, rural Andhra Pradesh, Colombo,
Sri Lanka, and Silicon Valley. Core studio staff included people with varied
training: MBAs, engineers, filmmakers, product designers, and economists.
Their friends included artists, activists, managers, and consultants. They
moved through education conferences, hackathons, and experimental cafes.
Through these varied sites, I saw how they worked to embody and champion
a form of entrepreneurial citizenship that answered the call of the state and
domestic capital while carving a moral or, more rarely, even a political path.[12]
I conducted fieldwork in the social worlds they moved through as well, interviewing their friends, family, colleagues, and collaborators across government
agencies, NGOs, festivals, and even homes. I followed people, design methods, and innovation practices as they moved. As I traced who put claims of
design, innovation, and entrepreneurship to work, I found a wider system of
public private partnerships, global trade agreements, and economic anxieties
produced by social forces (Marcus 1995). This is how I came to understand
DevDesign's work as just one response among many to the call of what I have
named entrepreneurial citizenship.

An ethnographic approach allowed me to see the diverse ways actors
oriented toward value, created knowledge, and worked to order their social
relations in response to social forces. I trace not only embodied, improvised,

contingent, and highly reflexive practices but also forces of habit and resources that structured those agencies and gave them form. Social forces shape grant cycles, project deadlines, government budgets, and political instability, and those conditioned what was possible in ways not always visible to practitioners day-to-day. Reflexivity and self-criticism were essential as entrepreneurial citizens told stories about themselves, adapted to changing circumstances, and forged partnerships. I do not treat those I work with like "cultural dopes" (Garfinkel 1967), but I also do not assume that they—or any of us—are fully aware of the forces that condition our actions (Bourdieu 1967). This book attends to entrepreneurial citizenship as a practice: of knowledge (Mol 2002; Fujimura 1988), as action organized in time (Bear 2016; Jeffrey 2010; Bourdieu 1977; Garfinkel 1967), and, crucially, as organized by social forces like finance and other resources (Bear et al. 2015; Bear 2015; Patel 2006, 2015; Maurer 1995; Marx 1978). Through ethnography, I worked to notice the patterned forms of marginality, exclusion, and hierarchy produced by innovation and entrepreneurship, even as their champions claimed openness, change, and chaotic unpredictability.

I interpret the utterances and practices of everyday life by contextualizing them in the histories and political economies that made those practices possible, sensible, and affectively compelling. Parts of this book will explain these conditions by analyzing, for instance, popular films that were meaningful in the sites and circuits I moved through. Other parts will rely heavily on historical analysis drawing on secondary literature coupled with close readings of planning documents, World Bank reports, and global consultancy reports. I pay particular attention to the changes in priorities and discourse in these documents over time and look to contemporaneous shifts in political economy, lost elections, or other moments of power shift to understand what drove the shifts in discourse. I do not privilege these documents as sources of truth claims, but I read them as attempts to consolidate and shape the direction of expertise and middle-class understandings of development. I also look for the subtle and most often unspoken conditions that haunted these attempts to plan and govern.

I wrote this ethnography not just for my scholarly fields or the "general public"—whoever that is. I wrote it for friends at DevDesign and beyond as they sensed the inadequacies of innovation practices in ways that manifested as cynicism, jadedness, or burnout. I wrote for those who see hope in the labor of making technologies in the struggle for a better life, but who might find wisdom and forewarning in the frustrations of the entrepreneurial citizens who people this book. Those I met in and around DevDesign responded to the call to be entrepreneurial, to build the nation as citizens, and to address "global" problems through development. And over the years, they grew frustrated with the limitations of development: funders clutching purse strings half a world away, impossible promises of a technological silver bullet, and the promising but always not-yet connectivity of digital systems. As an ethnographer, I turned my attention to wider histories of class, democracy, finance, and geopolitics that conditioned the possibilities of their actions. I also did this for myself. I began this project in 2009 as a technology designer who wanted to draw on anthropology and postcolonial studies to intervene responsibly in my world (see Irani et al. 2010). Early on, a project to design a water filter nobody wanted—a story I tell in chapter 6—exploded that fantasy. This book is an effort to replace that fantasy with something more grounded in reality.

Those I worked with in Delhi called on me to recognize the similarities between my biography and theirs. "You're just like us," a graphic designer and friend of studio members told me six months into fieldwork. I do not take this statement for granted but rather as puzzle. It was not an attachment to India per se but a shared attachment to design and a frustration with postcolonial conditions that sparked my collaboration with designers in India. With members of DevDesign, I began the project idealistic about the possibilities of design as a means of aligning technology with progressive social futures. I met members of the studio through a colleague at Google where I had worked as a "user experience designer" for four years. With Akhil and Ajit, the studio's founders, I shared a frustration with the provincialism of Silicon Valley designers and engineers, so certain of their global sensibilities and visions. A globalizing Google saw Indian designers as translators but not creativea authors. European designers accused Indian designers of mimicking when they failed to perform a European vision of Indianness. As an Iranian American, I knew intimately the sense of coming from the wrong end of modernity's time line, always catching up to Euro-American practices and knowledge. From these points of mutual frustration, and a mutual attachment to technology practices, DevDesign invited me to study their work. I neither went "native" in this fieldwork nor claim the distance of an "outsider." DevDesign found my presence useful as an emissary from California—a repository of information, gossip, and sensibility. I found in them skillful and brilliant people, tapped as ghostwriters and translators of Silicon Valley innovation reports. As I spent more time with them within and beyond the studio, I learned their ambitions exceeded recognition as innovators in a global profession. Their ambitions were to turn their fellow citizens from knowledge workers into innovators of a nation. Work was not just labor but a way of belonging in society.

The world around the studio moved in a mix of Hindi, English, and Hinglish—the practice of blending English and Hindi often associated with cities and Bollywood film (Kothari and Snell 2011). At the studio, Hinglish was the more intimate register in which I engaged with studio members day-to-day, and English was the dominant language of consulting work, conference calls, and most public talks. My primary informants interacted with lower-level staff or those Indians who were the target of their research in Hindi. Hindi was the language of domestic life, and of commanding the labor of others in Delhi. On occasion, DevDesign staff traveled to other regions of India where even they required translators to engage people in the field. Only rarely did DevDesign communicate its expertise to those who spoke only Hindi, whether their own research informants or their lower-level staff; on the rare occasions that they shared back research knowledge, they too consulted Hindi dictionaries though born, raised, and educated in India. The English-speaking "global Indian" of the managerial class already occupied a privileged linguistic stratum, and English was a key mechanism for delineating the distance between innovators and their others.[13] Of eleven conferences and workshops I attended, ten were primarily in English, to the point that participants used Hindi and vernacular languages as political interventions or reparative attempts to include the marginalized speakers at home in other Indian languages.

A limitation of my position in the field was that I had less extensive discussions with lower-level office staff. While I explicitly attended to divisions of labor and interactions between designers and lower-status workers, the cooks, cleaners, and couriers I spoke with joked about work and our relations but did not speak to me extensively about their work. They saw me (accurately) as strongly associated with their employers. These ethnographic refusals marked power relations within the studio.

Map of the Chapters

Each chapter of the book traces the practices through which different actors enroll or become enrolled in projects of entrepreneurial citizenship. After this introductory chapter, the book begins by showing how politicians and business elites—especially, but not only, from the high-tech sector—attempt to pose entrepreneurial citizenship as new kind of common sense in response to dilemmas of liberalized development. I read state documents, especially Five Year Plans, in the context of wider histories of politics and development in India. I show how meanings of entrepreneurship and innovation shifted in response to institutional shifts like patent law or political realignments. I argue that we should look at categories like entrepreneurship and innovation historically, rather than granting them a philosophical concreteness they lack. Entrepreneurship and innovation are not static analytic terms but categories forged through efforts by state and capital to manufacture common sense. Chapter 3 shows how elite reformers—here, education reformers, media elites, and intellectuals—take up this common sense and make it concrete through projects to remake Indian education. Reformers take up "design thinking" as a pedagogy that marries democracy and productivity for middle-class Indians haunted by communalism, labor market pressures, and the desire for development.

Chapters 4, 5, and 6 focus on the work of the entrepreneurial imagination at DevDesign. The book presents ethnographic analysis of innovators at work in the design studio, in the field, and in development workshops. As they worked to feel out opportunities, attract clients, and carry out projects, they remade themselves and the divisions of labor that sustained them. Chapter 4 shows how designers at the studio organized their lives, their relationships, and their self-understandings as they continually relearned how to "add value" in the context of shifting global divisions of labor and speculative hype. Life and leisure became resources for speculating in new forms of value. Chapter 5 turns to the history and political fallout of entrepreneurial urgency. Entrepreneurs privilege "a bias to action"—a manufactured urgency that treats opportunity as always about to disappear. An ethos forged amid the volatility of high-tech industries, the bias to action encourages trying many possibilities quickly, learning from collaboration, and accepting failures in the search for value. This ethos, I show, also encouraged people to bring diversity to the table while temporally foreclosing the slower work of democracy across difference. Chapter 6 turns to empathy and human-centered design—a way for entrepreneurial citizens to engage those for whom they design and innovate. Empathy, I show, generated inspiration and investment in innovation processes first and responded to the needs of potential users only to the extent that it aligned with investor interests.

Chapter 7 asks, "Can the subaltern innovate?" It calls into question how we know innovation: what counts as innovation as such, who designates it and how, and how these processes are embedded in relations of power and political economy. What makes some acts of technological configuration *jugaad*, or workarounds, and others proper innovation? What makes some designs innovative while others are characterized as derivative, inauthentic, or even copies? Put simply, I examine how, in contingent and everyday practice, people recognize some acts as innovation and others as not. I argue that we should examine innovation not as the search for value but as the recognition of value—a process of recognition inflected by caste, gender, regional identity, and class. I conclude the book by reflecting on entrepreneurial citizenship as a global project, promoted not only by Indian elites but also by the U.S. Department of State and global institutions of economic governance. I ultimately argue that the function of entrepreneurial citizenship is to subsume hope and dissatisfaction, redirecting potential political contestation into economic productivity and experiment.

2

Remaking Development

FROM RESPONSIBILITY TO OPPORTUNITY

WORKERS WERE causing problems again. On NDTV (New Delhi Television), English-speaking talking heads explained that to encourage entrepreneurship and economic dynamism, India needed to relax labor laws. Labor politics held back development. For decades, this had been the hegemonic refrain (see Rajagopal 2011, 1036). Planning Commission plans and papers reported that "jobless growth"—capital accumulation that registered as economic growth but failed to create jobs—fomented frustration among the masses. And those masses were always on the cusp of turning unruly.

Tata, for example, had been pushed out of a Bengali town called Singur (Kaur 2012; Menon and Nigam 2007, 105–6). The century-old industrial conglomerate wanted to build a factory to turn out the Nano, a US$2,000 car that had put India on the global map as a promising hotspot of "frugal innovation." The leftist government had tried to seize farmers' land under eminent domain—Tata and the state held up the organized sector and spectacular technology as in the interests of the nation as public, while they cast the democratic assertions of farmers protecting their means of subsistence as holding the nation back (Philip 2016; Kaur 2012; Sanyal and Bhattacharyya 2009). For decades, the state had cracked down on trade unions (Rajagopal 2011) and created special economic zones with reduced labor rights (Srinivasan 1997). Tata's escape to Gujarat was only the latest public declaration that labor held back (capital's) leadership and, by consequence, development.

The worth of democracy was also in question. Those with the voices most linked to mass media and state command—the English-speaking middle classes—argued that democracy was in tension with progress. The middle classes had grown impatient with democratic processes—protests, strikes, *bandhs*, lower-caste assertion at the ballot boxes, and demands for redistribution and affirmative action (Lukose 2009; Menon and Nigam 2007). Scholars had noted a postliberalization affinity among the middle classes for authoritarian developmental regimes; I'd shared cigarettes and drinks with people who wondered if Singapore or China, with their single-party systems, would be a better model (Fernandes 2006; Kestenbaum 2010). Comparisons between national styles of government—authoritarian and democratic— slipped easily into casual metaphors of corporate styles of management. At development seminars and design conclaves alike, professional elites considered "the Steve Jobs approach" to planning, government, and implementation. A national news journalist summed up a designer's approach to democracy at one conclave: "They don't know what they want, but when the designer gives it, they will want it."

For elites and the middle classes who looked to them, labor and democracy were two things that could get in the way of development as "opportunity": entrepreneurial action and the promise of vision, speed, competence, and innovation that went along with it. Entrepreneurship as a mode of development, however, was rarely explicitly debated in these terms. Rather, entrepreneurship appeared to be an expression of economic and cultural freedom—a positive addition to the world rather than an organization of authority and action. This chapter asks how this state of affairs became a commonplace taken for granted among the middle-class professionals I worked with and followed through India's centers of finance, planning, and government.[1]

The figure of the entrepreneur has been a dynamic tool used by policy and industry elites to legitimize liberalization and explain how development ought to proceed in shifting political economies. Before liberalization, the Indian state understood entrepreneurs as a stop-gap: producer-citizens who employed themselves in the interstices of the organized and agricultural sector (S. Roy 2007). The ongoing process of legitimizing liberalization drove policy and industry elites to redefine the entrepreneur as national hero, first as a captain of business (and, by implication, economic development) and later as a captain of "inclusive growth" who cared for the needy and the bottom line. This model inclusive entrepreneur extended century-old Gandhian theories that posed industrialists as trustees of the public—wealthy stewards and benefactors (Birla 2009, 103). Yet for Gandhi, trusteeship was the responsibility to shed wealth as philanthropic welfare (B. Chakrabarty 2011). After liberalization, trusteeship was, in the words of one CEO, an "opportunity" to accumulate wealth while developing the poor. I draw on Planning Commission documents, televised debates, and histories of Indian development to trace this shift. The shifting figure of the entrepreneur appeared not only in popular discourse but also in specific state policies created to support and even extend citizenship rights to those who fit the mold, as I will show in this chapter.

The chapter then turns to practice by showing how civil society responded to the state's call to entrepreneurship. Middle-class Indians put on festivals, conclaves, conferences, and workshops where they translated the call into consultancy, social enterprise projects, and activism in line with their own varied ideological orientations or situations. The proliferation of the norm of entrepreneurial citizenship in specific events, groups, and projects allowed people to pursue their freedoms and respond to their own frustrations in forms compatible with state-coordinated, industry-led national development. Entrepreneurs translated problems into opportunities, and dissatisfaction into exchange value. Policy makers saw entrepreneurialism as a prophylaxis against protest, dissatisfaction, and anger; the call to entrepreneurial citizenship redirected blame from structures of power to failures of imagination.

Development as Everybody's Responsibility and Everybody's Opportunity

Delhi during my fieldwork, spanning 2009 through 2017, seemed a development boomtown. Since India won independence from the United Kingdom in 1947, Delhi has been a center of development planning and calculation. In these early decades of independence, Planning Commissions and government offices calculated and directed schemes to modernize Nehru's "needy nation" (Roy 2007), implementing a series of Five Year Plans (FYPs) and import controls. Since liberalization in in 1991, those plans and import controls gave way to the coordination of capital investment and the cultivation of public-private partnerships (Corbridge and Harriss 2000, 120; Kohli 2006a; Rajagopal 2011; Chakravartty 2012; Jayal 2013). Since the mid-2000s global consultancies and banks like Goldman Sachs directed investors to India and other "emerging markets" (Wilson and Purushothaman 2003). Diasporic business school professors propagated images of India as teeming with potential, both as "bottom-of-the-pyramid" customers (Prahalad 2005) and as "billions" of entrepreneurs (Khanna 2007).

This promise of potential was the focus of the Indian delegation at the World Economic Forum (WEF) in 2011. The WEF, often called Davos after the city in which it takes place, brings together business, civil society, and governmental elites annually to discuss promising possibilities for and threats to capitalism as a global system. In 2011 the Indian delegation published glossy magazines with smiling Indian children advertising infrastructure development, manufacturing, and consumers as opportunity. On panels, elites debated prospects, risks, and how to address them.

The panel brought together government, civil society, the private sector, the press (the fourth estate), and—never to be left out—the International Monetary Fund (IMF). These institutions were embodied in the panelists on stage.

Palaniappan Chidambaram was the standing Indian minister of home affairs and former finance minister. Salil Shetty directed Amnesty International—the sole civil society organization on the panel. Chanda Kocchar was CEO of ICICI, one of India's largest private banks. Michael Elliot was the editor of *Time International*. And Chinese economist Min Zhu spoke as the special advisor to the IMF. In the audience were the heads of industry consortiums, elected politicians, and other elites in attendance at Davos.

I, of course, was not in Davos. I was in Delhi. NDTV, one of India's largest English-language broadcasters, was bringing these elite deliberations into Indian homes, training English-speaking Indians in global capital's modes of public explanation and logic. The mix on the panel was familiar to me; the Delhi development scene had taken me and the entrepreneurial professionals I worked with through World Bank offices, corporate conference rooms, and government planning offices, though we never had direct access to people working at the level on this televised panel. The broadcast let us hear how they understood the challenges of development.

Global unrest haunted the debate about the future of liberalized development in India. The Arab Spring was in full swing in the Middle East. The moderator, an NDTV television anchor, asked the panel: "We are of course seeing a lot of turmoil right now, in Africa and especially in Egypt, all that's happening out there. How do you see this entire question of growing fast enough but making sure people are being taken along in that growth?" The *Time* editor, Elliot, responded, "Oh absolutely. We're seeing the consequences of a generation of young people who feel that there is no substantial economic opportunity available to them."

This moment was the briefest acknowledgment of instability and inequality that haunted development debates in India. Liberalization had expanded inequality in India, giving the richest a growing share of national income (India Chartbook 2017). Economic growth rates nearing 10 percent had not brought sufficient increases in organized-sector employment; this "jobless growth" left the majority of Indians working in the informal economy. Progress in statistics measuring human development, including literacy and health, had stalled (UNDP 2017). Statistics aside, communal riots and independence movements in Kashmir and the northeastern states called into question the national project and worried investors. In these restive and resisting regions, the Planning Commission prescribed doubling down on economic development to offset the effects of military occupation and enroll the agitators in the national project. Planners' and investors' anxieties came with a sense of urgency, as elites understood India's youthful population to be an economic asset—"the demographic dividend"—whose potential diminished as it aged (Planning Commission 2012a, 11; Nilekani 2009).

"How do we share the growth?" the banker, Kocchar, asked, referring to India's growing income inequality. "Even if we have entrepreneur-led growth, and if we are expanding the services sector, if we have the right education given to people in the rural areas, you could have rural BPOs [business processing outsourcing] coming up. Then we get out of this constraint where 20 percent of the GDP has to feed 70 percent of the population. We have to ensure we provide ways and means in those sectors that are providing growth in the country." Kocchar took for granted that entrepreneurial activity would lead India's growth. But she also posed the impossibility of entrepreneurship as a way to profit and wealth for all Indians. There would be entrepreneurs, and there would be those whom entrepreneurs employed. Education, Kocchar argued, would lay the groundwork not for citizenship but for employability—readying the masses to enter into rural employment yet to materialize. Political economists argued that rural Indians most often felt the power of organized capital in the form of land dispossession and job exclusion (Jeffrey 2010; Sanyal 2007; Menon and Nigam 2007, 66). Kocchar held out the promise of rural entrepreneurship to legitimate capitalist development's depredations. New businesses, she argued, were the pathway to including the masses in the development project. She elevated the businessperson as job creator, employing those who could not employ themselves.

A bespectacled, middle-aged Indian man in the audience picked up on Kocchar's suggestion. The government minister on the panel called him by his first name, "Saurabh." Saurabh leaned comfortably back in his seat as he addressed the panel: "Each country has its own strengths and weaknesses; in India, our biggest single strength is our very entrepreneurial culture at the grassroots. If we look at the growth, it really comes from our entrepreneurs . . . what can we do in our legislation and policy mechanisms to encourage more and more entrepreneurs?" "Saurabh," as the minister called him, was Saurabh Srivastava, an entrepreneur and investor who had a long history of representing the interests of the Indian information technology (IT) and IT-enabled services (IT/IT-ES) industry. He was a former chair of NASSCOMM, the IT/IT-ES lobbying organization. The government had appointed him to official committees on venture capital policy (Planning Commission 2012d, 2006). He also sat on the central government's National Innovation Council, alongside prominent industrialists, business school professors, scientists, and filmmakers (Special Correspondent 2010). His casual comment at Davos was an iteration of a decade of advocacy for technology and venture capital to the Indian state.

Kocchar echoed Srivastava: "In India, it is the entrepreneurial spirit that has contributed to a lot of growth . . . how can PPP [public-private partnership] work together in every field? Health? Education? Expanding the sources of employment?" Referring to development, she continued, "It is a responsibility for everybody and an opportunity for everybody."

The audience erupted into applause. It was the only moment of applause in the whole panel discussion. Kocchar, Srivastava, and others offered entrepreneurial citizens as a force for economic development and as a substitute for the state. The private sector, they argued, could profitably provide what the state had promised under the banner of socialism but had strained to provide. Private citizens, as entrepreneurial innovators, ought to fill the gap. This was not the model of consumer-citizenship identified by political scientists and sociologists of the Indian middle classes. Those consumer citizens understood themselves as taxpayers entitled to state services in exchange (Lukose 2009; Fernandes 2006). Entrepreneurial citizens also wanted to fill the service gaps of the state.

As the applause faded, the state minister interjected with a correction: "There's an error in Saurabh's statement. The bulk of education and health care is in the public sector. Today, public-sector schools produce as good students as private schools. It was the public sector that eliminated the worst diseases before the corporate hospitals came." The state, Chidambaram argued, had a key role to play in fighting the inequality generated by free-market systems. He then shifted to a collaborative mood: "I welcome corporate social responsibility. I welcome public-private partnership. *But the role of the state cannot be underestimated or wished away.*"

It was true that the role of the state could not be wished away. However, among these elites, it was contested and malleable. And *nobody* underestimated the role of entrepreneurs as engines of development. Kocchar's call to entrepreneurial development—"a responsibility for everybody and an opportunity for everybody"—described a sensibility I recognized all around me in Delhi as I met professionals pursuing careers that allowed for volunteerism or private-sector development work, or renarrating their corporate work in socially beneficial terms (see also Sarkar 2016; Friedner 2015). At the end of this chapter and throughout this book, I chronicle the subtle cultural and labor politics of many such projects. But at a time when the promise of entrepreneurship seems ubiquitous, I first turn to a history of why the Indian state called on citizens as entrepreneurs. It was not always so.

A History of the Ideal Citizen after Independence

Planned Accumulation: 1947–late 1970s

The rhetoric of development as "everybody's responsibility" echoed the calls of decades past, when the Nehruvian state asked citizens to do their bit in the massive challenge of nation building. Jawaharlal Nehru was India's first prime minister and a left-leaning leader of the Indian nationalist movement (Zachariah 2004, xxi). His party, the Indian National Congress, ruled almost continuously until liberalization. Scholars of India broadly refer to the "Nehruvian" state as one that pursued development through economic planning and import substitution in the quest for national economic self-reliance and nonalignment with either capitalist or communist nations (Menon and Nigam 2007, 3). Planning was a key practice by which the central government attempted to manage India in its diversity and in the face of persistent colonial underdevelopment. Expert planners plotted economic parameters: inputs, outputs, import/export rules, and social policies, for example. Government actors, working with private industrialists, planned large-scale public undertakings such as factories, mills, dams, agricultural research, and production cooperatives.

This development formation posited a division of labor and intellect among Indian citizens. The middle classes were those administrative classes with access to English-language higher education in engineering, economics, sociology, planning, and design (S. Subramanian 2015). They worked as bureaucrats, planners, policy makers, rural reformers, social workers, and educators mediating national progress (Mazzarella 2005; Deshpande 2003; Hansen 1999, 52). Expert planners were to decide production targets, allocate of scarce resources, and choose industries and infrastructures to build. A cadre of bureaucrats, chosen through exams and insulated from electoral pressures, were tasked with implementing these plans largely outside of the domain of representative politics. Planning was the organ of development that made the government of India different from colonial Britain—accumulation would be developmental and nationally authentic, rather than extractive and foreign. In this way, historian Partha Chatterjee argues, planning became the seat of legitimacy for the postcolonial state as the organ tasked with rationally articulating the "single will and consciousness—the will of the nation" (1993, 205). Complementarily, government rituals, ceremonies, and rhetoric celebrated common Indians as workers, agriculturalists, and "producer citizens" (S. Roy 2007)—the engines driving these planned schemes to glory. These engines were the labor but not the reason of the nation. Films like Shyam Benegal's *Manthan* (1976) glorified the work of middle-class activists who showed peasant farmers the way to form thousands of cooperatives that led to India's "white revolution," the 1970s project that made India into the largest milk producer in the world. In stark contrast to contemporary figurations of entrepreneurship, the cooperative movement required cultural transformation through tenuous cross-class solidarities, group work, and active engagement of collectives who make up the nation.

In this Nehruvian period, entrepreneurs were of interest to planners but far from a priority or figures of widespread celebration. In India's Five Year Plans—public outcomes of national and state-level consultation and calculations—entrepreneurs featured only sparsely. Plans discussed entrepreneurs as India's business owners, from the richest industrialists to jobless engineers starting self-employment enterprises. The Third, Fourth, and Fifth Five Year Plans referred to "small entrepreneurs" in the same breath as cooperatives, artisans, and "small producers." Planners even worried that these entrepreneurs, private owner-operators, failed to be cost conscious (Fourth FYP) and damaged community resources in search of quick profits (Sixth FYP).[2] Entrepreneurship in this period was one means of producing employment and expanding production but not necessarily the best one.

Looking to Business: The 1980s

The central government began quietly looking to entrepreneurship as an engine of development in the 1980s. The Congress Party had won elections in the mid-1970s on the spectacular populist promise of *gharibi hatao*, which translates as "stop poverty." Its party institutions, however, were too weak to actually implement the policies (Corbridge and Harriss 2000, 67–80). In the face of regional unrest, the central government declared a national crisis, called "the Emergency." In the aftermath of the Emergency, the government decentralized control, relying on private industry to drive economic growth while formally integrating NGOs in development work such as education, health, and family planning (Kudva 2005, 244–45). Gandhi shifted from populist poverty reduction platforms to prioritizing the needs of business to stimulate economic growth, including suppressing trade union strikes (Rajagopal 2011, 1007; Kohli 2006a, 1255; Srinivasan 1997). This shift consolidated business's role as a prime driver of the larger project of development. The central government began to see the rights of the producer-citizen as at odds with the project of business-led development.

It was during the 1980s that the Sixth and Seventh Five Year Plans began to specify programs aimed at expanding India's "entrepreneurial base" in a wide range of "small industries," such as silk production, beekeeping, animal husbandry, and manufacture (Sixth FYP). These programs sought to close the gaps left by the organized sector by training people in establishing their own ventures. The Entrepreneurship Development Program, for example, trained underemployed science and technology graduates in small business creation (Seventh FYP). In the Sixth FYP, the Training Rural Youth for Self-Employment (TRYSEM) program aimed to train about one million low-income youth in agricultural enterprise creation. The Seventh FYP reported that TRYSEM trained 90 percent of the planning target.

It was also during the 1980s that the central government began restoring ties with the Indian diaspora abroad. FYPs looked to "Indians abroad" as repositories of management and technical expertise who could build out

India's telecommunication industries (Seventh FYP). U.S.-based telecommunication entrepreneur Sam Pitroda famously led the development of India's telecommunication networks during that decade (Chakravartty 2001, 79). The central government also implemented the NRI Portfolio Scheme, which enlisted people of Indian origin who were citizens of foreign countries as "nonresident Indian" (NRI) investors who could provide sought-after foreign exchange (Varadarajan 2010, 79). The state saw the diaspora as a favorable source of operating capital compared to the IMF, whose loans came with macroeconomic policy strings attached (Varadarajan 2010, 94). These shifts required refiguring the diaspora from "brain drain" and citizens of other nations to latent resources to be welcomed back as investors in the Indian nation-state, even as this refiguration threatened domestic Indian industry with new investors and competitors (Varadarajan 2010). These quiet turns to entrepreneurial, business-led dynamism became full-blown public celebration of entrepreneurial citizens only when economic liberalization threw up legitimacy crises for the Indian state in the next decade.

Legitimizing Liberalization in the 1990s: Forging the Entrepreneurial Citizen

With liberalization in the 1990s, the central government continued the decentralization of the decade prior but suddenly opened up its financial and consumer markets to global capital. For decades India had privileged domestic, privately owned firms and public-sector firms in key industries through import-substitution policies. The occasion of a foreign reserves crisis in 1991 gave World Bank– and IMF-trained technocrats in the central government the occasion to push through economic reforms (Corbridge and Harriss 2000, 146). The reforms began a process of selling off public-sector undertakings, deregulating foreign direct investment into Indian companies, and exposing domestic firms to competition with the introduction of foreign goods into domestic markets.

Factions of domestic capital balked at the reforms. The reforms faced resistance in the parliament, the political body responsible for approving the 1991 budget that would set the reforms into motion. Factions of domestic capital reliant on domestic consumer markets resisted the opening up of India to foreign competition (Varadarajan 2010, 110–22; Kohli 2006b, 1363). Liberalization threatened to expose domestic firms to competition by multinational firms, and domestic investors to competition for vehicles for financial accumulation. Critics argued that the reforms opened India up to recolonization by economic means (Varadarajan 2010, 122).

By contrast, the faction of domestic capital representing the high-tech and software industries, the Confederation of Indian Industry (CII), welcomed liberalization. CII contrasted itself with family-based industrial houses, representing itself as a "modern," technology-based Indian sector (Jackson 2013). It worked closely with policy makers, offering solutions and draft policy to the central government. Liberalization promised to facilitate and expand the ability to establish multinational technology agreements and export contracts (Varadarajan 2010, 119–20; Pedersen 2000; Kochanek 1995).

Liberalization's architects employed the figure of the entrepreneur to reframe opening capital markets as a testament to the maturing of India and its citizens. In 1991, for example, then minister of finance Manmohan Singh told the parliament, "After four decades of planning and development, we have now reached a stage of development where we should welcome rather than fear foreign investment. Our entrepreneurs are second to none. Our industry has come of age" (quoted in Varadarajan 2010, 128). In the same year, Prime Minister Narasimha Rao cautioned that the Indian state had to "formulate a policy not on the basis of an inferiority complex but on the basis of a certain national confidence" (M. Singh 1991, quoted in Varadarajan 2010, 129). Fears of liberalization, they argued, indicated colonial "inferiority complexes" and an absence of confidence. Singh and Rao challenged parliament on psychological and temporal terms. When the Eighth Five Year Plan assured that "the private sector has now come of age" (1992b, 5.3.1), what domestic industrialist would want to stand up and publicly deny that claim?

Champions of liberalization—government technocrats and CII—proffered a new ideal citizen to reconstruct nationalism in the face of contested globalization. This ideal citizen was the global Indian (Kini 2014; Varadarajan 2010; Mazzarella 2005, 158–59; Chakravartty 2001). This ideal citizen showed up in advertisements (Mazzarella 2005, 158–159; see figure 2), policy debates (Varadarajan 2010), and aspiration-generating business and policy books (e.g., Nilekani 2009; Khanna 2007; Das 2001). Its gender was usually (but not always) male. Its job was often software entrepreneur (Philip 2016). Companies such as Infosys and Wipro became symbols of new industries that could spring forth when skilled Indians didn't "wait for the government" to plan growth (Upadhya 2009, 79–83). Abroad, successful Indians in Silicon Valley became nationalist symbols of masculine, technical, and business achievement (Chakravartty and Sarkar 2013; Poster 2013; Dasgupta 2008; Philip 2005, 216; Chakravartty 2001). "The global Indian" could compete anywhere in the world while still maintaining affective ties to India as home (Mankekar 2015; Bhatt, Murty, and Ramamurthy 2010). These achievements signaled fuller participation in a universal modernity of development and progress through capitalism, while India became not an anticolonial national project but an agent of development and victorious competitor in the global game of the market.

FIGURE 2. An English magazine advertisement for the State Bank of India
pictures two suited men walking through a towered cityscape, confident, collegial,
with briefcases in tow. The ad reads: "The Indian entrepreneur has made the
world his backyard—so wherever he lands, his business acumen and skills lead
him to success. He overcomes language barriers, the foreign environment and
local competition." The ad honors the entrepreneurial citizen celebrated by
a liberalizing state after 1991 but prior to the rise of "inclusive growth."

The figuration of the global Indian was backed by concrete transformations to the law to support citizens who would be globally mobile, Indian in identity, and developmental in financial and technical capacities. The Citizenship Act of 2003 created two new legal categories of person, commonly referenced as Non-Resident Indians (NRIs): "Person of Indian Origin" (PIO) and "Overseas Citizen of India (OCI)" (Citizenship [Amendment] Act 2017). [3] PIO and OCI programs allowed people with citizenship outside of India to travel, buy property (except agricultural land), seek education, and invest money in India. People with Indian citizens as parents, grandparents, and, in the case of PIO, great-grandparents, were eligible.[4] OCI was originally available to Indians in only fourteen countries—wealthier industrialized countries where highly educated Indians had migrated since the 1960s (Varadarajan 2010, 138). These policies attempted to incorporate the resources of diasporic Indians—their capital and their high-value technical knowledge—into territorial nation building through NGOs, high-technology partnerships, and private-service firms (High Level Committee 2001). The initial act turned away from the larger numbers of diaspora—more often in labor or mercantile work—in Africa, the Middle East, and Asia who sent larger volumes of remittances to India than did the diaspora in richer countries (Jayal 2013; Van Der Veer 2005). The state prioritized those who could offer large investments and managerial expertise, implicitly prioritizing those with accumulated caste and class privilege. In 2005 the Citizenship (Amendment) Act expanded PIO and OCI eligibility to any country other than specifically excluded ones, such as Pakistan (Varadarajan 2010, 138). Though the law appeared to construct the diaspora as citizen, its history of exclusions belies the state's attempt to sort potential citizens according to their capacities to contribute status, expertise, and capital—in short, innovation—to the nation. The state was less interested in large remittance flows in small increments than it was in large investments by managerial entrepreneurs who could set up industrial projects.

The economic reforms of the 1990s also called on the public sector to reorganize itself as a series of public-private partnerships in the name of "fiscal discipline." The central government sought to "inspire confidence" among global investors and banks (Sunder Rajan 2006, 82). The financial terms of World Bank and IMF loans to India included stipulations that the state rely on the private sector, allow capital to flow across borders, repay debt and accrued interest to banks, and manage market infrastructures. This fiscal discipline was a significant shift from Nehruvian policies in which the central government distributed money to states or loaned on multidecade repayment schedules (Bear 2015, 34–36). With liberalization, the central government pitted regional and local levels of government against each other to attract private investors in what would have otherwise been state projects. As the Eighth Five Year Plan (1992a) put it:

> The public sector was assigned a place of commanding height in the Indian economic scene. . . . In the process, it has made the people take the public sector for granted, oblivious of certain crucial factors like efficiency, productivity and competitive ability. This has eroded the public sector's own sense of responsibility and initiative. . . . While there are several social and infrastructural sectors where only the public sector can deliver the goods, it has to be made efficient and *surplus generating*. It must also give up activities which are not essential to its role. The Eighth Plan has to undertake this task of reorientation. (emphasis mine)

In her study of a river port in India, anthropologist Laura Bear (2015) describes the "entrepreneurial society" of government officials and family capitalists who make the maintenance of public infrastructure into an opportunity for public-private partnership, creating projects that promise quick investor returns while sacrificing worker safety or infrastructural durability. State politicians' work of generating patronage and promising futures was no longer restricted to constituents and power brokers within India. They now had to travel to global centers of capital to pitch projects, construct promises, and attract investors (Sunder Rajan 2006, 86–89; Cross 2014). On the home front, bureaucrats and political parties facilitated the dispossession of peasants to make room for these promising, high-impact projects. The central government, in turn, relied on these projects to generate revenue to service international sovereign debt. The cosmopolitan Indian who could make deals in every country was competing not only in a market to make products and profit but also to gather the resources to do the work of the developmental state.

Legitimizing Intellectual Property in the 1990s: Intensifying the Call to Innovate

As India privatized state projects during liberalization, it also faced pressures to "harmonize" its understandings of knowledge, culture, and technology with international intellectual property (IP) regimes. It was through struggles over these shifts that innovation became both a source of value and something that every Indian ought to produce.

Prior to liberalization, innovation marked a process of change. In the 1980s, for example, the Sixth Five Year Plan described innovation could mean the adoption of technologies from elsewhere as well as new ways of organizing and administering development in the NGO, public sector, and private

sector. Through the early 2000s innovation remained a word that broadly referenced organizational novelty—something the state called for in the spirit
of modernization.

By the early 2000s transformations in trade policy, intellectual property,
and communication technologies created contradictions elites attempted to
resolve by calling for "innovation." With the global projects of expansion of the
internet and liberalization of trade, software companies and film and media
industries based out of the United States and Europe could now see Asia as
a market, reachable because of both import-friendly trade policies and computer networks. To secure these markets, however, they would have to displace
the networks of shop workers, hawkers, and local technicians who had been
distributing film and software in the absence of official channels. U.S.-based
multinational media corporations lobbied with the U.S. government, World
Trade Organization officials, and government elites to craft and push policy
that advanced their interests globally (Sundaram 2010, 110–12). They did not
limit their efforts to the law. They also fought culture in the field of discourse,
labeling diverse and often legal reverse engineering and distribution practices
as "piracy" (Philip 2005; see also da Costa Marques 2005). They positioned
"Asia" as a pirate continent with respect to U.S. and European interests.

India came under pressure to transform its intellectual property regimes to
align with those pushed by the United States and the World Trade Organization. India's intellectual property regime had historically privileged access and
wide manufacture of inventions over novelty. Since the 1970s it had enforced
"process patents" but not "product patents" (Surie 2014; Ramanna 2002; Mehrotra 1987). The Indian Patent Act of 1970 transformed India's IP regime to
prioritize access over monopoly rights. It forbade product patents in areas
crucial to national sovereignty such as food, drugs, space technologies, and
atomic energy. Instead, it allowed for process patents. This provision ensured
that India could produce equivalent versions of existing drugs and technologies without paying royalties, as long as companies invented an alternative process to produce equivalent products (Sunder 2006; Das 2003; Ramanna 2002;
Mehrotra 1987). Writing about similar policies in Brazil, historian of technology Ivan da Costa Marques (2005) describes this as "rights to creation"—the
right to create that which people use by controlling the labor, extraction, and
knowledge processes required to ensure the supply of a product.[5] These policies also allowed India to produce generics that drove down drug prices across
the developing world, making India one of world's largest pharmaceutical producers by the mid-2000s (Sunder 2006).

The collapse of the Soviet Union left developing countries like India vulner-
able to pressure from the World Bank, the WTO, and multinational corporations to move to product patents. Since the late 1990s the World Bank had

developed a set of "knowledge for development" (K4D) policy frameworks that emphasized the role of education, literacy, internet connectivity, science and technology funding, and scientific publishing as indexes of development potential (Radhakrishnan 2007). Crucially, K4D frameworks also included patent production and royalty payments as key to ranking countries (World Bank Institute 2008; Chen and Dahlman 2005). The WTO's preferred patent regime was the Agreement on Trade-Related Intellectual Property Rights (TRIPS)—an agreement that would ease the enforcement of product patents across national borders. The financial promise of the biosciences intensified the stakes and urgency of TRIPS negotiations (Sunder Rajan 2006; Hayden 2003). Indian NGOs and policy experts sounded alarms as U.S. firms attempted to patent the materials of everyday life in India: turmeric, basmati rice, and neem. Social movements, NGOs, and activists mobilized against these intellectual property regimes and their claims on life with appeals to human rights, public health, environmental rights, and distributive justice (Sunder 2006; Hayden 2003, 37–42; Shiva 1999). The Indian government fought those patents off in court and through diplomacy with the U.S. government (Fish 2006, 200).

Amid strong criticisms of IP regimes, domestic capital in the high-tech and pharmaceutical industries began to see the potential for patent monopolies through new drug development. India had already become a service export powerhouse in call centers and software outsourcing. Patents born of research and development promised value out of property rather than labor. Harmonized patent regimes meant that Indian companies could also expand into more lucrative work such as drug discovery work, algorithms research, and technology design in partnership with multinational companies invested in strong IP (Ramanna 2002). This section of Indians emerged as pro-TRIPS voices in the debate. Among activists as well, one set of voices—most famously Vandana Shiva and Anil Gupta—argued that the "innovation, creativity, and genius" of the poor ought to be recognized as IP (Shiva 2001, 49; Philip 2008, 257). TRIPS changed, in turn, to grant "traditional knowledge" and "indigenous" resources the status of property (Planning Commission 2012a, 259; Sunder 2007, 111–12; Ministry of Science and Technology 2003).[6] Under humanitarian and activist pressure, TRIPS also began to allow for countries to take measures to accommodate health crises (Sunder 2006, 293).

With this new inclusion of rural Indians, craftspeople, and the poor as potential creators of intellectual property, India's alignment with TRIPS appeared to be in everyone's interests—not just that of high-tech capital.[7] By 2005, India brought its law into alignment with TRIPS. In a shift that took place over a decade of political and policy struggle, its patent regime shifted from "process patents" to "product patents." This forbade the production of equivalent goods. The production of novel products became a legal and moral imperative (Sunder 2006; Ramanna 2002; Mehrotra 1987). Far from boring technical details, this shift in patent policy transformed the mechanisms by which Indians could convert labor into value and accumulate assets. It would no longer be fruitful to engineer a cheaper or more sustainable process to produce a good patented elsewhere.

The concept of innovation gained cultural power through news media, through its priority in policy, and through institutions of education. By 2003 Science and Technology Policy called for a "national innovation system" and declared support for patents, copyrights, and intellectual property to "ensure that maximum incentives are provided for individual inventors." The policy targeted not only the laboratories of technoscience but also "traditional knowledge" and "indigenous resources" (Ministry of Science and Technology 2003; see also Surie 2014, 47–48). The policy carried forward the long-standing priority the postcolonial state placed on "technology"—electrification, production machinery, telecommunications, and computing. Media scholar Paula Chakravartty (2004) calls these state-led projects to outfit the masses with technology "techno-populism." Technology, as a concept, named those kinds of machines and techniques by which modern societies defined their difference from putatively premodern, racialized ones (Oldenziel 1999). Innovation, however, was not only techno-populism. It prioritized monopolizable novelty. Innovation called on all Indians to see themselves and the social knowledge around them as sources for cultural and knowledge property for the nation (Kaur 2016). And it was one justification for extending some rights of Indian citizenship to diasporic "global Indians"—the highly trained, technological elites who benefited most from TRIPS (Radhakrishnan 2007).

Innovating for the Other: "Inclusive Growth" as Poverty Capital after 2004

As the economy grew between 1991 and 2004, so did inequality (Kohli 2012). The elections of 2004 pitted the Congress and left parties against the ruling Bharatiya Janata Party (BJP). Congress ran on a platform of liberalization coupled with social programs called "inclusive growth." The BJP, the incumbents, ran with the triumphant slogan "India Shining." The slogan attempted to sell an economic optimism built on economic growth rates and the expanded consumption of the middle classes (Wyatt 2005). Many expected the BJP to stay in power. As the votes were tallied, voters shocked elites by handing the BJP a stunning loss, stripping the party of one-third of its seats (Ganti 2013). "This is a verdict against globalization," one member of parliament told the press (Ramesh 2004). Growing inequality had dealt a blow to the legitimacy of the liberalization project. Economic growth would have to produce development the masses could feel.

The "inclusive growth" promise that Congress had ridden to victory in the 2004 election demanded a different kind of "global India." The triumphalist entrepreneur or business tycoon no longer appeared an inclusively *national* victory—the masses rejected "India Shining" and "the global Indian" dominated by upper castes and classes. It was during this period in the aftermath of the election that the figure of the ideal citizen took on the qualities of *developmental* entrepreneurial citizenship—benefiting not only oneself or the economy but also other citizens. This vision of the ideal citizen had long been part of technocratic ideas of how NRIs and OCIs could contribute expertise to nation-building projects. But it was only in the second half of the 2000s that this reformed entrepreneurial citizen—the entrepreneur as leader of the masses and agent of development—became iconic in public and policy culture. It was during this period when I carried out the bulk of fieldwork informing this book. As I did my fieldwork, I saw the rhetoric of "inclusive growth" all over big cities, newspapers, and in professional discourse in India. Newspaper columns, television programs, McKinsey reports,[8] and economics research all oriented around the question of inclusion. But what did inclusion mean?

The World Bank introduced "inclusive growth" to the global development lexicon in 2000. It did so after a decade of antiglobalization struggle between social movements, the IMF, the World Bank, and developmental states. The early 1990s were a time of elite optimism about liberalization as the universalization of liberal economic and legal regimes—so much so that Francis Fukuyama declared 1992 "the end of history" (Roy 2010, 15–16). Actually existing liberalization, however, generated hunger, health, and human welfare catastrophes as well as social movements resisting capitalist expansion and disciplines (Roy 2010). A group of economists, including Mahbub ul Haq and Amartya Sen, developed the "human development index" to track and express human welfare, education, and health as concisely and spectacularly as economic growth statistics (Sen 2000a; Sen 1999). By the late 1990s World Bank leaders had gotten the message and declared poverty a looming crisis (Rao and Walton 2004, 19; Stiglitz 2002).

Rather than roll back liberalization, advocates of inclusive growth sought to mitigate its toll on human welfare. Under Congress, this meant an election platform called the Common Minimum Program that guaranteed basic rights to food, education, and land. Such interventions promised to keep the masses out of crisis if not out of poverty (Prime Minister's Office 2004). The informal economy, however, posed a problem for economists. The category of "the informal" marked those who labored outside the organized sector, away from labor regulations and industrial zones where economists and policy makers had long focused their calculative attention. Informal workers might manufacture parts, produce baked goods, or fold dumplings. Five-star hotels or local children might buy their products. But their activities take place in complex outsourcing chains and in gray areas of the law (see Sanyal 2007, 195–208). With the turn to "inclusion," technocrats and business elites renarrated the informal economy, long considered to lag behind the modern, organized sector, as a dynamic site of enterprise and innovation (Ananya Roy 2014; Sanyal 2007). Business school professors, consultancies, and corporate executives painted India as a nation of entrepreneurs, naturalizing informality as potential.

Champions of entrepreneurship thereby attempted to manufacture a common sense that conflated the divergent interests of poorer Indians—"the entrepreneurial poor"—and high-tech entrepreneurs as being one and the same. This conflation of capitalists and the poor was starkly evident in the cover of a Planning Commission Report in 2012 titled "Creating a Vibrant Entrepreneurial Ecosystem in India" (2012d). The committee that authored the report represented the state, high tech, and high capital. Government officials representing science, small enterprise, and revenue were joined by Saurabh Srivastava (the NASSCOM founder who sang the praises of Indian entrepreneurs at Davos), lawyers, management consultants, and venture capitalists. The report opened with two promises of expanded entrepreneurship: the creation of some of the ten to fifteen million jobs sought by planners in the next decade, as well as "innovation-driven . . . solutions" to India's myriad social problems. The remainder of the report argued for policy frameworks and government programs to facilitate start-up investment, at both investment and exit or sale stages. Start-ups, here, could include "social impact" or conventional high-tech ones. In the dry pages of bulleted text, the primary beneficiaries of these policies are entrepreneurs who seek large-scale finance. Committee members framed these primary beneficiaries as having secondary beneficiaries—workers employed in the new enterprises and the poor who would benefit from their "solutions."

The report cover, however, graphically promised a very different primary beneficiary—the informal producer presented as entrepreneur (see figure 3). A vivid color photograph showed the hands of a South Asian woman as she scooped powder dyes out of a set of bowls arrayed on the street. She dispensed vibrant India's commodities into small bags suitable for consumers with little money to spend. For those with more money, stacks of large powder dye bags sat ready for purchase on the street. The cover was a version of what Ananya Roy describes as poverty capital's hero: the third-world woman as microfinance borrower and bearer of risk (Roy 2010, 72; see also M. Murphy 2017;

Creating a Vibrant Entrepreneurial Ecosystem in India

Report of The Committee on Angel Investment & Early Stage Venture Capital

June 2012

Government of India
Planning Commission
New Delhi

FIGURE 3. The cover of a Planning Commission report, "Creating a Vibrant Entrepreneurial Ecosystem in India" (2012), presents a street-side pigment seller as an icon of India's entrepreneurial potential, even as the report focuses on the needs of high-tech finance.

Moodie 2013). It not only justified microfinance but also suggested that India's informal economy was a source of potential and strength. Nation branders such as the India Brand Equity Foundation frequently published such images to distribute to elites at Davos or other trade-related conferences, even as urban middle classes cracked down on actual street entrepreneurs to bring aesthetic order to their real estate (Rajagopal 2002).

This conflation of capitalists and the very poor was routine in elite arguments about entrepreneurship. Economists often presented the informal economy as a "breeding ground for entrepreneurship" (Oberoi and Chadha 2001, quoted in Sanyal 2007, 205). Some credited the absence of labor laws and regulations—informality itself—as key to its creativity, generativity, and potential; domestic capitalists held labor laws and due process of India's organized sector as an impediment to innovation (Maiti and Sen 2010, 7). Planning Commission task force members blamed proworker regulations for slowed start-up creation (2012d, 7). Informality promised flexible value creation and innovation; vulnerability was recoded as sustainability. The conflation of the informal micro entrepreneurs and high-tech capitalists was also useful to those rushing to present India as a site ripe for capital investment.

This conflation persisted despite well-reasoned arguments against it by economists of different stripes. Abhijit Banerjee and Esther Duflo, highly respected in development economics, argued that informal merchants were less "capitalists without capital" than people investing in their comfort when profits were exceedingly hard to come by (2012b, 208). They devote a chapter of their bestselling book *Poor Economics* to why entrepreneurship won't lift the poor out of poverty. Marxist economist Kalyan Sanyal (2007) underscored that capital among the informal poor barely accumulated. Those in "the need economy" made enough to feed themselves and reproduce their lives but not enough to invest and accumulate. Why, when Marxists and liberal experts agree, was the idea so persistent? Banerjee and Duflo offer one explanation: "The idea of the entrepreneurial poor is helping secure a space within the overall anti-poverty discourse where big business and high-finance feel comfortable getting involved" (2011b, 207).

A wide array of projects emerged to capitalize on the poor. Ananya Roy (2010) calls these "poverty capital." These projects were fueled by World Bank networks that began to generate expertise on the poor as debtors and consumers. Industry and expert speakers often retold tendentious studies, selectively spinning studies and stories into hype (see Srinivasan and Burrell 2013). These partial truths were promissory hype that fell short of fraud (Sunder Rajan 2006). Roy (2010, 23) identified two contrasting paradigms of microfinance: the Grameen Bank's rights-based loans that favored the poor versus Bill Gates's "creative capitalism" that positioned the poor as a market. The first frames the poor as entrepreneurs who can produce goods and services if only they had access to capital. The second frames the poor as consumers of a benevolent, technocratic capitalism. In the world of social enterprise that I studied, these paradigms were rarely in competition; rather, projects simultaneously assumed and experimented with both models.

Outside of India, Wall Street turned its attention to "poverty capital" as a way to offset aging consumer populations and slowing economic growth in highly industrialized countries (Wilson and Purushothaman 2003, 2, 17). This was well before the U.S. and European financial crises that would come half a decade later. The Goldman Sachs report "Dreaming in BRICs" (Wilson and Purushothaman 2003) issued forecasts to the management consultants, industry pundits, and executives who made up its readership. It predicted that by 2050 the BRICs would become the world's biggest economies (as measured in U.S. dollars), a shift away from a global economy dominated in size by the United States, the United Kingdom, Canada, France, Germany, and Japan. The report was only one marker in a proliferation of reports, business school books, and shifts in business pedagogy that directed global management to the potential of the global poor as a market of consumers, debtors, and investable lives (Ablett et al. 2007; Khanna 2007; Prahalad 2005). For Wall Street, even social welfare programs like National Rural Employment Guarantee Scheme Act (NREGA), the Congress-led program to provide a hundred days of guaranteed rural employment, became a signal of rural consumer market opportunity (Ablett et al. 2007, 83–84).

Beyond Wall Street, "inclusive growth" extended long-standing business family traditions. During the independence effort, Mahatma Gandhi—patronized by industrialist families—called for a "trusteeship" system in which the wealthy became stewards of resources for those around them. This system called on the wealthy to benevolently regulate concentrations of wealth through philanthropy on behalf of an abstract public (Birla 2009, 104–5; Zachariah 2005, 167). Crucially, Gandhi did not trust workers to organize their own lives or production; trustees, he argued, accumulated wealth and mastered workers through their "intelligence and tact" (B. Chakrabarty 2011, 67, quoting Gandhi 1921). In the mid-2000s elites transformed trusteeship into something that could itself generate profit while managing the poor. Business school professor C. K. Prahalad's book *The Fortune at the Bottom of the Pyramid* (2005) suggested that businesses could create products and services for the poor, serving them as customers rather than communities to whom trustees had duties. Companies began to experiment with using NGOs, social networks, and self-help groups to distribute products (Elyachar 2012a, 2012b). Prahalad had pitched this vision to the National CII conference in 2003 ("Indian Industry" 2003) during an event whose agenda focused on more near-term profit concerns like marketing, product quality, and service industry differentiation (Mahindra and Khanna 2004; Vidyasagar 2004).[9] With the Congress victory in 2004, CII suddenly centered Prahalad's vision, actively adopting the rhetoric of inclusive growth. It staged conferences and began to issue press releases framing Indian industry as a steward and agent of rural development

("CII Outlines" 2004). Domestic capital began to emphasize promises of rural development alongside promises of growth in the gross domestic product.

The Companies Act of 2013 made this promise of responsibility into a legal requirement for the largest Indian companies. The act was primarily designed to shift the responsibility of corporate oversight from the government to company shareholders (Roy and Celestine 2009). It also created a legal category for the iconic start-up as "one-man company," but few commented on this technicality (Dash 2016; Ministry of Corporate Affairs 2013; National Knowledge Commission 2008, 80). The act's most spectacular and highly publicized provision required the highest revenue companies to donate 2 percent of their net profits to corporate social responsibility (CSR) projects (Balch 2016), including nonprofit health, education, housing, and welfare initiatives, as well as technology incubators in central government institutions (Bahl 2014).[10] The 2013 act did not include technology incubators, but the BJP-led parliament amended the act in 2015 to cement the status of technology start-ups as a social good even in the eyes of the law. CSR work included remedies for dispossession, as in a mining company offering housing and services for those displaced by its extractive work. Implicitly, the Companies Act required large companies to become a new kind of trustee, allowing them to burnish their own legitimacy through selective exercises of public duty (Lok Sabha 2010, 158). CSR gifts allowed industrial discretion and brand building in contrast to the alternative—higher taxes and government distribution and provision of services formally accountable to political processes. The passage of the act, industry analysts estimated, made US$5 billion available for the social impact sector (P. Shah 2013); this bolstered the promise that entrepreneurial citizens would find funders and investors in their designs for development.

From Planning an Economy to Governing a Movement

Entrepreneurship formally supplanted planning in national government language in 2015. That year Prime Minister Narendra Modi's government closed the Planning Commission (PC) and replaced it with the National Institution for Transforming India, or NITI Aayog ("On New Year" 2015). In Hindi, *niti aayog* sounded like the words for "policy commission." Plans direct futures, while policies condition them (see, for example, Baumol 1990). The mandate of NITI Aayog was "to provide advice and encourage partnerships between key stakeholders and national and likeminded Think Tanks," and "to create a knowledge, innovation, and entrepreneurial support system" (Press Information Bureau 2015).

The Planning Commission stood for Nehruvian planning to achieve distributional outcomes, though its role had shifted over the decades. Since its start, the PC had employed the most sophisticated economists and statisticians in India (and, by consequence, the world) to calculate the inputs, outputs, and money flows that could rapidly industrialize and develop India. The PC was staffed by permanent members chosen for expertise in selected areas; thus the commission's reports and activities were less subject to shifts in political parties. As India turned toward liberalization, the work of the commission shifted from "command" to "coordination." With this shift, some saw the postliberalization PC's unique role as making policy prescriptions for welfare and social justice, including emerging regional inequalities as states competed for investment and resources. The Planning Commission had the power to allocate funds to ministries and state governments, giving its recommendations some heft, though it had no capacity or power to implement its prescriptions directly. As such, it had the capacity to serve as a stable, technocratic counterweight to elected politicians, as well as ministries with more domain-restricted priorities. By contrast, NITI Aayog lost funding allocation powers, strengthening elected officials' hands. NITI Aayog convened state chief ministers, producing vision and statistical documents to facilitate coordination among them (M. Sengupta 2015).

In many respects, NITI Aayog's organization simply symbolized transformations that had already begun with liberalization in 1991 as the PC shifted from setting private and public industry targets to coordinating them with the state in a more liberalized regime. NITI Aayog formalized this coordination function, symbolizing the break from Nehruvian top-down planning and the Congress Party legacy. One PC report, called "Scenarios: Shaping India's Future," modeled the Indian national assemblage as a flotilla: "The many diverse communities that compose our nation (class, caste, region, etc.) can be imagined to be sailing in ships in a flotilla on a sea that is often rough" (2013, 6). The sea was meant to symbolize the national and global environment and a context of "stress on the earth's resources." With proper reform, the report argued, the flotilla would be governed by a system that could break impasses and come to consensus about direction:

> The ships are manned by inventive crews, empowered to try new ways to speed up their ships. With good communications between ships, new ideas from one ship are transmitted quickly to others. . . . All ships have a map, know what route to take, and have good instruments to guide themselves, and coordinate with others. (10)

The language of the report echoed proposals published by then commission member Arun Maira under his own name across books and op-eds over a decade (Maira 2009, 2015).

The "Scenarios" report optimistically described an assemblage of actors in charge of the work of governance. Maira's own career in management consulting, at Davos, and at the PC traversed the web of corporate and policy expertise characteristic of governance assemblages (Ong and Collier 2005). The Indian state has long relied on NGOs and, later, public-private partnerships to extend its reach. As it came to rely on entrepreneurs as well, these varied entities—for-profit and not-for-profit, private and public—became ships in a flotilla, making history but not in sailing conditions of their own making. The report modeled how these agents could, while acting in the interests of their own organizations, coordinate with each other to fulfill those interests in ways legible as nation building. The flagship—the Indian state— would set the course while allowing NGOs and private actors to follow community interest and self-interest, respectively.

What is the work of the setting the course? What does governmentality (Foucault 1991; D. Scott 1995) look like when it is organizations, firms, and citizens—not just population—that become objects to be guided and steered? Planning Commission documents described the role of the central government as "enabling" this array of actors through "good governance." The Twelfth Five Year Plan (2012a, 299) poses the problem as one of "stimulating a 'movement' . . . across a large, diverse, and democratic system." Entrepreneurial citizens appear animated by their own, authentic aspirations and inspiration, yet the state remains, working to steer and stimulate them in some directions and not others.

Following World Bank guidelines, this vision of the Indian state minimized state intervention, allowed market institutions to distribute resources, and acted as a check on excesses (Planning Commission 2007a, 223–24; see also Baruah 2012, 3–4). This did not necessarily mean that the government receded. In India it also meant that the government focused on service delivery or even guaranteed employment when markets seemed to have failed (Roy Chowdury 2013, 86). These minimum-level-of-care policies ensured the legitimacy of the state and a consumer market for Indian products. The private sector, however, would otherwise provide the material means of living; this way, the nation's use values could register, through exchange value, as economic growth. The work of rule expanded beyond experts and the elected to all kinds of professionals, and entrepreneurial ones at that. Diversity in wealth and poverty, region and religion, promised innovation for the nation, even if the rewards were unequally distributed.

The terms of entrepreneurial citizenship fit with a broader professionalization of politics through "governance." Partha Chatterjee describes governance as rule mediated by expertise: "the body of knowledge and set of techniques used by, on behalf of, those who govern" (2004, 4). He builds on Michel Foucault's account of governmentality (Chatterjee 2004, 35; Foucault 1991) and particularly the production of expertise about populations through categories like tribe, community, or minorities. These forms of expertise mediate the "pluralization of the state" (Chandhoke 2003, 2964, quoted in Datta Gupta 2013, 67)—here, through what I am calling entrepreneurial citizenship. In India, the pluralized state governed people through assemblages—projects that extended transnationally but took form and significance locally (Ong and Collier 2005). NGOs, civil society organizations, agencies, and private institutions performed governmental functions (Datta Gupta 2013, 67; Ferguson and Gupta 2002) and sometimes legitimized the Indian state by managing surplus populations (Sanyal 2007). The language of governance allowed diverse organizations to speak to one another in exchange, absent a coherent suprainstitutional authority (Ludden 2005, 4048).

Financial regimes also disciplined this assemblage (Bear 2015; Ludden 2005). International development agencies shaped agendas, setting the bounds within which NGOs and social entrepreneurs could express their goals. CSR funding allowed corporations to extend their authority to citizens through assemblage (Mosse 2013, 238–39). (Chapters 3 and 6 explore how entrepreneurial citizens optimistically search for opportunities while disciplined by the interests of funders and partners who resource their projects.) World Development Reports, Millennium Development Goals, and the manufacturing capacities and interests of companies seeking fortune at the bottom of the pyramid all shaped which efforts at progress could be recognized as "opportunity," which appeared as threat, and which could not be heard at all.

Proliferating Entrepreneurial Citizens

On a visit to the Delhi Science Center I saw how the central government extended a nationalist pedagogy of innovation, renarrating knowledge in entrepreneurial terms as opportunity and value. As I strolled through the center, groups of school children scurried chaotically around displays that placed India in a universal history of science. A room called *dharohar*, or heritage, produced for India a scientific past long denied by Eurocentric historians. A historical exhibit explained ancient Harappan architecture and planning patterns. A glass case displayed printouts of scholarly articles on histories of Indian technology, as if to offer scholarly support for the claim that India belonged in a global scientific history. Another gallery extolled the "information revolution" and the life sciences; a brain model the size of my body presided over the gallery, labeled "Seat of Intellect." Behind glass double doors festooned with words like "motivation," "creativity," and "vision" stood an Intel-sponsored "Innovation Space" (figure 4). The space was available to children only by appointment; passers-by without an appointment could read through the glass doors a wall-sized panel that diagrammed an intellectual property cosmology: "Idea to Product: The Process of Patenting Your Ideas" (figure 5).

FIGURE 4. The Delhi Science Center opened an Innovation Space in 2014. The double glass doors were festooned with the words "motivation," "innovation," "build," "develop," "explore," "vision," "practice," "inquisitive," "creativity," and "action." Entry was for "members only." Through the double doors, those on the outside faced a diagram explaining a cosmology of intellectual property: "Idea to Product." (Photograph by author)

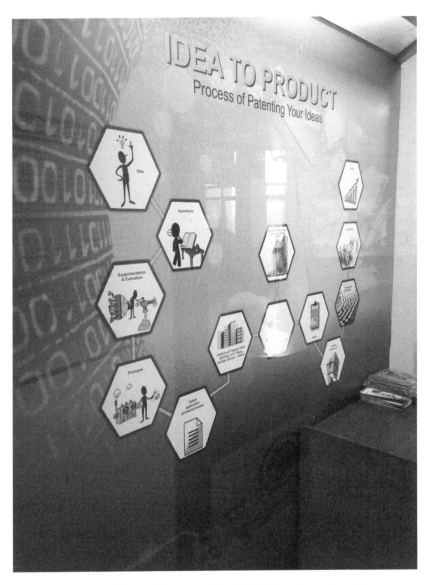

FIGURE 5. At the immediate entry of the Delhi Science Center Innovation Space, visitors and those peering in would find a map: "Idea to Product: Process of Patenting Your Ideas." (Photograph by author)

The map "Idea to Product" depicted a chronotope of innovation that erased workers, natural resources, and risk. The map sequentialized product development to explain it to children: "Idea—Hypothesis—Experimentation and Evolution—Prototype—Patent application (product/process)." From these schematics of intellectual property production, the path moved through a number of institutions that consecrated the invention and inventor: "Intellectual Property Office Building G.S.T. Road, Guindy, Chennai—60032—World Intellectual Property Organization—International Preliminary Examining Authority," represented by tall buildings and slick logos. From there, the idea would become a "Patent," then "Product Development" likened to a Rubik's Cube puzzle. Next, the hero's journey went to "Commercial production," symbolized by an assembly line packed with thousands of bottles—the idea reproduced in matter. The penultimate step was "Marketing" and the last step, "Profit," with the proverbial graph that went up and to the right in the background. This map was of a piece with the consistent lionization of software entrepreneurship in English-language newspapers, broadcasts, and bookstores in India (see Philip 2016; Upadhya 2009). Absent from the map of innovation were natural resources and labor, taken for granted to the point of erasure.

The map visualized the cosmology of value favored by the state, the World Bank, and the thought leaders of domestic capital. Scientists, technologists, and managers were its heroes. Knowledge-as-value could take the form of start-ups traded by commercial capital (Sunder Rajan 2006, 7–11). It could take the form of patents that could be traded or used to monopolize production of a product. It could be found in designs for products and services that approached the poor as consumers through a market.

The entrepreneurial citizens I knew called on more diverse politics and histories of engaging in people's science movements, open source, and appropriate technology movements. Arun, one DevDesign cofounder, turned to design as an attempt to turn away from editing media for corporations like MTV. He cited as inspiration Barefoot College of Tilonia, a school that trains rural people in skills of engineering, water testing, and health care to serve their communities (Bhowmick 2011; Roy and Hartigan 2008). Bunker Roy, a founder of the college, borrowed the model from Maoist China's barefoot doctors. Others I worked with looked up to Poonam Bir Kasturi, a Bangalore-based designer turned waste activist who took a more overtly political stance in her work. Her NGO, the Daily Dump, designed composters that craftspeople could build out of inexpensive, local clays. She made her designs freely available through open-source licenses. A fierce critic of corporate product design (Kasturi 2002), she and her group also conducted waste tours to encourage more sustainable consumption among middle-class Indians. Still others celebrated P. Sainath, a rural journalist famed for covering farmer suicides, debt, and the violence of the market economy (Sainath 1996). Curiously, champions of social entrepreneurship celebrated Bir Kasturi and Roy even though their projects did not register as economic growth, new firms, or large-scale job creation in the organized sector. Bir Kasturi went on to win the India Social Entrepreneur of the Year Award in 2015 (Lucchi 2015)—an award given by a "sister organization" to Davos and judged by Indian business executives, government officials, and nonprofit leaders. Promoters of entrepreneurship also claimed Roy. He won awards and grants for social entrepreneurship from the Schwab Foundation in 2003 and the Skoll Foundation in 2005 ("Barefoot Evangelist" 2006). These awards singularized activists and their movements in entrepreneurial leaders. In doing so, the awards pluralized entrepreneurship beyond high tech, beyond Silicon Valley, and beyond business schools, widening its appeal even to critics of capitalist systems. The projects offered legitimacy to entrepreneurialism and inspiration for new models of innovation and productivity. Innovation as policy, however, focused on the production of knowledge and technology as value: product, patent, and investment vehicle.

Conclusion

As postindependence India intensified its exposure to global capital and property regimes, entrepreneurial citizenship offered a pervasive answer first to the withdrawal of the state from development tasks and later to the forms of exclusion generated by Indian capitalism. Good citizens built their own wealth while also acting as trustees of poorer others. Industrialists in India, guided by Gandhi, had long imagined themselves in this way. Whereas the Gandhian trustee treated the poor as objects of responsibility, the entrepreneurial citizen treated them as opportunities—markets in the making. With shifts in India's political economy, the state and domestic capital have refigured the ideal citizen in turn.

The turn toward entrepreneurial innovators was not a break but an extension of long postindependence histories of "betting on the rich" (Ludden 2005, 4047; see also Kohli 2006a). The Congress Party had long pursued investments and labor policies that encouraged the private sector to produce the nation's needs. Gandhi's trusteeship system tasked the wealthy with setting agendas for workers and the poor. With liberalization, the state prioritized the needs of high-tech capital, enabling their service exports and technology acquisition while opening up other domestic industry to foreign competition. The figure of "the global Indian" narrated this political shift as the opening of possibility for Indian economic triumph. When liberalization's fruits failed to reach the much poorer, voting masses, the ideal citizen had to shift again from an agent of wealth and power to a new, speculative trustee—the visionary steward of development.

Entrepreneurial citizenship hailed the middle class—largely those employed by and managing the private sector that liberalization served—as agents of governance. As the state parceled off its functions to the private sector, entrepreneurial citizens built networks, learned to speak the language of governance, and proliferated investable vehicles for offering services and commodities. In some cases, markets of consumers would judge which innovations would succeed. In other cases, entrepreneurial citizens sought to subcontract for the state itself in development projects, managing lines of credit for micro entrepreneurs or providing health services, for example. Even the home became a development workshop; anthropologists Amy Bhatt, Madhavi Murty, and Priti Ramamurthy (2010) observed that middle-class women in Bangalore took it on themselves to impose family planning and financial responsibility pedagogies on their domestic workers. In each of these cases, entrepreneurs became agents of governance, but outside of formally accountable structures of state policy implementation.

Historian David Ludden (2005, 4048) argues that as states have lost their disciplining power to markets, they have lost their leadership role in development as well. Territorial boundaries no longer define the "participants, populations, and priorities" in the development process. Even as funds from the Gates Foundation, multinational corporations, and venture capital roamed India searching for fortunes "at the bottom of the pyramid," nationalist imaginaries, as well as caste, labor, and gender relations, guided middle-class imaginaries and enactments of development work. Entrepreneurial citizenship took its particular forms—at the time of my fieldwork, innovation as inclusive growth—as the product of a dynamic process in which high-tech capital, political actors, and the middle classes worked to manufacture consent for transformations in India's political economy.

3

Teaching Citizenship, Liberalizing Community

POLICY MAKERS intent on liberalizing India from the 1990s on looked to entrepreneurs to become engines of infrastructural development, economic growth, and "vibrant" order.[1] To them, India's population could become vibrant or violent. All hinged on whether the nation's billion was figured as a mass ready to work, start up, and consume, or as a frustrated surplus of people in need of employment, food, and education. Those on the right saw occasional eruptions of communal violence as unfortunate but understandable; those in the center sought to marshal those forces toward orderly and secular forms of development; those on the left lamented the suppression of political energy by a state that saw organized labor as a damper on growth. From right to left, middle-class commentators characterized the national education system—the valorization of engineering schools, the relative absence of liberal arts, and the culture of exams—as deadening creativity, producing alienation, and generating civic intolerance, failing to serve Indians and the nation alike.[2] Critics figured India's population as a kind of potential energy—and not always positively. By the late 2000s entrepreneurial citizenship promised to turn this energy toward constructive ends.

This dilemma was nowhere more acute than in the city of Ahmedabad, where communal riots in 2002 had killed thousands of Muslims and a much smaller number of Hindus. Ahmedabad was the home of Gandhi's Sabermati Ashram, from which he had started his famously nonviolent salt march protests. It was also the home of India's premier business, planning, and design schools. And it was where alumni of the National Institute of Design (NID) set up schools, contests, and museums to cultivate and evangelize entrepreneurial forms of civic voluntarism to heal the city and secure the future. Ahmedabad was but one city where conferences, workshops, and educational institutions worked to make liberal, development-minded Indians. And they did so in the idioms of design and innovation. Design and innovation even had national policy pull: the Ministry of Human Resources Development issued a "Design Manifesto" calling for Indian Institutes of Technology engineers to align the technical and the social through design pedagogy (A. Sharma 2014).

This chapter shows how and why "design thinking" became a model for the ethos of entrepreneurialism. Entrepreneurial citizenship called on Indians to turn development into an opportunity, pursuing nation building and economic growth at once. Design became a powerful metaphor for steering these entrepreneurial energies with reason, aesthetics, and civic care. The conference called Design in Education was held at NID in 2011 and featured prominent professors, filmmakers, and NGO founders all advocating for design as civic pedagogy. Its conveners promised that every child could be an entrepreneur, improving India "in line with a vision of a democratic society," as one convener put it in her keynote. They saw entrepreneurial design as secular, optimistic, and individuated channel for Indian energies that might otherwise pursue politics based on regional, caste, or religious identities. They borrowed practices from product design and technology innovation to make these secular pedagogies of development. Design, and in particular "design thinking," drew together the cultural and the technical into an optimistic orientation toward the world as a problem and as a set of possibilities for improvement. Advocates of design as a civic pedagogy of entrepreneurship translated development, planning, and governance into a pedagogy of imagination, entrepreneurial action, and a contagious civic sense.

This chapter analyzes conference talks, films, and family histories of activism to show how design became a model for remaking relationships between middle-class citizens and broader communities in India. I pay special attention to the Design in Education conference in 2011 as a place where elites reworked ideas of citizenship, community, human capacity, and civic belonging. The conference's message attracted coverage in national newspapers, from Indian parliamentarians, and from the Technology, Education, and Design (TED) conference. I chose this conference as a place to see entrepreneurial citizenship in the making for several reasons. First, it staged oft-told and promising stories of development that were in much wider circulation in India and abroad. For example, the convener's TED Talk about making kids entrepreneurial had over one million views. The ideas represented here traveled: I had seen another speaker, an education entrepreneur, at two additional innovation conferences in Delhi and Bangalore. Second, the conference was a place where I could see how teachers and NGO workers reacted to these proposals; I often observed them react favorably, or at least with interest. In the accounts of the conference that follow, I show how civil society actors translated development into a problem of the entrepreneurial ethos, and how they drew on the legitimacy of Silicon Valley entrepreneurialism and design to strengthen their message. This is the work of articulating an entrepreneurial vision of development and the work of attracting others who could make that vision into a reality. I show how this vision translated large-scale challenges of development, planning, and governance into localized problems that called for "entrepreneurial action" among citizens. Design offered a set of techniques, success stories, and a prestigious skill set that married private interests and public benefit.

Design techniques and entrepreneurial metaphors traveled well because of what they promised and what they obscured. They married care for potential users with the legitimacy of Silicon Valley innovation and the making of services and commodities. They appealed to NGO workers, schoolteachers, activists, and elites alike as a form of rationality accessible to all—simply a "way of thinking that anyone can do," as one teacher put it to me. The universality of this promise was possible, however, only by obscuring the very structural forces that produced the difference and inequalities design sought to remedy. Design improved the world by adding to it—adding initiatives, products, and options. Lost in the frame were questions of unequal starting points, uneven distributions, or reparation. It promised this additive transformation by intervening in desirable ways, rather than inconvenient or even objectionable ones. Design and entrepreneurship were linked practices; together they proliferated products, managed risk, and promised novel sources of value. As design and entrepreneurship became civic pedagogy, a model of management became a model of care, community, and speculative experiment. The skills of innovation and the skills of substantive citizenship were, in these formulations, one and the same. Entrepreneurial citizenship subsumed political desire into productive potential—the potential of speculative value production that blurred the economic, personal, and cultural.

Remaking Education: From "Outsourcing Worldview" to Unleashed Authenticity

The morning of the conference, two hundred teachers, journalists, school administrators, and NGO workers assembled in an NID auditorium to learn how design could transform Indian education. The convener was NID alumna and now private school founder Kiran Bir Sethi. She brought together Indian elites—including a blockbuster Bollywood screenwriter, Indian Institute of Management professors, Harvard-educated education entrepreneurs, and even Stanford University design professors (via Skype), as well as her own students—to make the case and spread the message.

Bir Sethi beamed from the podium, wearing cosmopolitan linens and energizing the audience with an intense smile. Her image as a model entrepreneur had already traveled widely. She had spoken at TED Global in Bangalore, and her video had circulated widely. Her work had been featured in *India Now* magazine, established by the right-led government and continued under the center to promote an image of an investor-friendly India (S. Singh 2010). In the auditorium that day, she recounted her story of starting Riverside, the Ahmedabad private school "where common sense is common practice" (Townsend 2014). She had been working happily as a graphic and interior designer, she explained, until her first child went to school. Dissatisfied with the values and discipline inculcated by her son's teachers, she took matters into her own hands, starting the school that she wanted. She recounted Riverside's origin story as an exemplar of entrepreneurship in pursuit of actualization for self and community.

According to Bir Sethi, the Indian self was in trouble, and India with it. Throughout the conference, alienated children were presented as robots, as puppets, as suicidal, as dulled followers. The Indian child was alienated by the disciplined competition of the Indian educational system. Indian children were synced with national time but out of sync with their own desires, with the problems local to them, and with their energy. India was a product of this alienated child, multiplied in the millions.

Bir Sethi presented her own students as energetic and progressive models of what other Indian children could become. They danced. They choreographed. They chose their own music. They campaigned against the use of child labor in the production of *agarbati*, or incense sticks. In blue polo shirts, freshly washed, they took the stage one by one, explaining to the audience what students needed to build a modern India while becoming their best selves. As a small sea of bright blue shirts, the children appeared from a distance as a relatively undifferentiated citizenry—full of potential and their differences obscured. Standing under bright lights, a teenage girl took the stage and in very careful English explained: "Students need plurality in identity so they won't just be a number," speaking a truth apparently so self-evident that even a child could teach it. Bir Sethi cheered her on from the seats below. The girl continued: "Well-rounded students are happier." Projected starkly on the screen behind her were words, unspoken but haunting: "Student suicides." The next speaker, a professor from the prestigious IIM-Ahmedabad, resurrected suicides as a signal that Indian youth in high-pressure, elite institutions were barely surviving in prestigious professions for which they were often ill-suited. India's hierarchies of prestige and class mobility—and those who made the pressures real for children—were alienating India's future.

Bir Sethi then mobilized the voice of youth again, screening an award-winning film produced by a group of NID animation students. The film, *Unni: The Plight of a Kid and Many Others*, had won national awards and had gained press coverage for its coverage of "tuition culture" (Jose et al. 2007; see figure 6).

FIGURE 6. Stills from National Institute of Design student
film *Unni* (2007). (NID Animation Film Design)

The film opens with the dawn breaking through the bedroom window of
a young kid. The alarm clock rings unforgivingly. A trophy stands perched on
the nightstand, standing guard over a photograph of the same trophy, clutched
by the kid. It's five o'clock, Sunday morning. Time to work. The parents come
into the bedroom and show the kid his schedule. They brush his teeth, bathe
him, and, with unremitting time discipline, drop him into a desk chair. Mom
places a pencil, a book, and milk in front of him. The kid's job is to sit there
as tutor after tutor comes through, droning and drilling about national curriculum subject materials. The first tutor glides inhumanly into the room,
casting a long and foreboding shadow. A looming chant, "kooooyannisqatsi,"
announces his entry. The chant is taken from *Koyaanisqatsi: Life Out of Balance* (1982), an art film popular with NID students today. As the camera pans
to the tutor's face, the ladies around me—all teachers themselves—burst into

laughter. The tutor is a Hitler doppelganger! He is a windup robot putting the kid through his paces.

The tone of the animation changes markedly at 4:58 pm. It's break time. The kid gets up from his desk, a bit shell shocked. He walks into his room, puts on his Mozart record, and floats away in a fantasy of passionate creativity. Imagined kid Mozart gives way to imagined kid Elvis. And kid Elvis gives way to kid Zakir Hussain in virtuoso Hindustani tabla performance. The timer rings; break is over. The parents come in to usher the kid to the next study session, but not before noticing his affinity for music. The kid takes his position behind the desk for the expected science tutorial. Instead, a parent drops a tabla on the table. A happy ending! Our young protagonist's education is taking his own talents and passions into account.

As the film screen went dark, the audience in the auditorium burst into applause. Teachers called out from their seats and a few stood up. The film had struck a chord, and not just one but many. Robotic systems of discipline. Alienated children. Artistic passions, like weeds trying to push their way through the pavement. With these images, the film vividly reiterated the critiques of Indian educational achievement advanced by the other conference speakers on previous days. One ponytailed adolescent wearing the blue Riverside School polo shirt spoke carefully under the bright lights of the stage, reiterating the message again. *Unni*'s young animators symbolized adult instructors as crushing, alienating machines destroying youth potential.

The problem of the mass-alienation machine reappeared during a dinnertime dance performance. The performance began with drably dressed Riverside students twitching mechanically on stage. They danced as puppets in synch with each other, limbs pulled in unison by invisibly tugging strings. A single puppet master descended from above, joining the children he controlled. Slowly, the rhythms of the music grew more complex, and two sparkling green creatures burst into the ordered dance, pirouetting and jumping with sparkling, leaf-like skirts flying behind them. They darted about the stage, tapping each of the puppet children one by one. Each puppet awoke suddenly, suddenly finding movement in individuated dances of their own but moving to a common song. The puppet master withered away in defeat.

In both *Unni* and the staged dance, robots represented the routine, the mechanical, the repetitive, the unemotional, and the uncreative. The tutors droned through material for which they had no feeling. The student learned math and English not because of feeling, passion, or desire but because the schedule said so. The student was subject to the time and bodily discipline of middle-class Indian achievement: go through twelfth standard, take competitive national examinations, go to college, and get a job in the private sector, the voluntary (NGO) sector, or government. Sit at desks, drink milk, and develop a hunchback that tells the tale of your childhood rigors. This was also a casted image of childhood—the stereotype elsewhere described to me as the Tamilian Brahmin or "TamBram" child. The dancers, in their drabs and grays, moved to the tugs of the puppeteer. The puppeteer represented the external force that repressed the children's energetic and varied inner dances. The puppeteer symbolized the Indian education system and middle-class achievement norms: time discipline, passionless rehearsal, and a singular telos of achievement. These strictures, the argument went, suffocated the potential of Indian children to develop themselves and develop India.

Throughout the conference, speakers reiterated these harms to—and loss of—a generation of Indians alienated from their authentic selves. The concerns articulated at the conference reappeared in public culture in works ranging from Bollywood films to government planning documents. While the Indian education system had produced a globally mobile elite of successful technical workers, critics argued that it psychologically alienated the masses and failed to cultivate the capacity to innovate—particularly among masses who aspired to reach the top levels but for whom there was no space. These concerns broadly formed the problematic backdrop to which Design in Education stood as a solution; these were also some of the concerns that motivated organizers of other conclaves and festivals promoting design, entrepreneurship, and the arts, including the DevDesign festival I discuss in the next chapter. For these reformers, the professional practices and discourses of design offered a way to make civic and innovative Indians.

These arguments represented a middle-class critique of postindependence educational policies and present-day institutional realities. To train the engineers who would build the infrastructures, manufacturing tools, and products of independent India's economy, Nehru invested heavily in elite educational institutions, the most famous of which are the IITs and IIMs. The National Institute of Design, Center for Environmental Planning and Architecture (CEPT), and School of Planning and Architecture (SPA) were also products of this moment, set up to train the engineers, managers, and planners of the new nation. These institutions provided reliable paths to elite status and cosmopolitan mobility so middle-class families helped their children gain entry, supporting a thriving industry of private coaching classes and tutorials that turned privilege into "merit" (A. Subramanian 2015). The schools taught primarily in English, a rare form of cultural capital in India that was historically the province of commercial urban classes and government administrators (Chopra 2003, 436). Though NID, CEPT, and SPA are also very competitive, they fit strangely among the IITs and IIMs. As single institutes, they graduated only a few hundred students a year and did not hold a position of national prominence and aspiration the way engineering schools did when Nehruvian industrialization valorized engineers, as did global technology industries later on. Nor did design have the prestige and mobility promised by management degrees during postliberalization corporate expansion. Design and planning students often saw themselves as marginal, artistic mavericks within the elite.[3]

Unni, the tale Bir Sethi screened of Hitler-like teachers and creative redemption, critiqued the constitution of "a kid and many others." The educational regimes the film decried were ones designed to train the managers of modern India. According to sociologist Satish Deshpande (2003, 138–39, Indian higher education institutions in the first decades of independence trained an English-speaking cadre of professional citizens who could act as the educated "proxy" for primarily rural Indians), doing their bit for India by engineering while the masses worked in their factories and construction projects as "producer-citizens" (S. Roy 2007, 110–23). After liberalization, these educated classes took their cultural capital and technical skills abroad, sending money, accolades, and a more self-interested politics back home (Fernandes and Heller 2006; Deshpande 2003, 148). The speakers and organizers of the Design in Education Conference and the NID students who created *Unni* were members of this very class, having tested at the top 1 percent of applicants to make it into NID. Though they had made it, they critiqued the formation they had entered. However marginal within the elite, design students still carried forward the mantle of managing Indian development for the masses. Yet they wanted their educational entitlement to allow them to develop their unique aspirations, capacities, and desires.

Beyond the walls of the conference, criticism of educational policies was widespread. Public anxieties about Indian futures cropped up in film, newspapers, and public policy. Student suicides, invoked at the conference, also made major metro news stories and blockbuster film plot points. These symbolic tragedies often went along with stories of failed exams, frustrated familial aspirations, or harsh instructors. The Bollywood blockbuster *3 Idiots* (2009), for example, told the story of three engineering students, all alienated in various ways by their high-pressure, joyless educations. In the film the students are alienated from themselves by mainstream education and familial duty: one student wants to be a wildlife photographer, but his father wishes him an engineer; another sees engineering as a path out of poverty; a third student actually has a genius for gadgetry and mechanical systems, but his passions find little outlet in the institute's textbook memorization routine and lectures. Only after one of the friends attempts suicide—torn between duty and affections—do the friends find the courage to pursue their dreams openly. A commercial success within India, *3 Idiots* also found a massive following in East Asian markets with similarly tight links between educational achievement, class aspiration, and liberal projects of self-styling often in tension (Chumley 2016, 151). The film made sense of a structure of feeling linking class, modernization, and selfhood. Abhijat Joshi, the film's screenwriter and weaver of powerful tales, was also at the conference, discussing its ideas, proposals, and critiques. Attendees listening to him at a dinner session applauded his film; we learned that he had left the aspirational middle-class track of engineering college to pursue writing, drama, and the arts.[4] Joshi represented the apotheosis of the educational possibilities sketched by Bir Sethi.

Suicide was only the most extreme cost of the repression of authentic, individual selfhood in Indian education. Indian development—from appropriate technologies to good jobs—was figured as a problem of individuating Indian selves. At the Design in Education Conference, for example, Bir Sethi encouraged educators to find individual children's talents and interests as a means for unleashing children's creativity toward development. Similarly, the DREAM:IN conclave in Bangalore called on Indian education, business, and design elites to focus on Indians' aspirations and dreams rather than deindividualized needs such as food, housing, literacy, or economic growth numbers. In this vision, India needed not working masses but billions of endeavoring, unique selves. These lofty messages were often situated in specific complaints about Indian middle-class social mobility: high-pressure education prepared students alienated from themselves, focused instead on getting into an IIT and working for a Indian multinational service export industry. Entrepreneur Ashish Rajpal, a speaker at Bir Sethi's conference, at Bangalore's design-centered DREAM:IN, and at DevDesign's OpenLab festival, diagnosed Indian culture as stuck in a "BPO worldview." BPO stands for Business Process Outsourcing, an organizational structure that contracts large volumes of business data work to an external company, usually one with lower labor costs than the client company. Such tasks include data analysis, revising PowerPoint decks, and data entry. The BPO worldview called for dutiful obedience to foreign clients and "executing on someone else's design," displacing creative self-expression in work (Rajpal 2008).

This achievement system failed to cultivate Indians' capacities to innovate. In public debates about India's national future, commentators argued that the nation was bursting with diverse and undocumented knowledge and creativity; hidden in the cities and the countryside were entrepreneurs who must be "unbound" to develop their ideas and enterprises (e.g., Khanna 2007; Gupta 2006). The intense competition to get into schools directed these energies toward test taking and cramming rather than learning skills that enabled people to be useful to the nation (e.g., "India Has Exam System" 2011). Test culture taught social skills that worked against the teamwork and idea sharing taken to be constitutive of business innovation (see Thrift 1997). According to the critics, students clawing their way up the national exam rankings would prefer to step on each other on the way up rather than exchange disciplinary and tacit knowledge among lives made entrepreneurial experiments.

Reinforcing these perceptions, the government's National Knowledge Commission (NKC) issued a report in 2008 arguing that the Indian education system failed to emphasize "creativity, problem solving, design, and experimentation," ultimately impeding entrepreneurial activity. The report primarily cited American management scholars, including nonresident Indians teaching abroad. Heading the commission was Sam Pitroda, an engineer famous for returning from his U.S. successes to develop India's telecommunication infrastructure in the 1980s. A report by the Yash Pal Committee (Pal 2009, 10) called for IITs and IIMs to offer a full range of university courses to prepare students for flexible, interdisciplinary futures adapting to changes in job markets. Other government bodies echoed these calls for interdisciplinarity, suggesting tactics such as university cross-registration schemes and the creation of a national knowledge network (Planning Commission 2012a, 280; 2007c, 436; National Innovation Council 2011) to create what then prime minister Manmohan Singh called "'new minds conducive to the growth of innovation" (National Innovation Council 2011). Interdisciplinarity—here a bridging of technology and the liberal arts to make adaptable subjects and organizations (Stark 2009)—promised to open Indian minds and values to create new prospects for value.

These critiques of the education system were a structure of feeling grounded in the experiences and voices of those who had made it. For those located outside the middle class, trying to claw their way in, we might imagine a number of other critiques: there aren't enough spots, the private tutoring needed to be competitive is unaffordable, an education isn't enough without other forms of privilege such as caste or family connections (Jeffrey 2010). Millions of children in India do not even have access to basic compulsory education; implementing the Indian constitution's right to education clause is an ongoing and only recently invigorated project. The speakers at Design in Education seemed to suggest that even if those children could access the existing mainstream system, the system would crush their individual potential. Overall the conference depicted a privileged group, benefiting from India's state-supported educational institutes, stunted in personal growth, and whose personal growth was assumed to drive the progress of the nation.

"Spreading the I CAN Bug": Political Pedagogies of Design Thinking

Bir Sethi—both in her TED Talk and in her educational practices—wanted to transform India's institutions from the singular hierarchy of progress and success to one that accommodated the varied talents, desires, and visions of its citizens. She carried forward a vision of progressive innovation both in continuity with older projects of progressive humanism and translated into alignment with contemporary political economies. NID, India's first postindependence design institute, was meant to produce designers who could work with available craftspeople and natural resources to fashion the material culture of an authentically modern Indian nation. Bir Sethi, herself a graduate of NID, wanted to turn every Indian into a designer—a resourceful mediator of modernization. Rather than designing for a massive nation-as-community, Bir Sethi argued, young Indians ought to proliferate designs for an India as variegated as the children themselves. In contrast to Nehru, who had famously called "every Indian . . . a problem" (S. Roy 2007, 110), Bir Sethi argued that inculcating design thinking could turn every Indian into a solution.

On the last day of the Design in Education Conference, Bir Sethi made her pitch. As the lights went down, the auditorium of people faded from view and I saw only her on the podium under the spotlight. "Design thinking is not a tangible idea," she began. She began telling the tale of Rahul, a schoolboy on a journey to civic engagement.

Rahul, as Bir Sethi told it, was bothered by the garbage around his neighborhood. But when he tried to take action to clean it up, he found only discouragement.

"No no no," his mother scolded, "do this someday, not today."

"This isn't part of your studies," his teacher admonished him.

"Can I?" Rahul asked himself. "I CAN'T!" he concluded.

Bir Sethi went on: "And all those dreams of being superman and changing the world were replaced by excuses. And life became dull and gray and nobody noticed anything. Because you see, Rahul did not know, we live in a world called ProcrastiNation where everybody said 'someday.'"

On screen, a cartoon wooden sign read "ProcrastiNation"—the first half of the word in white and "Nation" in yellow—to drive the message home. The sign pointed left—a direction I read as backward, against the left-to-right directionality of the English words on the screen and, by implication, moving the nation backward in time.

Rahul's cousin, Poonam, lived in a different world, as Bir Sethi told it. Rahul went to visit her and found her house filled with love, laughter, and light. Poonam had taken matters into her own hands. She was cleaning the neighborhood trash. Miseducated Rahul asked her why she did not just wait for the government to clean it up.

"Why should we wait when we can do it ourselves?" Poonam replied.

On the screen behind Bir Sethi, a new sign pushed aside the backward-pointing "ProcrastiNation" with a forward-pointing "ImagiNation" sign.

The new sign had the same white and yellow typography to make the substitution clear.

"Poonam," Bir Sethi explained, "lived in a world called ImagiNation—where everyone said 'I CAN' and everybody said 'TODAY instead of SOME-DAY.' Poonam took Rahul to the land of imagination where children from all over the world were changing the world and making it better."

Bir Sethi's story abstracted the specific histories, relations, and positions of actual Indian children into abstracted, line-drawn figures—abstractions into which the audience might project multitudes of children. In the actual world, these children might be spotted in uniforms, t-shirts, kurtas, or singlets suggesting varied caste, class, or regional locations.

With abstracted civic children setting the frame, Bir Sethi began to show the audience videos of actual children improving their communities. She had created a program called Design for Change to spread this pedagogy internationally. The program, whose sponsors included Stanford, IDEO, NID, and Disney, translated "design thinking" into a process of "Feel, Imagine, Do, Share." Workbooks instructed teachers on how to organize students to "feel, imagine, do": to locate problems, imagine solutions, and intervene in their communities. The last step, "share," turned the students and teachers themselves into evangelists of this civic pedagogy.

And share the students and teachers did. Bir Sethi showed us video of Nepali children cleaning up trash in their own neighborhood. She then showed a home video of Finnish children mobilizing against packaged food in their schools. "Children all over the world," she declared, were making their communities better. Her Design for Change slide showed a Mercator projection of the world with India at its center; a red dot marked Ahmedabad radiated red pulses that spread over the world.

"Design was happening," she concluded. "We showed example after example and made connections in line with a vision of a democratic society. . . . But even though we reduced our waste, something still bothered us. What about other schools? So we shared! We presented at a principals' conference, UNICEF Bhutan, national television, and school . . . after school . . . after school."

"Every child an entrepreneur!" Bir Sethi declared.

But in this vision, simply being an entrepreneur was not enough. The problem was not only to make people into productive citizens. Bir Sethi also called on these transformed citizens to evangelize this mode to others. Design for Change was not only a discipline or an ethos; it was also a virus: "Contagious is a good word, even in the times of H1N1. . . . Passion is contagious," Bir Sethi explained in her TED Talk (2009). This entrepreneurial contagion was matched to an age where dangerous affects and viruses threatened nation-state borders and citizen-making projects, jumping national boundaries by plane, by touch, and via commodities.[5] Entrepreneurial contagions could move through media too, like Design for Change stories and TED Talks. The entrepreneurial citizen built up the nation, but also helped make the whole world a better place.

Bir Sethi returned to her story of Rahul in the world. Rahul's mother and teacher were wrong. Superman is not a fairytale. Superman was in every child. "But what was the key to the "I CAN bug?" The key, Rahul's friend Poonam revealed, was that

> You don't need anybody's permission to change the world and make it better. It's very simple. All you have to do is feel, imagine, do, and share. First, feel anything that bothers you. It can be loneliness, children bothering each other, garbage. Look beyond yourself and feel not only with your mind, but with your heart. Then you have to imagine a way to make it better. Brainstorm with your friends. Be bold. Out of the box. Fresh ideas. Courageous thinking. Think of ideas beyond the obvious. After that, you simply have to go and do. Go out and change the situation. Even if it is changing the life of one child, one community, one problem, that is great. Because remember Rahul, you can't change anybody's life without it changing your own. Have fun. The most important part, share. So this way, other children get infected with your ideas and your energy. This way, you're saying not only I CAN and I DID but YOU CAN.

This was how, Bir Sethi concluded, 250,000 children in twenty-four countries had become change makers. It was in this way that citizens could overcome ProcrastiNation to achieve ImagiNation—the nation recomposed through entrepreneurial passion, a bias to action, and design.

"Design thinking"—a loosely defined set of techniques and work styles popularized in California by IDEO and Stanford—allowed Bir Sethi to articulate individual authenticity and passions with the national and even transnational development, both economic and social. Bir Sethi offered design thinking as an alternative educational stance that develops children's ability to sense their environment, develop a situated ethical practice, and engage in work that is personally meaningful while political and culturally constructive. In place of the planner who saw culture as a sector separate from economy and reason, the design thinker saw culture and economy as inseparable and central to projects of improvement and mobilizing others. Design left room for entrepreneurial citizens to mobilize their own intuitions and desires in the development projects.[6] The jump away from technocratic planning, however, was not so far as to completely break with middle-class frames of legitimacy. In forums like TED, *BusinessWeek*, and *Harvard Business Review*, design thinking stands for a critique of rationalistic, impersonal, and quantitative forms of corporate knowing. It argues instead for corporate employees, educators, and even government actors to combine their professional understandings of their work with empathy for those whom they seek to sell to, educate, or discipline. From IDEO and Stanford's Product Design program, technology creation practices guided by applied ethnographic techniques have in design thinking been abstracted to an emotionally attuned ethos for guiding anyone who seeks to transform a situation into a problem amenable to their particular forms of knowledge and perceived agency in the world. This abstracting move distilled away the labors of fabrication and commodity distribution (Irani 2018)—the materialized social relations that make designers' agencies ideologically plausible in industrialized economies. As production labor, and worker-citizens, became invisible in middle-class culture, the design thinker could come to seem an icon of civic agency.

Casting design thinkers as entrepreneurs rendered Bir Sethi's proposals desirable to middle-class constituencies who saw the private entrepreneur as a symbol of national triumph and possibility. As Indians gained prominence in high-technology industry both at home and abroad, both nonresident Indians and domestic middle-class Indian media seized on the high-tech entrepreneur as a symbol of masculine, global, and technical achievement, embodying the image of an economically dominant India to come (Chakravartty 2006). Like Poonam, the figure of the entrepreneur didn't "wait for the government" (Upadhya 2009, 79, 83). The entrepreneur's ascendancy marked a shift in the role of the middle class in Indian public discourse, from a "proxy" of the interests of India's rural and poor citizens to a "portrait" of the nation (Deshpande 2003). The entrepreneur also enjoyed currency in international development and NGO circles as the favored driver of grassroots, large-scale social change—figured in those discourses as collaborative rather than agonistic, technical rather than political, and constructive rather than complaining (Drayton 2011; Bornstein 2007; see Ferguson 1994 for a discussion of antipolitics in development). It was through the figure of the entrepreneur that private desires and passions were framed as the motive force for creating broader public benefit. A properly cultivated sense of empathy alongside an aversion to "ProcrastiNation" would direct self-interest into community and national interest. Feeling, intuition, and passion—Poonam's world in Bir Sethi's story—served twin purposes in discourses of design thinking and entrepreneurship. As students learned to "feel, imagine, do, and share," feeling was the capacity to be moved by the world, empathy was the capacity to intervene in alignment with others' feelings, and passion was the motive force that erased the labor and dangers of taking action and championing change.[7]

Returning to the Design in Education Conference, we see that Bir Sethi elevated the affective practices of design production into a form of civic morality or citizenship. Skeptical about the relevance of new media production practices to civic participation, I asked two social workers who worked at a school for urban poor children if they saw these practices as relevant. They told me they did, explaining that design thinking is largely "about how one thinks or talks and so anyone can do it." An IIT grad I met in Delhi, off to Stanford for a master's degree in design, echoed that design thinking was more portable than design practice—that because it was a way of thinking, it could apply to any situation.

Bir Sethi argued that young Indians have been disciplined, dulled, and habituated into unhealthy, unproductive relationships with their environments and communities. Children had the means and opportunity to improve their worlds; they simply lacked permission or invitation. Authenticity for her was not so much a question of being true to some preexisting self but to the self that emerges in full and conscious interaction with others and the environment. Bir Sethi, educated at NID, drew on figurations of designers in European history; from the Bauhaus on, elites positioned designers as a more conscious, more sensitive, and more experimental cultural avant-garde responsible for steering mass culture (A. Dutta 2007; Findeli 1995).[8] This reformed, conscious, and entrepreneurial citizen would be, for Bir Sethi, in line with "vision of a democratic society."

At a time when Delhi made the news for middle-class corruption protests and for government scandals, this citizen figure invested little faith in the government (see also Lukose 2009; Fernandes 2006). It was not so much that Bir Sethi denied that government had a proper role. She had collaborated with the municipal corporation and the police when her NGO aProCh shut down city streets to put on a festival day for children (Sethi 2009). She had married into a family that used the courts to seek justice for Indians who suffered from caste and communal violence. Yet the pragmatic pedagogy of design and the failures of the developmental state together called for children to build themselves up by building up the nation. This call figured the nation not as an imagined community nor as a collective of "builders" through labor but as the participatory project of a billion endeavoring selves, productively adapting themselves to the circumstances they found themselves thrown into by myriad unnamed social and economic forces. These multitudes developed themselves while animating—infecting, by Bir Sethi's metaphor—those around them with "ideas and energy."

These billion selves—the very demographic dividend that could power economic growth—also threatened to explode. The contagious feeling Bir Sethi sought to channel toward civic ends expressed her antidote to communalism—caste- or religious-identity projects—that haunted discussions of design, entrepreneurship, and Indian civic life. The city of Ahmedabad had seen communal riots in 2002 that left thousands of Muslim residents and a much smaller number of Hindus dead. The riots were widely acknowledged even in Delhi when I did my fieldwork, as people discussed then chief minister of Gujurat Narendra Modi's level of connection to the deadly killings. Even ten years later, in office chatter, designers who trained at NID somberly remembered the plumes of smoke rising all around the city. At a Bangalore social enterprise conference, a journalist exclaimed, "Today there is so much energy in this country, the right amount of channelizing and you can go on to bigger things." (Channelizing was an Indian English word I encountered often to describe the marshaling and directing of people's energies.) In an interview with an NID magazine, institute director Pradyumna Vyas warned, "By 2020, the average Indian age will be 29. This means that, at present, a lot of creative youthful energy is readily available. If this is not channelised, it may become destructive" (2009, 5).

Though the riots were never mentioned during the Design in Education conference, Bir Sethi's extended family included activists dedicated to promoting secular humanism through human development and legal work. Gagan Sethi, Bir Sethi's father-in-law, had sued the Gujurat government on behalf of riot victims and has founded and headed several NGOs concerned with human rights of women, religious minorities, and lower castes: Dalit Foundation, Janvikas, and the Center for Social Justice. Bir Sethi's sister-in-law, Avni Sethi, had worked with Mr. Sethi to design the Conflictorium, a public museum in Ahmedabad designed to provoke attendees to choose their identities and empathize with those different from them. Recall the "plurality of identities" the Riverside student called for. The elder Sethi argued that Indians identified first with gender, caste, religion, and other "choiceless identities." Violence, he argued, erupted when people identified with a side they saw as losing; the transformation of identification—through work on empathy and on the self—could redirect the energy generated in conflicts to a search for "solutions" (American Jewish World Service 2012). Among his influences were his training at American social psychologist Kurt Lewin's National Training Laboratory in the United States (interview with author). Lewin's teams also came to Delhi in the 1950s. Their task was to socialize new in-migrants to the capital, retraining potential communal, caste, and regional affiliations through programs to facilitate what anthropologist Matt Hull (2010) calls "democratic technologies of speech" that could foster communities not of kind but of place. These projects of democratic citizen making laid a foundation—one older than the rise of neoliberalism—for the entrepreneurial citizen who could lead, problem-solve, and innovate in place.

Debates about Indian education, and in particular the place of the liberal arts, have focused on the relationship between these destructive energies and the science and technology focused education of India's elites. Speaking with a journalist about the rise of the Hindu right in 2007, political philosopher Martha Nussbaum argued that interdisciplinarity could have calmed the communal violence that had erupted in India over the previous decade: "There is not enough attention on critical thinking and independence of mind in India. Not enough on stimulating the imagination. We all have the capacity to inflict pain on others. But this capacity needs to be trained and developed through the arts—dance, music, theater. Tagore understood that, Nehru less so" (Chaudhury 2007).

Nehru sought to train peasants in the "scientific temper" to drive out their superstitions and indisciplines (S. Roy 2007, 110). Rabindranath Tagore, a lauded Bengali poet and nationalist from the landowning classes, promoted arts, literature, and aesthetics as postindependence priorities. Bangalore-based scholar-activist Gautam Bhan, quoting Nussbaum elsewhere, argued that the liberal arts would liberate the Indian mind from "mere habit and tradition" and cultivate the ability to empathize with differentiated, independent, liberal others (Bhan 2013). This break from habit and tradition was, in this logic, the substance not of innovation but of citizenship. Authenticity in identity seemed key not only to economic growth but also to politics.

This liberal project had an illiberal discipline at its heart. Admonishing "ProcrastiNation," Bir Sethi echoed a public urgency fueled by the demographic dividend. This urgency meshed well with entrepreneurial production styles, often called the bias to action (see chapter 5), but it also legitimized middle-class, illiberal political styles (Fernandes and Heller 2006). In wider discussions of Indian politics, some citizens argued that the Indian state ought to act urgently and with a strong hand, militarily and economically, to channel demographic dividends before it was too late (Modi 2017). At a time when the low-caste groups were mobilizing electorally, the middle classes began to deride politics as a domain of corruption, handouts, and imprudent policy making. With this, some turned toward authoritarian styles of government. These middle-class Indians often cited Singapore and China as models of Asian development: single-party systems that could implement programs at speed (Kestenbaum 2010; Fernandes and Heller 2006, 497–98). At another conference—this one a symposium on civic design in Delhi—some even called this the "Steve Jobs" model of governance, citing the famously authoritarian, self-actualized, spiritually attuned late CEO of Apple. A national news journalist summed up the design approach to governing at one conclave: "They don't know what they want but when I give it, they will want it." Design could mean caring for the other, but it could also mean that privileged, if empathic, vision overcame public pushback. Thus an illiberal rush to development lay at the center of Bir Sethi's liberal pedagogy of entrepreneurship through design.

Building Up the Ideologies of Entrepreneurial Citizenship

The Design in Education Conference drew together a number of social worlds, including education, entrepreneurship, and design, to work out relationships among individualism, citizenship, and innovation in India. Convincing Indian parents to discover and invest in their child's authentic skills, talents, and desires was no small feat. Bir Sethi brought together a set of techniques, discourses, and practices to articulate, make sensible, and legitimate this promise of a new kind of citizen. Her designing citizen builds on a number of diverse and circulating understandings of the self, development, and cultural change. Exemplars of such empathetic, entrepreneurial citizenship circulated in both transnational circuits of "innovation" culture (e.g., TED, design blogs, the *Atlantic*) and Indian English-language media. Bir Sethi's own TED Talk (2009) has been watched over half a million times on the TED website (https://www.ted.com); hers was a popular story. Yet not all figures circulate as well or make sense to others. To understand why the conference stories were sensible and appealing to the audiences I met there, we have to examine not only the rhetoric at the conference but also the way it sits among and draws from existing narratives in Indian public culture.

It would be tempting to interpret Bir Sethi's vision as a simple story of cultural diffusion from Silicon Valley to its IT margins. Indeed, the Design in Education Conference emphasized its connection to Stanford University and Silicon Valley by placing design thinking at the center of its pedagogical project. Yet to see Silicon Valley as emanating everywhere would echo the historiographic problem of reproducing as originary and innovative those cultural locations that are already recognized and credited by powerful people (Philip, Irani, and Dourish 2012). It would miss the ways in which social actors bring together specific flows of media, people, and finance for particular cultural projects (Appadurai 1996). While Bir Sethi's conference drew on Silicon Valley and made its influence visible, it also articulated a relationship between self-actualization and developmental citizenship in response to older middle-class dilemmas that endured in contemporary India. She drew on a number of contemporary and historical cultural projects, all variously transnational and some with direct ties to India, to which we will now turn our attention.

The tension between authentic selfhood and community manifested in middle-class film and public culture. They were central to, for example, the successful Bollywood film *Zindagi Na Milegi Dobara* (Akhtar 2011)—a film whose title means life won't come again. The Hindi film featured three young professionals—Kabir, Imraan, and Arjun—on a road trip through Spain to send Kabir off into married life. The terms of the trip are as follows. Each friend chooses an extreme sport. Each of the choices—sky diving, scuba diving, and running with the bulls—taps into deeply held fears that must be overcome and are overcome, testifying to the power of individual will and excellent safety equipment. The most difficult fears, however, are not bodily dangers but familial and psychological ones. Arjun and Imraan suspect Kabir's unreadiness to marry. They sit him down for a truth trial—a word association test meant to extract Kabir's true feelings. Asking "What do you say, Dr. Fraud?" Arjun fires words at Kabir. Kabir verbalizes, seemingly without premeditation. Translated: "Job / Money. Sea / Salt. Friend / You. Sex / I like. Marriage /." Here, Kabir breaks his gaze with Arjun, looks away, and responds "uhhh family." Kabir's inauthenticity has been detected! Arjun's clever mispronunciation of Freud— "Dr. Fraud"—foreshadows the inauthenticity; Arjun isolates the passions of Kabir's id using improvised psychoanalytic devices. Kabir's inauthenticity revealed, his friends demand he be honest and rescind his marriage proposal. Only when facing imminent goring by a Spanish bull is Kabir able to promise to be honest with his fiancée.

This pursuit of authentic personhood in *Zindagi* is particularly framed around recognizing and validating one's affects, passions, and desires as bases for action while removing supposedly traditional barriers of duty to family or resistance to change. Anthropologist William Mazzarella (2005) argues that a key debate around the construct of the postliberalization middle-class has been about the role of affective, consuming desires. These desires are most often characterized as focused on mobility, prestige commodities, and the production of urban space sanitized of the poor (Menon and Nigam 2007; Fernandes 2004). This is a sharp departure from the ethos of capital savings and secular dispassion promoted by Gandhian austerity and Nehruvian socialism, respectively (Nigam 2004, 77; Fernandes 2006, 30–36; Mazzarella 2010b, 16). *Zindagi* narrates this personal desire as, at once, an engine of personal growth and a source of tension with norms of family, development, and responsibility.

Design in Education takes the desiring citizen as its point of departure but constructs a model that adapts Nehruvian norms to entrepreneurial times. While *Zindagi* focuses on exploring the world and testing one's desires and bodies against it, the Design in Education Conference advocated for expressive cultural production and a social reform approach to daily life. Yet the experiences scholars refer to as consumer-citizenship were not completely disavowed; affect and desire were the motive force in Bir Sethi's stories of

Rahul's desires for a tidy neighborhood and for students moved to mobilizing neighbors to clean. Bir Sethi's story put those affects in service of an entrepreneurial form of citizenship that cares for and uplifts others, rather than simply developing *Zindagi*'s self.

Themes of individual authenticity and self-development could not only be found in the sphere of popular culture. They had also long been part of elite educational discourses—discourses Sethi drew on as well. Utilizing Harvard education professor Howard Gardner's Multiple Intelligences (MI) theory, Bir Sethi and others in her network made the case that the production of innovative Indians required an understanding of intelligence attuned to a wider range of capacities. This more capacious sense of intelligence recognized a wider variety of children, as well as a more flexible skill base for the production of innovation. This understanding of intelligence was particularly meant to persuade parents aspiring to hegemonic, upper caste-dominated visions of merit in the form of school achievement and test scores (Subramanian 2015; Fernandes and Heller 2006, 500). Rather than the psychometric notion of scholastic intelligence measured by IQ, MI advocates argue for various kinds of intelligences, including verbal-linguistic, logical-mathematical, bodily-kinesthetic, musical, and interpersonal. Children's varying capacities for each intelligence warrant personalized forms of nurture and education. The MI theory offers scientific legitimacy to the idea that Indian children have a variety of talents that go uncultivated by the existing educational system and its status regimes.

Ashish Rajpal, a speaker at the Design in Education Conference, was one of Gardner's most active champions within India. Despite not identifying as a designer, Rajpal spoke at three design conferences I attended in India in 2011 alone. The Gurgaon-based entrepreneur left multinational corporate management to obtain a degree in education from Harvard. Both his business credentials and his Harvard degree substantially added to his stature and opportunities to speak. Returning from Harvard, he started his educational training and curriculum company, XSEED, to deploy Gardner's theories of development. XSEED's programs included corporate leadership training, standardized "experiential" primary school curriculums, and outdoor camps to impart "confidence for life." During my fieldwork, Rajpal stirred considerable excitement among the designers I worked with by bringing Gardner to India for a speaking tour. The tour sold out auditoriums in seven cities.

Gardner's Harvard credentials conferred legitimacy on MI theory, and MI theory in turn conferred legitimacy on the idea that intelligence can take a range of forms. Rajpal draws on metaphors of biological propensity when he explains MI's theories of child development to wider publics. He framed the instructor as a gardener (the pun on Gardner's name isn't lost on Rajpal). The gardener adds water and supportive soil to the seed; yet only with sunlight, water, and freedom will the seed take its authentic, healthiest form. "Chid ke beej men se, deodhar toh niklega nehi," as Rajpal explained to a national news host. The aphorism ("from a pine seed will not come a deodar tree" in English) warned against those who would try to misdirect the propensities distinct to a person. Bir Sethi drew on such verdant imagery as well, contrasting plants, vines, and flowers to the inauthentic machinic.[9]

Though Gardner's influence was the most vividly advertised during the time of my fieldwork, other individualist theories of development also shaped the practices I studied. Rajpal explicitly cited a number of thinkers as influential in developing the XSEED approach; alongside Gardner, he cited Gandhi, Swami Vivekananda, Maria Montessori, Jiddu Krishnamurti, and Sri Aurobindo—all philosophers from the early 1900s.[10] Swami Vivekananda, a Hindu philosopher, understood the development of India as the spiritual development of its individuals. Maria Montessori, an educational reformer, emphasized education through practical play rather than didactics. Jiddu Krishnamurti, a philosopher of relation, founded several schools in India that trained students to develop a global outlook and connections with others and environments. The most famous of these, Rishi Valley, produced many designers and artists. Krishnamurti also taught Pupul Jayakar, a close associate of Nehru's daughter Indira Gandhi, a prominent advocate for Indian craft, and a major force in the founding of NID. I emphasize these influences to unsettle any assumption that entrepreneurial education is a simple mimicry of Silicon Valley ideologies—ideologies themselves shaped by knowledge from India, Japan, and other places.[11]

I now turn to Sri Aurobindo, not because of his outsized importance but because he was just a link or two away in the design worlds I studied. Aurobindo's projects, followers, and institutions stood just in the background of XSEED's efforts, life at the DevDesign, and alternative technology worlds in India. Many designers I had met, particularly at my focal field site, had passed through institutions founded by Aurobindo and his followers. Aurobindo's views on education and social progress paralleled Bir Sethi's in many ways. I focus on them here not to claim them as the original source of her views but instead to show how individualism that might seem to be a product of market-based consumerization or American psychology has also been foreshadowed by much older discourses and projects.

Aurobindo was a British-educated Bengali who rose to prominence in India as part of the Indian freedom movement in the early twentieth century. Though sent to England for his education, he argued for a universal form of human life achieved through worldly works and meditation. In his writings on Indian education, he took a futurist stance directing readers to look past "moribund" European modernity in order to develop human capacities with the "past [as] our foundation, the present our material, and the future our aim and summit" (Ghose 1921a, 8). Aurobindo advocated for the evolution of humankind through the evolution of individuals in a regime of educational, bodily, and social practices; he attributed to each individual "a nature of its own and a law of that nature, a Swabhava and Swadharma" (Ghose 1921b, 16) Swabhava, for Aurobindo, was the essential law of an individual's nature—something to be discovered through virtuous work in the world. Swadharma, he argued, was the individual's own quality of spirit, which found expression in action (Ghose 1997 [1922], 507–11, 514). Like Bir Sethi's promise of transforming India from ProcrastiNation to ImagiNation, Aurobindo also articulated a transformation of the nation through a transformation of its people according to their individual capacities and interests. The evolution of individuals, drawing from the wisdom of East and West but rooted in the authentic worldly experience of the individual, promised a path to rebuilding India's "true self" through the transformation of its population.

Aurobindo's writings mirror Bir Sethi's and Rajpal's stories in a number of ways. Aurobindo rejected "the idea of hammering the child into the shape desired by the parent or teacher" as "tyranny over a human soul and a wound to the nation" (Ghose 1921a, 5). In his 1920s recommendations on developing a decolonized educational system, he argued for the importance of developing a nation by developing its citizens to their fullest individual potentials. To do otherwise, he claimed, would be to impose on the world the "imperfect and artificial, second-rate, perfunctory, and common" (Ghose 1921a, 21). Though separated by almost a hundred years, Aurobindo and Bir Sethi both indicted the standing education systems of their times as teaching the rote application of Western knowledge rather than moral practices. Aurobindo and Bir Sethi alike advocated for the pursuit of a moral but worldly interest rather than the deferral of self to duty. Like the young student depicted in *Unni* pursuing musical aspirations, Aurobindo wrote in 1916: "I do not think the Gita would . . . bind down a Vivekananda to support his family and for that to follow dispassionately the law or medicine or journalism. The Gita does not teach the disinterested performance of duties but the following of the divine life" (Ghose and Khetan 2003, xxii). This pursuit of a "divine life" was, for Aurobindo, a "spiritually alert working in the world"; this work of "integral yoga" developed each person's unique mind, body, and spirit (Shinn 1984, 240–41). Through such worldly development of one's given capacities and passions, a person would evolve to higher levels of understanding; it was through the transformation of individuals en masse that human civilization would reach the next stage of evolution.

Varied interpretations of Aurobindo's philosophies have been institutionalized in India through a series of schools, ashrams, and intentional communities, as well as in NID itself. A number of people I came across in my fieldwork,
especially at my focal field site, had spent significant time in these spaces.
Some founders of DevDesign had attended the Mother's International School
on Delhi's Sri Aurobindo Ashram. One of them had also attended primary
school at the even more experimental Mirambika School for the New Age.
Mother's and Mirambika included sport, music, craft, and meditation activities alongside a more traditional academic curriculum. Mirambika offered an
open curriculum in which students set the course of their activities. Another
DevDesign product designer had spent a year working on solar power in Auroville, an intentional community founded in the mid-twentieth century to live
out Aurobindo's teachings. The Indian government and UNESCO sponsored
Auroville; Aurobindo's universal humanism fit with early UNESCO's pursuit of "world civilization" through the support of international elites "owing
their best allegiance not to nations, but to humanity" (Huxley 1948, 6). Auroville attracted a number of designers to projects in textiles, solar power, open
source, and photography.

These institutions differed widely in how they rendered Aurobindo's
teachings practicable; they all, however, had stood for decades as an alternative to mainstream Indian educational systems and models of development.
The teachings had also long stood for a theory of global transformation, not
through mass mobilization but rather through the mass evolution of individuals. According to Aurobindo, these individuals would manifest neither "poor
and futile chaos" nor "mechanical falsity" (a prefiguring of *Unni*'s imagery) but
instead would show a "real, living, and creative upbringing" (Ghose 1921b, 13).
These pedagogies prefigured aspects of Bir Sethi's proposal for entrepreneurial
citizenship. Design in Education drew on these existing forms of common
sense in proposing a vision for a postliberalization citizen.

In addition to these discourses from the world of education, Bir Sethi
also frequently drew on the figure of Mahatma Gandhi to narrate the link
between personal disciplines and historical agency. This was not unique to
Bir Sethi. *The Times of India*'s Lead India initiative—a nationally visible set of
TV spots and competition shows—depicted an iconic image of Indians following Gandhi in the salt march, but with a man in shirt and tie in Gandhi's
place, leading the masses into the future. Gandhi represented vision, leadership, and nation building; Gandhi, in the historiography of Indian nationalism,
was the figure who consolidated and disciplined mass support for bourgeois
nationalist demands for independence (Guha 1991). A poster from the Design
for Change competition depicted a reversal of these icons of Gandhian leadership, also taken from a salt march photo. This image depicted a silhouette of

a child pulling Gandhi along the beach: "the father of the nation" in pursuit of the innocent embodiment of the nation's future. In her TED Talk, Bir Sethi (2009) conveyed the significance of her vision by linking design to Indian nationalism: "I have to end with the most powerful symbol of change: Gandhi-*ji*. Seventy years ago, it took one man to infect an entire nation with the power of 'we can.'" Nationalism, here, was an idea gone viral.

Beyond the Design in Education Conference, Gandhi had become an icon of ethical leadership that moved the masses to action through empathy (Bornstein 2007, 48–61; Drayton 2006). Ashoka, a global nonprofit that cultivated "Innovators for the Public," promoted Gandhi as a transnational icon of "social entrepreneurship" who created change through the ethical refashioning of individuals rather than violent challenges or state redistribution (Bornstein 2012). Not coincidentally, Bir Sethi was one of 2,500 international Ashoka Fellows named since 1980. Bill Drayton, Ashoka's founder, calls his work the building of "the citizen sector" to replace the "squalor of the social sector"—his name for the welfare state whose dismantling he celebrates in his writings (Drayton 2006, 6). (He locates the watershed moment with the Ronald Reagan administration in the 1980s.) His vision of a "citizen sector" would do the work of the state better than the state could. Drayton counts empathy and moral fiber as virtues that both regulate these private leaders and compel their followers (Bornstein 2012; Drayton 2011, 2006). As in design thinking and in the pedagogy of the conference, empathy in Drayton's view signaled a flexible ability to understand the other and propose transformations that would enlist them rather than coerce them (Drayton 2011). (I take up the question of empathy as a technique for managing politics in greater depth in chapter 6.)

Gandhi was also a globally legible symbol of decolonizing processes. In the lead-up to independence, Indian nationalists debated the merits of communism, socialism, and capitalism as setting the direction for postcolonial policies. Within these debates, Gandhi argued that all these systems flattened human spirituality and will within massive, urban, and alienating formations. He worked with a vision of polity as soul energies to be purified and mastered through bodily practices, and social affections to be ordered and directed toward national efforts (B. Chakrabarty 2011; Guha 1991). Bir Sethi and others built on this understanding of the polity when they spoke of channeling energies and directing them properly. A closer examination of Gandhi's politics, however, also reveals two hierarchies at the heart of his national project: the first placed the village above the city as a site of Indian authenticity; the second placed the wealthy above the masses, charging the wealthy as trustees of a common wealth. Entrepreneurial citizenship transforms the first but sustains the second in modulated form.

In privileging the village over the city, Gandhi proposed that cities were places of corruption, alienation, disease, and loss of identity (Jodhka 2002, 3346). Like the global economy, which promised both economic growth and moral decay, the city was the site of accumulation but also spiritual corruption in Gandhian thinking. By contrast, Gandhi posited village India as model communities that married production, spirituality, and politics. Bir Sethi argued that authenticity lay not in the heart of the village but in the authentic heart of the citizen who responds and leads her neighbors in change. Her iconography relied on Gandhi, but placed India's everychild before him, leading him along new paths.

Gandhi also articulated a social hierarchy in which elites were to steward wealth for the benefit of the masses. He called this system trusteeship. Gandhi argued against nationalizing the holdings of well-off industrialists, arguing that the wealthy were people of talent who ought to hold and steward their wealth for the benefit of the nation (B. Chakravarty 2011; Birla 2009; Zachariah 2005, 167). Gandhi idealized what anthropologist Ritu Birla (2009, 103) calls "Indian Economic Man"—one who must meditate and "try to act" on this ideal of putting wealth in service of the nation and the poor. The trustee system attempted to avert class war while legitimizing hierarchy (B. Chakrabarty 2011, 63). Gandhian economist J. C. Kumarappa (1958) also articulated this hierarchy in an economic theory that stratified society according to social duties and time horizons that shaped one's actions (Zachariah 2005, 180–96). At the top of the hierarchy were those who took a view across generations and took actions that potentially caused harm to themselves in the interest of society. Just below were those who subsumed self-interest to that of their collective, such as cooperative society members or members of joint-family businesses—trustees. Below them were agents of enterprise—those who produced for themselves and also exchanged with others, producing mutual benefit but only within the material realm. The lowest were those who were predators and parasites, taking from or even harming others for their own gain. This group could include financiers or petty thieves (Kumarappa 1958, 1–30). This hierarchy necessitated that trustees gather wealth and use it in the interest of those below them. The poor, in Gandhian philosophy, were poor not because of exploitation but because they lacked "intelligence and tact" (Gandhi quoted in B. Chakrabarty 2011, 66).[12] Gandhi's concern for the masses stopped short of trusting them with power.

Bir Sethi's articulation of entrepreneurial citizenship echoed these long-standing Gandhian visions of individuals as trustees of wider communities. When citizens found a gap in social care or order, entrepreneurial citizenship called on them to dedicate their own energies and resources to civic care. This was, to echo Bir Sethi, "in line with a vision of a democratic society." And, as

I have shown, it is in line with enriching the self. Entrepreneurial citizenship, like trusteeship, located social progress in personal ethical disciplines rather than reorganization of property, exchange relations, or distribution of wealth (Zachariah 2005, 196).

Hero Historiographies: The Erasures of Entrepreneurial Citizenship

Bir Sethi's message of citizenship traveled well in middle-class spaces because it offered a message of collectively oriented individualism—nonpartisan at first glance—that married broader duties of progress to self-actualization. Its politics were agnostic as to causes of collective injustice or unequal distribution of harms. If Bir Sethi's message had a politics, it seemed to be the politics of the self-actualized guided by one's own moral sentiments.

On closer examination, however, entrepreneurial citizenship shares a number of elective affinities with existing forms of middle-class politics in India. Narratives of design and entrepreneurship share a common structure—that of an achieving hero who is the leader, author, or initiator of a course of events larger than himself or herself. Understanding social change in this way elides the role of privilege and capital in making designers and entrepreneurs possible. Instead, entrepreneurial citizenship valorizes individual enthusiasm, energy, will, and leadership as the source of social progress. In doing so, it obscures at least three dimensions of how social change happens: the role of collective politics in social change; the role of social, cultural, and economic capital for political actors (Bourdieu 1993; Bourdieu and Wacquant 1992, 118–20), and the violence and labors of producing social order. I will elaborate each of these dimensions in turn.

First, entrepreneurial narratives focus on personal initiative over collective identity and alliance. The work of politics might be understood as the work of having conversations, mobilizing others, negotiating platforms and positions, and building up collectivities. In contrast, designers often narrate social change through individuals who take the lead and influence others to take up their visions of change—visions that come from an empathic, aware, and educated child-citizen, in Bir Sethi's account. The privileging of designed change came as broader middle-class discourses decried caste- or religion-based electoral power in India. Just as Dalit caste groups in certain states have turned their collective voices into state-level electoral power, India's middle classes have begun to frame electoral politics as the site of corruption, patronage, and inappropriate "communal" politics (Fernandes and Heller 2006, 497–98). In the context of this backlash against popular power mobilized through voting and messy street politics, Indian discourse favors merit (as legitimated by educational attainment [Subramanian 2015]), rational planning, and authoritarian implementation in accordance with a unitary vision.

Second, the stories of civic change by design at the Design in Education Conference recurrently elided the role of social, cultural, and economic capital in making the changes on display possible. As *ideological* discourses, stories of entrepreneurialism elide and naturalize the conditions of privilege that make heroic acts possible, rendering it invisible to those who enjoy those privileges and pathologizing those who do not. Recall the story of Bir Sethi starting her Ahmedabad school, fired up by an idea to improve education and the passion to better educate her own son. The story exemplifies the kind of entrepreneurship advocated through the conference. What was left out of the story was kinship, class position, and property—the material conditions and means of influence by which Bir Sethi was able to develop and sustain her school. To give just one example, Bir Sethi's school was built on her grandfather's estate. In a second story, Bir Sethi told of her project to make Ahmedabad a "child-friendly city." In this project, to close down the streets of Ahmedabad for a children's day, she gained cooperation from city police and municipal administrators—precisely the segments of government over which India's middle classes exert influence. In the chapters that follow, we will see that entrepreneurial efforts take much more than spirit and chutzpah. Their success is enhanced through the meting out of tedious tasks, spending money for marketing, and drawing on powerful networks to enable cooperation. Stories of entrepreneurship often elide these broader privileges and labors, producing a new form of middle-class merit that legitimizes middle-class power (see also Subramanian 2015).

Third, entrepreneurial narratives explain social change through social influence and leadership, glossing over diverse social relations and labors by which these efforts are realized. Recall the model of contagion, the powerful force that Bir Sethi argued could make transformation in the local become transformation of the nation or even the global. Contagion, as philosopher Sara Ahmed argues (2004, 10), describes a sociality where emotions possessed within individuals move from person to person through proximity, touch, or contact. The story of contagion flattens the very different positionalities of actual children pulled into these projects. Telling the story of entrepreneurship as one of a viral enthusiasm makes differential oppressions problems to be overcome by passion and self-confidence. Further, those lacking entrepreneurial passion become problems for a nation figured as in need of optimism to develop. As Ahmed has written elsewhere, the one who names the problem can become the problem. Design in Education champions argue that the one who names the problem must solve the problem—lest he or she becomes the problem. This claim waves away questions of violence, coercion, caste, class, or gender—the structuring processes by which the work of making social order actually gets done.

These narratives valorize initiative over labor; in doing so, they construct an origin point for progress, eliding the labor and the power relations that produce it. For example, Bill Drayton characterizes an entrepreneur as "someone who brings a pattern change. Instead of measuring how many children you teach, it's about whether you introduce a whole new pattern of education" (Rajadhyaksha 2013). This is the logic of the manager, the engineer, the Schumpeterian seer of opportunity who produces disjunctive change in patterns of production, whether social or financial (Schumpeter 1934). Drayton borrows from Marxist and earlier anthropological understandings of modes of production (Marx 1978; Morgan 1877) but strips away questions of resources and power. In this vision of change, the entrepreneur defines and does the conceptual work that makes all the difference. Those who work with the entrepreneur are simply laborers, followers of instructions, and executors of a vision. This model of change posits the entrepreneur as the author, the pattern maker, and the conscious will.

This language of leadership, persuasion, and influence also masks the multifarious and violent ways in which social orders are pulled into place. This mirrors the way global microfinance projects claim to use grassroots community to encourage loan repayment; years into these programs, reports have surfaced that some grassroots NGOs have employed upper-caste collectors in villages who retaliate for nonpayment with violence. Others document gender-based violence in the collection of loans (Roy 2010, 29). Historians have also complicated the narrative of Gandhi as charismatic nationalist by finding traces of how upper castes coerced others into boycott and noncooperation through the denial of professional and religious service (Guha 1991, 17). Leadership narratives so common to social entrepreneurship mask as persuasion myriad power relations by which leaders pull people into line.

Bir Sethi herself (2008) noted the limitations of such methodological individualism in the telling of change. On a web forum, she described teaching her students the difference between "the man" and "the mahatma." Kavya, in grade 7 at Riverside at the time, posted to a forum asking, "Let's ask ourselves—WAS IT JUST HIM??? What about the others???" These nuanced reflections aside, the vision of "every child an entrepreneur" circulates through powerful institutions, funded by philanthropists, the World Bank, and media forums like TED, endorsing a vision of empathic change without discomfort or violence—a vision of change that promises value for everyone. Bir Sethi's project distills design thinking to offer a model of an empathetic, entrepreneurial leader in every child. The story of citizenship she tells travels easily, leaving thorny questions of how collectives are to be forged or where social problems actually lie to the remainder that only reveals itself in practices as people try to bring the vision to ground.

This chapter has traced how champions of entrepreneurial citizenship remake education, proposing that the skills of producing innovation and the skills of taking civic action are one and the same. These educational reforms promise that "every child" can be an entrepreneur, adopting ethical norms of care, a bias to action, and a sense of oneself as unique rather than communal. This model appears democratic in that it expands merit or success beyond narrow visions that locate merit at the apex of the IITs or global corporations (Subramanian 2015). At the same time, it naturalizes privilege and resources as leadership and passion. Entrepreneurial citizens appear simultaneously as empathic leaders of entrepreneurs' others and as portraits of what all Indians ought to become. Those who do not lead India, implicitly, should follow. Design in Education, in its optimism and its pitfalls, offers a view into the limits of entrepreneurial citizenship. This form of citizenship promised a model of change, but it also was a new mechanism for development without disturbing existing social orders.

4

Learning to Add Value
at the Studio

THE PREVIOUS CHAPTERS introduced the figure of the entrepreneurial citizen and presented the political, cultural, and economic contexts in and from which it emerged. This chapter begins to explore what entrepreneurial citizenship looks like in practice: what it takes to become an entrepreneurial citizen, and to become recognized as one. It takes us to the everyday work practices of the Delhi design consultancy I call DevDesign. To the designers who worked there, it was often known simply as "the studio." I followed the studio over five years, working there daily (and sometimes nightly) for eleven intense months. Over this time, DevDesign expanded and contracted. It adjusted and rebranded. Its leadership recalibrated the studio to make entrepreneurial citizenship something that, at once, paid the bills, built up the nation, and developed members as authentic selves.

I first met members of the studio because they had subcontracted with Google, the global technology company I had worked at before entering graduate school. Google had wanted to understand Indians' information practices so that it could explore ways to expand and deepen its reach into India as a market. DevDesign had planned and conducted qualitative research—such as observations and interviews—and produced reports about how the lives of others could become sites of innovation. It had organized the study and worked with the Google team to interpret the results in line with the company's needs. This service—sometimes called design research, sometimes innovation consulting, sometimes management consulting—was something many Indian firms offered and many multinational corporations sought. To many at the studio, the work was more than just making a living. It offered them ways to enact the civic sense that Kiran Bir Sethi was trying to cultivate, as described in chapter 3. Through their design work, they hoped to improve India. Unlike Bir Sethi's child citizens, adult entrepreneurial citizens had to motivate their work by the concept of *value*: the value they could provide to clients, to the nation, and to themselves.

Trade liberalization brought competing calls to Indian middle classes. On the one hand, liberalization processes called to Indians as consumers. Options for consumption proliferated on shelves and streets. Foreign and local brands competed by calling on consumer desires. As products multiplied, so would desires, the brands hoped. With liberalization, Indians began to see themselves as consumers whose desires ought to be catered to, whether by private industry or by the state (Nigam 2011; Lukose 2009; Fernandes 2006). On the other hand, liberalization processes called on Indians as laborers. The growth of networked telecommunications made India "an outpost of the global economy" (Upadhya and Vasavi 2008) where English-speaking Indians could find work in call centers, software consulting, and business processing offices, through which Indians offered services to companies and people abroad (Vora 2015; Nadeem 2011; Upadhya and Vasavi 2008; Aneesh 2006). The globalization of service work required Indians to work for the comfort of distant people and time zones (Vora 2015; Aneesh 2006). Many of those attracted to entrepreneurship felt that liberalization's jobs suppressed Indian energy and ingenuity into forms acceptable and palatable to those abroad. They had to adopt "neutral" accents, American cultural references, and less-valued work to serve the needs of employers outside of India and their managers at home (Aneesh 2015, 2006; Jodkha and Newman 2007).

The entrepreneurial citizens who formed DevDesign were against all this. They chafed at service work that demanded price sheets and "neutral" accents (Aneesh 2015). They wanted clients to hire them not as "vendors" of prespecified services such as translation, but as expert "consultants" and researchers who were hired for the promissory potential of their advice. They continually reflected on how they and others "added value," or didn't, as they worked out how to articulate themselves as knowledge workers within global value chains. Every few months, they also reflected on whether their projects offered the "creative freedom" they personally desired. This reflexivity was a core means by which they monitored and recomposed themselves, their relationships, and their civic ideals to climb the value chain.

Echoing Bir Sethi's exhortations for students to be encouraged to pursue their unique passions, studio members maintained an emphasis on personal "authenticity." For some, this was interest in art well beyond the commercializable. For others, it was an interest in politics and justice. For others still, it was the pleasures of working with friends rather than for a boss. Members worked vigorously to develop a "scene" for design, art, and innovation in Delhi; they saw a scene as the context of partners, shops, and work spaces that lent inspiration, resources, and credibility to their own individual studio. And they honed a sense of the kinds of people who added value; good degrees, English, and disciplinary knowledge were not enough. People who fit in at DevDesign demonstrated an experimental curiosity and vigor, signified often through photography, music production and consumption, topical obsessions, or even optimistic criticism (here, perhaps, was my value to the studio). As individuals attempted to turn themselves and their relationships into value, value did not obliterate difference or critique. It thrived on it. Studio members' capacity to innovate was in part their difference from clients; they could see and evaluate potentialities in the world that clients could not, simply because of different standpoints, routinized ways of seeing, or values. Building a life of experiment and engagement beyond the remunerative became crucial to demonstrate the capacity to innovate at the top of a global value chain.

This chapter reads everyday talk about work and value in a context rarely made explicit: global supply chains formed through multinational corporate practices, trade policies, and racialized and gendered modes of valuing labor. Anthropologists of capitalism have demonstrated how firms distribute labor through complex supply chains, moving value, representations, and material around to further accumulation at global scales (Bear et al. 2015; Tsing 2015b). Management theorists call these chained subsystems of production "value chains" (Orta 2013, 695). Unlike the metaphor of supply chains, value chains are hierarchical. Countries attempt to climb higher on the value chain. Companies reorganize their production to control their competitive advantage—what makes them unique in customers' eyes—while outsourcing the rest (Kogut 1985). Companies like Nike, for example, keep what they see as their core value—branding, advertising, marketing, and design—within the corporate center. The rest they outsource through supply chains of extraction and manufacturing enabled by free trade zones and capital mobility. It was in the highest level of global capital's value chain—the planning and marketing level—that DevDesign strove to position itself. This was the level where actors located value and planned its capture. This was the level at which "opportunities" were discerned and their pursuit initiated.

This chapter explains the form of expertise in such possibility that the studio cultivated over a decade and the moral economies (Daston 1995; Thompson 1971) and divisions of labor that made this expertise possible. It also shows the symbolic, organizational, and affective work by which DevDesign staff climbed a global value chain. The staff almost never spoke of value chains or supply chains explicitly. It was like the air we all took for granted but occasionally found irritating. Delhi landscapes, throughout the duration of my fieldwork, were suffused with headlines about economic growth, industrial development, becoming a "knowledge superpower," and development statistics. Policy documents instructed Indian industries to "move up the value chain" (Planning Commission 2012a, 194; 2007c, 434). These lent moral importance to value chains and the position of individuals and firms within them. On a day-to-day basis, the work of pitching the studio and its projects meant identifying why the client should hire *this studio* with *these people* and not another. This was the work of articulating the unique value of self or collective, and how one could open new horizons of value for the client. This was the work of "adding value."

Good entrepreneurial citizens didn't only find value for themselves and for their clients; they added value to the nation. They channeled their developmental desires and hopes into forms—programming, design, intellectual property, new business creation—that ascended to the highest rungs of a global capital's hierarchies of value. Value was far more than a measure, made concrete in price. It was also a word with moral and promissory charge. Those who added value to the nation, to the design studio, and to client projects were those to cultivate and include. Those who failed to add value were understood instead as sinks, as mouths to feed, as jobless masses, and as failed potential. These middle-class ideologies suffused news, policy, client expectations, and everyday talk. As ideologies and as everyday pressures, they shaped the everyday practices of organizing and valuing work and workers in the studio.

A Decade of the Studio: From Knowledge Workers to Experts in Possibility

"We have cracked the design research thing enough that we can get clients like [the] Gates [Foundation] coming to us now," Mukta declared, sitting on the porch with me, another longtime staff designer, and an intern. "But if we are experts," she continued, "what are we the experts of?"

The question surprised me. DevDesign was a firm that competed with IDEO, a globally known design firm based on Silicon Valley. IDEO was often in the news and featured in business journals like *Harvard Business Review*. But the studio went toe-to-toe with IDEO in competing for clients, and often it won those contracts. Sometimes the contracts were for qualitative research into potential user practices. Sometimes they extended to translating findings into proposals for actual products. Sometimes schools, governments, and private-sector managers hired the studio to run workshops to teach "design thinking" to others. Sometimes the studio studied middle-class consumers; sometimes, people "at the bottom of the pyramid." DevDesign reliably and convincingly performed this affective, future-oriented form of expertise, but Mukta could not articulate what exactly that expertise was. The studio had mastered a habitus (Bourdieu 1977) but struggled and sought to articulate what it was and what it was for.

Such lingering, reflexive, and skeptical conversation about work was routine in the ground-floor studio. It too was part of the habitus. People often gathered unofficially, and sometimes officially, to discuss how things were going, whether the studio was accommodating staff interests, and how to explain themselves to clients. The answers to these questions shifted over time, as did people's interests, development industry trends, and client demand. In the decade since I met DevDesign's most senior members, one idea had stayed fairly constant. Mukta reiterated it that day on the porch: "The point of DevDesign is to create a space where each of us can put something of ourselves into the work that we do." These aspirations echoed Bir Sethi's call for children tuned in to their feelings and desires. The echoes were not coincidental. These ideals linking the civic to the self moved through India's design networks, particularly out of the National Institute of Design, its faculty, and its alumni flung far and wide—including at DevDesign.

This openness to the interests of its members, however, caused dilemmas. The studio offered design research consulting for NGOs, companies, and governments. That was clear enough. It also organized festivals, coached and mentored students, and supported staff members' side projects—including a small experimental restaurant, pop-up public photography exhibitions, toy design, and a coworking space for aesthetic and technical experiments. Some studio members were trained formally in design. Others had engineering and management degrees. Still others had studied liberal arts and film. The size of the studio always ranged from six to twenty design staff, supported by four other staff who kept the studio running day-to-day by cooking, cleaning, driving, and keeping accounts. At times when the design staff was larger, the intense, reflexive relationships that formed the social infrastructure (Elyachar 2010) of this self-actualizing workplace were more strained. The variety of projects and interests was both the reason studio founders had left corporate jobs to form the firm and also the thing that risked pulling the studio apart. At the time Mukta voiced her uncertainties about the studio and its expertise, the studio's identity as a "design and innovation" consultancy was under strain.

The studio was not the factory, the office park, or the cubicle farm. It was a place for mapping and pointing client compasses forward in time. For example, it did fieldwork for a London-start-up working on hand sanitation innovation for "emerging markets," starting in India. It coached young entrepreneurs searching for low-tech health interventions that people would want to use. Designers here were mediators who calculated market preferences; their task was to help clients sort out which futures suited the clients' organizational capacities. The word "studio" marked the promise and purpose that each project would be a little different, intellectually engaging, and socially purposeful. For many years, the staff worked out of the ground floor of a house in Delhi, close enough to the neighborhood market to buy *momos* (dumplings) and take-out from street food carts. They later moved to an office space with a smoking balcony overlooking gorgeous trees and ancient monuments. In the studio, professionals worked alongside each other as a community of peers and experts in possibility. They conducted fieldwork, experimented in art and culture, and deliberated on how to steer parts of India's future.

The studio tweaked the terms of recognition over a decade, rearranging words like design, innovation, strategy, research, collaboration, and interdisciplinarity in marketing materials that attempted to attract the right customers and deter the wrong ones. In the mid-2000s it described itself as "a multidisciplinary design studio" working in "film, communication, and research." By 2009 it rebranded itself as "design-led business consultants," and six years later, a "design thinking and innovation consultancy." For those making the studio, however, it was a more than a space, a business, or a source of expertise. "The studio" was a project, an aspiration, and a way to invoke dreams about the integration of work, life, and progress. Linguistically, the phrase "the studio" was far more stable a term of affiliation among members of DevDesign than was the term "designer." Studio members sometimes turned these aspirations into financial value for themselves and for clients. Sometimes they turned that value into support for other, varied aspirations and personal experiments.

Situated in Delhi, the studio consulted with the central government, NGOs, and global development institutions. Delhi had long been a center of development planning and calculation. The Planning Commission was there. The World Bank and Ford Foundation were there. So were parliament and the offices of national government. These offices had long calculated needs and strategies to usher what Nehru called "a needy nation" (S. Roy 2007) into modernity. More recently, the Gates Foundation and key development NGOs also kept offices there. DevDesign became part of this calculative work of decentralized governance as the central government distributed planning and implementation work through public-private partnerships, NGOs, and entrepreneurs (see chapter 1). The studio's work was largely located in the speculative "dream zones" (see Cross 2014) of consumer capitalism and development. It attended to the present—potential consumers' habits and hopes, clients' reputations and production lines—and attempted to highlight where opportunity lay in the future.

The studio steered the future from the ground floor of a house in Delhi. The house was zoned for residential use, but small professional firms often chose location, beauty, cost, and convenience over legality. The studio had several shared office rooms with doors that could close. Its double doors opened up to a wall of bulletin boards pinned with members' latest preoccupations. A magazine rack lined the wall, displaying graphic design, business, and technology magazines. Nobody read these, but they set the tone for visiting partners or clients. The boards divided the entrance from a large, common table where staff, visitors, and friends could collaborate, pitch, take breaks from their desks, or even just work side by side. Bulletin boards and whiteboards surrounded the table, housing sticky notes, scribbles from meetings, and pinned pictures and cards with research observations yet to be put in an order clients could understand. The table was the heart of studio life. The design staff gathered daily to eat lunch around it. (The lunch was prepared by Dinesh, the office cook, and he ate out of sight in the kitchen with others—the driver and the cleaner—who made the office a working infrastructure.) Other spaces in the studio also supported exploration and play. Throughout the building, people watched films, drank beers, cooked photogenic ramen, and built darkrooms. On the backyard porch, they could be found debating everything from current events to font ligatures late into the night. Some members experimented with public art, film screenings, and dance events. They used studio cameras and projectors as infrastructural perks that extended their creative capacities.

Though members of the firm were all invested in "design" or "design thinking," only some had been trained in any kind of design. All were graduates of competitive Indian universities, but few had design degrees. However soon or late members had come to design, many had described part of their coming as a revolt away from more mainstream, respectable, middle-class career paths. Kritika graduated with a degree in product design; she chose design school because, as she put it, she did not want to do engineering. Mukta started as a history student at prestigious Delhi University but felt frustrated and flunked out; the next year she switched to the prestigious National Institute of Design in Ahmedabad. Brashly funny and charmingly prone to rants, she constantly experimented with materials and techniques—sculpting body-sized pillows out of plastic ties, making films out of software glitches, and weaving tapestries with twigs. Akhil, the studio founder, and Vipin, a senior partner, had both taken the highest-prestige path through Indian education: the Indian Institute of Technology, topped off with an Indian Institute of Management MBA degree. Tara had met Akhil at IIM after receiving a degree in literature; Paolo Freire and beat poets graced her bookshelves. Arun, a cofounder, studied film—one of the studio's signature storytelling and documentation techniques. While some of these academic pathways accredited studio members as design experts, other pathways accredited them as capable technocrats, technologists, and cultural workers. Their fluency in English—the medium of elite postsecondary education in India—placed them in cultural circuits where they learned to speak the language of governance, Hollywood movies, and post-Fordist corporate practices like "design thinking" and "brainstorming." All these fluencies were crucial for communicating with and securing the confidence of clients, usually multinational for-profit companies or not-for-profit organizations, who were unsure of how to evaluate design but wanted to find new options for pursuing their agendas.[1]

The studio's composition was interdisciplinary in two senses that mattered. First, its members were disciplined. Each member of the design staff had finished at least one college degree in English, polishing their fluencies in the vocabularies and civilities of global technocratic cultures. Second, the content of staff knowledge varied. The interdisciplinary collaboration allowed people to bring "multiple orders of worth" into dense interaction. The "creative friction" that resulted helped studio members arrive at new understandings of the world that identified within it potential assets or profitable sites of intervention (Stark 2009, 80–90). Entrepreneurship channeled difference into opportunity but required people whose affective bonds kept them pleasurably interacting in labor and in play.

"Not a Living but a Life"

The studio was one project in a series of experiments in how to pursue "not a living but a life." These words were Vipin's, a former management consultant with a background in physics who had come to DevDesign after his start-up went belly up. At other times he had told me he was interested in how technology design could "create deep change" in people, and he considered both academia and the studio as places to explore this. One afternoon like many others, I stumbled across Vipin in Kritika's office as he described the germ of a social enterprise idea to her; he wanted her help developing a brand for a social venture. The idea was so tentative that he waved me off at first, but he allowed me to stay when I reached out to offer him water on the hot afternoon. He took my gift and offered me a place and a voice in the conversation. The project was to start a summer program to teach students "to be authentic to themselves. . . . The idea is to make people who are wise, not just knowledgeable." He imagined a trip out into the mountains. Students would hike, contemplate their lives, marvel at nature, and learn the pleasures of teamwork and communication. I knew that Vipin had a brother who was a banker; Vipin felt that his brother was too fixated on making lots of money and was not grappling with "the deeper issues in life." Vipin fully admitted that his dreams were of transforming the consciousness of a minority of middle-class elites, but he felt it justified. First, he felt that this minority affected India heavily both through its consumption and through its participation in the work of governance. Second, he felt that he may as well start with what he knew well—his own class section. He imagined that his endeavor could become a for-profit social enterprise, an NGO, or just a one-time voluntary project. Civil society and for-profit projects could go on blurred for quite a while; figuring out how to add value to the nation did not require that one directly accumulate profit.[2] Even the founding of the firm blurred these boundaries. The founders had considered creating an explicitly nonprofit arm of the studio but backed off, daunted by the paperwork and accountability burdens.

Vipin's career path was just one example of a set of experiments and entrepreneurial moves that sustained his middle-class status while striving to generate social and ethical surplus. Other studio members had left jobs at video-editing companies, large Indian banks, technology start-ups, and multinational corporations with a foothold in India. The studio allowed members far more flexibility than did working in a company where managers directed their actions. One studio founder described this as the project of letting "smart people find interesting work" for themselves. An architect close to the studio summed up DevDesign's "philosophy of practice" as "collecting talented people and finding work for them, rather than finding work and finding people to do it." On a visit to California, Ajit, Mukta, and Akhil tacked on an extra day after a client presentation to explore Berkeley and Silicon Valley. We sat in the rumbling BART train as the three of them discussed the studio as more than a place of work, and more than a place of design narrowly construed:

> The actual project . . . is not the end product. The actual project is to live your life. The studio is a chance for us to do it collectively and give all of us more. . . . At least for me, that's what it is. It gives you time to do it as a collective of people where you're not like trying to harm the other or get in the way of the other—at the very least don't impede someone else's journey. For me, that is the thing we are trying to do. . . . A lot of people [other designers] get obsessed with being creators and purveyors of beauty.

The goal for these studio members was not to produce a narrow conception of beauty but to live a creative life that absorbed the influences of others— through friendship, or through fieldwork (see chapters 6 and 7)—and produced new lines of flight forward.[3] In this way, they were like Bir Sethi's child entrepreneurs creating in dialogue with those around them. A more recent addition to the studio, Vivek, echoed this ideal when explaining how he had come to understand the studio. Its founders, he said, designed it "to support what we want. We can use the space to do our own thing." Vivek had come into the studio as a close friend of Kritika, another junior designer. Through this friendship, he had known of the studio ethos before arriving. He and Kritika had taken an apartment as roommates near work and often stayed late, cooking, talking with other late-night stragglers, and working on side projects. He offered his job interview as an example of how studio work was about more than remunerated work—it was about how they developed as individuals, "authentic" to themselves but also expressive agents of development.

"I very clearly remember it. It was fifty-fifty," he recounted. The interview had not simply been a trial peppering him with questions and tests. He had also talked to a number of designers who spent a lot of time talking about themselves and the projects they were getting. "Mukta asked about my experience in college, in Auroville—what I've learned through those experiences." (Auroville was a UNESCO-recognized South Indian alternative community, structured around the principle of world transformation through individual development and freely chosen work.) Vivek continued that Mukta "told me how she came to where she was today. There was an openness to sharing. It was not just taking in another worker, or another person into the group." He described the interview process as less one of accounting for oneself as an expert in any particular disciplinary or professional domain and more one of accounting for one's experiences as processes of active reflection, flexibility, and learning. Mukta sought to understand Vivek's potential not only as a consultant but as a person who could change with the studio and could change the studio as he changed.

Vivek made the cut as "authentic" and experimental, of a kind with other studio members. The two founders saw the studio as nothing short of an institution for "free will" and the expression of personal "authenticity." Akhil explained to me that when he founded the studio with Arun and Ajit, they agreed that it "should never curb a person's free will. What the studio does will evolve and take shape by every new person who joins." Akhil contrasted the studio to his last job at one of India's largest banks. There, protocols and organizational hierarchy restricted his ability to pursue what he felt was best for a project. The organization, he felt, lost the chance to benefit from employees' insights. Employees failed to grow as agents of development in turn.

Akhil and his cofounders often invoked free will, even if as a mocking joke to mark how their labors were falling short of the ideal. On a retreat the studio took together, Ajit, Arun, and I were eating breakfast and discussing whether to take a long hill hike. Ajit asked if I wanted to come and I hesitated in responding. "You should only come if you want to come! The studio only works if everyone has free will." Ajit was usually exhausted from music gigs and late-night catch-up on consulting work; noticing the irony, he added that he tried to make sure that the free-will meter is rating high, though he thinks he was "only coming in a five right now." My compulsion as a fieldworker and social exhaustion did not align in that moment, but I joined in the hike anyway. As Ajit and I walked through a wide yak field, Ajit yelled ahead to his cofounder, "Hey, Arun, what's your free-will rating?" Arun yelled back, "Two or three at *most*," adding half-jokingly, "I have no free will!"

Studio members traced the contours of "authenticity" and "free will" by also lodging accusations against people and practices they saw as inauthentic or imitative. Objects of ire were often the icons of postliberalization economic growth: call centers, outsourcing, service exports, and the ostentatious Swarovski crystals. Mukta complained that her fellow middle-class Indians just wanted foreign products out of malls. The enemies were those citizens who had gained the ability to want and consume products from abroad after liberalization. When consumers craved the foreign, who would buy the work of Indian designers? The globalization of consumption created new opportunities for Indians as workers for multinational firms, but those I worked with saw these as confining. For design graduates, LG and Whirlpool were near the apex of corporate design jobs. They offered designers stability and a role making highly sought-after consumer electronics. But Mukta preferred DevDesign to those stable corporate houses; at DevDesign, she had an in-built community with whom she could tinker in music, art, and space design alongside remunerated projects: "I like new things. I don't question why. It all feeds back into the studio eventually. And it works better for me than LG or Whirlpool." Srila, a graphic designer, contrasted the freedoms of small studios with the confined roles at large corporations: "They have a cubicle life [at the corporation]. They want to get out [of corporate jobs] and learn stuff."

For studio members, the Indian government and multinational capital stood in the way of free will. One studio cofounder blamed the government for capitulating to global capital. Once I asked Arun what he thought of India's National Design Policy (2007)—a government declaration of design's importance as a service export industry and a source of "value addition" to products. Arun sharply replied, "The government wants us to be whores." Ajit, after we had just watched *X-Men* at a Delhi mall, complained that Bollywood star Aishwarya Rai sounded like she had been coached in an Anglo accent as she advertised L'Oréal skin products. Though studio members prized chances to go abroad, they also expressed frustration at how foreigners' expectations typecast them and their creative works. Those they met abroad, including designers, curators, and fellow travelers, sought exemplars of authentic Indianness. Curators and academics, for example, often asked them, "What is Indian design?" This question held no interest for them. Mukta explained her frustration in such situations: "We're Indian, not *India*." This invocation of "authenticity" differed from Hindu majoritarian interpretations (Hansen 1999), as well as Nehruvian ones that located authentic India in the home and in the village (Chatterjee 1993). This understanding instead located authenticity in the desire of the individual, a product of culture but not an exemplar. The nation would be composed of its individuals, and composed *by* its individuals as founts of creativity.

While megabrands and foreign goods suppressed the authentic creativity of the nation, development projects targeting the poor had long-standing status as contributing to nation building. Studio members often looked to uplift projects as a more ethical way to pursue life and livelihood. Water filters, craft design, and toilets always promised developmental progress. These projects were sometimes in tension with free will. Mukta bristled as development project commitments extended from months to years. But, she explained, "We're at peace with what we're doing now. Not everyone gets what design is. But they get that it is social. My grandma gets what I do now, 'Oh! You give poor people water!'" Longer histories of middle-class duty conditioned what appeared as good work to do.

Design's global ascendance also helped studio members explain its value to others. I stood with Akhil one day as he tried to convince Neera, a family acquaintance, to rent out her spare room to me. I vividly remember Neera's look of horror when Akhil told her that he was a "designer." "Fashion design?" she exclaimed. Delhi had fashion design institutes, but they were associated with gay culture and textile export rather masculine engineering and nation building (Varma 2015). Akhil scrambled to repair his reputation: "No, ma'am, I went to IIT and IIM." Over the next decade, however, IDEO, *Harvard Business Review*, and even Indian government bodies began promoting design as associated with engineering innovation rather than textiles. Design connoted the synthesis of technology, culture, and progress DevDesign sought in contrast with their corporate work experiences. Over the years of my fieldwork, other middle-class Indians began to see design as a more legitimate participant in nation building as well.

Even in pursuit of free will and authenticity, the studio could not completely take making a living out of the picture—rent, power bills, and food had to be paid for, and parents had to be supported. Studio members sustained themselves economically while pursuing projects they felt aligned with their varied, personally authentic interests. In the collective, they drew on each other's support, diverse knowledge, and friendship to make "not a living, but a life." The studio was a machine for turning affective ties, diverse knowledge, and varied values into productive potential.

Climbing the Value Chain: From "Vendor" to "Consultant"

If "free will" was a motivating principle for studio members, they climbed "the value chain" to expand their sense of autonomy. The studio spent half a decade working toward projects that granted them greater creative autonomy, raising their status from "vendors" to "consultants." The studio began in 2005 as what anthropologists Carol Upadhya and A. R. Vasavi (2006) call "an outpost of the global economy." With the growth of internet-enabled outsourcing, the studio began working as vendors for international clients seeking cheaper graphic design work or Indian expertise to localize products. Vendors, studio members explained to me, had to meet tightly specified deadlines and deliverables. Several years in, studio members had achieved a full project pipeline, but they felt the work had little meaning. The studio had grown to twenty staff during this time, employing animators, film editors, and graphic designers along with management consultants, product designers, and artists. Their projects included interstitial TV clips advertising upcoming shows, logo and illustration work, and the occasional product localization campaign for multinational corporations (see Mazzarella 2003). Studio clients included famous names like National Geographic, Discovery Channel, and beverage conglomerates. These multinationals kept core creative decisions at their headquarters but outsourced well-defined tasks to lower their labor costs (see also Amrute 2016). The studio thrived financially, but the founders were dissatisfied.

Frustrated with these projects, they wanted ones with "more creative scope"—work that made studio life feel different from the corporate jobs they had left behind. The founders decided to purge. They stopped bidding for the work they had been getting, unless it would lead to more substantive consulting relationships with "interesting" clients. These clients included NGOs, other design research consultancies, and commercial projects that offered the chance to do some version of good or stretch members' skills and curiosity. The studio manifesto announced the new attitude: "Be extremely selective in the projects we take. We are not creative whores. (Even though we are creative at times and whores at times.)" The freedom to be picky required firing the majority of studio members. The founders chose to shrink the studio, reduce overhead expenses (salaries, materials), and retain only staff who could consult broadly in the language of markets, consumers, meaning, and product concepts. They let go the people expert in editing, graphic design, and animation; they could subcontract people with those skills if a project demanded it.

The cuts to the studio were massive and were the first step in DevDesign's climb to more highly valued services in a global value chain. They understood this climb as moving from vendor projects to consulting. Vendors offered commoditized services. A vendor, according to one founder, had price sheets for fixed services like video editing, transcriptions, or image production. They competed with other vendors on price. By contrast, good consulting projects were the ones where studio members could advise clients, make presentations, and define unique deliverables rather than creating prespecified media commodities. Consultants tried to compete not on price but on the potential value they would promise to those who hired them. Tara and Mukta, two senior members close to the founding team, explained to me that they wanted projects where they had "meaningful conversations with a client." For example, they worked as the local research team for a lauded California product design firm. They traveled, conducted interviews, interpreted data, and commanded the ear of clients who lacked the local knowledge to challenge DevDesign staff's interpretations. As subcontractors, they were never publicly credited for their research. The credit and applause went to the California designers who knew little of India. But at least studio members felt authority about India within the confines of the project. They could pursue the development projects in earnest; they felt that the results of the work meant something, not only to their clients but also to themselves.

Designers had a joke about their expertise—and its illegibility to clients: "A client came in and asked for a website . . ." I recognized this joke from my own days working as a designer in California, having trained in a mix of interaction design, psychology, organizational studies, and computer science. The client wanted a website, but we designers saw our remit as so much wider. A website was a knowledge commodity—a fixed end, and a dead one for designers. Clients thought design was a collection of finished products with polish. They often had little awareness of the range services design studios offered. They thought only of the most obvious objects of design: clothes, websites, and logos. Designers, however, wanted to advise clients not only in form but in strategy, message, and even corporate vision. In the shift from vendors to consultants, DevDesign members helped clients construct corporate souls, including mission, values, and personality, that could be communicated through product form, brand, and communications planning. Designers often had to educate clients in a different process for planning product development in features and material form. They wanted to make strange clients' business models and product lines. They wanted to open up new markets rather than new product versions for clients. They sought to stretch open their clients' assumptions to make more room for their own visions and expression. Clients came in for a website, but designers wanted to sell them a long-term relationship that could affect all of their business decisions.

In the years that followed, DevDesign built on a series of successes by drawing on social connections, the prestige of the staff's education, and reputation from completed projects. The firm also drew on a very real, multigenerational accumulation of skills (Subramanian 2015) in English, management sensibilities, and American and European literature and pop culture that smoothed its circulation among elite transnational clients. One of the founders had met a Swedish designer online through their mutual interest in children's toy design; that Swedish designer had gone on to work at the famous Silicon Valley design firm IDEO. Through that friend's networks, the studio began acquiring work as on-the-ground design research translators for American design firms meeting to subcontract design research in India. Through an IDEO connection, they met a designer at Google who hired them to research middle-class technology use in India. Back in California, the commissioning Google team erased DevDesign's role, taking credit for themselves. But DevDesign staff were able to draw on these connections and experiences to pitch to global health NGOs and philanthropists. Through this kind of design research ghost writing, as well as extensive reading of design blogs and research papers, studio members learned to walk the walk and talk the talk of firms like IDEO at a fraction of the price and with far greater understanding of India. Their networks, their linguistic and cultural competencies, and their financial capacity to turn down "vendor" projects enabled studio members to climb the value chain to ultimately compete directly with IDEO.

Articulating the "Value Add"

The work of climbing the value chain suffused the social categories of the studio and similarly positioned professionals. To climb the value chain, they had to learn not only to "add value" but to articulate that "value add" to clients and partners. Their articulations of the value of their work shifted over time as they gained experiences and articulated their biographies to shifting market needs and conceptions.

They pitched projects, showing examples of past projects and market opportunities they had discovered or cultural insights that had helped clients reframe, reprice, or redesign products around opportunity, possibility, and failure risks. This was the labor of everyday studio work, but people's willingness to hire the studio and work for it also hinged on shared stories about what the studio did. The corporate story as mission and vision has long been both part of management theory and the butt of workers' jokes. At DevDesign, the story of what the studio did came not as a top-down effort to manage the culture and loyalty of thousands of engineers, as in Gideon Kunda's (2006) studies of corporate attempts to "engineer culture." DevDesign ranged between six and twenty people, not thousands. And DevDesign workers had to both believe their story and sell parts of that story to potential clients. Authenticity was more than a moral claim or the satisfaction of personal desire. Studio staff saw it as essential to generating creativity and being able to sell it. As Ajit explained, "If it isn't coming from somewhere real, inside, you can tell because it is cliché—it's about things that didn't happen to them." Authenticity, Akhil felt, was the studio's competitive edge: "You can't copy this because it is so relationship driven. There is a lot of tolerance and trust that people share. You can only focus on doing what you are best at in a point in time." Studio members joined and stayed at the studio when they demonstrated this ethos in their own biography. Each member was expected to tinker within this culture to help the studio innovate its forms and practices in response to changing trends, winds, and situations.

Reusable pitch decks and documents meant studio members did not reinvent their story every time they had a pitch. Sometimes, however, the story stopped working. Being an "innovation and design consultancy" with both business and design skills was relatively unique in India when the studio started in 2005, but the field soon grew crowded with competing consultants. Furthermore, as the portfolio of projects the studio completed grew to include water, employability, and sanitation, some studio members wondered if they were going to get pigeonholed into design at the bottom of the pyramid. They wondered if they needed to narrate their history differently to attract a more varied scope of projects. This was part of how they emerged out of the "vendor" phase I described earlier in the chapter. It was partly through shedding labor, and partly through shifting story.

The stories came out of the ongoing, thick, almost familial interactions among members of the studio. All the time, people would talk about how they felt the studio aligned with their lives, or how projects were frustrating or boring them, or what projects seemed exciting to pursue. They ranted over lunch. They cribbed in the car or on the metro on the long commutes home. They hung out at each other's homes to eat and displayed what they were working on. They knew each other's parents in many cases. They stayed up late nights after a meal with conversations that wandered through project work, intellectual interests, political questions, and how the studio was going for them.

These reflective flurries also happened in more structured, periodic forms. When I first visited the studio, there was one day when Akhil let me know that I shouldn't come. I did not know the content of the meeting but heard later that everyone sat in the backyard to talk and that one cofounder cried. A year later I traveled with studio staff to Northeast India for the annual studio vacation. Intense, loud conversations among some of the senior members could be heard coming from a hotel room. Later conversations around the campfire referenced these conversations about the studio's direction even as people rolled joints and drank beer. By the time we went to Sri Lanka for a development conference together, I was working on projects with the studio and was included in these intense reflective circles.

People at the studio knew they were doing something that interested them more than the marketing, film editing, or engineering from which they had escaped. But a total articulation often evaded them. Kritika explained: "Design for a lot of us here has been a reaction to something that you don't want to do. It's not like 'we are so cool, be like us, offbeat.' But whatever you're doing, don't be a drone. Be mindful about you're doing. Lots of people see life as an escalating ladder. Go to college, get a job, get a house, do this and that. We're about questioning what you do."

This indeterminacy and openness was common among those who stayed with the studio over the years. But so was the commitment to mindful intention, and design as a vehicle for channeling those intentions and energies into transforming the world around them. In a studio where intentions were diverse and projects kept changing, members had to attune to and track each other and the world so they could keep turning toward ways to add value.

Sometimes outsiders told the studio what their value was and, consequently, what their value was not. This was a disciplinary strategy clients or partners employed to contest expertise studio members claimed. I saw this over and over as I observed workshops where the studio presented its findings to foundations and to World Bank staff. These were sites full of experts—economists, sociologists, loan officers—and not all of them understood design as a form of expertise. The studio presented their contested design expertise under the imprimatur of their powerful funder. At one workshop on open defecation, for example, the design team described their four months of interviews with people living in *bastis* (poor neighborhoods). They translated their learnings to principles for the design and operation of a latrine that would attract use. In short, the team had to design a community toilet that would be nice enough to compete with an open field or beach under a blue sky. Akhil and Vipin in particular were excited to draw on their MBA training to develop operational models: revenue strategies, organizational structures, and human resources management. Economists at the meeting seemed to bristle at Akhil and Vipin's intrusion into their professional jurisdiction of pricing and operational models. One Ivy League economist interjected in Akhil's operational proposal, recalling an earlier story Akhil had told about a rickshaw driver. "We have this picture of nice open fields," the economist began, "so will this guy be willing to actually pay to have three walls around?" The program officer who commissioned the studio, Erica, interrupted to elaborate the economist's intervention. "THAT," she emphasized, referencing the user stories, is "something that I think YOU guys have a lot of value add on . . . your value add on that question are mental models of health." Twice she told the studio what their "value add" was. In workshops with the wider project team, clients and others also used "value add" to imply what advice and expertise they wanted and what they didn't. It became a term by which clients and investors disciplined designers—a way to impose boundaries on designers' credibility, expertise, and value.

In other cases, the question of value was an invitation and a gentle demand. At a sanitation conference in Sri Lanka, another foundation officer attended the studio's research presentation. I was in attendance, taking notes and help-ing the team prepare for the presentation. As we had drinks after the presenta-tion, the officer, Gerald, asked Vipin and Akhil what the studio wanted to do now that they had completed the research phase. I had seen Erica have very similar conversations with the studio, working with it to craft projects that would appear legitimate to the funding foundation and generate credible find-ings about the future. In some ways, this was an ideal relationship—a thick, trusting relationship where the studio advised the client on exactly the sort of work it wanted to do. Akhil told Gerald that they had identified a city admin-istrator in Nanded, Maharashtra, who was interested in implementing the stu-dio's designs. Gerald pushed the studio to articulate what its "value add" would be in the implementation phase: "Is that a product? What is your deliverable? What is your value add? It seems like the Nanded MCD [Municipal Develop-ment Corporation] would own the project and you would be hired as project managers." Gerald probed skeptically about the value for the foundation in funding DevDesign as project managers on an urban toilet. He continued: "It is hard to see the coalition [between DevDesign and the MCD] as a product. It is hard to see a book about integrated development as a product. It would be more interesting to have a model you can replicate elsewhere. There are enough UN books on urban design to fill a bookshelf."

The foundation sought replicable models of development it could export elsewhere. Gerald assumed that reports, presumably unread, added no value. Nor did the construction of real, working infrastructure add value. The foun-dation understood this as the job of the MCD, and it wanted to direct the state in certain ways but not substitute for it: "At some point Nanded would have to say 'we like the design' and hire contractors. The foundation would not want to be involved at that point. It's not our job and it isn't sustainable."

Gerald's challenge to DevDesign drew on the logic of value addition. First, he worked to impose a particular ideology of value—the foundation's—on the studio. The foundation already organized its activities by this ideology of value. What the world needed was not more books. What was valuable were business plans and management models—governance. And even *more* valuable were business plans and models that could be replicated elsewhere, extending the foundation's claim to affect lives in the global South. This could also extend the studio's claim on resources from the foundation. One had to justify how they added value—the foundation's money, private budgetary oversight, contracts were involved—even in the absence of direct pressures of capital accumulation.[4]

The articulation of value, then, was not only a descriptive task. It was the task of negotiating with clients and partners what role others would value and accept, and what roles would be unacceptable. The struggle to articulate value was the struggle to find the overlap between what one wanted to do and what others would value. It was the struggle to find a niche in a system of production. And it was the struggle to articulate this value so others would recognize it. Entrepreneurial citizens had to tell their story, even sell it, to earn their keep. Some were more skilled at this than others.

Adding Value as Interactional Style

The call to add value disciplined not only careers and justifications but even everyday forms of verbal interaction. The sorts of selfhood privileged at the studio were neither natural nor frequently found, as evidenced by the studio's difficulties hiring and retaining new recruits. It was hard to specify in advance what made someone a good colleague for those already at DevDesign. To keep someone on, studio members had to feel that the new addition added value in some way. The value one added could equally be from contributions to compensated work as to uncompensated work. "Free will," hobbies, and experimental life were not just perks of the job; they were required as the engine that kept the studio changing, experimenting, and keeping up with the ever-moving cutting edge. Moreover, members had to be present, playful, and social with others at the studio. This allowed them to monitor others' work so they could develop the abilities demonstrated by more senior members (Lave and Wenger 1991), demonstrate the unique abilities they brought to the group, and more broadly make their lives, hobbies, whims, and political interests a resource for innovation work at the studio.[5] To innovate, one had to sense and develop oneself in tune with but in excess of the needs of the studio and the market. To only do what one was told was to be considered a burden or even, in Kritika's words, a drone; members expected each other to manage themselves. They expected each other to add value in surprising ways—bringing promising, unanticipated differences to the work of the studio and the work of innovating.

This dynamic was clearest to me in the short career of Rupa, a young woman just out of a top Indian design school. She lasted at the studio for four months—the duration of her first project. She came to the studio with an impressive portfolio. She spoke and wrote English well. She had won an honorable mention in an international social design competition for a yearlong participatory design project in rural South India. She already knew a bit about the studio from participating in its festival in its inaugural year; she had gotten on well with the other fellows of a two-week workshop the studio had put on. I expected Rupa to do well at the studio.

Rupa and I were on a handwashing project team with three other designers for several months. The project was to help British tropical physicians find a hand sanitation product people in India would use. We had involved design master's students in Pune in the project, teaching them qualitative design research methods while integrating their interviews and prototypes into reports for the British clients. The project had Rupa, Kritika, Mukta, and me living together in small Pune apartments—away from Delhi—for weeks at a time. We developed and revised curricular materials, adapting to problems the students raised and encountered. We shared observations about the students, looking for trouble spots on the teams. And we listened to and made sense of the students' research findings, developing an ever-evolving story that we reported back to clients on conference calls and on their occasional visits. We figured out our tasks and divisions of labor on the go, as we had not taught a full course before. We also had not worked with these particular students. Our work often stretched from mornings through nights in the service apartment we shared.

Kritika and Mukta, the seasoned DevDesign members, showed sparks of frustration with Rupa as the project wore on. One night at the apartment, we all sat face-to-face around the kitchen table, the crumbs of dinner tiffins all around us. We had to develop the teaching plan for the next day. We each had our laptops open. I was on Wi-Fi and ready to type, send, search, or upload as needed to get us to the goal. We didn't start with a plan, and Kritika, Mukta, and I talked quickly, and in incomplete sentences, about how to introduce the students to ethnographic methodology.

"What about showing them *Powers of Ten*?" Kritika asked. The film—a 1960s film about scale by Charles and Ray Eames—was shared background among us that demanded no explanation. I had been shown it while training at Stanford. Kritika and Mukta had seen it in different design schools in India.

"How do we sensitize the students?" Mukta asked.

Flipping through a directory of teaching resources we copied from Ajit's computer, I suggested, "What about the newsletters—"

Mukta cut me off. "What about sending them out onto the campus to take notes?"

We went on like this for about ten minutes. During the fast-clip exchanges, Rupa sat quietly, oscillating between watching us and watching her computer screen. At times it seemed that she was composing emails that we needed to send to the students soon; at other times we could not discern what she was doing. She was not interjecting. Mukta, Kritika, and I were grasping for a lesson plan. Rupa did not seem to be grasping with us. Mukta suddenly turned to Rupa: "What do you think? You haven't said anything."

Rupa looked startled. "You guys haven't said anything that I disagree with," she responded. "I don't have anything to add." This was not the first time Mukta and Kritika had tried to draw Rupa out; I had seen them single her out on a number of occasions. Upon a pause in the conversation, someone would turn to Rupa and ask for a commentary on the debate—"What do you think?" In our months together at the studio, Rupa rarely interjected to interrupt the aggressive and fast-paced exchanges of group work conversations.

These energetic discussions were how studio members produced critiques, proposed connections between topics, committed their labor, and constructed, deconstructed, and reconstructed design dilemmas. During Rupa's tenure at the studio, Kritika and Mukta continually urged her to speak up. I had already seen two other studio hires let go in part because they were quiet in such venues, distinctly preferring written communication—from reports to whiteboard lists—over fast verbal exchange. Quieter members met with critiques that their value to the studio was unclear. "I don't get what she's contributing," Mukta complained to me of an intern helping me organize a festival. Rupa was under suspicion of adding little value to the studio. The question "What do you think?" was both a pedagogical elicitation and a test.

Kritika pushed Rupa on more than vocalization. She often prodded her to develop creative hobbies and to get involved with personal projects others were doing at the studio. One afternoon Mukta had gone to work on an installation for Ajit's nightclub gig that night. Kritika urged Rupa to take the subway to the club to help Mukta out. Rupa dutifully complied. A few weeks later, Kritika announced to Rupa that she had a present to offer. Kritika thrust a film camera into Rupa's hands. Kritika, Vivek, and a friend had converted a studio bathroom into a darkroom for developing film and pinhole camera prints. The gift was not simply an expression of thoughtfulness or even an establishment of mutual obligation (Bourdieu 1977) but rather a signal that Rupa had little excuse not to join in on the kind of creative hobbies studio members pursued. Rupa had an obligation to demonstrate free will—the generator of experiment and promising difference.

Three months into Rupa's tenure at the studio, Mukta and Kritika met with Rupa to volunteer "feedback" on her performance at the studio. When Akhil, as managing director, asked staff designers their opinion on Rupa as a permanent hire, Kritika recounted the feedback to him: "We told her she needs to speak up and have an opinion rather than just sitting there and waiting for us to decide. Her response was that 'You guys are awesome! I don't have anything to add!'" Akhil frowned, implicitly agreeing by responding, "Well, I guess she has a few weeks to work on that."

Rupa felt overwhelmed in the culture of fast-clip interjection and exclamation at the studio. When I interviewed her apart from the group, she addressed the criticisms of her demeanor: "It's not that I don't have a point of view. I take some time. I'm not loud about it. When these guys are talking, it is hard to speak. People think I'm quiet, but I'm not. It's possible for a person who isn't vocal to get lost here." "Point of view" was a term of art; it described the distinct perspectives—ideas, experiences, and values—designers brought to projects, expressing their will in their labors. Rupa's words echoed Ellen's to me six months before; Ellen, a photographer with degrees in anthropology and development studies, had worked at the studio six months. She had also cited difficulty interjecting in fast-paced studio exchanges as well. She had been let go from the studio.

Rupa continued, explaining that she entered the studio unclear on expectations of design staff: "Eventually I figured out that I won't be given tasks. I have to say 'I'll do that.' It's not a good thing or bad thing, but at some level, I like to know. I like to be organized in my head about what I'm going to have to do." Mukta and Kritika had expected her to figure out what to do herself, as an expression of her own interests in the work at hand. That was how she could show her calling and passion for the work as a source of personal growth—a way of living a life.

Rupa and Ellen both left the studio for good jobs. One went to work for a philanthropic foundation. The other worked as a researcher for a well-established, more hierarchical marketing firm where the structure of work allowed her to demonstrate her skills. They fit as part of the broader "scene" of design and innovation, part of the larger milieu of developmental and entrepreneurial enthusiasm but embedded in work relations where they added more value. Rupa's and Ellen's careers revealed that the capacity to add value was not intrinsic to the individual or their skills but was relational to the norms in their milieu.

Necessary Labors: Devalued, Disavowed, and Pushed on Others

Not all staff at the studio were valued for their relationships, their connections to a cultural pulse, or their experimental ethos. Other labors were essential but did not extend the promissory value of the studio. Dishes had to get done. People had to be invited to events. Computer graphics had to be processed and compressed. Travel had to be booked. Finances had to be tracked. Organizational roles at all levels of the hierarchy had more and less interesting parts. Studio members, however, enacted hierarchies of value and prestige in how they talked about their own work and that of others. Power manifested as the capacity to push less interesting and devalued labors onto others.[6] This section attends to the labor practices that sustain the drive to add value in economies that privilege innovation, change, and competitive differences.

The studio employed a cook, a driver, a cleaner, and an accountant, who were paid far lower salaries than the client-facing studio members. These infrastructural workers were not seen as having unique knowledge, nor did their work obviously enhance the reputation of the studio. Rather, they kept the studio clean and functioning. Studio members recognized neither these workers' voices nor their unique desires as part of the production of value. Nobody expected them to express "free will" in their work.

Studio members also had work they considered low value, whether boring, repetitive, or unlikely to generate prestige. They often called such work "sweat-shop work," "menial tasks," or even "donkey work" (see also Xiang 2007, 5). Examples of this work included booking plane tickets for festival speakers, saving hundreds of animation graphics for an animation, or fixing HTML code for a project deliverable. This work was necessary; it was even impressive and virtuous when very senior members took on their parts of such tasks, demon-strating a willingness to get their hands metaphorically dirty. But such work alone was not sufficient to earn one's keep as a member of the studio.

Ellen, the quiet photographer, casually used the phrase "sweatshop girl" to volunteer for a particularly tedious set of tasks in the project we worked on together. Ellen and I, along with a short-term studio visitor, Anna, worked together to orchestrate a festival put on by studio members. Upon announcing the festival, we began to publicize it through emails diffused to studio friends, family, and colleagues, as well as through Facebook. Ajit had purposefully accumulated several thousand Facebook friends through his exposure as an electronic music performer; he encouraged us to share the festival page with his contacts. I sent an email with a list of launch tasks, including contacting Ajit's contacts, to Ellen and Anna. Ellen and Anna began an email exchange taking responsibility for various tasks:

From Ellen, 3:03 pm December 7:
I've got Ajit's login details on Facebook so when you give me the go-ahead, I can be the sweatshop girl and sit and invite his whole friends list to the festival Facebook page—plus the rest of the studio should try to do the same with their own FB friends lists. I can also sit soon and follow a bunch of people on Twitter and start promoting that way as well. It's tedious, but effective.

From Anna, 3:06 pm December 7:
Ellen, if you don't like doing that stuff, I don't mind it. . . . Also, if you have his login details, can you make me an admin of the Greenery page?

From Ellen, 3:09 pm December 7:
No no, I don't mind it, just tedious. :)
Yep I'll go ahead and do that!

Ellen volunteers for a task, even as she marks the task as unfortunately tedious; this is not the kind of work that expresses a point of view or develops her interests. Ellen's and Anna's offers to absorb the tedium establish their *esprit de corps*, while with "sweatshop girl," Ellen disavows the labor as beneath the studio ideal.

RK, a graphic designer, similarly disavowed some of the graphic production labors necessary to his project as "donkey work." The project was a museum display, and RK had learned programming languages, space installation, and "sketching in code" through the project. His software, however, needed dozens of images in multiple file formats. RK would have to generate these files; this was the donkey work. As he foretold his suffering to me, he explained the repeated file-processing steps and mimed repeated mouse clicks, emphasizing his displeasure.

Studio members did not completely disavow repetitive, craft, or manual work. Several studio members cooked photogenic meals and experimented with recipes from abroad. Ellen decorated the studio space with textiles. Mukta and RK spent hours engaged in the manual labor of tying zip ties, winding yarn, and nailing wood to create experimental typography and sculptural installations. These "hobbies" constituted, in part, the experimental life. Though tailors, carpenters, and peons earned little, designers did craft and manual work as a means of developing "one's interests." Unlike manual workers and cooks, studio members had the luxury of choosing when to dabble in such work. Tinkering, making, and manufacture could provoke innovative approaches or signal creative quirks, but manual labors became value only when appreciated by wealthy patrons or consumers. Designers' cultural capital could transform manual production into value, but this was labor intensive and more often an experimental hobby.

RK and Ellen drew distinctions between the work they aspired to and these necessary but disavowed labors. The work they aspired to allowed them to perform their distinct, added value to the studio. Work others could do— clicking invitations, processing data—had to be done but denied them the chance to show the difference they uniquely could make.[7] Such work was not only below the station of the studio but below the station of humans as idealized in (at least) Western history and philosophy. From Roman slavery to Marx, animals and barbarians have occupied one side of a nature/culture binary, citizens and rational man on the other (Zuboff 1988, 25–30; Arendt 1998 [1958]). Within these systems of meaning, designers figured themselves as ideal humans—intentional, less alienated laborers creating value out of their free will and intellect. Even as they dabbled in cooking, crafts, and chores, they had the freedom to stop when they felt like it because they hired others to perform less valued but necessary tasks that kept the studio running.

In this scheme, the Hindi-speaking staff could not make claims to free will. They furnished the labor that stabilized the workplace, providing food, bodies, and maintenance that freed the studio members to experimentally create. These staffers had been with the studio for years. They included the cook, Dinesh, the driver, Manas, the accountant, Rajnit, and an office peon,[8] Anil. They were employed for various support functions: Anil cleaned the office before studio members arrived; Manas drove members to business and personal errands and also delivered and picked up visitors and packages; Dinesh cooked lunch each day, kept a steady stream of chai cups circling through the studio, and cooked for individual studio member requests; Rajnit managed the ledgers, issued checks, and existed in an awkward relationship between the service staff and the English-fluent designers. While Rajnit issued orders to the service staff, all the studio members barked orders at Rajnit, ranging from "Turn on the fan!" to "Make me a copy!"

This tier of staff did not refer to DevDesign as a studio but rather as an office (the linguistic distinction was meaningful in Hindi as well as English). Studio members did not expect the Hindi-speaking staff to personally invest in their work or enact free will and point of view in their tasks. Kritika would occasionally offer Dinesh recipe directives, and studio members would joke and complain in English that Dinesh's food was particularly boring certain days, but Dinesh did not shoulder the expectations to express an opinion or explore in his work. This staff played table tennis with designers, hung out on the patio during self-selected breaks, and vigorously made fun of each other (often involving me as a culturally incompetent prop). They did not, however, interject opinions on design projects or business decisions. They did not engage in photography, art, music, film, drawing, or other expressive or romantically creative practices in the space of the studio.

The free will designers pursued in the studio relied on the steady and reliable infrastructural labors of the service staff. Despite liberal efforts to recast innovation as collaboration (see Isaacson 2014), innovation always required others not quite equal to the collaboration—others not quite part of the scene. These others provided the devalued labor of social reproduction (Vora 2015), manufacture (see also Varma 2015), and the stabilization of infrastructures necessary for innovation work (Irani 2015a). Incorporating the service staff into the experimental life would destabilize the steady flow of food and drink, the freedom to focus on more highly valued tasks, and the conviviality of never having to fight about who would clean the common area. Free will relies on unfree labors. Nobody at the studio imagined that these infrastructural workers would one day become entrepreneurial citizens, freely contracting and moving according to their will. These workers were, rather, those who enabled entrepreneurial citizens to intensify their freedoms and production of value. They made possible the infrastructure, resources, and flows on which entrepreneurial citizens relied.

Conclusion: Articulating Selfhood and Social Life to Value

Learning to add value meant learning how to monitor one's relations, how to make one's value visible, and parlaying present conditions into steps up the value chain. It also meant setting up one's work to push less valued but essential infrastructural labors onto others who could perform them with minimal oversight and management. As people turn their lives and aspirations toward "value," they articulate themselves to a larger system of production—the production of innovation and the commodities and logistical networks that might follow from it (see also Cross 2013). The cherished practices of the studio—interdisciplinarity, living optimistically and experimentally, searching for unique selling propositions and ways of adding value—are the disciplines of entrepreneurial innovation. Sociologist David Stark (2009) calls innovation the search for value among multiple orders of worth. Studio members' "free will" generated of experiment in service of innovation. Their emergent rubrics of authenticity were their yardsticks of worth in assessing possibilities and opportunities.

We can trace DevDesign's operation as a way of examining the labor of ascending a value chain in which global capitalism elevates branding, advertising, and the construction of markets through design research and business planning. The labors necessary to make designs and innovations into reality—manufacture, maintenance, and even product design (once a zenith of creative production)—were more standardized or available from larger labor pools pitted against each other in competition (Irani 2018). Thus as DevDesign climbed the value chain, it distanced itself from what it called this "vendor" work—the work that stabilized infrastructures for client organizations. Even within the studio, members distanced themselves from the components of their work that they recognized—in day-to-day practice—as failing to contribute to the uniqueness of their skillset or portfolio of projects. This was the donkey work. This was the sweatshop girl work.

Scholars of globalization debate how global institutions and projects reorder the world and recompose people's lives. This chapter shows how entrepreneurial citizens respond to these global structures as they calibrate their lives to align their varied aspirations with what clients and patrons can recognize and compensate as valuable. In styling themselves as a consultancy, studio members exemplified the flexible ethos identified by sociologist Richard Sennett in his *The Culture of the New Capitalism* (2006); for Sennett, the figure of the consultant is characterized by its capacity to move from project to project, quickly work on problems, and "move along." DevDesign did demonstrate this ethos of flexible work and flexible relations. The idea of flexible relations, however, fails to capture the stability of social relations that made possible the work of rapidly interpreting culture in pursuit of opportunity. As studio members worked to make a living while making a life, they cultivated friendships, explored politics, and formed communities with the express purpose of finding inspiration, accessing knowledge, and even finding material support in the entrepreneurial quest to refigure their authentic selves as sources of value. The studio itself reflected this stability: since 2009 five members have formed the core of the firm and the social relationships that make the reflexive search for value work. Others have left the studio but remained within reach, extending the networks of familiarity and trust out of which the next project might come. And the social orders that stabilize the studio's infrastructures reflect the social orders of caste and class that reproduce India's cultures of servitude (Ray and Quyum 2009). The next chapter turns to how studio members look beyond the studio to explore possibilities and partners for entrepreneurial projects.

5

Entrepreneurial Time and the Bounding of Politics

AGAINST THE VOLATILITY of innovation, there was often little time for democracy. Since independence, nationalists posed development as a rush to catch up with the West. What shifted over time was how Indians justified this rush, and what kinds of projects this rush justified in turn.

By the early 2000s Indian policy elites cited the "demographic dividend" as one reason for urgency. Economists coined the demographic dividend to name the growth effects of a large working-age population with relatively few elderly or child "dependents." The dividend promised a boon to economic growth if governments channeled working-age people into jobs or entrepreneurship (Planning Commission 2012a, 12; Nilekani 2009). But populations age; the dividend would not last forever. The window of demographic opportunity would shrink. And, some warned, those promising young people could turn to crime or Maoist rebellion if opportunities to match their aspirations failed to materialize (Nilekani 2009, 52).

This public urgency fueled and legitimized both particular forms of production and particular political styles. Some citizens argued that the Indian state ought to act urgently and with a strong hand, militarily and economically, to channel demographic dividends before it was too late (Modi 2017). Many in the middle classes supported authoritarian styles of government. At a time when the low-caste groups were mobilizing electorally, the middle classes came to deride politics as a domain of corruption, handouts, and imprudent policy making. These middle-class Indians often cited Singapore and China as models of Asian development: single-party systems propelled by rational planning and authoritarian execution (Kestenbaum 2010; Fernandes and Heller 2006, 497–98). At symposiums on civic design in Delhi, some even called this the "Steve Jobs" model of governance, citing the famously authoritarian, self-actualized, spiritually attuned in late CEO of Apple. While projects with endpoints, by definition, create pressures to cease deliberation and act, it was a newer, classed phenomenon to valorize action over deliberation entirely.

The surge of interest in "emerging markets" also made the present particularly ripe with possibility. In the mid-2000s a wave of books, reports, and talks pointed to the potential for profit latent in countries thought too poor to have masses of consumers. C. K. Prahalad's *The Fortune at the Bottom of the Pyramid* (2005) was the most famous of these. Goldman Sachs (Wilson and Purushothaman 2003) and McKinsey (Ablett et al. 2007) sounded the "emerging market" drumbeat among the transnational capitalist class. Geographer Ananya Roy (2010) calls these projects "poverty capital." Multinational companies' turn toward "emerging markets" generated buzz in major Indian cities like Delhi, Bombay, and Bangalore. Middle-class professionals with good English and good networks found companies like Abbott, Lockheed, Proctor and Gamble, and CitiBank looking for consumer insights and local corporate and entrepreneurial partners. Development agencies pursuing ICT-driven "Development 2.0" agendas sought software developers and designers to develop digital connections to the poor (Gajjala and Tetteh 2016). They also found European cultural institutions and trade ministries seeking to fund conferences and shape Indian agendas. Many professionals who otherwise would have gone abroad for jobs decided to stay in India, sensing it was where the action was (Saxenian 2006). The founders of DevDesign, graduates of prestigious Indian schools and fluent in English, were part of this generation that considered and deferred a move to the United States. Acknowledging that times were flush in the Delhi development scene, the managing director of DevDesign quipped, "There's nothing wrong with a bubble if you are in at the beginning."

Entrepreneurial citizens looked for the opportunity in these bubbles and windows. As the studio and its members sought ways to add value, they sometimes did this by rearticulating their skills and stories. They also experimented with paid and unpaid projects in development, marketing, design, and arts, and with partners. People spun off side projects to the consulting work. Ajit started a restaurant that doubled as an art space. Vipin carried around a digital pitch deck of projects—creativity workshops for bureaucrats, crowdfunding for NGOs, for example—to pitch to his ideas to funders and partners he happened to meet as he moved through his day. Mukta and Kritika looked for ways to actually make stuff, from hosting skill shares in Delhi coworking spaces to doing art installations at clubs. Vivek kept up with his friends in solar power NGOs, helping on projects when he had time outside of DevDesign. People kept their hands on many projects and relationships, at the ready in case one of them bore an opportunity whose time had come. Entrepreneurs prized timeliness: at the level of interaction when one found a partner or investor to make an idea real, and also at historical time scales of bubbles and demographic dividends. The director of DevDesign, for example, had forgone chances to work abroad after attending IIM; to him, the time seemed right in India to grow a business. He saw the possibility of a bubble, but he wanted in early.

This chapter is about the forms of productive activity and styles of politics that emerged out of these public urgencies. Those I met at design studios, hackathons, and development workshops sometimes spoke of "the bias to action"—a temporal ethos that valorized the production of venturesome experiment and derided longer deliberation, political demand-making, or the extended work of meaningful political inclusion. This "bias to action" was familiar to me from my time at Google and Stanford; its ethos deflected the work of care with the adage "ask for forgiveness, rather than permission."[1] The bias to action was popular across Silicon Valley. Facebook famously invited employees to "move fast and break things" (Fattal 2012, 940). Google encouraged employees to "launch early, launch often" (Hill and Jones 2007, C94)—a style of software development pioneered by Linux developers to maximize contributions while trusting communities to find problems (Raymond 2001, 28). Beyond the expert-driven world of open source, Uber experimented with public life, flouting regulations and democratic procedures by launching illegally in several cities (M. Scott 2015). Critics point out that this "do first, ask forgiveness later" breeds crisis after crisis as companies pursue actions that favor their vision with little patience to anticipate and accommodate public concerns (Sherman 2010). I agree with this critique, and it was only during fieldwork that I came to realize the extent to which I had incorporated this bias as an embodied habitus. My work with DevDesign reveals illiberalism rendered innocent by this optimistic, speculative, investment-friendly ethos.

The bias to action was a regime of being-in-time (Adams, Murphy, and Clarke 2009) that emerged in responses to shifts in political economy. It fit with the wider middle-class sense that saw opportunity in a bubble and cherished action over deliberation and careful work; I call this public sense entrepreneurial time. In India, it was not at all clear how to turn the masses into markets. Start-ups experimented with many strategies for monetizing the poor (Cross 2013). The design staff at DevDesign experimented in how to add value—to clients, to one another—given their connections, resources, credible expertise, and personal aspirations (chapter 4). A bias to action urged entrepreneurs to experiment with varying alignments among products, money, and people to find those combinations that seemed most promising. For investors, the bias to action generated a churn of informative experiments, and they could choose to invest only in the most successful. The bias to action described an ethos demanded by multinational corporations since the 1990s. In the face of the volatility brought by technological change and trade policies that enabled outsourcing, supply chains, and global competition, corporations sought a new kind of worker. This worker would be able to intensify innovation, reduce risks, and manage themselves and collaborators amid shifting policy, technology, and market conditions (Brown and Eisenhardt 1997; Wood 1989; Peters and Waterman 1982).

This chapter focuses on the consequences of the entrepreneurial bias to action for the practice of citizenship and democracy. To witness these consequences on the ground, I examine a hackathon—one of the ongoing, speculative experiments at DevDesign—as a site of pedagogy, labor process, and civic engagement. The hackathon was a multiday event in which entrepreneurial citizens gathered to get to know one another, brainstorm around a theme, and develop a prototype of a technology in search of investment. In this way, the hackathon staged a ritual of entrepreneurship—a purified moment of intense, convivial creation. The event kept at bay the grind of making investors, customers, and workers happy. More than a ritual, the event was one of many through which participants explored possible futures, built their networks, and investigated what of the possible was viable as an opportunity. I show who joined the hackathon, why, and toward what ends—and what happened when one member abruptly abandoned the effort. The departure, and reactions to it around the DevDesign studio, made visible political sensibilities implicit or only hinted at among entrepreneurial citizens but rarely articulated in formal discussions of entrepreneurship. I argue that the bias to action, amid a wider public sense of entrepreneurial time, renders social movements, deliberation, and planning as barriers to innovation. Participatory models like the hackathon or user-centered design ostensibly open the doors to innovation to all but invite participation only so long as it does not delay the demos, prototypes, and promising projects that count as action. I show how these temporal and social disciplines align high-tech production skills with contemporary Indian middle-class political imaginaries (see also Lukose 2009; Fernandes 2006). I demonstrate that the entrepreneurial bias to action mobilizes liberal or even social justice desires toward innovation but with illiberal effect.

"Likeminded People": Scenes as Social Life Made Productive

The artists, consultants, and designers of DevDesign mingled in wider networks peopled by management consultants, art curators, playwrights, independent bookstore owners, designers, and development workers. As they inhabited the dance floors, bars, readings, screenings, hackathons, and "skill shares" of Delhi, they moved through several scenes. At TED conferences and development workshops, they mingled with experts, journalists, and policy makers from across sectors. Ajit, Mihir, and Mukta also moved in experimental art and design scenes. Tara, Vivek, and Ajit kept in touch with old friends from the Indian Institutes of Technology and Indian Institutes of Management. Scenes like these kept studio members inspired. They kept them connected to new ideas. They were sites where studio members found and vetted project partners, friends, and patrons. These scenes were where political rants could turn into project ideas. They were where history, literature, and critique could occasion friendships that became new ventures and collaborations. They were places where members could remind themselves that they were more than their projects for Dunkin Donuts or Samsung. And in those scenes, they could meet "likeminded" others who also wanted to be more than their work for multinationals and had similar tastes for self-actualization, developmental good, and nation building.

Professionals produced these scenes as they moved, tangled, and made place—scenes are knots formed by lines of people's practices, in Tim Ingold's sense (2009). The scenes were a cultural infrastructure for the production of innovation (Turner 2009), useful for how they offered an outside from work among others who, in turn, could be helpful *for* work. These scenes generated the social fabric and shared sensibilities that underpinned entrepreneurial citizens' capacities to translate their lives into value.

Sociologists of space and subculture have analyzed the role scenes and spatial formations play in supporting creative production, for example, of new media start-ups (Neff 2012), Burning Man (Chen 2009), fashion design (Currid-Halkett 2007), and high-tech production (Florida 2002). Long before these sociologists pointed to the importance of scenes, artists and subcultural sociologists reflected on them (e.g., Hesmondhalgh 2005; Straw 2001; Irwin 1977). These sociologists demonstrate how flexible, creative workers make connections, find partners, and find future projects and jobs on the dance floor, at restaurants, and at networking events. As early as the 1970s, musician Brian Eno theorized "scenius" as the intelligence produced by groups of people (Albiez and Pattie 2016). In India, architect Charles Correa (2012) and M. P. Ranjan (interview with author) similarly argued that cities enabled a critical mass of special, unusual, innovative people to gather. Annalee Saxenian's work on "regional advantage" (1996) also identified the importance of "the ecology"—of suppliers, of employees, of people moving across firms—to producing innovation; Saxenian's analysis has entered into high-tech capital's self-conscious understandings of itself. Eno, Correa, and Saxenian all drew on cybernetic images of organizations as networked ecologies. This way of figuring the social erases power relations among actors and generated through institutions and economies (Murphy 2006, 132–60). Sociologists Gina Neff and Sharon Zukin point out the erasures that accompany the celebration of scenes and entrepreneurial ecologies. Cities that prioritize the productivity of creative classes, they argue, often deprioritize those who sustain less celebrated infrastructures and services—the dishwashers, the print shop workers, and the textile workers, for example (Neff 2012, 124; see Zukin 1996).

These less celebrated others were important sources of labor for those in Delhi's creative scenes, and sometimes they were even a source of information and inspiration. Designers often sought and produced critiques of their own categories by chatting with craftspeople, chaiwalas, and rickshaw drivers—innovators' others could inform the production of creative novelty (see also Becker 1978). But nobody talked about these poorer workers as part of the scene. Entrepreneurial citizens titrated openness to these others, keeping boundaries just porous enough to generate inspiration and novelty without introducing frustration or people who "just don't get it" into these scenes. For aspiring innovators seeking company among likeminded people, the invisibilities of innovators' others could be a source of guilt but were essential to the pleasures and productivity of the scene.

On one night like many others during my fieldwork, I happened onto a late night hangout that blurred any lines between labor, fantasy, and therapy. I was returning from a long day crisscrossing Delhi, visiting old friends; that week, I was in Delhi for DevDesign's OpenLab festival. One architect, a friend of a studio founder, called the festival "a scene to bind all scenes" for its capacity to draw people from the arts, nonprofits, design, and business. DevDesign organized the festival as a way to stage inspirational talks, development workshops, food experiments, literary discussions, and music performances; their goal, as Ajit put it, was to attract and "turn on" entrepreneurial citizens.[2] I returned to OpenLab to participate as a friend, as a critic of design, and as someone who had a stake in the making of other possible worlds (Haraway 2008; Uncertain Commons 2013; Escobar 2018; Rosner 2018). I had thought I was done with observation and came to have a seat at the proverbial table. My friends at DevDesign had put me up in a guest house on the edge of a tree-shaded Delhi park with a handful of others who had come to Delhi for the festival.

As I walked through the door and tossed my backpack in the corner, I found my suitemates slouched, cups of *chai* in hand, on velveteen cushioned benches designed for more formal comportments. Our guesthouse had no beanbags or couches, iconic furniture of the new media workplace, but we brought our habits with us anyways. Krish, a software engineer, was hanging out with Gustav and Erik, German NGO workers. I knew Gustav and Erik because they had hired DevDesign to work on a sanitation education project the previous year. Krish lived in Bangalore but knew Vipin, a DevDesign principal, from Vipin's IIM-Bangalore days. Krish was a surprising software engineer, soft spoken even as he was enthusiastic. He painted and read Rosi Braidotti, a feminist philosopher of technology, for fun. I had met Krish only because we were both in town for the OpenLab festival. Krish had only just met Gustav and Erik, but they had found plenty to talk about.

I sat cross-legged next to Erik on a chair facing Krish and Gustav. Gustav regaled Krish with horror stories from the development industry; Dutch aid agencies were in his crosshairs. The agencies, Gustav explained, had requested informal help on workshops and sanitation policy. Gustav offered the help uncompensated; when donor staff seek favors, nonprofit workers feel they have little choice but to offer. When it was time for the agency to formally contract for a sanitation initiative, Gustav thought his nonprofit would get the contract.

"The money went to Dutch copycats!" Gustav railed.

"Can you get revenge?" I asked conspiratorially.

"Development is a small world," he told me shaking his head tersely. "Nobody wants to see a fight. But I will get my revenge. I could plant a shit bomb." A seasoned development worker, Gustav witnessed a constant stream of small scandals and compromised ideals that would send spin doctors into overtime.

As our conversation wandered, we talked about risk-averse development funders. Erik told us about his time in Occupy camps in Berlin, and how he wished the occupiers were more politically pragmatic.[3] Stories of Occupy begat stories of cardboard bicycles and sustainable technologies. Stories of technologies and politics sparked conversations about prototyping—the production of inexpensive test models—as an art of exploring "what's possible."[4]

Erik, needing to prepare for the next day's workshops, went off to bed.

Krish and Gustav returned to stories of partnerships gone wrong, and the problem of practicing global development that required them to partner with NGOs in unfamiliar parts of the world. They noted a shift: funders no longer expected small NGOs to operate as an expression of local civil society. NGOs had once been seen as an expression of local voice—a check on global markets and government corruption (Fisher 1997, 442). Now funders wanted small NGOs to act as on-the-ground partners to implement global development initiatives. NGO workers like Gustav, located in Europe, now needed to locate partners across regions and languages; moreover, they had to find local partners they could trust and collaborate with. As they hung out, Gustav asked Krish for leads on just these kinds of partners. Earlier in the night, Gustav had peppered Krish with questions about organizations they could seek out for their sanitation work in the Indian state of Maharashtra. Gustav was planning sanitation pedagogy across India, based on models his NGO first developed in Africa. Krish knew Maharashtra only from a two-month bike ride across the state, but no source of leads was too tenuous for Gustav. Potential partners, however, were not created equal.

"For a long time," Krish explained, "a lot of NGOs were left-wing activists. Now there's also a lot of NGOs who work in the cultures of philanthropic corporations like Tata." One style of NGO would send you to protest; another style would allow for efficacy monitoring and reporting. Krish noted that he needed to know which was which.

"In UP [Uttar Pradesh, an Indian state]," Gustav interjected, "We found strong partners through WaterAid." WaterAid was a multinational sanitation NGO with offices based in London and operating in dozens of countries ("Why We're Here" 2018).

"Ah," Krish cut in, "common partners make it easier to make the connection."

Krish and Gustav began imagining possible tools as they talked. Talk about the past easily sparked talk about possible design futures. A map of NGO and activist groups, Krish speculated, would let you browse "ground partners" by locations or by "particular domains." I began to extend this newly conjured mapping tool. I drew a map surface in the air with my hand—I traced a flat screen and NGOs dotting it with my finger—and suggested that users could filter the NGOs by region. I started getting excited; much of my training as a designer had taught me to think about organizations and information. And puzzles, like engineering problems, were fun for me. They promised resolution—so long as you bracketed contingency, power, and social forces. And bracket we did! The designer buried in me took over, carried away with the puzzle; "It sounds like it's hard to find trusted connections," I replied, pointing back to Krish and Gustav's earlier complaint. "Maaaaaaybe," I wondered out loud, "you could select NGOs through partner organizations you have in common."

"That could be very helpful!" Gustav got excited.

Krish sat up stick-straight, his eyes wide, his voice excited. "That's a great idea. *Let's do it!*" A thrill charged through me. Did this software already exist somewhere in the world? Was the data we needed available? Did we actually have time to tackle a new project alongside our other commitments? We did not know, and in the effervescence of that moment, I did not think of those questions. Nobody raised them. The pleasure was in the possibility, not the labor of production and maintenance.[5] We shared an itch. Management experts called it "the bias to action." Pedagogues of civic entrepreneurship like Kiran Bir Sethi (chapter 3) called it "the 'I Can' bug." I had honed this propensity during my time in Silicon Valley. Gustav, an Ashoka Social Enterprise Fellow, thrived in a development economy that demanded constant pitches, promises, and grant proposals. We sensed, explored, and played through acts of planning, anticipating, and tinkering. It was more fun to do so among the "likeminded"—with sufficient similarities in habitus, language, and points of reference to share stories, knowledge, and advice. We had just enough similarity to get along productively and just enough difference to be interesting and even inspiring to each other. The bias to action rendered this sociality fuel for the furnaces of entrepreneurial experiment.

The Hackathon: From Talk to "Actually Doing Something"

The NGO partner map we dreamt up that night never made the transition from late-night brainstorm to bits. We jumped straight into OpenLab workshops that were meant to generate future projects. The next morning, Gustav went to meet with his OpenLab group—a team of designers, artists, and entrepreneurs who wanted to explore and prototype theater for development education. Krish and I departed by subway to the design studio to join our OpenLab group; we had signed up to spend five days before the festival as part of a hackathon on "open governance." The OpenLab workshops had in common that they brought together people who did not know each other to spend a few days dreaming of development projects, and then making those dreams concrete as demos, plans, and presentations. Whereas late-night brainstorms often went no further than a single conversation, the OpenLab workshops convened people who wanted to spend a few days working together around a theme. The hackathon was one workshop, and it invited us to tinker with software to produce demos that would only partially work but would serve as promises of fully developed software to come. Hackathons were one way of taking the energies of experimental life and channeling them into tangible things.

DevDesign was hosting the hackathon in its studio. The convener of the hackathon, Vipin, was a senior partner at DevDesign who, like several of his colleagues, had escaped from tech start-ups and management consulting to work at the firm. He saw design and development consulting as personally meaningful ways of contributing to social good, broadly construed. Like other studio members, he had spent his life and career located domestically in urban India but working alongside multinational corporations with American management theories and U.S. internet publications in tow. The hackathon was one of Vipin's many ideas for how to innovate for social good and one of the few he was able to pursue alongside his full-time studio work; unlike his larger project ideas, the hackathon was only a few weeks' commitment.

Vipin recruited other hackathon participants through his personal networks and through an "open" call application. He circulated an English-language call through the festival website, nonprofit sector mailing lists, and

European "knowledge economy" distribution lists. Not surprisingly, all thirty applicants to the event were professionals or university students, fluent in English, and were involved in design or software work. Only 4 percent of Indians were fluent in English, so this was an elite group.[6] Krish certainly fit this profile. I partially fit it; my prior work experience and my Ph.D. program rendered me legible as a designer, even though I also approached the hackathon with a sense of disillusionment and ethnographically informed alienation. The one who did not fit the software design profile was Prem, a political anthropologist. Prem was Indian American, raised in Bangalore but college educated in the United States. I had recruited him to apply because of the relevance of his work to the theme.

The goal of the hackathon was to come together as a group and, working within the theme of "open governance," to choose a design direction and drive toward a demo. Within that remit, we had the freedom to prototype whatever software we could. "Governance" was World Bank lingo that framed the state as an efficient manager of market-led development, rather than as a political entity (Kiely 1998). This was the technocratic idiom in which Vipin and Akhil were particularly comfortable. Vipin recruited several institutional partners to the project: a Ford Foundation–funded legal research NGO to consult on questions of Indian parliamentary processes, as well as a software consultancy to help with digital media programming. These partners promised both to receive the demo after the hackathon and to shape our imaginations so our open-ended work would result in a demo more suited to their agendas. I also organized a visit to the Planning Commission during the hackathon so our team could understand how government technocrats saw the legislative process and political participation in it.

On the first day of the hackathon, six of us convened at the studio. We gathered in wicker seats around a large glass table surrounded by whiteboards. Few of the participants knew each other, so Vipin had each of us introduce ourselves by explaining what we sought from the experience. Our motivations were varied, but each of us articulated the desire to "make a difference," though we would discover as the hackathon unfolded that our visions for difference and the politics of achieving it diverged significantly.

Dev, a young web developer from Bangalore, explained that he wanted to see if he could affect the functions of the Indian government. With all the "complaining" he heard about how the government "doesn't work," he saw this as "a chance to see if we can make a difference." Nikhil, an ex-start-up founder and now Gurgaon-based software consultant, wanted to transform how government officials responded to "technology" writ large through the demo we would produce: "This could be just jamming the door. Getting the technology in. Ease their lives a bit with technology. So then in the future, even if it is not

[Vipin's studio], they'll be more receptive [to other technology initiatives]."
Dev's and Nikhil's optimism about technology was broader than personal
desires for software contracts; they both echoed broader middle-class optimism about technological potential for government transparency and rural
economic development (Mazzarella 2010a). The demo, Nikhil hoped, would
give government officials a taste of what was possible.

Next, Benoy, a design graduate student from Mumbai, spoke. Like Prem,
he was attracted to design's promise of tangible intervention, but he had found
that design school rarely delivered on that promise. "I want to see if design
can actually save the world instead of just making posters for clients about it,"
he explained.

Prem, a political anthropologist, echoed Dev's and Nikhil's hope of making
a difference through the software: "Anthropologists sit and critique things but
they never get around to doing anything." All the speech act theory Prem used
in his own research had left him still wanting to experiment with other forms
of intervention; the performativity of speech and knowledge production left
him wanting. The promise of design and making seemed palpable even to
those on the political and academic left.

I was there because I wanted to see what my training in software design
could offer when not commissioned by a tech company or a multinational
philanthropy, the cases I usually studied and the work I had done prior to the
Ph.D. degree. Scholars at the intersection of science, technology, and society
and design had long argued that design and making could be one way to
work toward more desirable worldings and agencies, whether motivated by
feminism, racial justice, or political liberation (Haraway 2008; Fouché 2006).
I was inspired by Lucy Suchman's recasting of design as a humbler form of
"reconfiguration" (2007), as well as approaches to design that emphasized
the values held by groups (Knobel and Bowker 2011; Borning and Muller
2012; Friedman 1996). After a year of fieldwork at DevDesign, following
others' leads in design consulting, the hackathon invited me to the promised power of making, of intervening, and of translating commitments into
persistent objects.

Each of us, in different ways, sought to intervene in the operations of the
world through "action." In different ways, what was at stake for all of us was
performing the promise of collectively instantiated agency in a messy, complex
world through some kind of building. We differed in how we understood the
significance of our technical practices, whether as an extension of our own
intentions, as a proving case for information technology, or as a way of entan-
gling with others at a distance. We all wondered about our technological agencies, but we imagined different ways technology might travel, different effects a
technology might have, and different ways the social worlds outside the studio

operate. Some of us were actively disinterested in reproducing Silicon Valley values as we wandered hopefully into this experiment in hacking. After all, whether we even could make a difference was in question. The Delhi hackathon, then, staged the promise of agency—of making a difference by making promissory technology. But it did so by inviting divergent imaginaries to come into temporary, experimental contact.

The promise of agency was central to the OpenLab festival, as well as the assemblage of competitions, fellowships, and programs like Ashoka, Echoing Green, and TED.[7] Our demo would live beyond the hackathon in the gallery of the OpenLab festival as a celebration of social entrepreneurship and design in potentia. The hackathon was one of several "fellowship" projects preceding the festival, all of which would showcase their outcomes in the festival gallery during the peak of the festival. OpenLab organizers intended that the fellowships would produce friendships, induce self-exploration, and offer a taste of entrepreneurial experimentalism through weeklong projects all over India. While it was uncertain whether the fellowships would actually spawn projects, the conveners hoped the experience would transform the participants as subjects. While other OpenLab fellows worked on textiles in an experimental community and with NGOs at urban ashrams, we would hack software in Delhi. "We want to show that all this design thinking is not just idealistic; it's something you can actually do with success," a graphic designer organizing OpenLab explained to me. OpenLab talks during the festival were meant to inspire audiences with case studies of long-term activist, artistic, and entrepreneurial projects. The fellowship outcomes, by contrast, would show what small groups of people were able to achieve in just a few days. These disparate practices were temporarily tethered together under the OpenLab banner of "alternate" paths to "creative thinking and action" to transform India and the world. The demo to be displayed in the festival gallery would stand as a symbol of walking this fertile path.

The demo was more than just a symbol. It was also a promissory object meant to occasion storytelling and attract investment. As we began our work at the hackathon, some of us anticipated that it would have a chance at life after the festival. Vipin—well connected through his prestigious IIT, IIM, and family civil service networks—promised to circulate the demo among Delhi philanthropic funders and government officials after the festival. "I think we can get funding from the Ford Foundation," Vipin assured us, "I was having lunch there. There are young people there in their thirties looking for inspiration from a good grant." Vipin's position at a design studio reassured future funders that he could attract and manage skilled technology workers to build out the project. With a promising demo, Vipin hoped to transform his social and cultural capital (Bourdieu 1984) into financial capital for the implementation and maintenance of a more durable system. The rest of us banked on his ties to bolster the promise of making a difference through a week's hacking.

Finding "Room for Innovation," Getting to a Demo

Though we had signed up for a hackathon on "open governance," most of us had little knowledge of legislative processes so we worked to familiarize ourselves. A Delhi think-tank friend of Vipin's, Anil, explained the protocols of bill drafting in the Indian parliament. We read through and critiqued a recent road safety bill draft to put ourselves in the shoes of possible law-reading users. Vipin pushed a stack of books on "open government" and e-government, exclusively containing American case studies, to me and told me to skim for anything "that interested" me.

These activities were interwoven with expressions of time anxiety. Someone, most often one of the software engineers, would ask us to sketch a production schedule for the next few days. How long could we talk about the law? Could we set a limit on the time of debate to assure ourselves that we could produce "the demo"? As we negotiated milestone deadlines, Vipin pushed sticky notes around the board representing a provisional agreement for milestones such as "features decided," "first working demo," and "refinement of features." These milestones set temporal bounds on our deliberations; they also affirmed our commitment to arrive at a demo, come hell, high water, or team conflict. The sun passed over the sky, casting shifting shadows on the studio whiteboard. Our laptops and meal breaks kept our time.

When we began talking about law, it become clear that we held very different views of how politics should work. The common ground we had seemed to share receded to the background; conflict raged to the fore. Vipin, the convener, saw the law as a sort of code determining the actions of the governed but riddled with logical loopholes. What if we made a website where citizens could read and point out weaknesses in bill drafts? Redressing loopholes would, by Vipin's argument, refine incentive and punitive structures that would manage India's population in turn. Vipin saw the law as a kind of computer code, buggy but logical. Fix the legal code, improve the country. This deterministic understanding of the law was foundational in Vipin's imagination of agency through the hackathon.

Vipin's argument also drew on visions of internet crowds that could power the system. Drawing an analogy from social media on the web, he called for a way to "crowdsource" the law. "Expert" Indians all over the country, Vipin envisioned, could see drafts of bills and consult online to point out loopholes, bad budgets, or unimplementable provisions. Another engineer summed up

Vipin's proposal as "like a Wikipedia for the laws." Vipin's vision of participation drew from production models of open-source software. Vipin hoped to apply an open-source design adage to the design of legal code: "all bugs are shallow, given enough eyeballs." In India, these eyeballs would have been the highly educated, English-speaking elite with the tenacity to untangle legal declarations. Phrases like "crowdsourcing" elided the uneven conditions of access, whether knowledge, skill, or infrastructure availability, that shaped just who could be in that crowd.

Prem's stories turned Vipin's account of the law on its head, and with it Vipin's imaginary of agency. Prem's Ph.D. degree fieldwork had tracked land rights law from the ministries of Delhi to the village outposts of Maharashtra. He described the laws as ambiguous and conflicting resources for local power contests between mining companies, police officers, landless peasants, and land rights activists. "At the local level," Prem concluded, "these guys can do pretty much whatever they want [with the law]." The law as text was little match for the contingencies and power plays in which it was invoked. Prem, and many of us with him, did not share Vipin's faith in elite experts in substituting for the politics of the poor. Prem explained how networks of activists connected cities and rural areas, mobilizing pressure to hold elites accountable to poorer Indians on issues like water and land access. Rather than empowering technocrats, Prem proposed empowering poor people's movements to hold technocrats accountable.

Prem and Vipin got into a heated debate, and many of us sided with Prem. Vipin argued that Prem simply wanted to disseminate information to activists. This, Vipin felt, was just more of what Indians had been doing for a long time.

"I don't get this view," Vipin said of Prem's proposal, "I feel we're reinventing the wheel."

Prem countered, "But I don't see any evidence that getting better information to the parliament will help when there is already a lot of good information around."

"It's not evidence. It's information," Vipin retorted. "It's human information. Stories. The special information environment in parliament can be dramatically improved—there's so much room for innovation." Vipin, like so many design-thinking advocates, argued that the difference between a good and a bad technocrat hinged on their access to empathy.

Vipin wanted parliament to be more like the design studio—filled with stories from the field, emotional tales that could compel a more integrative and holistic ethos of legislative reason. To Prem, empathic stories might motivate small tweaks, but the exigencies of accumulation drove the state's logics. Only constituent pressures and threats—politics—could redirect these drives. Vipin wanted to transform elite consciousness. Prem wanted to transform possibilities for social movement building.

Working with and through Prem's ethnographic cases, our interactions that followed were peppered with the subjunctive: "what you *could* do" and "what if we." Taking advantage of Vipin's absence for a few hours on the hackathon's third day, we developed a concept called *Jan Sabha*. *Jan Sabha* would allow organizers to document face-to-face deliberations of poorer constituencies around central government issues. On the whiteboard, Benoy sketched a "bill page" that activists across India could use to track the progress of a bill as well as commentary on it. Citizen activists could use the site to track their elected officials' involvement in it. A "petition page" would allow activists to publish feedback and demands from constituency meetings. Prem knew that these meetings were often already happening; the "petition page" would offer a quicker way for groups to make their voice and pressure visible to those in Delhi and to people in other parts of India. In Hindi, *jan* meant people and *sabha* was the name for the nation's house of parliamentary representatives. We sought to turn middle-class politics on its head by drawing populist pressure closer to where Delhi intelligentsia and politicians could feel it. The hackathon, it seemed, could accommodate a more leftist politics.

But there was one other big limit to taking any software approach. As long as we were talking about the web, Prem warned, we wouldn't reach most Indians, "at least [not] directly." As we hacked away in Delhi, only about 10 percent of Indians accessed the internet (D. Sengupta 2012), to the consternation of organizations like Google, Facebook, and Wikipedia (Tejaswi and John 2012). Our fantasy of social change through web-based software was predicated on a fantasy of universal web access. Silicon Valley companies had been working to make this fantasy a reality through industry-wide initiatives such as Internet.org (Rosenberg 2013; see also Fattal 2012), but the fantasy was laughable in many parts of the world, including India. "Digital India" was not only a dream but a requirement if India's software engineers were to build systems for the nation.[8]

Without the web connecting publics, how could we software makers connect Indians with legal processes, as we hoped to do? What if we could get the bill drafts into existing NGO and activist networks who could organize people around the process? Could we work with them as a way of getting noise and voice into the bill-drafting process? We imagined a website that would alert activists and NGOs to drafted bills and collect photographic and digitized paper evidence of constituency demands. The responses would be grouped by the politician elected to represent that constituency. In other words, our software could make documentation of deliberations and demands visible as electoral pressure. But, Prem warned us, this proposal would require "some REAL footwork" to get "on the street" and work with existing organizations thinking in terms of political participation. As the sun sank deeper in the sky, we realized we had little time to reach out to NGOs or activist networks. We had little time to understand their information practices or to build trust with them. We could not even promise maintenance of any demo that came out of a potential collaboration.

For that week, however, we weren't on the street. We were in the studio. The time, tools, and skills in the room were geared toward "code work," not "foot-work." Even the kinds of code work we could undertake were limited. Krish, a software engineer, explained to us that in the long term, the project could get into rural areas through interactive voice-response phone systems, rural kiosks, or SMS-based systems. "In Andhra, there's a women's radio station," he told us. "The scope of what we want to envision is THAT. What we implement in five days is probably a website. So we're going to go to a conversation where we'll chop off everything. Cut. Cut. Cut. Cut. But if there's a master document accompanying this chopped up little thing—" Krish trailed off, implying that the remainder—what we could not code—we could simply write as intentions for some future. (We never did make such a document.)

Our hackathon—and the bias to action it taught and ritualized—was premised on the proliferation of the internet industries' software libraries, cheap servers, and skilled programmers. Kiosk and radio prototypers were in far shorter supply than web developers. The growth of new media industries meant that we had at our fingertips masses of already built web application code modules and software engineers with the skills to use them. Software consultants well versed in platforms such a Drupal, Wordpress, and Ruby on Rails could whip up web-based applications quickly. These programming environments had evolved along with the growth of the web industry; they allowed developers to quickly draw together server hosting, databases, user authentication systems, and web interfaces to build blogs, content manage-ment systems, and dynamic web content. An experienced programmer could get a Ruby on Rails website with a working user-authentication system, forms to enter data, and web-based displays of the data in thirty minutes so long as they adopted Rails's default presentations. These were the infrastructures that made our hacking possible. But what infrastructure enables it also torques; torque, according to historian Geof Bowker and sociologist Susan Leigh Star (1999), describes how infrastructures twist and transform the very practices and biographies that they support. Our bias to action meant we twisted our visions to accommodate infrastructures at hand.

As we negotiated our ideals, Prem's frustration with the hackathon quietly escalated. On the third day he decided to abandon the hackathon. Prem was shocked that the group accepted as fun the prospect of working for a whole week unpaid. Nor did he appreciate morning-to-night sociality with only

other engineers. Prem had both grant-writing obligations and family obligations weighing on him each day as he participated in the hackathon. After a
particularly long debate with Vipin, he walked out—he had decided that the
convener was a stubborn technocrat mistrustful of popular will. Like me, he
anticipated the demo would have an afterlife. Unlike me, he was skeptical that
Vipin's stewardship of the demo would align with his political commitments.
"Vipin's like the Tucker Carlson of India," Prem exclaimed. (Prem knew Carlson as a smug conservative talk show host famous for bow ties, bad-faith arguments, and confidence in his own intelligence.) I laughed at this comparison
but implored Prem to stay, optimistic that the broader group leaned toward
Prem's politics rather than Vipin's. "Why," Prem replied incredulously, "would
I trust him to follow through on our vision?" Prem decided to cut his losses
and walk away.

Prem went further, challenging my optimism and investment. He cast into
high relief the energy I had invested more out of habit rather than explicit
commitment; I had leaned into the demo and the team, privileging the team
and "action" over political purity. My political ideals aligned with Prem's.
But absorbed in the intensity of real-time practice (Bourdieu 1977), I had
not seen how the push toward the demo had produced a thousand compromises. Cut. Cut. Cut. Cut. I had my ideals, but Vipin would have my labor
once the demo was built. He could use the demo to generate investments.
Though trained half a world away, I seemed to share habitus with the engineers (Bourdieu 1977); I found it easy to walk the walk, talk the talk, and
keep the pace at the hackathon. We problematized the world, imagined fixes,
and took pleasure in the craftsmanship of building hopeful experimental systems. My undergraduate training in computer science had been like a long
chain of hackathons: in the intense, team-based projects, we were most often
handed an assignment and expected to code it to function, never questioning
the terms of the project. Questions of ethics and politics never reframed the
practice of producing software—how fast we did it, with whom, and with
what accountabilities, except as they informed content and design. Ethical
and social concerns were always covered in a separate course, sequestered
away from the ongoing pedagogy of hacking toward a vision. The pedagogies of computer science reinforced the bias to action and the exclusions and
assumptions it entailed.

That night, I tried to make sense of Prem's departure—and my own persistence—with my roommate, Roshni, at the guesthouse. Roshni was at Open-
Lab to participate in Gustav's prefestival workshop on sanitation theater.
She was also well-known in the wider Indian design scene as a thoughtful
critic of the design professions. Roshni attributed Prem's departure to political inflexibility—something she explained as a well-known issue for design.

"Hardcore" "ideological" people, as she put it, were a known danger to projects. She told me a story about a student at the National Institute of Design, the premier institution in Ahmedabad where she did her degree. Design education required students to produce lots of work with teams under tight deadlines—not unlike my computer science training. She described a "hardcore" socialist student who had been admitted to NID. The student's tenure became infamous for tensions with many "urban" students; "urban" here connoted privileged cosmopolitans (Nadeem 2013, 61; Jodhka 2002). Roshni described the socialist student's struggles as "mentally and politically self-destructive," as well as damaging to other students' educations. The faculty at NID, she went on, took the issue so seriously that they adopted psychometric admissions interviews to filter out morally inflexible students. (I verified this with faculty later, a point I will return to.) Ideological commitments like Prem's, she implied, were a known hazard to the productivity of design.

When I returned the next morning, many in the group were compelled by the vision of activist and NGO support we had developed with Prem, despite his departure. Even as the inclusive visions of software I had hoped to realize fell out of scope, the rest of us persisted while Prem walked. After all, the hackathon was a stage for us to test if we *could* make a difference. It was not the hackathon that was on trial; it was the force of our will, optimism, collaborations, and technical skills. Even as Prem tried to pull us back to the problematic presuppositions of the event, we seemed optimistic by habit. We wanted to get to the demo. Many things, at that point, *could* happen, we thought.

I worked with the other designer, Benoy, to put together a set of graphical renderings of what such a software interface might look like. The software engineers worked on coding pieces of what they hoped would become a database-driven, interactive software demo. They threw themselves into the kinds of demo work that their skillsets allowed. They agreed to a set of milestones that would let the rest of the team test and adapt the software before the demo's launch at the festival.

The night before the launch, neither I nor Benoy had seen a working demo. When we saw what the engineers had built by the morning, it was a page with some broken links, some sample text, and a database sitting behind it that didn't seem to do much. Benoy and I quickly jumped into rescue mode, resuscitating our graphical renderings into a slide presentation we could walk through at the launch—a scaled down but still illustrative promise of software to come. Over the next two days, we took shifts in the festival gallery and walked attendees through our software concept, usually for just a few minutes at a time. We gathered some business cards, basked in some peer approval, and went to have a drink and see a design talk together. Two years after the festival, the demo sat in storage on my laptop. The dispersed participants stayed connected through LinkedIn and Facebook and could list themselves as "fellows" at the festival. Nikhil emailed me more than a year later, asking if I still had the mockups. He had some free time, he told me, and wanted to tinker with building a working version of our demo. Although I sent him the mockups, he has not built a prototype to date. The demo ultimately spawned no projects, no grants, and no working software systems. The failure to spawn a working system might seem like a disappointment, but it surprised no one; by the time of this book's writing, none of the OpenLab fellowship projects had spawned lasting projects. Relationships forged in the fellowships did prove more useful. Krish's software-consulting firm did a contract job for Vipin the following year; the job was a sanitation website Vipin produced for Gustav's German NGO. Events focused on technological production produce scenes and relationships even when they don't produce technologies.

We saw the demo less as a failure and more as indeterminate in its futures. We hoped the demo would have an afterlife: as inspiration to other festival goers, as the kernel of a future working system, or simply as an advertisement for the promise of e-government. These were some of the ways we tried to "make a difference" through making—making objects to remake ourselves as change makers. Days after the hackathon, Krish spoke on the festival stage and proposed a traveling bus full of educated Indians who could go from Indian village to village, pursuing a series of small, fast reform projects—like a series of hackathons on wheels. Beyond the festival, hackathons continued to proliferate, as do other social philanthropic, corporate, and state efforts to stimulate entrepreneurial citizenship as a vehicle for economic and social development.

Conditions and Cosmologies of "The Bias to Action"

How could we imagine making a difference through these acts of urgent making? What were the conditions of possibility for these acts of faith and investment?

The Feeling of Agency, the Possibility of Complexity

The hackathon offered a micro world in which we could imagine ourselves as historical agents—in a multitude of ways—through the production of the demo. Agency, here, is not a fundamental attribute of persons or things but rather an effect and attribution of causality and efficacy—an effect of material and semiotic configurations (Mialet 2012; Suchman 2007) and mediations (Barad 2003). Our capacities for agency depended on tools and platforms that congealed others' labor, as well as the promise of others' future labors of implementation, maintenance, and repair (e.g., Dominguez Rubio 2016;

M. L. Cohn 2013; Jackson, Pompe, and Krieshok 2011; Edgerton 2007). These configurations can produce particular ways of acting and speaking but also can produce an individualized agent by obscuring these intersubjectivities and infrastructures with which one acts (Cartwright 2008, 161; Jain 2006; Helmreich 2000, 170–72). The event of the hackathon, like the activities of the design studio more broadly, purified the experience of design, planning, and prototyping by pushing other necessary labors elsewhere, far away and out of mind. From the confines of the studio, internet connections connected us to programming tools, other people's code libraries, and cloud computing services that could speed up the production of software and make it available to unknowably large publics. To understand ourselves as making a difference with a demo, we had to locate agency in instigation, in seminal moments, in technological authorship (Philip 2005), and in software source code (Mackenzie 2006, 83). Designing and building the demo offered us an immediate sense of control over pixels and code. Examining the act of programming, Paul Edwards (1990) has argued that agency through coding depends on the pleasures of immediate control through the representations programming languages make available. Yet these pleasures became available only after women, who in the 1940s generated computer instructions out of (male) scientists' math, wrote the very computer code compilers that automated them out of a job (Chun 2005). Women (and people of color) still played an important part in the pleasures of man-machine, but they no longer translated others' human intention into code. They moved into the manufacture and assembly of the world-simulating machines. With personal computers, we hacked on machines that made us feel we had the world at our fingertips. We thus mistook computers for tools rather than media knitted out of and sustained by others' labors (Sharma 2014).

A cosmology of complexity also sustained hope in entrepreneurial, rapid, and experimental approaches to change. The hackathon, the festival, and the design and management theories surrounding them described the world as an interconnected system of actors; design pedagogues from India's National Institute of Design to Stanford's d.school taught this view of the world as "systems thinking." This systems perspective enabled entrepreneurial citizens to imagine that small actions could create effects by sending perturbations through extended networks and across scales. One India TEDx conference, for example, took as its theme "the butterfly effect," in which a butterfly can flap its wings in one part of the world and create a storm in another. Along similar lines, a well-respected design theory book, *The Design Way*, was subtitled *Intentional Change in an Unpredictable World* (Nelson and Stolterman 2012).

Sometimes DevDesign staff explained this promise of interdependence as "everything is connected." They showed the Eameses' film *Powers of Ten*

(1968) when instructing students of design, business, and even engineering because it offered a powerful illustration to teach this multiscale ontology.[9] The film depicts a couple picnicking at a park. It then slowly zooms down into their skin, into their molecules, and into their atoms. Reaching the smallest scales, the camera then begins zooming out. Atoms, molecules, skin, bodies. The camera zooms out to the couple on a picnic blanket, then the couple in the whole park, then the city, the continent, the whole earth, and the galaxy the couple occupies. My design teachers—innovation consultants from Silicon Valley—had also shown the film at Stanford. They even taught students a method called "Powers of Ten" as an exercise in querying the nestings and connections of a given design problem. The National Science Center in Delhi displayed stills of the film's scalar vision. In the 1950s this film underwrote understandings of societies as part of a whole earth (Turner 2006); in Cold War India, "whole earth" understandings spurred elite debates on the international nature of dependency, environmental policy, and communication, as well as anxieties about maintaining national identity—a topic I turn to in chapter 7. In the context of speculation in postliberalization India, interconnectedness augured not only responsibilities for the state but also opportunities for small-scale actors to trigger large-scale change.

While this view enabled individuals to imagine that they might provoke large-scale change outside of social movements or formal politics, the view also suggested that people could not predict, control, or confidently model nature. Instead, subjects in a complex world must work between order and chaos, trying and learning as a part of complex adaptive systems (Merchant 2003, 201; Maurer 1995, 114). Cultural responses to this complexity have been many. Silicon Valley entrepreneurs took up Zen Buddhism as a way of learning to be present to the world. Mind mapping and sticky-note brainstorms were techniques to document complexity's endlessly fragmentary knowledge. They incorporated this pedagogy into design thinking—a topic I return to in the next chapter. It was to these limits of reason amid the uncertain to which the bias to action was an answer.

"The bias to action" was an actor's category originating in the work of management consultants Tom Peters and Robert Waterman, Jr., on how to manage corporations in the face of the failures of rational, predictive, linear models. Their book *In Search of Excellence* (1982) made concepts like "the bias to action," "lean staff," and "innovation champion" into everyday talk in business and management circles.[10] The world, they argued, was one of complexity and rapid change. They advised that managers ought to quickly research, implement, experiment, and learn rather than run into "analysis paralysis." These "new wave management" techniques (Wood 1989) eschewed both worker participation and hierarchical organizations; they instead favored entrepreneurial individuals who take decisive action in networked workplaces. This way of orienting toward the world and toward time was often called "the bias to action." In India, the celebration of action over ideological commitment was not entirely new. In the aftermath of independence, Nehru saw modernization as an urgent task that called for men of action and managerial reason rather than village politicians (Vatsal 1970). What was new in the era of entrepreneurial citizenship was complexity, uncertainty, and normalization of failure. Melissa Gregg and Carl Disalvo (2013) argue that hackathons may normalize failure among civic volunteers in the United States. The normalization of failure, however, is not just a product of hackathons but rather a product of these new forms of management and the forms of uncertainty and failure they demand workers accommodate (Mazzucato 2013, 5–7; Neff 2012, 4). These uncertainties were different from risk. Risk is calculable, knowable, and manageable contingency (Neff 2012, 4; Adams et al. 2009; Patel 2006). Instead, uncertainty demanded a worker who could muster belief, find open options, and sense quickly when options went bad. The design field, business schools, new media corporations, and philanthropists had institutionalized and attempted to disseminate this orientation. A Danish business school called KaosPilots most vividly illustrated this worldview; the school claimed to train students who could pilot the chaos of rapidly changing markets and operating environments. One did not manage. One did not overthrow. One navigated.

Subjects in this complex world saw any action as having multiple possible effects as it perturbed multiple systems. Our demo could have many possible futures: as charismatic object, as educative failure, as a throwaway that meant less than the social ties, serendipity, and scene it strengthened. At the same time, failure to achieve desired effects was no cause to critique one's own process in wider systems understood as capricious and difficult to predict. Seen through the lens of complexity, entrepreneurial citizens' mistakes were hardly cause for critique. Rather, they were expected costs of experimentation in pursuit of social progress.

Speed, Creative Friction, and Mining the Social

There were two sets of reasons for the bias to action. First, people most readily reflected on what they saw as its subjective, epistemic, and emotional benefits. Benoy, the young product designer, explained, "Sometimes better things happen when the time frame is ridiculously short." Ajit, the studio's founder, had described something similar as he told me how he had prepared a talk for a local instance of the TED. Intimidated by the task and overwhelmed with other kinds of work, Ajit locked himself in his hotel room for twelve hours until he completed the piece while on a trip to Goa. As he pulled out his laptop to show me a film of the talk, he told me that "creative work has to happen in a day." This was his practical reality. He juggled several roles as a designer, teacher, performer, and restauranteur. He understood moving quickly not only as intensifying productivity but also as getting ahead of analytical self-censure and anxiety.

The bias to action was also an organizational response to the sense that markets, technologies, and culture were always changing. Entrepreneurs had to sense, envision, and build intensely, seizing opportunity before its time passed. Geographer Nigel Thrift (1997) identifies a range of managerial practices and ideologies that underwrite this response to capitalism since the 1980s. Broadly, he calls these "soft capitalism." Under soft capitalism, workers are not only sources of labor—sheer time applied to a problem—but also sources of rich, sensory, and culturally mediated knowledge. The job of the corporation becomes, in part, organizing knowing workers to elicit and recombine this knowledge in service of innovation. Pragmatic problem-solving exercises put these workers into provocative interaction, drawing unmined intellect into the open so it can be harvested by the corporation (Thrift 2008, 29–46). The hackathon, like the other OpenLab fellowships, drew people from different industries, disciplines, and regions into problem-solving encounters as a way of mining this rich, varying social knowledge.

Sociologist David Stark (2009) elaborates the problem of innovation as organized dissonance. Stark conceptualizes innovation as the search for "terrae incognitae"—the search for novel possibility through open-ended inquiry (2009, 4). Like Thrift, Stark identifies collaborative, fast-paced work as central to the practice of innovation. In a study of New York web start-ups, Stark and his collaborators documented the collaborative, exploratory practices of organizations probing possible futures. Conflict and difference rendered these spaces productive, to a point. Conflict was useful for generating feedback about risks and opportunities to the project. Conflict could even generate new ideas. These were the spaces where multiple orders of worth, in Stark's words, were "densely interacting" to produce friction. Out of this "creative friction," knowledge workers came to new understandings of how to make value out of assets, partnerships, and technologies within and beyond the firm (80–90). At the same time, start-up workers had to be "pragmatic," tabling tricky issues while eliciting just enough fruitful friction to better understand their contexts (108–11). Under capitalism, the business of innovation was the making of value in collaboration with some and in competition with others, amid shifting technological and policy conditions. It required workers who spoke openly and dissonantly and tried things quickly, shunning both structured participation and autocracy, proposing decisive action, execution, and iteration instead. Stark calls these organizational forms heterarchies: "cognitive ecologies that facilitate the work of reflexive cognition" (5). Hackathons, like design projects more broadly, organized dissonance so that groups could quickly locate, assess, and pursue value.

Organized dissonance offered a way to mine the social in search of possible profit. Recall that DevDesign hired people who interacted vigorously, speaking openly with the others; these practices served heterarchy. This "bias to action" even made it into DevDesign's own job postings. Not all social relations, however, were equally promising of value. DevDesign, like Google, Facebook, and other companies that prized the bias to action in its hires, were notoriously selective companies. They needed workers who could make open-ended social connections to bring in ideas, expertise, and partners. DevDesign cultivated a scene around itself, porous enough for "likeminded" people to flow in and around it. But the taste cultures of music, art, and books subtly attracted those with cultural capital and an entrepreneurial ethos while keeping others at a distance.

Sometimes those who did not "get it" showed up anyway. The boundaries of the scenes were porous but within tacit limits. A restaurant near Ajit's studio served as an epicenter for a scene that attracted journalists, designers, artists, and the professionals who liked them. When the son of a recently wealthy Jat landowner in the neighborhood—someone sociologists might categorize as petty bourgeois but without professional credentials (Fernandes and Heller 2006, 500)—showed up, the bouncer denied him entrance. Theories of creative friction and forethought would suggest the landlord's son could be useful as dissonant information and cultural knowledge. But the scene operates not only on knowledge but on comfort—friction had to be managed and could not disrupt interclass relational norms. In the creative scenes of Delhi, innovators' others were to be designed for but were much more rarely included in the social world beyond prescribed roles of informant, user, or worker.

Organizations mined the social in a second way. They called on participants to search themselves, their communities, and their resources to construct opportunity. In the case of the hackathon, I recruited Prem, a good friend I knew to be expert in questions of politics in India. Vipin called on Krish, someone he already knew had useful skills and sensibilities. I called on the Planning Commission consultant who offered our team an orientation to how planners thought about policy and pressure politics. Each of us brought individuated knowledge and the ability to draw on relations and resources. Entrepreneurial voluntarism drew sustenance from the accumulations of privilege that enabled us to be in the room. It drew sustenance from the structures of labor and kinship that freed us, but not others, from the obligations of care work. And it drew sustenance from our histories of social dreaming and political aspirations that motivated our voluntarism. These forms of organizing mined our labor, our cultural knowledge, our social bonds, and our "good sense" (Gramsci, Hoare, and Nowell-Smith 1971, 321–22) for the production of innovation.

When Passionate Production Displaces Democracy

These rhythms of entrepreneurial production—what Sreela Sarkar (2017) calls "passionate production"—required easy, fast social relations to proceed. "Moving forward" toward the demo required only getting the people on your project team onboard. If people coming together were sufficiently similar, sufficiently flexible, and sufficiently few, hackers could "get to the demo." The hackathon required fast trust, fast talk, and consolidated free time. The participants all spoke English fluently. They had obtained at least college undergraduate degrees. And several had trained as engineers—the degrees that granted the most symbolic capital after liberalization (Subramanian 2015; Fernandes and Heller 2006, 514). All had jobs that more or less allowed them time to participate in the hackathon. All but Prem were relatively free of care obligations. On top of all this, we had the patronage of DevDesign and its funders housing us, feeding us, and providing our infrastructure. These forms of capital built us resumes and institutional biographies that made our networks so promising—chock full of funders, fellow engineers, and academic legitimation. The bias to action made sense only because of the ease with which we were mostly able to get on—an ease that was a product of our middle-class positionalities. The "real footwork" of developing partnerships with other organizations and activists, by contrast, would not come so easily as the energetic imagining of the hackathon and in the wider scene. Though we could build some software over a few days, there was little time to go explain our developing goals to members of activist networks. There was no time to build coalition, align frames (Snow et al. 1986), or build trust with activists, NGO workers, landless villagers, or frustrated city dwellers.

The culture of innovation practiced at the studio and in its wider entrepreneurial networks derided "ideological" people—those whose commitments took too much time to negotiate. Political desire—whether left or right—could drive the work of innovation, revealing new paths forward or possible impediments to success. But political desire that halted the progress of the project itself had to be calmed or expelled. Political desire could inform innovation, but it ought not impede the bias to action. Social entrepreneurs and designers I met through my fieldwork counterposed themselves to varied stereotypes of Indians who fail to demonstrate the bias to action. Among those described as lacking in the bias to action were Bengalis, Malayalis, Brahmins, and academics. By talking about these others, they reasserted their own difference as entrepreneurial citizens.

Benoy, himself a Bengali, contrasted the hackathon participants with a stereotype of Bengalis: "You see, the people of Bengal are lazy and don't do anything, but they'll just sit for eight, ten hours and talk, talk, talk . . . people are quite satisfied to talk." Benoy offered *adda* as an example of this laziness. Historian Dipesh Chakrabarty (2000) describes *adda* as a space where men talk and debate, working out modern selfhood in capitalist modernity. Benoy's assessment, if self-deprecating, echoed European colonial assessments of colonized tropical people as lazy and uninnovative (Adas 1989, 257). The British Victorians criticized Bengali *adda*, claiming that endless gossip distracted from productive work and self-fashioning individualism. Those characterizations haunted middle-class citizens still.

Another designer linked the problem of talk to the problem of intellectual activity. The designer described his home state of Kerala as "the land of all talk, no action. It's the land of the intellectual. People say there are two sides to any coin. In Kerala, there are six sides to the cube. It is impossible to get any project done." Since trade liberalization, members of Kerala's professional classes have articulated their politics in terms of economic productivity and shun forms of resistance such as *bandh* (strike) (Lukose 2009). This hostility to strikes and street protests was a middle-class form of political talk. Kerala, a state that regularly elects Marxists to power, has high literacy and health indicators but a smaller economy than other Indian states. Pundits speak of the Kerala paradox—high levels of well-being with low economic growth; the paradox reveals the assumption that business development entails human development.

Academics, like the men of Kerala, were also seen as protesting too much, though by different means. While planning the OpenLab festival, one studio founder resisted inviting a well-known Indian think tank to speak, saying that it seemed too "cerebral" and "focused on public education and awareness" rather than entrepreneurship, activism, or intervention. Designers set themselves apart by drawing distinction to academics' propensity to dwell, interpret, critique, and teach. On another project at the studio, a designer and her client decried an "education Ph.D." who, to their minds, had set their project back four months. The project was an online training program to prepare low-income, young Indians for retail work in cities. The Ph.D. holder, herself a member of the team, had called the training "brainwashing." "I wish education Ph.D.s were more grounded in the reality of the situation and would not get so deep into ethical questions," her teammate griped. Pragmatism, designers thought, required a willingness to table issues and put aside differences in favor of moving projects forward.[11]

Designers bounded contestation—just enough, but not too much—in workshops and project teams as well. Designers routinely convened workshops to generate feedback and buy-in among partner organizations, investors, and academics, and at such events a modicum of contestation produced new information about situations and risks. As Vipin convened a global health workshop, for example, he sought NGO partners, funded organizations, trusted experts, and "some creative types" to review and offer "feedback" on the studio's work on a sanitation system. Contestation as informational feedback was welcome. However, contestations as commitments to something other than the project were far less so. He explained that inviting people to the workshop "ends up coming down to comfort because there isn't time. When there isn't time, you don't want to bring people into the room who are too different from you, who see things differently, or you think might create conflict." On project teams ranging from education projects to water sanitation, I saw designers break down in frustration when faced with academics—people with Ph.D. degrees and committed to political economic critique—who slowed down implementation discussions with persistent questions about larger structures beyond the system designers' reach. Workshops, hackathons, and entrepreneurial teams worked when there was easy difference—creative friction but not contestation. In this organizational ideology, contestation threatened productive rapport and legibly productive outcomes.

Recall that Roshni, my roommate during the OpenLab festival, had pointed out that NID had institutionalized political geniality as part of its admissions rubric. NID conducted written exams and interviews of prospective students, probing their abilities to draw, to make decisions, and to respond to interpersonal challenges. When I went to a senior faculty member to confirm this, he sketched out how the interviewers might probe morality and rigidity: "So sometimes when we look at things like—sometimes we crack a very racist joke and then say, *What do you think about this? How would you react to this?*" The faculty dismissed students who reacted with moral indifference; they also downgraded those "with a very strong opinion" as "rigid" and "not open to anyone else's point of view or ideas." Engineering and business education similarly institutionalized an ethos that elevated completing projects over deliberation and contestation through its pedagogies of problem sets, time-bound projects, and more recent celebrations of entrepreneurial, team-based practices.

This ethos aligned with middle-class and, implicitly, upper-caste political practices and sensibilities. The middle classes in India are numerically in the minority, but they are powerful—though they do not always feel so. Prior to liberalization, the middle class consisted of bureaucrats, scientists, engineers—beneficiaries of an Indian education system that invested intensely in public, English-language higher education to train its leadership cadre (Fernandes and Heller 2006, 510; Mazzarella 2005). With liberalization, salaried private-sector workers joined these ranks in growing numbers. The culture of India's middle class at its highest ranks was, as Nivedita Menon and Aditya Nigam (2007, 7) put it, "steeped" in the "normative world and etiquette of Western modernity" and charged itself with the task of ushering in Indian modernity (Fernandes and Heller 2006; Chatterjee 1993). Beginning in the 1980s, lower- and middle-caste Indians began electing their own into political office in a "democratic upsurge" (Fernandes and Heller 2006, 497). Fernandes and Heller argue that the middle classes reacted both in discourse and practice. Discursively, the middle classes began denigrating electoral politics as debased—"dirty, dishonest, corrupt, criminal, and vulgar" (510).[12] I heard these sensibilities take slightly gentler shape during my fieldwork in the form of comments people made about politicians who trade computers or water for votes; implicitly, the interests of the middle classes—world-class cities, corporate jobs, and economic growth—were supposed to be the interests of the nation. They cast poor people who voted in their own material interests as inadequately deliberative or in conflict with the national interest. They cast protests and strikes as destructive, rather than constructive, politics (Lukose 2009). The bias to action gave middle-class Indians license to ignore contesting voices in the name of experiments in progress.

Members of the middle class were able to turn to the courts and civil society organizations as institutions to assert their interests, particularly through a rhetoric of rights—rights to consume, rights to clean air, and rights to the city (Lukose 2009; Menon and Nigam 2007; Fernandes and Heller 2006). The right to the city was not the right to the city for all but rather the struggle for a "world-class" city through the clearance of street hawkers, slum dwellers, and poor people from middle-class spaces (Baviskar 2003, 2009; Baviskar, Sinha, and Philip 2006). In the name of clean air, citizens groups went to court to force the relocation of industrial sites and, by consequence, workers away from Delhi (Menon and Nigam 2007, 77; Baviskar 2003, 90). This middle-class style of politics mobilized bureaucratic, corporate, judicial, and mass media networks, influence, and know-how to transform India (Benjamin 2000, 54). We practiced precisely this classed form of resourcefulness at the hackathon as we worked quickly to marshal what influence, information, and patronage we could to sustain the demo.

Entrepreneurial citizenship celebrated the deployment of cultural capital and social ties rather than popular movement building to push for social change. The hackathon, in particular, also rode the energy of euphoric faith in ICTs (Thomas 2012; Chakravartty 2012; Mazzarella 2010a). Vipin, recall, drew in a friend as the hackathon's NGO partner. He promised his Ford Foundation ties as potential sources of funding. Jan Sabha, the protest-mobilizing platform, eschewed this middle-class style of politics.

But entrepreneurial time contained the agonism and populism implicit in Jan Sabha. And if NGOization required sustaining funding, entrepreneurial enterprises were open not only to philanthropy but to profit in the name of "sustainability." Even when the content of our design imaginaries departed from these middle-class tendencies to render problems technical, the bias to action disciplined and contained our politics while mining our relationships, skills, and hope to render us entrepreneurial instead. Demo-oriented hackathons were one process that produced the kind of entrepreneurial subject celebrated in development and NGO circles: collaborative rather than agonistic, technical rather than political, and constructive rather than complaining or demanding (see Drayton 2011; Bornstein 2007; see also Ferguson 1994 for a discussion of antipolitics in development).

Innovation's Labor Pedagogies

These entrepreneurial qualities—the bias to action, collaboration, and technical fluency—relied on labors kept at a distance from innovation scenes. The agencies and fast action celebrated at the hackathon relied on hidden labor buried in digital infrastructures, ready at hand but maintained out of sight: 24/7 servers, code libraries written and maintained by others, Foxconn workers, and metal mining. We barely questioned how parliamentary bills would be transcribed, cleaned, and formatted for the web; that kind of data labor has become especially cheap in BPOs and microwork systems like Amazon Mechanical Turk. This is not exclusively a feature of the digital realm. Designers working in the studio similarly developed product design plans in plastic and metal at a great distance from the extractive, factory, distributional labors that enabled an idea to actually materialize for the masses. Labor questions mattered only when they threatened the authorial intentions of the designers and engineers, as when they impinged on manufacturability and cost. Like those workers who search for ways to add value at the studio (chapter 4), we could take for granted that supply chains, platforms, and underpaid contract workers were off in reserve to materialize our visions.

The organization of labor *as infrastructure* underwrote our feelings of agency and creativity as we stitched technologies and stories into demos. Infrastructures, following Bowker and Star (1999), are those tools and systems our practices rely on. They materially support and implicitly standardize aspects of those practices as people come to depend on them, but, crucially, they usually slip into the background of our awareness. The studio became a space of creativity for some only because the cooks, drivers, cleaners, and accountant stabilized the workplace as an infrastructure, as I showed in chapter 4. The hackathon also consolidated our claims on authoring these technological futures by excluding unfamiliar others who might dilute our visions, make their own claims to authorship, or slow down work toward the demo. Those in the studio designed the demo; those outside—the system administrators, code library authors, future website and server maintainers, and even the users who shaped the meanings and purposes of our work—remained at a distance and largely taken for granted. Networked computing infrastructures and black boxed computing labors sustained our belief in technological authorship as a practice of changing the world. We bracketed past labors that made our present hacking possible. We bracketed future labors that would manufacture and maintain our hacks as working software. We learned the labor politics of entrepreneurship by practicing the labor phenomenology of networked computing. The pace, pattern, and tempo of social life (Sharma 2014)—here entrepreneurial production—was possible only because of computing made modular (Blanchette 2011), with sedimented code, system administration, and maintenance kept at a distance from sites of hacking.

The hackathon also offered a pedagogy that favored low-hanging fruit over longer investments in transformative infrastructures. The complex technologies at hand for entrepreneurs had taken shape not for needs of postcolonial nations but for the interests of imperial ones. In 1990s New York City, web workers searched for ways to commercialize technologies and infrastructures—internet protocols, fiber cable, programming languages—that were the products of *massive* U.S. state (and especially military) investment over decades. Those workers were trying to discover what extensions to that infrastructure might be valued by consumers (Neff 2012; Stark 2009); political scientist Mariana Mazzucato argues that this is precisely the substance of entrepreneurship (2013). Entrepreneurship builds no heroic infrastructure; it does not organize basic research. Venture capitalists have no patience for work that does not promise high returns. Rather, entrepreneurs search for ways to make use value out of inherited infrastructure and research. From India, we see that these inheritances have been forged for the benefit of the wealthiest nations.

The shift to entrepreneurialism after liberalization has not served Indian infrastructure well. In the first decades of independence, the government made sustained investments in large-scale infrastructure for periods measured in decades, not years (Bear 2015). With liberalization and the decentralization of planning, the government began to structure infrastructure projects as public-private partnerships. Infrastructure had to do more than serve the nation or region, as judged by technocrats. It also had to generate value for private investors or banks. Like the projects entrepreneurial citizens generate, these public-private partnership infrastructures had to earn their keep. Laura Bear illustrates how infrastructures begin to take strange forms as these rapid-return financial disciplines transform what engineers find it possible to build. A riverboat needed to carry pilots to shore, in one particularly illustrative case, also has to double as an ornate pleasure boat for entertaining politicians. The pragmatic search for value to be built on extant infrastructure turns enterprising citizens toward opportunity but robs the social endowment of maintenance, upkeep, or larger-scale changes that might serve many but serve no patron's interests in particular. Recall the lack of low-cost radio expertise or toolkits for our team to hack on. Cut. Cut. Cut. Cut.

Conclusion: Bounding Politics with the Bias to Action

This chapter has shown what the bias to action does to politics, with a hackathon as an illustrative case. At a hackathon, participants imagine themselves agents of history—of development, of social change, or of nation building—part of a larger narrative collectively produced by TED Talks and funded by large foundations, NGOs, and corporations alike. The hackathon was in part a site of speculation and in part a site of pedagogy. The pedagogy privileged a bias to action, civic responsibility, and enthusiastic speculative labor (see also Gregg 2015)—precisely the pedagogies of the Design in Education Conference spreading "design thinking" out of Ahmedabad (chapter 3). It is tempting to call these projects antipolitical. James Ferguson (1994), interpreting Foucault, calls development antipolitical for the ways it transforms conditions of politics and history into bounded problems amenable to putatively apolitical, expert technique (see also Li 2007). There are plenty of entrepreneurial projects that fit this description, attempting to mobilize expert technique in search of a social fix. The hackathon, fueled by Prem and Vipin's fights, testifies to how the projects of entrepreneurial citizens can also draw sustenance from political hope. In this case, participants' politics generated the epistemic friction and affective motivation that fueled the labors of innovation. The sociotemporal form of the intense, entrepreneurial projects—small groups working intensely—contained those politics and channeled them into productivity. Entrepreneurial citizenship thus does not erase politics so much as it channels and directs it toward the making of enterprises, though as it channels, it also contains. Over time, the designers at the studio started, ended, and flirted with projects, events, and start-ups. The sum of these beginnings amount to more than the debris of failure. They also amount to an entrepreneurial scene of "likeminded people" whose relationships and shared sensibilities could be mined for potential value.[13] They amounted to a coalition within civil society that vied to speak for and make the nation as they worked for themselves.

The practices described in this chapter produce entrepreneurial rhythms, but they only made sense for those close to resources. Delhi's middle-class entrepreneurs could deploy their cultural and social capital to attract funding and patronage as consultants to European cultural organizations and multinational businesses seeking a foothold in India. For these well-heeled professionals, promises of projects for "the near future" (Guyer 2007) sustained the studio financially. This ability to turn speculative investments into a steady living was not equally distributed. In his ethnography of India's smaller cities and towns, Craig Jeffrey (2010) shows that young people with college educations, rural land wealth, but few urban social ties wait for their preparations to turn into jobs promised by economic growth rhetoric. The "bias to action" celebrated by design works because of the kinds of networks, labor configurations, tools, and systems designers can mobilize quickly, extending their agencies out into the world. The bias to action is possible only because others labor to clean, cook, and sustain the infrastructures so hackers can purify their experience of creativity. Entrepreneurial time separates—discursively, spatially, and temporally—valorized moments of creative freedom from the "donkey work" (see chapter 4) and infrastructural labors on which such creativity relies.

In entrepreneurial forms of design, the moment of creativity becomes the moment of political hopefulness, urgently channeled into innovation potential. In this urgency, entrepreneurial citizenship renders social movements, deliberation, and even extensive research and planning as potential barriers to development and dilution of vision. This is the case not only in hackathons but also in the forms of entrepreneurship predicated on the construction of opportunity, the authorship of ideas, mass distribution, and speculative investment. Champions of the bias to action urge entrepreneurial citizens to proliferate experiments out of their lives, out of their social relationships, and out of their encounters with the poor. These relations become the "living lab" (Schwittay 2008) for experiments in adding value in the for-profit and nonprofit sectors. At the same time that entrepreneurial citizens reach beyond their salaried jobs and into civil society and development, they worked in entrepreneurial time—amid a manufactured urgency that made democratic processes a threat to self-actualization and a threat to value.

6

Seeing Like an Entrepreneur,
Feeling Out Opportunity

"HOW DO YOU BEGIN to get acquainted with four billion people?" This was the question posed by DevDesign's client, a global health NGO. The NGO wanted "clean water" for the world's poor, and it had the funding from the Gates Foundation to get it. Its challenge was to find a design that poor people all over the world would want, buy, and use. Hence the challenge for DevDesign—to get to know four billion potential consumers. DevDesign specialized in moving out of the design studio and into villages, schools, workplaces, and homes to locate glimmers of innovation potential in everyday life. In keeping with human-centered design more broadly, it advocated empathy for potential users. It understood the worldviews of those it studied not as targets for reform but as resources for innovation.

Empathy, however, did not imply democracy. Innovation called on entrepreneurial citizens to translate needs and desires of potential users into product and service opportunities rather than democratic demands. This was the work of rendering the world as entrepreneurial projects. Shiny new water filters presented an opportunity for manufacturing partners and investors. Citizen demands for repair to existing public infrastructures did not (see Anand 2011). To investors, a need common to a few thousand was too small to be of interest. A need shared by a million piqued their interest. Though DevDesign documented needs, aspirations, and practices in the field, these findings became opportunities only as designers cycled back to investors, clients, and manufacturing partners—those with the institutional, financial, and labor resources to make an idea come to matter on wider scales. At expert workshops, designers transformed their travels into films and stories, and they worked to produce empathy for potential users in their clients and potential partners. Guided by the dual motivators of empathy and institutional interests, those who sought to intervene could begin to see opportunities in the snapshots of everyday life and desire collected by designers on the ethnographic trail. Opportunity existed in the overlap between the desires of the poor they hoped to uplift and the agendas of partner institutions, investors, and enterprises.

This chapter shows how "human-centered design" (HCD)—a form of ethnographically guided, experimental design practice branded in Silicon Valley—operationalizes empathy to guide entrepreneurial actors toward opportunity to transform the world "at scale." Both empathy and opportunity were key ways that enterprising people oriented toward the world they hoped to transform. Empathy promised to guide development along the grain of the masses' developmental desires rather than against them. Empathy here was a distant cousin of psychosocial techniques for attempting to understand another's mind. As part of design, it became a model for understanding not just one person but many people. Design-minded citizens needed to mingle among targets of development and hypothesize vectors of mass affect—widely held desires, fears, or ways of making sense—that suggested areas of opportunity surfaced risks to development projects. Capitalism's reformers proposed empathy as the moral sentiment that could, at once, uncover others' wants while steering away from capitalism's excesses (see, for example, Grant 2013; Gates and Gates 2014). Empathy guided speculation to refine the perception of opportunity.

Human-centered design not only was the province of design professionals but had spread as a discipline for practitioners of a highly optimistic, networked, and experimental form of development. HCD had evolved in Silicon Valley, in the crucible of rapid high-tech change and global economic volatility, as a set of techniques for generating ideas, testing them quickly, and keeping teams optimistic and adaptable. It was one method for surviving the search for value amid technological, economic, and cultural change (see Stark 2009; Brown and Eisenhardt 1997). CitiBank's foundation had funded the Grameen Bank to train its extensive network of NGOs in HCD techniques of qualitative interviewing, brainstorming, prototyping, and user testing to sharpen innovation skills in the development sector.[1] The Knight Foundation similarly trained winners of its journalism innovation competitions in HCD to prepare them to invent the future of networked journalism and civil society. The Bill and Melinda Gates Foundation, the Rockefeller Foundation, and Britain's Nesta all had funded the production of toolkits, workbooks, and case studies to train NGO workers, government workers, and social entrepreneurs in HCD techniques for innovation. School reformers, as we saw in chapter 3, taught human-centered design as a pedagogy of citizenship to teach Indian children how to build the nation while building the authentic self. Even nonprofit projects employ empathy in service of sustainable—read value-generating or firm-legitimating—public-private partnerships and corporate social responsibility projects.

This chapter argues that, in the context of entrepreneurial citizenship, empathy functions not as an orientation toward compassionate solidarity but rather as the mining of intimacies for projects of value creation. It examines how this human-centered design ethos becomes central to entrepreneurial citizenship—a form of seeing, sensing, and reasoning that "problematizes" (Li 2007; Ferguson 1994) the world to construct it as a site for design "opportunity." In my fieldwork, I observed that to see like an entrepreneur meant to study people's lives to learn of their social relations, everyday practices, and desires. Design-minded entrepreneurs imagined product forms and distribution practices that glided along these grooves of practice rather than fighting against their grain. This was thus a form of expertise by which entrepreneurial citizens could engage people as users or customers while smoothing out frictions and mitigating resistance. Entrepreneurial citizens exercised their ethical feelings (Redfield 2015) and engaged across difference (Escobar 2018). NGOs, philanthropies, and companies put these affects and labors to work in the search for opportunity.

I conclude the chapter with a reflection on techniques of knowledge, design, and power in the transnational assemblage that combines government with profit. I argue that to see like an entrepreneur in this way is radically different from what James Scott (1998) calls "seeing like a state." The high modern, authoritarian state attempted to design better futures by sensing citizens as universal objects of technical expertise, extracted from social bonds and the value systems of communities. Instead, human-centered design teaches an art of seeing and acting that turns bonds, values, and differences into resources, rather than impediments, for entrepreneurial innovation. Entrepreneurs do not seek to formalize and control but rather to profitably align with and incorporate. They seek to render the world as entrepreneurial opportunities.

"Rich Media": Promising Empathy in Global Health

Empathy was DevDesign's calling card. The studio always talked about its empathic film and media style as core to the work it did, but I saw the most surprising evidence of this in the hallways of a sanitation conference in Sri Lanka in 2011. I was passing out workshop invitations with Kritika, a quick-witted junior designer. DevDesign and their foundation funder wanted to invite the NGO workers, government officials, and academic experts roving the hallways to learn about the foundation's approach to sanitation. The invitation was a detailed photo card of a latrine, pictured close up and made gorgeous by the bright plastic cleaning supplies framing the porcelain. Kritika, turning twenty-four that day, nudged me toward a group of men in suits: "You're white so they'll think it's important."[2] Such were the pragmatics of expertise in development work.

DevDesign had spent the prior year studying how poor people washed, defecated, and used—or did not use—toilets in five cities. Its client, a major foundation, had hired it to find ways of innovating sanitation technology; open defecation in India made national and international news as an index of modernization,[3] and the foundation could bend the ear of government ministers of competing Indian Congress and BJP Parties to discuss sanitation issues.[4] The foundation had sent DevDesign's team to this Sri Lanka meeting to present its design research work, generate buzz, learn about other best practices, and influence sanitation development practitioners.

As I returned to Kritika having deployed my whiteness, another design team member, Vivek, ran up to us. "How did it go?" I asked. Vivek, eyes wide, leaned in excitedly: "Duuude! A bunch of people had already heard of it [the workshop]." Vivek met a woman from UNICEF who already knew of the studio from a video it had produced and circulated online. In the video, a cameraperson followed a rickshaw driver on a morning visit to open defecation fields. The woman recounted to Vivek the moment that had seized her. As the camera trailed the driver through the muddy grass, the view through the camera suddenly quaked and plummeted. Then, with barely a pause, the view stabilized and trailed the man again. The falling shot implied the camera person tumbled to the ground in the defecation fields. The fleeting moment lasted less than a second in the tightly paced film, but the point was made.

"Nobody ever goes to where people defecate!" the UNICEF staffer exclaimed to Vivek. "They [researchers] may go in the home, but that's it!" Vivek had been that invisible camera man and now he was ecstatic. "That was me!" Vivek had told the woman. She grinned and gave him her card: "Call me in Delhi!" Vivek and Kritika high fived as he recounted the invitation. Just hours before, they had been hunched over laptops, burning CDs, making presentation slides, and muttering about "burnout." Vivek's encounter charged them with optimism about the potential of the toilet project, the potential of the studio, and the potential of their efforts to come to something.

Studio members showed this film often, both when pitching to clients and when evangelizing design and entrepreneurship to Indian students and professionals through their festivals. They saw "rich media" as central to their practice of informing and mobilizing clients and partners. Though the electronic music soundtrack gave it a glitchy, futuristic feel, audiences still reacted sentimentally to it. The film served as evidence of Vivek's intrepid empathy. He had violated purity taboos and social norms, taking a camera into the fields in search of a more intimate landscape of possibility for sanitation development.

This video, like other ethnographic films the studio produced, promised an empathic form of development that would be wise to the rough-and-tumble of people's lives. There was a substance to this style (Silverstein 2003); development workers and designers recognized the style as promising innovation. The style was similar to those of ethnographers and designers from technology firms like IDEO, Intel, and Nokia. Each image offered evidence of both the event depicted and the mentalité (Pinney 2008, S34) of those who took the photo. The "rich media" contrasted starkly with other media displayed at the conference: graphs, statistics, and success stories of gleaming sanitation infrastructure. The videos were not really meant to document the present, however; they were instead meant as emotional provocations to investors and partners to imagine innovative futures for the lives on screen.

When the Medical Anthropologist
Met the Software Manager

The Bill and Melinda Gates Foundation (BMGF) was one of the many organizations invested in innovating development through design and entrepreneurship. The foundation contracted with several design studios in India, including DevDesign. It also orchestrated entrepreneurial passions in the government-adjacent NGO, media, and professional worlds of Delhi. BMGF contracted research, organized competitions, and staged TED conferences (M. Gates 2011). It organized a Social Innovation Lab with the government of the Northeast Indian state of Bihar (Raje 2011; Datta and Sood, 2014). It cultivated networks of NGOs and entrepreneurs in global interchange; for example, the foundation sent DevDesign project members to Kenya to learn from sanitation projects and share methods. It also disseminated human-centered design pedagogy globally; the foundation commissioned California design firm IDEO to develop and disseminate human-centered design as "toolkits" (worksheets and guide books for NGOs) (see Brown and Wyatt 2010, 34). These activities allowed BMGF to shepherd civil society, the private sector, and the state in alignment with foundation agendas.[5]

BMGF was not alone in advocating for entrepreneurial approaches to development. The Rockefeller Foundation and Britain's Nesta also funded production of HCD and innovation toolkits. Acumen Fund promoted "patient capital"—a venture capital approach that invested in social entrepreneurs who pitched projects that could affect one million lives or more. The U.S. Agency for International Development had also turned to entrepreneurial experimentation in India, shifting from grants and contracts to "creative platforms" that would "identify, test, scale, and diffuse development innovations proven in India" (USAID 2012, 8). Ashoka, a nonprofit dedicated to cultivating social entrepreneurship, awarded entrepreneurs and brought training in design and empathy to schools all over the world.

In these ways, global development institutions called on entrepreneurial citizens from the private sector and nonprofits to experiment in promising opportunities to move toward global development goals.[6] India has been made into a laboratory of experiments before, first for scientific studies in population control (Williams 2014), and then for pharmaceutical research (Sunder Rajan 2005) and corporate experiments in ICT products for the poor (Schwittay 2008). These calls to entrepreneurial citizenship, however, sought not only to conduct experiments but also to proliferate enterprises in the name of development.

Development celebrities Melinda Gates, a former software manager, and Paul Farmer, a famed medical anthropologist, announced the power of empathic design to a global, English-reading public in a *Wired* interview entitled "The Human Element: Melinda Gates and Paul Farmer on Designing Global Health" (Roper 2013). Farmer, well-known as a cofounder of NGO Partners in Health and a Harvard anthropology professor, stood for culturally and historically informed development in action. His cofounder, Jim Yong Kim, a Harvard anthropology Ph.D., was named president of the World Bank in 2009—a highly visible testament to the perceived value of cultural knowledge even as the bank remained dominated by economic reason (Mosse 2011). Gates had come to lead the Gates Foundation with her husband, Bill, after a career in software management at Microsoft.

The *Wired* journalist asked Gates, "What innovation do you think is changing the most lives in the developing world?" Gates's answer, presented without equivocation: "Human-centered design." She continued, explaining HCD as "meeting people where they are and really taking their needs and feedback into account. When you let people participate in the design process, you find that they often have ingenious ideas about what would really help them. And it's not a onetime thing; it's an iterative process."

The enthusiasm was not Gates's alone. Farmer added an example of a "design approach" to development practice. He described hospitals in Haiti where patients might wait three days to see a doctor, resting their heads on found objects and waiting without food. "We have to design a health delivery system by actually talking to people and asking, 'What would make this service better for you?'" He continued: "As soon as you start asking, you get a flood of answers."

Farmer and Gates's optimism countered a pessimism about development that was unspoken in the *Wired* interview. Books like *Dead Aid* (Moyo 2009) and *The White Man's Burden* (Easterly 2006) argued that development did not work. A group of prominent economists, including MIT's Abhijit Banerjee and Columbia's Jagdish Bhagwati, published a slim, popular volume titled *Making Aid Work* (Banerjee et al. 2007), betraying anxieties about development. The pessimism so threatened the public legitimacy of development in wealthier nations that BMGF had created campaigns called "Living Proof" and "Impatient Optimists" to restore public faith in foreign aid outlays (United States Senate 2010, 44). Without faith in development, entrepreneurial citizens would not step up to the charge.

The critiques of development made sense to designers in India as well. There, popular films like *Peepli Live* problematized efforts by cynical or distant politicians to produce development through spectacular but poorly conceived programs. Vivek, Kritika, and their friends invoked the film on several occasions to articulate how the government failed to take a "systemic" view of development or to see India's poor as "consumers" who need solutions to "just work." The state, they believed, ought to design development better, but poor management and political corruption got in the way (see also Chakravartty and Sarkar 2013, 61–62).

How did design become such a promising practice for development in trouble? Design at once seemed rational and systematic yet in touch with human emotions, needs, and desires. Design promised to take a social, contextual, and embodied understanding of people and their practices and turn it into large-scale interventions, systems, and products to transform human life. HCD promised intimate alignment with experience and community life and yet paradoxically also promised that this alignment could scale for mass consumption. Design wove together two genealogies of how the social sciences have been put in service of transforming human life, joining anthropology's relationship to development with other histories of social science engagements with computer systems design.

Engineering the Acceptance of Development

Design was a recent answer to a long-standing problem in development, from colonialism to the present. How should development institutions involve people in their own development? The legitimacy of development and the stability of reigning orders were at stake. Colonial and early developmental projects drew on the social sciences to manage top-down projects, including extraction, rule, and infrastructure development. These are the histories that produced concepts of culture (Birla 2009), tradition (Fabian 1983), and *adat* (a word that connotes habit and forms the backbone of colonial-era customary law) (Goh 2006; Mamdani 1996). Colonialism, then, worked by both managing culture and managing *through* culture.

As colonized people formed formally independent nations, development emerged as a way for American-led capitalist nations to keep people of the poorer nations away from communism (Prashad 2012; Goldman 2006).

Development agencies oscillated between bottom-up and top-down approaches. Community-based and cooperative development experiments thrived in in the 1950s and 1960s amid postcolonial optimism and fear of citizens bound to nonnational identities (Mansuri and Rao 2013, 3; see also Hull 2010). Dissatisfied with the results of these experiments, development agencies turned to large-scale agricultural and industrial investment by the 1970s (Mansuri and Rao 2012, 3). Soon it became clear that these top-down projects registered poor results and radicalized peasants. Development agencies began to require grassroots participation approaches and "social soundness analyses" as a way of enlisting consent and managing resistance (Escobar 1991, 662–63). Though participation emerged as a response to social movements and the radical demands they made of development institutions, it withered over the decades from a language of people's "control" to people's "influence" over development (Hickey and Mohan 2005; Cornwall 2000).

In 2013 Gates and Farmer advocated a notion of participation that drew on its latter sense, not to generate shared control but to generate acceptable innovation in large-scale technological interventions. This turn to the poor for "ingenious ideas" fit a broader shift to what anthropologist Julia Elyachar (2012a) calls "development after development" in which the poor are seen as repositories of tacit knowledge, "next practices," and opportunity for agencies and corporations alike. Human-centered design rode on the legitimacy of poor people as knowing subjects who ought to have a voice in their future but translated those voices not into political control but into sources of marketable ideas.

Engineering the Acceptance of Software

Human-centered design also rode on a second history of top-down projects negotiating bottom-up resistance: the history of the computerization of everyday life. Bill and Melinda Gates were not just any sorts of philanthropists. They were also software engineers and product managers. While they rarely cite software production as a pedagogy for development, I found frequent crossings between the worlds as I did my fieldwork. As a former software engineer myself, I might have been a magnet for such connections. As I studied projects in BMGF's orbit, I met several foundation program officers who had no history in development but came from software engineering and design at Microsoft. I also met economists—economics was a more usual background for program officers—who had become interested in human-centered design after stints at Google.org, Google's technology-focused nonprofit arm, or after meeting designers through information science fields. The Gates-funded NGO operating the water-filter project I will introduce later in this chapter employed ex-Microsoft software interface designers to work on a nondigital filter. That same NGO also sponsored university human-computer interaction (HCI) researchers to develop design methods for sanitation interventions; those papers were published at the leading conferences in the field of computation design (e.g., the ACM SIGCHI Conference). Clearly, HCI had enough legitimacy to extend and adapt its expertise to noncomputational domains.[7]

Early HCI in the mid-twentieth century was a top-down project situated in military and industrial expertise. Researchers of "man-machine systems" studied complex technologies—weapons systems and airplanes, for example— with "humans in the loop." HCI was the science of reducing human-generated error and inefficiencies that hampered system performance (Harrison, Sengers, and Tatar 2011; Baecker et al. 1995). By the 1980s a second wave of HCI research focused on theorizing the human as an information processor embedded in work systems with other people—office jobs and information work, for example (Card and Moran 1995; Olson and Olson 1995). Foundational in this turn were psychological and microsociological approaches to understanding human action and the production of social order. Whether in the military or in the office, computer users rarely had a choice about whether to adopt computing; instead, they were workers whose performance had to be optimized to improve the system.

A technology industry in search of growth pursued new frontiers of computerization, from the managed workplace to people's cars, homes, and pockets—spaces where management did not yet coerce workers to take up computing systems (Grudin 2005). This was HCI's "third wave," in the field's parlance: a turn to humans as social, cultural, and embodied actors who invent, appropriate, and make meaning out of technology (Dourish and Bell 2014; Harrison, Sengers, and Tatar 2011; Salvador, Bell, and Anderson 1999). By the late 1990s researchers and designers extended their view from cognition and information processing to gesture, sociality, embodiment, and affect. This expanded, social view still largely imagined "the user" as the center of analysis (Satchell and Dourish 2009), translating the social into the phenomenological as "user experience" design (Goodman, Stolterman, and Wakkary 2011; Harrison, Sengers, and Tatar 2011; Wright and McCarthy 2008; Suri 2001; Segal and Suri 1997; Winograd 1996; Ehn 1988; Winograd and Flores 1986). This incarnation of HCI extended earlier microsociological approaches, adding anthropological concerns about culture, meaning, and reflexive action. This was the HCI in which I had trained, and whose reflexive approaches to power and positionality (e.g., Lindtner, Anderson, and Dourish 2012; Cohn, Sim, and Dourish 2010; Irani et al. 2010; Sengers et al. 2005) prepared me to understand design as reflexive practice and unfinished project, rather than crystallized expertise.

One product of this turn to user experience was the operationalization of empathy as a tool for design. Designers, including those at DevDesign, described empathy for users as what distinguished them from engineers whose affections were for technology itself; designers sought to know human difference and bring technology into closer relations with it (Goodman, Stolterman, and Wakkary 2011; Patnaik and Mortensen 2009; Suri 2001; Salvador, Bell, and Anderson 1999; Segal and Suri 1997; see Taylor 2011 for critiques within HCI). Designers devised a range of techniques for understanding users' interior lives, including embodied role-playing to simulate the other, qualitative interviews to understand categories and narratives of the other, and design coproduction to engage the other in experimental future making. This empathy was largely a one-way project; designers needed to empathize with users to understand why they behaved as they did. With that understanding, they generated designs that might align with a larger set of users. Designers, after all, almost never designed for just one. As they had in development's participatory turn, these methods invited reflexive engagement with knowledgeable users. But empathy usually did not assume users knew what was best, only that they felt they knew what was best, and that their feelings determined the success of the product. Again as in development, empathic designers invited users to exercise influence, but they rarely shared design *control* with users (see Beck 2002; Bjerknes and Brattentig 1995 for exceptions).[8] These twin trajectories of social sciences in the computing industries and in development work came together as designers looked for opportunities that could tap into local desires, manage local resistances, and promise large-scale developmental "impact" on human life.

Design Ethnography: The Politics of Empathy When Impact Means Scale

DevDesign members made their living conducting HCD research for entrepreneurial actors who were turning toward the poor. In the earliest moment of my fieldwork, in 2009, a "clean water" project jarred me—then a student aspiring to contribute to design methodology—into recognition of the limits of empathy at scale. The studio's task was to test existing water filters by placing them in the homes of poorer Indians. The teams would study how people used and maintained the filters—or didn't—to inform the design of a more ideal, desirable filter people would buy, keep, and use. The teams employed human-centered design as a way to get to know the "four billion"—the imagined constituencies of global health projects—by studying a few hundred people in rural India. Not surprisingly, empathy often came into tension with opportunities to intervene at large scales. Institutions and investors taught and enforced the call to intervene at scale.

The promise of scale fueled the entrepreneurial imagination, making even small tweaks appear full of potential. A small dent in the carbon production of billions of poor people, a studio intern explained to me, could address global warming. It was too daunting, by contrast, to seek dramatic changes in the life-styles of the middle class, who were a global minority anyway. To the aspiring change agent, small dents at fantastically large scales appeared more tractable than thoroughgoing changes in ways of life.

The client for the water-filter project was a reputable global health NGO based in the United States that I will call HealthWorks. HealthWorks saw the project as a first step in developing a "market out of thin air" for usable, afford-able commercial water filters for poor consumers across Asia and Africa. The project merged market making with global health goals; expanding filter use, the logic went, would curb waterborne illness. This was the project in which a HealthWorks report posed the problem thus: "How do you begin to get acquainted with 4 billion people?" Four billion was not just any number. It was the population of potential consumers business school professor C. K. Prahalad promised augured "fortune at the bottom of the pyramid" (2005, xii). The number marked the audacity of the organization's ambition, as well as the size of its potential market. Behind the photographs, statistics, and user stories in the report were months of labor by DevDesign researchers and NGO staff in India. I had accompanied the researchers into one village with interview protocols that I had helped prepare; I also analyzed data when they were back in the studio.

Here is how you get acquainted with four billion. DevDesign's team drove hundreds of kilometers from village to village in the Southeast Indian state of Andhra Pradesh searching for participants. The imagined study recruit, according to the lead designer, was "fairly poor," getting "water from the dirty river," often sick from waterborne illness, and lacking a filter. Few indi-viduals matched the client's image of poverty. What the design research-ers found instead were villages where people seemed relatively happy or even proud of their water, claiming that they were acclimated to it. They boiled water for elderly people, infants, and sick children, and during the rainy season. Designers found few people complaining about illnesses such as diarrhea or parasites. It appeared that designers were seeking a solution without a constituency.

In a number of villages, the design team *did* find a pervasive, but differ-ent, water problem. Even better, they also found a design constituency: those they interviewed—from physicians to farmers to itinerant rickshaw pullers—resoundingly articulated a desire for a solution to the problem of fluorosis. Many villages got their water from bore wells—wells bored deep into the ground to access groundwater. For a variety of reasons, including industrial pollution, dams, and wells dug too deep into mineral deposits, the water had an excess of fluoride. Activists had agitated in the area, asking the government to install fluoride filtration facilities, but the local government had not done much.

The politics of impact and scale mediated what designers could hear, interpret, and act on in the project. The NGO commissioning the design team had already decided not to address fluoride early in the project. The reasons were many, and overlapping. The NGO had a US$17million grant to develop household water purification. In global health worlds, "clean water" usually meant free of diarrhea-causing and waterborne disease; researchers inscribed the urgency of those diseases in DALYs, or disability adjusted life years, and those DALYs in turn informed philanthropic strategies that sought to fund areas with the largest impact on health. The question of impact, here, was mediated by DALYs calculated at a global scale and multiplied by aspirations for the global spread of water treatment systems. The NGO was running pilots in Africa, South Asia, and Southeast Asia. Fluorosis, even if it affected millions in India and China, seemed local by comparison. The immediate, present need for fluoride filters was seen as a diversion from the global imaginary of development impact.

Further, addressing fluorosis risked the NGO's project timeline. The NGO, one of the lead designers told me, was "on a timeline to prove themselves to [the foundation] so taking the fluoride project is too risky." Existing fluoride filters required electricity; engineering filtration that could work without electricity could take an unknown amount of time. By contrast, the bacterial filters the NGO wanted to market to the poor ran without power and were already being sold at higher price points to wealthier consumers such as middle-class Indians and American hikers. The bacterial filtration mechanism already existed; the NGO sought to find the design, distribution, manufacturing, and financing strategies that would make it desirable to four billion poor consumers (see also Redfield 2015). Humanitarianism here meant valorizing the existing manufacturing capacities and technical knowledge honed for people in wealthier places. This was as true in the hackathon as it was in design.

Ultimately, the design team reinterpreted people's requests for fluoride filtration as a "perception." As a perception, fluoride became yet another aspect of user beliefs that might influence the desires for and expectations of a bacterial water filter. Even if the team could address the fluoride problem, to empathize became to treat overfluoridation as a feeling rather than as knowledge.

The feeling that there was too much fluoride in the water became like the feeling that metal was more beautiful than plastic, or the feeling of confusion at which part of the filter contained the processed water. These feelings about materials, about bodies, and about aesthetics were what designers were interested in and needed to understand in order to generate new products that were likely to land. These feelings were users' personal truths, but they implied no ethical demands on design teams. As one designer put it, "[Overfluoridation] may or may not be valid. The perception of fluoride is just another perception being made." The NGO could not address the fluoride problem at the scale of impact it hoped to make, but empathy became a tool for managing people's perceptions that bacterial filtration was not what they needed.

The design team, trained in engineering and product design, did not worry much about the omission of fluoride. When I raised the issue again years later, Kritika and Vivek suggested that other NGOs were tackling that problem. During the time of the project, however, nobody mentioned the problem of bore wells, dams, and activists' efforts. The project did not open the frame of "clean water" to include concerns about how to support fluorosis projects in Andhra Pradesh. To design with global reach, designers had to translate the embodied, the voiced, and the local into opportunities with reach, scale, and promise for partners. Empathy meant taking people's voice not as declared will but as symptoms of opportunity and risk. (Chapter 7 shows how common conceptions of innovation and development legitimize this refusal.)

Stakeholder Workshops: Constructing Opportunity, Generating Investments

After the research that happened in the field, research workshops were an additional key site where designers mobilized empathy—this time that of potential partners—to construct promising opportunities. Clients and designers held workshops to convene varied stakeholders around their findings. These stakeholders included people from within the client organization, or the client's broader network of partners, collaborators, or experts. At the workshops, invitees could offer critiques in a semiprivate space. They could offer informal or well-guarded information or contacts. Workshops were where clients tinkered with how DevDesign's findings could generate insights for their own operations or for their partners. Most important, the workshops were where participants could explore ways to collaborate, partner, and pursue projects where their interests overlapped. This was the work of mobilizing empathy to construct opportunity and generate investments.

DevDesign's work on the water-filter project earned it a reputation for the design of sanitation technologies. As the filter project concluded, BMGF contracted the firm to study toilets. A year into the project, DevDesign staff found themselves touring World Bank offices, Ford Foundation campuses, and five-star hotels presenting their research as it developed.

At one workshop in a posh Delhi hotel, designers worked to generate empathy to find where the opportunity in sanitation lay. The scene of action was a five-star hotel, designed so global professionals could feel at home in Delhi whether they hailed from Sri Lanka or Seattle. An ecology of carpeting, air conditioning, filtered water, and wireless internet reproduced the global habitat of transnational professionals' deliberations. This particular workshop was not about water filters but about toilets. The foundation program manager, Erica, had invited fifteen participants to spend two days together behind closed doors. Among the participants were foundation grantees, academic colleagues, and staff from NGOs doing related work. These included program managers from a U.S.-based global health NGO, an economist from an Ivy League university, a sociologist from Delhi focusing on gender and health, researchers from a U.S. development economics institute, and a number of other professionals from global sanitation NGOs. Studio members had met some of the participants in prior conferences but not others. I experienced this workshop from its margins. There was room for only six from the studio at the workshop; an American studio intern and I had to stay home. Back at the studio, I participated in the late-night rants, analyses, and midcourse adjustments between the first and second day of the workshop. Kritika, Vivek, and Mukta, a more senior designer, also videotaped the proceedings at the hotel and shared their notes with me. They wanted help understanding the foundation's motivations and pressures as much as I did, and I had been to enough of these workshops to contribute from a distance.

Everyone in the room was connected through their acquaintanceship with the foundation program officer (and their shared ability to work in English). They all had reasons to get along in a flexible and competitive funding environment where being on granting agencies' good sides was key. The studio members entered the workshop hoping to locate potential partners for projects that could come out of the research; partners could include supportive NGOs who could help deploy designs or funding organizations that could sponsor follow-up work. DevDesign staff also wanted to learn how these partners worked and saw the world so that they could design the studio's future reports and deliverables to have an impact. DevDesign's research, the studio director explained, should "speak to" attendees and "inspire their work." The studio's objective, after all, was not to design toilets. Its objective, and the foundation's, was to produce research and models that would provoke entrepreneurs elsewhere to design and scale better toilets.

The beginning of the presentation was fairly boilerplate; as managing director of DevDesign, Akhil described the studio, as I had seen him do routinely when presenting to potential and actual clients. DevDesign, he explained, was a multidisciplinary studio that drew together expertise from business, design, and technology. Through the presentation, he told the audience, he would share the experiences studio researchers had gathered in their five-city, four-month defecation study. He worked through the timeline of the project, showing that the team was in the middle of their plans. They intended to refine their insights with attendees' feedback and then transition from "insights to action" in the weeks ahead by collaborating with architects, urban planners, and product designers to develop design concepts.

Akhil then moved into findings, primarily organized over the past few months by Kritika, Vivek, and Mukta but also edited late into the previous night. The findings were organized into groups around higher, summative "takeaways" exemplified by photographs, films, and stories from the field. One set of slides, for example, showed Vivek's film of traveling to the open defecation fields. The slide that followed showed dirt hills and verdant green foliage against a gray morning sky; six men with *dhotis* hiked up or pants pulled down squatted in the field. The field was separated from the neighborhood by a wall. The slide title read "Key Takeaway 01" and the photograph was captioned: "Standards of privacy are elastic and highly tolerant in certain contexts." Another photograph showed a group of women and one man bathing at a public water tap, the man's head covered in soap pouring water out of a mug and the women near him wearing *kurtas* as they washed their bodies and clothes, killing two birds with one stone. The caption read, "When bathing, a sense of cover is enough as opposed to blanket cover." Throughout the presentation slides, the audience interrupted Akhil to comment on the findings, sometimes expressing intrigue, sometimes warning that the statements were "provocative," sometimes cautioning that the team might have jumped to conclusions.

A later slide showed, again, a green pasture against a jewel-toned sky. A single person squatted at the center of the frame, mostly a silhouette holding an umbrella. The caption read, "Defecation in open fields is the idealized reference for toilet experience." He had touched a nerve. Critics began to call the novelty or accuracy of the observations into question. As Akhil talked about moving from "insights to action," several of the workshop participants told him to slow down. Academic attendees told him that some of their insights, such as "clear ownership [of toilets] drives responsibility," were old hat in development circles. Though DevDesign testified that it had seen the principle at work in the field, this did not, the economists told Akhil, constitute a finding. The Indian sociologist asked if DevDesign could bring a trained anthropologist on the team, critiquing it for not studying any neighborhoods in India's contentious northeastern region. A gender activist pressed the team to produce activist films on the strength of hard facts and concrete stories. Another argument erupted when an economist asked whether open defecation could really be desirable, or whether it is the last resort of desperate people without access to toilets.

Erica, the program manager who had commissioned the studio, cut in to manage the disagreement and to reinforce DevDesign's worthiness as a team. She urged the group to think of open defecation as an experience that millions of people *valued* and to see their challenge as understanding what attributes of that experience could be emulated to "trigger behavior change" in people. Development practitioners and the millions who defecated in the open seemed to have disjointed orders of worth (Stark 2009, 13); the task of the studio was to find a path where those distinct orders of worth—both moral and evaluative—overlapped.

Erica also intervened on behalf of the studio's expertise, not as development experts or makers of positivist truth claims but rather as people who could bring the worlds, habits, and orders of worth of the poor to the foundation. She had seen DevDesign's work on a prior NGO project; she recounted how in that project, DevDesign had shown how poorer Indians thought about water filters as short-term durables rather than long-term household investments. That finding had jarred the project manager—a Ph.D. in economics—into a different way of understanding sanitation infrastructure, and it was that generative jarring toward a "user experience" perspective that she hoped the team would produce today.

The foundation director, John, turned to the economist who had suggested people defecate openly for lack of access to toilets. "I wanted to push back," he began, "because it sounds like you're assuming everything will be happy using hotel toilets." He pressed on; part of what the workshop had opened up, he explained, was that people may actually desire the open field, open sky experience; they may not be choosing it for lack of resources.

John turned back to the DevDesign team. "I think the tension you're hearing," he began, "is that we would actually rather at this point you *err on the side of innovation.*" The emphasis here is mine. His advice obliquely referenced earlier challenges to the studio's expertise—the challenge that the studio should bring an anthropologist onboard, for example. The anthropologist's knowledge of culture, gender, and political economy might be less valuable, he suggested, than errors of interpretation that lead to innovation. "There is just not enough of that sort of thinking," he continued, "where people are open minded and start from a user's perspective. . . . So I guess we're not as eager to come up with the direct solution now as we are to

SEEING LIKE AN ENTREPRENEUR 157

have a process that would seed a bunch of ideas that might eventually come up." The ranking officer and funder of the convening had spoken; nobody countered him.

"Erring on the Side of Innovation": The Generativity of Naïveté

This conflictual assembly of competing forms of knowledge and sensibility— the gender activist alongside the economist, for example—was not a planning mistake. Workshops like these were designed to generate both dissonant feed- back—information that would inform the search for solutions—and buy-in. Films, storytelling, and ethnographic observation, designers believed, offered people denser bundles of symbolic departures for imagining futures than text did. These kinds of media practices were common in innovation research— work characterized not by mass production but by the collaborative search for opportunities amid multiple possible orders of worth (Stark 2009, xvii–xviii). This dissonance among multiple orders is what sociologist of innovation David Stark calls "bountiful friction" (108). The sorts of tensions the director marked and managed were common features of such gatherings. Like in the hackathon, the challenge was to make sure that arguments about *what was* did not get in the way of arguments about *what could be*, that participants practice "discursive pragmatism" (108–111) rather than pose a political challenge to the foundation.

The foundation client and studio members considered the studio's lack of specific topical expertise an advantage for understanding the worlds of users. After the workshop, Mukta, Kritika, and Vivek griped over drinks about the attendees who challenged the absence of existing literature and case studies in their presentation: "No we didn't cite your research. We started fresh." Excited, Mukta gestured as if she were picking fruit off of trees. "We're going to run out into the field, start grabbing something, organic and bottom up. We don't know which parameters are going to be important." Mukta, given to passion- ate, micromonologues among the familiars of the studio, continued:

> Seeing the reports is scary! You think, "Oh, all that has been done!" It's like designing when you've been staring at pretty things. Then you think, oh, how do I make something that is as nice. It's scary. It's better to just spit it out. . . . Not to diss other people's work, but this has to be coming from inside me. I incurably have no idea where this is going but that's good. It's like when we get clients who say they want this but we tell them, "No, you want that!" Collectively, all of us are myopic. We have a different myopia than their myopia, which is why they come to us. [The foundation] comes to us because 300 people have done it and none of it has worked.

If they had done all their homework to read the extant literature and studies, they would begin to inhabit the "myopic" perspectives the people already working on the sanitation problem had, leading to approaches that, Mukta added, had not worked anyways. In that scenario, what fresh perspective would they bring? What would they add to what the foundation could imagine? What would be the point?

The program officer independently echoed Mukta's assessment when I interviewed her after the workshop. The program officer had a Ph.D. degree in economics and understood the academics' unease about the rigor of DevDesign's research, yet she reinforced the value of its work:

> They're not coming at it through an academic discipline. Their naïveté is an upside to an extent. You just have to calibrate that right. Their naïveté helps them ask questions and get answers to them that might—someone who is saying I have a model of human behavior and that's gonna be my lens—you might miss something. . . . You could have had an anthropologist do this. . . . You know, they would have come at this with a particular worldview. I think these guys are kind of worldview free. I don't think they're coming at this with a worldview except that people are customers and consumers—they're not just passive beneficiaries.

To see people as consumers was a historically specific but widespread form of naïveté—a generalized kind of social category around which turned middle-class discourses about Indian citizenship, private industry expertise, and transnational development practice. Many anthropologists and sociologists would have come ready to critique this formation, bringing to bear analyses of neoliberalism, marketization, privatization, and individuation of subjects in relation. By hiring designers, the foundation could focus not on the politics but on the technology design that could evade becoming the object of political awareness, contestation, or even just disuse.

What Erica called naïveté—freedom from the constraints of existing work and models—generated an optimism central to designers' motivation and productivity. Recall Mukta: "Seeing the reports is scary! You think, 'Oh, all that has been done!'" The history of other attempts to improve human life was at best an inspiration—a source of energy, excitement, or associative ideas—and at worst intimidation that diminished the optimism that one's design experiments could really develop legs and find a place in the world. Though history could suggest ways to avoid failure in the future, these lessons were uncertain at best—what failed in one set of hands might succeed in another—and came at an affective cost in a culture that encouraged the bias to action and failure over deliberation and "analysis paralysis" (see Peters and Waterman 1982).

Mukta, Erica, and others at the workshop noted that naïveté enabled them to approach the field with an untrained eye, sensitive to the possibilities immanent in this place and moment that might be ignored by others. In new-age terms, designers trained in being present. Designers actually trained and taught this naïve form of perception, attentive to detail and wary of assigning value judgments that occluded users' own values. This naïve eye promised to discern newly relevant features of the situation that suggested promising paths forward. In conditions of competition, these paths would be novel and unknown to competitors.[9] This was more than simply bringing the fresh perspective of outsiders to development; DevDesign had worked on development projects for half a decade. This was a stance of privileging the concrete present—however naturalized by power—over intellectually mediated perceptions. It was an ideology of consciousness widespread in the design and entrepreneurial cultures that oriented toward Silicon Valley. Recall that IDEO and DevDesign alike taught students to "see through the eyes of a beginner"; this adage draws on Zen writings from the San Francisco Bay Area, particularly Shunryu Suzuki's *Zen Mind, Beginner's Mind* (1970). Stanford product design professor Rolf Faste often referred to Zen teachings in explanations of design research techniques, even writing an unfinished book titled "Zengineering."[10] This epistemic stance called for a peaceful mind that attuned to the present, letting go of ego, rank, and abstractions. Prior research and knowledge of failures threatened the beginner's mind. If designers approached a problem without expertise, they could facilitate communication among experts, pose questions to them, and attempt to generate design ideas informed by the information elicited. The beginner's mind ought to notice that which others had learned to ignore. The beginner's mind also suspended judgment; its politics were pliable.

The effect of naïveté was to bracket out questions of history and politics. This was a boon for clients seeking products that appealed to very large markets. The foundation in this instance worked on "global health" and sought to identify technologies and approaches that could be established in particular locales but then implemented at scale. DevDesign abstracted its research on sanitation practices in particular neighborhoods into general hypotheses about the relationship between human behavior and the qualities designers could fix in objects, spaces, or policies. Investors celebrated the power of social enterprise and design projects to change the world at wide scales through mass manufacture or diffusion. The lure of the global or "four billion" required designers to systematically ignore histories of places and politics since these threatened to unprofitably localize the framing of the problem at hand. Careful naïveté, then, became empathy—a strategy for getting past the occlusions of one's own values and expertise to locate opportunities for portable interventions.

Designers understood naïveté not in the language of lack but as a positive orientation toward "facilitation" and the production of "insight." Speaking to students, Akhil once put it: "It's always a good sign when the designer did not come up with the big idea.... The designer's role is that of a facilitator. He's in charge of creating tangible visions for [potential users'] aspirations and needs and a synergy amongst the team members." Design offered a sensibility and set of techniques by which people could communicate, visualize, and strive toward "tangible visions" at the points where their interests aligned. These visions were opportunities for entrepreneurial development.

The facilitation role complemented the beginner's mind. Professional designers facilitated the sensing of the world, coupling the fresh inputs and questions afforded by their naïveté with the knowledge of other kinds of experts. Designers then drew on these inputs to construct alternative possibilities, ranging from new products to new states of the world. They could materialize these alternatives—in sketches, in prototypes—so that people could reason about these alternatives or put them out into the world as transformations of people's material and symbolic environments. Designers acted as sensitive and visionary mediators, facilitating and accelerating the judicious choosing of futures for the many.

This view of design work emerged out cybernetic accounts of the subject and change processes, now highly influential across computer science (Winograd and Flores 1986), evolutionary biology, economics (Helmreich 2000; Maurer 1995), and even parts of the qualitative social sciences (Escobar 2018; Boyer 2010). This view posed subjects as agents, and the world as a system in which they operate (Galloway 2014). Agents sense their environments, calculate alternative futures, and choose among them to act on the world. Sensing the result, agents incorporate the feedback into the next cycle of action. Such is the cybernetic individual; the organization can also be rendered as a cybernetic system in which designers embed. With the world rendered a system of feedback relations, design could seem a universal approach to interacting, navigating, and stimulating reorganization. This view of design as the facilitation of agency within a system can be traced at least to the 1950s views of decision theorist Herbert Simon and American designers Ray and Charles Eames.

Simon's highly influential account of design as "a science of the artificial" famously argued that "everyone designs who devises courses of action aimed at changing existing situations into preferred ones" (Simon 1981, 54). Despite this putative universality of design, he called for its perfection through mathematics, decision sciences, management, and artificial intelligence (AI). These fields, he argued, needed models of how to optimize for "what ought to be." Artificial intelligence would, for him, model the planning problems that designers too needed to solve. When some artificial intelligence researchers abandoned AI in the 1980s, they invented the field of human-computer interaction (Winograd and Flores 1986). They abandoned hope for an algorithm that could intelligently plan, instead placing their hope in human designers (Winograd 1996). Good design, in their view, took in as many parameters as possible and made good decisions in reasonable amounts of time. Good design, in other words, judged, mediated, and governed based on various inputs and ongoing learning.

Ray and Charles Eames also saw design as a kind of mediation of and transformation of complexity. They too were influenced by research in computation, communication, and cybernetics (Eames and Eames 1959). They articulated design as a kind of cybernetic mediation of sensing the vividly communicative environment and shaping it in turn, through form, texture, and symbol.[11] The Eameses helped found India's National Institute of Design at the request of Nehru and with support from the Ford Foundation. Their *India Report* (1958, 12), a document still read and debated today, argued that designers "should be trained not only to solve problems—but what is more important, they should be trained to help others solve their own problems. One of the most valuable functions of a good industrial designer today is to ask the right questions of those concerned so that they become freshly involved and seek a solution themselves."

The Eameses authored the document at time when cultural elites, including India's leaders, anticipated chaotic reconfigurations of culture through accelerating communication and transportation technologies. Designers offered a process for steering the masses through cultural transformation, governing change through facilitation. When postcolonial and radical critiques made top-down modernism untenable, designers turned to empathy as a way of steering culture and technology by setting up environments so freely choosing consumers choose as they ought (Turner 2013, 251).

Eliciting Investments in the Project

Designers not only facilitated the construction of opportunities but also generated affective investments that could turn into resources or partnerships. They saw "rich media documentation"—films and photographs of ethnographic work—as core to how they elicited investments from others. As they workshopped their research among varied stakeholders—activists, manufacturers, businesspeople, or government officials—designers facilitated a conversation that bridged representations of user practice with the agendas and investments of those at the meetings.

One video DevDesign members often showed—known internally as "the heart-wrenching potty video"—was an affective workhorse of the sanitation project. Designers had honed the film over time. The film generated optimism about their project. It demonstrated the studio's credibility as tour guides into the lives of potential users. And it provoked multiple, contradictory interpretations. This ambiguity was not a flaw but rather a feature. It allowed designers to draw out many possible investments viewers might have in entrepreneurial futures of sanitation.

Back at the five-star hotel, Akhil had been fielding challenges to the "takeaway" slides. Recall the economist: "Do people idealize open defecation because the enclosed toilets are so bad?" Another asked: "You've documented what's there, but did you ask about their aspirations?" Each takeaway was a claim, and each claim seemed subject to question by a development economist, a sociologist, an NGO worker—all of whom had seen many projects and had many theories. Akhil noted these questions and told those in the room that they would return to them after they got through this section of the presentation. At the head of the conference room, he gratefully acknowledged questions, but I could hear the edge in his voice.

He reached down to his laptop to start a film already cued up. Mukta turned the lights in the room down as the film started playing. The camera follows a thin, older man wearing a white, sleeveless shirt and a dhoti. Ambient electronic music eases viewers into the scene as the shot follows the man down the road at a rapid clip—editors accelerated the film to intensify the pacing of his movement. An auto rickshaw speeds by. With a towel slung over his shoulder and bar of soap in hand, he navigates an alley crowded with a vegetable market and cycle rickshaws. Guitar music layers in, adding a quick rhythm over the ambient tone. The beats of the music combine with the skipped frames to create a frenetic pace for this morning journey.

Arriving at an area crowded with men and boys, the man walks over to a hose, slings his towel over a ladder, and pauses to look at the camera. He hangs his towel near some water hoses where a crowd of boys bathe. He turns to the nearby toilet stalls, locates an empty plastic can, and returns to the water hose to fill it. He selects a stall, places his can in front of it, and, when the stall's occupant leaves, enters. The film cuts to the man as he exits the stall, pays the toilet attendant, and returns to the water hose where his towel still hangs.

The man strips off his tank top and dhoti, leaving on his blue boxer shorts. He waits to use the hose as a boy fills his own can. The man then grabs the hose, wets his hair, and soaps up. Others come and circulate the hose to fill their cans while the man rubs the soap into his hair and face.

Eyes squinted shut and covered with soap, the man stops soaping and reaches out with cupped hands. A boy filling a water can redirects the hose's flow into the man's cupped hands before returning to his task. The hose again goes back into circulation, moving among others' hands. The man then reaches out for the hose again and another dhoti-clad young man places it in his hands. As the man rinses off, two streams of water spring from the hose, spraying water at the crowd around him. The men standing around break into laughter.

The young man grabs the hose at the leak, sealing it while the older man finishes washing the soap away. Occasionally the hose goes taut while the elder and younger bathers laugh. It is not clear if the tugging competition is intimate humor, a struggle for resources, or both. The film cuts to the man changing under cover of his dhoti, slipping off his soaking shorts and pulling on fresh ones. He leaves the water point, walks back through the alley and onto the street as the screen fades to black.

This film was like many others shown by the studio to clients and students. "Time compressed and exaggerated" films, as Kritika described them, gave a sense of the structure of how bodies moved through spaces and infrastructures. Studio members composed these films to "give a feel for context" and replay evocative moments from the field in the space of workshops. The films moved fast and were rich with details—some fleeting and some demanding full attention. They were not, however, meant to stand for generalized patterns. With these films, designers invited workshop attendees to attempt an empathic immersion in others' practices. With a "feel for context," workshop participants posed new questions and imagined new relations their firm or organization might forge with those on film and those like them, and then imagined how they might intervene. The films, in other words, enabled designing viewers to fantasize about changing the lives of others. The film was an evocative document—one that generated excitement, curiosity, and affective investments. It helped workshop participants feel out opportunities.

With these films, designers powerfully shifted moods among experts, activists, and technocrats in the room. In contrast to the frequent interruptions, questions, and challenges studio members fielded when they spoke, nobody ever interrupted a film. The MBAs, engineers, and liberal arts graduates were not experts in development, economics, or sociology. But the latter experts lacked what the designers had—detailed representations of embodied practices. These were the practices—of water consumption or of handwashing, for example—that those in the room sought to transform in those potential users not in the room. DevDesign staff expected the films to speak for themselves. They did not pause the film to ask if everything was making sense as they might have during a speech. I never saw anyone challenge the authenticity of a film's representation of reality, even though DevDesign staff knew well the power of editing. People frequently commented on the apparatus that produced the film—the cameraman falling in the open defecation fields was only the most obvious case—but only to note that the filmmakers went where other experts rarely did.

Why did no one interrupt these films? Intensified time lapses pulled audience members along lest they stop to think with losing the plot altogether. The details of digital interfaces also mattered. The digital film clips ran on standard software—VLC or QuickTime player—that enabled films to be played and paused in a click. Compared to slide software like Keynote, it was much harder to click back to particular segments or rewind without fumbling in the space of professional presentation. In workshop and conference settings, these film segments keyed a moment of performance—a patterned, special mode of address where audiences know that their social role is to direct their energy to the performer. These patterns of address offer performers control over situations (Bauman 2001, 182–183). Studio members used films to focus audience energies on vibrant, dense, and quick action. They used film to entrain audiences on worlds of user experience and possibilities for innovation rather than on historical, structural, or political questions. These documents helped organize time, sociality, and agencies (Hull 2003) for workshop participants, attempting to mobilize empathic investment from them in the process.

These films were a variation of a widely recognized design practice of grounding design deliberation in storytelling. Storytelling was a kind of cultural practice valued in the innovation industries as an organizational skill for persuading audiences and subtly managing them. TED, IDEO, and Ashoka, for example, all offer storytelling pedagogy to instruct designers in this technique.[12] These storytelling pedagogies often focus on stories as a means of influence. Design practitioners, however, articulate storytelling as part of a more open-ended choreography whose aims go beyond simply driving home a point. In 1996 a researcher at Apple, Tom Erickson, published "Design as Storytelling." I knew of Erickson's work; he was highly respected in HCI. Ajit, a studio head, also quoted Erickson in pedagogical worksheets for students. Erickson posed storytelling as a "tool" to get varied constituencies—users, managers, engineers, and even designers—talking about the contours of problems in interaction design. Anticipating DevDesign's headaches at the workshop, Erickson explained that "findings" or "design principles" will "elicit arguments about validity and generality from the skeptical." By contrast, stories seemed "to sidetrack the debates about methodology" (1996, 35). Storytelling also addressed the "confusion and unease" that plagued early, highly uncertain stages of design (Erickson 1995). Ajit had quoted Erickson on this as well. Erickson wrote at a time when filmmaking required cassette tapes, large cameras, and expense; DevDesign honed the power of storytelling with small cameras, cheap digital memory, and laptops powerful enough to edit film.

Designers honed their storytelling films to maximize polysemy, both to elicit investments and to maintain optimism about the projects among elite viewers. The films never included demands, calls to action, polemics, or explicit pedagogy. Rather, they offered a charged-up phenomenological portrait. They presented close-up views of user activities. Bodily surfaces and movements held center stage. Histories of how life came to take those forms were never featured. These moving portraits of the present allowed viewers' divergent readings— Stark's "bountiful dissonance" (2009)—to coexist in parallel. People's reactions to the films offered clues as to their political and organizational commitments, anxieties, and growth impulses. Film discussions, and research discussions more broadly, were peppered with low-commitment future talk: "what if we could" and "maybe." Maybe there could be a way to draw on community behaviors to share responsibility for facilities; we could put some kind of sanitizing mat at the exit of the toilets so those leaving stalls don't drag germs to the bathing facility; there's a new compound this company is developing that we could use; and so on. This proliferation of imaginings, grounded in polysemic media artifacts, was what people often called "getting inspired."

The polysemic films also kept designers' options open. DevDesign staff crafted workshop programs to elicit imaginative investments from attendees. Films were a common ground around which viewers could discuss and imagine futures they might mobilize around—or at least futures they would not block. By staying close to bodies, things, and spaces films allowed elites to project their political and institutional assumptions onto targeted others; these became targets open to a wide range of imaginings—of institutional agendas, of expert practices (Hyysalo 2006), of likely courses of action (Callon and Law 1982, 617), of ethical aspirations (Fortun and Fortun 2005), and of profit motives. When people spoke of "sustainable" and "viable" opportunities, it was this alignment of agendas to which they referred. That which was not viable faced institutional enemies, technical challenges, or major risks. Projects were accused of unsustainability when they failed to earn their own keep. Designers crafted films to burn no bridges and allow viewers many lines of flight into imagining viable futures.

The films also stimulated broader, vaguer optimism and ethical commitment among viewers. Though this was harder to pinpoint in the room, I found evidence of it in the films' afterlives. The week after the workshop ended, Erica gave me thirty minutes to interview her about it. Many of her responses to my questions felt like warmed-over public rhetoric about the power of design. As she described the specific work of the studio, however, she paused and vacillated; she seemed to grapple with the significance of design and innovation given DevDesign's specific challenges at the workshop. As I wrapped up the interview, she interjected, "I think there's one really cool thing that I think summarizes some of the power of this stuff [the studio's work] in terms of us listening to our clients." By clients, she meant the users, managers, politicians, and maintainers who would ultimately sustain the technologies the foundation funder specified. She began to reflect on the film of the man bathing:

> He uses this hose and he has to keep giving this hose to other people and competing....
>
> And he manages to bathe, wash his hair, everything. You never see his privates. He's been doing this for a million years. He knows exactly how to do it.
>
> And it was soooo touching. Like you felt, it was a private thing in a way you shouldn't look at. He still managed to totally still be dignified while doing it. It really made you think about—it was embarrassing to watch it. It was hard to watch. It wasn't really something that anybody—we should all have our privacy when we have a bath. And this guy doesn't. And a lot of people don't.
>
> I actually talked to our senior colleague who was also at that meeting. And she knew exactly which video I was talking about. It is really compelling....
>
> So [the video] was a really powerful way to be forced again, even for cynical old jaded development professionals, to be forced to think anew about dignity and poverty.
>
> And so I think that's a really special, unique thing for—yeah—for development funders. It might be that kind of thing that is the most valuable stuff out of this, not the hypotheses. Help people who are cynical and jaded get struck all over again by these issues.... [Hypotheses] matter ... this intangible stuff matters too.

To Erica, the film was more than ethnographic proof. It was a salve for the "cynical old jaded" development worker. She read the film as evidence of human dignity, of the universality of privacy, and of the particular grace of this bathing man to whom, in her mind, these universals were denied. The senior colleague Erica referred to had been one of the harshest toward DevDesign during the workshop, yet she too had been compelled by this emotionally intense view into the lives of others. This was "the intangible stuff" that made the work—and workers—stay engaged. This was how she experienced the power of empathy.

DevDesign staff interpreted its film differently from Erica. Mukta, Kritika and Vivek had not made the video to elicit humanitarian compassion for the dignity of the individual. On the contrary, they sought to challenge those assumptions with a collective portrait of interdependence, shared infrastructure, and conviviality. Yet when the team learned of the vastly divergent readings the film enabled, they continued to present the film to clients. They did not contextualize it to avoid readings like Erica's. "The heart-wrenching potty movie" became the film's slightly sarcastic nickname—a reference to the soft if universalizing hearts of development practitioners.

This was not the first film in which the studio's subtle critical intervention had failed to land. Another film, a short time-lapse piece, depicted the ebb, flow, interaction, and friction of sari-clad women circulating around a community water tap, filling fluorescent plastic lota pots over the course of an afternoon. Mukta, well aware of clichés of village India as a site of tradition, stasis, and authentic culture, chose the clip to showcase the iconic lota pot in synthetic plastic colors; she overlaid a blippy track by British electronica duo Autechre to emphasize the coeval modernity of the village. The film was a qualified hit with the Seattle public health clients who saw it. They liked the film enough to share it with Bill Gates during a short audience with him; however, they edited the soundtrack, replacing Autechre with a Bollywood song. DevDesign used the films to do emotional work on their clients, and their clients used the films to do emotional work on their own patrons in turn. For the film's affective power to move with it, people subtly tweaked it along the way. These tweaks reveal how empathy is an experience in the viewer rather than knowledge of empathy's object.

Film was also part of how designers restored their own faith in their projects when they felt pessimistic, disappointed, or "mindfucked." To get mindfucked was to be drained of inspiration, frustrated by thwarted promises of getting from research to product, or disillusioned about the virtue of their work. Mindfucked designers smoked, snacked, ranted, and talked late into the night; they critiqued development officials and entrepreneurs. During one long studio work session, Kritika implored Mukta: "If I'm still doing this in five years, slap me!" Amid such feelings, designers rewatched and made new films to renew their fascination as collectors of experience and opportunity. Kritika made this explicit to me when admiring my short documentary of a woman washing the dishes in a courtyard. In the film, I had caught a woman quickly washing a staircase to prepare it as a drying rack. I had not even been sure what the moment meant, but I had caught it only on reviewing video and thought this reappropriation of form might inspire ideas for the sanitation project; Kritika gasped at the sweep of the woman's hand, telling the rest of the team, "When we get mindfucked over, like coming up with ideas, we can just watch that again and get inspired."

This was the representational work of constantly restoring the promise of opportunity. This promise attracted investments. This promise propelled designers and entrepreneurs to work harder. And this promise facilitated consent to systems that spoke in terms of imagined "user need" but refused to address clearly articulated needs like fluoride filtration.

Entrepreneurial Empathy: Making Innovators, Managing Their Others

At the studio, human-centered design posed empathy as inspiration, as care, and as social glue for project teams. On a broader scale, philanthropists also posed design practices as ethical remedies for the depredations of capitalism writ large. Bill and Melinda Gates addressed ambitious Stanford graduates at the 2014 commencement in the heart of Silicon Valley. The gap, they conceded, between the rich and the poor was widening. The solution, they asserted, was empathy. "If empathy channeled our optimism," the Gateses told the audience, "we would see the poverty and the disease and the poor schools, we would answer with our innovations, and we would surprise the pessimists" (Gates and Gates 2014). The Gateses promised that empathy could bring entrepreneurial citizens in alignment with the (tacitly less entrepreneurial) poor.

The actual empathy documented in this chapter paints a different portrait of entrepreneurial alignment. In practice, empathy was not about what consumers *wanted* (Akrich et al. 2002, 200–201). People wanted fluoride filtration. The NGO and design team recoded that want—even need—as a "perception." Empathy in the entrepreneurial mode sought inspiration in the texture of people's everyday lives. Empathy in the entrepreneurial mode transformed ethical feeling into productive investments. Workshop attendees—economists, activists, company representatives—empathized when they imagined productive courses of action and risks to the success and legitimacy of their interests and roles. In short, empathy generated productive relations among entrepreneurial citizens by keeping *representations of people* nearby while keeping actual demands from people far away.

This entrepreneurial empathy served geopolitical goals. In Cairo in 2009, President Barack Obama launched a now-annual Global Entrepreneurship Summit focused on building "mutual interest and mutual respect" between Muslim-majority countries and the United States (Obama 2009). The Trump administration continued the practice, sending Ivanka Trump to Hyderabad, India, to speak on the power of women as entrepreneurs. The U.S. Department of State described the summit's aim as to "showcase inspiring entrepreneurs and investors from around the world creating new opportunities for investment, partnership, and collaboration."[13] The State Department had a second purpose for promoting entrepreneurship globally. Hillary Clinton's

Department of State under Obama cultivated global networks of entrepreneurs as a way of mitigating ugly feelings that could metastasize into terrorism. Bill Gates and former U.S. president Bill Clinton advocated for this new model of soft power as well. Clinton testified to the U.S. Senate Committee on Foreign Relations in 2010: "We cannot kill, jail, or occupy all of our adversaries. *We have to build a world with more partners*" (United States Senate 2010, 20). Philanthropies, NGOs, and innovation champions diffused pedagogies of entrepreneurship through conferences, workbooks and toolkits, and funded projects and competitions. Human-centered design was one of the key pedagogies; it taught would-be entrepreneurs to observe and listen to others, translate lives into sites of opportunity, and optimistically find the "mutual interest" that could become the vein of *viable* opportunity.

The entrepreneurial ethos is also micropolitical. Human-centered design offers entrepreneurs a way of engineering and marketing change while managing resistance and "perceptions." Management practitioners have, for decades, employed empathy as a skill of "soft capitalism" (Thrift 1997)—the skill of managing individuals without resorting to violence, coercion, or bureaucratic authority. HCD channels these skills both into the designed form of objects and into the institutional organization of development. These projects conjoin the production of social order and the production of financial value; all the while, they work to ensure that project targets and subjects feel creative, participatory, and free.

Poor people, Melinda Gates told *Wired* in 2013, have "ingenious ideas about what would really help them." But entrepreneurial innovators need more than ideas—even ones that come from poor people. They have to translate the interests of investors, manufacturers, and powerful institutions into forms desirable and acceptable to potential users. This is a far cry from shared control.[14] This empathy for potential users does not imply responsibility to the other. It is an empathy that treats others' lives as inspiration, expanding how companies, NGOs, and entrepreneurs see their own interests and scopes of action. It is an empathy that seeks to entice unruly users to behaviors preferred by development agencies and manufacturers. It is an empathy that seeks to work along with some habits and transform others. It is an empathy in service of the conjoined tasks of market development (Cross 2013; Elyachar 2012a) and development governmentality (Li 2007; Scott 2006; Foucault 1991).

To understand the politics of empathy as a technique for regulating entrepreneurial citizens' powers to affect, we might compare these practices of mass empathy to a different political ethic. Feminist philosopher of science Donna Haraway (2008) argues that the work of political collaboration across difference requires the forging of relationships among beings—animals, humans, and other lively subjects. The design team might not have known about fluorosis, but once they learned about it, what responsibility did they have to respond to the people they spent days interviewing when those people said they need flouride water filters? Design, we saw, did not imply responsibility or accountability to such calls. The intersecting patterns of design work, global health work, and mass production and distribution made the ability to respond—what Haraway calls response-ability (71)—unimaginable at worst and unviable at best. Neither I nor the designers on the team discussed how we might exceed the client's directions to collaborate with fluorosis activists in the region. Our professional habitus occluded the possibility. My absence of imagination in that moment haunts me and this book.

Instead of holding themselves responsible to others, innovators moved their conceptions of the other into the studio and into expert workshops. At a distance, innovators could render others' lives as "inspiration"—as a source of excitement, redolent detail, and novel lines of flight. As inspiration, these socially dissimilar others could not threaten the creative energies of experts in vibrant inspiration and innovative fantasy. These others could not question the priorities and sensibilities that excited the producers. Empathy was not an understanding of the other. It was the *feeling* of understanding the other—a feeling more stable as a memory rather than as the reality of the lives of others. What a foundation officer from the United States with a resume spanning work in Africa and Asia can empathize with is limited by what she can imagine from her own experiences and what her grantees will labor to teach her. She comes from a world that enshrines European and American individuated dignity, privacy, and self-possession as universal human values. Designers too are limited by their classed and casted histories, even as they are hired on as empathic mediators. The studio and the workshop were far away from those places where targets of development could call inspiration into question or to account.

Entrepreneurial citizenship—here mobilized through human-centered design—stimulates and shapes the affects of those called into its productive, futuristic circuits—its affective economies (Ahmed 2004). Sara Ahmed conceptualizes affective economies to point out how feelings emerge in interactions conditioned by history. Affects, for Ahmed, are capacities of relating among people that do not originate in subjects—they take shape in histories, media, and reactions to environments and things—but form subjects in the interaction. The empathy DevDesign facilitated—through "the heart-wrenching potty video," for example—rode on myriad histories of social relations. It fed on the developmental desires of middle-class Indians. It fed on NGO workers' sense of duty as activists. It fed on nationalist histories that told of educated elites—lawyers, engineers, social workers—serving India's villages. It fed on frustrations with state and corporate corruption that make entrepreneurialism feel like a form of restorative direct action.

Entrepreneurial calls to citizenship seem open-ended, allowing them to feed on these diverse hopes and histories. While the open-endedness of these agendas makes them seem open to reformulation, feedback, meetings, and workshops bring designers and project participants' hopes back into line with the larger foundation-funded projects. The affects put to work here are historically and culturally mediated (Mazzarella 2009, 2004; Ahmed 2004). A variety of desires, hopes, and forms of mobility can, through HCD and social entrepreneurship, be subsumed into the kinds of research practices that grease the wheels of development with even more intimate knowledge and integration with existing social relations. Concepts that claim universality like development, like capitalism, encounter friction everywhere they try to root (Tsing 2005). Design research offers entrepreneurial citizens a set of techniques for attempting to reduce this friction, or even turn friction into inspiration and the multiplication of opportunity. What differentiates mere perception from opportunity are the interests, capacities, and tolerances of those with accumulated resources to invest.

7

Can the Subaltern Innovate?

THE OXFORD *English Dictionary* defines innovation as "the introduction of novelties; the alteration of what is established by the introduction of new elements or forms." This definition takes for granted what counts as new, what counts as old, and the social processes that make the difference. Left out of this definition are the ways political economy, class relations, and national ideologies shape what counts as desirable forms of newness and beliefs about what novelties ought to be contained.[1] Recall from chapter 1 the three different prescriptions for Indian development from three elite policy actors. Their visions were varyingly capitalist, socialist, and Gandhian; yet they shared a belief in entrepreneurial innovators as vehicles for national growth and distribution. Arvind Subramanian imagined an India with glittering software towers and an industrializing economy. Sam Pitroda called on engineers from the Indian Institutes of Technology to apply their engineering training directly to the problems of villages—a vision dramatized in the Indian film *Swades* (Gowariker 2004). And Anil Gupta, the kurta-wearing professor, led elite students at the Indian Institute of Management Ahmedabad on annual walking journeys to discover inventors living in rural India. Each of these figures imagined innovation as the introduction of novelties, but the novelties took different forms from different social locations. Furthermore, each of these key figures imagined innovation primarily through technology. This too has been contested. The Global Innovation Index, a creation of business school professor Soumitra Dutta (2017), responded to technology centric indexes by adding other cultural products such as film, textile designs, and music as innovations that should be measured and stimulated through governance.

Some counter that innovation is overvalued (Russell and Vinsel 2016; see also Edgerton 2007). Recent turns in science and technology studies, sociology, anthropology, and information studies highlight the work of maintenance in the material world. Such work tends to the material world's infrastructures, relations, and forms, repairing what decays and recalibrating arrangements as surrounding conditions shift.[2] They augment studies of domestic work-ers, repair technicians, and janitors with studies of code maintainers, system administrators, and network cable layers to expand our vision of the labors of living collectively and sustaining worlds over time. They grant that innova-tors—inventors, authors, and creators of the new—do exist, but they draw care, configuration, and articulation work to the fore.[3] In critiquing innova-tion, however, these arguments still render the definition of innovation—a valorized category in need of revaluation or supplement—as unproblematic in itself.

This chapter calls into question how we know innovation: what counts as innovation as such, who designates it and how, and how these processes are embedded in relations of power and political economy. What makes some acts of technological configuration jugaad or workarounds and others proper innovation? What makes some designs innovative while others are character-ized as derivative, inauthentic, or even copies? The answers I offer to these questions are not philosophical ones; they are ones drawn from everyday practices among designers, rural people, instructors, and policy influencers in India. People mark the line between innovators and their others in every-day practices. Drawing the line is an act of cultural and economic power, scaffolded, as I have already shown, by legal and political projects. This chap-ter, then, approaches innovation not as a process of making new things, as the dictionary and common usage would suggest, but as a designation of agency, discerned in sites of social interaction. Put simply, I examine how, in contingent and everyday practice, people recognize some acts as innovation and others as not. I argue that we should examine innovation as a process of the recognition of value rather than granting it concreteness it does not have in practice.[4]

This analytical move owes a great debt to anthropologist Lucy Suchman. Suchman, an early researcher at a major Silicon Valley research lab, subjected the lab's figurations of futures and of work to anthropological analysis (Such-man 2011; Suchman and Bishop 2000). Many at the lab, including managers and researchers, understood themselves as needing to innovate, but rather than taking these claims to innovation at face value, much of Suchman's work asks what counts as innovation, and what projects of power are served by calls to innovate. In the everyday talk of the research and design lab, Suchman explains, researchers justified themselves by giving accounts of what was "orig-inal" and "new" about their experiments. Experimental systems that recom-bined existing systems were not inherently "new"; they could be judged old hat. And systems judged exciting and new invariably combined putatively old things. "Just as translation invariably produces difference," Suchman (2008) explains, "novelty requires imitation or likenesses to familiar forms." To claim something as new, one makes claims that other things are similar. Similarity or difference, then, "is not inherent in things but an achievement of relevant discursive and material practices" (Suchman 2011, 15).

I also build on historians of technology who call into question what counts as technology and innovation. Ruth Oldenziel (1999) shows how "technology," as a valorized social category, emerged when industrial elites in the United States and colonizing elites in Europe needed a category that favorably distinguished between "the machine age" of "enlightened Europe" and material cultures of people putatively occupying earlier stages of development. Prior to this moment, agricultural elites in the United States valorized "useful arts" like fish mongering, machine building, and dress making, but these activities sank in prestige, if not in material importance, with the "machine age" and the ascendance of industrial capital. Historian Rayvon Fouché (2006) further argues that the historiography of invention in the United States is a white one, in which patent officers, collaborators, and historians denied African American people credit for their inventions and African American people were often denied positions of agency over whole technological systems, so that their technological creativities often took the form of resistance and appropriation. Historian Clapperton Mavhunga (2014, 10–14) argues that historians of technology have similarly erased Africa as a site of innovation, instead writing histories that abet imperial projects and racialized stereotypes. He analytically turns to African creativities and mobilities as "the means and ways with which ordinary people engage in creative activities directed toward solving their problems and generating values relevant to their needs and aspirations" (7–8). With these scholars, I turn to the question of whose creativities count as innovation in India. I do not, however, assume the intrinsic importance of innovation or creativity, and thus I do not seek to make the social category of innovation more inclusive. Rather, I work to show the limitations of innovation as a grounds for establishing the value of people and their lives.

This chapter takes practices such as household work, design research, graphic production, and sewing as its objects of analysis. I observed these practices while embedded with the DevDesign team as they conducted user ethnographies. These activities take place in rural, peri-urban, and urban India. They take place in the home, in informal sites of production, and in studios. In each case, I detail the social interactions that deemed these practices either proper innovation or its other. Some practices were designated grassroots innovation, a kind of marked variant of genuine innovation. Practices seen as craft or jugaad were marked as other to innovation. In each case, I show how the construction of innovation was a practice of recognition, contingently situated in improvisational interaction but conditioned by class, caste, and gender, and nation-building projects and histories.

The first two cases I examine compare two methods of cooling vessels and their contents. Designers from DevDesign encountered the first method—a lota (a curved vessel commonly used to carry and store water) cooled with wet cloth—during fieldwork. I show how the designers drew distinctions between jugaad practices of rural householders and what counted as proper design, sanctioned by widespread ideas about what constitutes proper innovation for India. The second cooling method was a clay cabinet also cooled with water, but that object was branded, it was produced on larger scales, and government agencies made a national hero out of one of the men who invented it. With these two cases, I probe the difference between what could be recognized as productive novelty and therefore as innovation. I then turn to two cases that illustrate how Indian aesthetic objects—the products of graphic designers and craftspeople—may be judged novel but also seen as inauthentic or derivative creations. These two latter cases are, put simply, ones in which people are told "nice work, but doesn't look Indian." To judge something as innovation, then, is not just to recognize it as new but also to judge the authenticity of producer in ways mediated by assumptions about caste, race, region, and ethnicity. My findings show that those who pulled off the performance of innovation had to do enormous cultural work to establish the uniqueness and then authenticity of their productions. Ultimately I conclude that while people create in myriad ways, the conditions of recognition and reward for such innovation are powerfully constrained by histories of colonialism, contemporary capitalisms, and other forms of social hierarchy, exploitation, and oppression.

Provincializing Innovation

Contemporary use of the word "innovation" comes with distinct historical baggage; it conjures trajectories of technology, of intellectual property, and heroic agencies. In preceding chapters I attended to the others that innovators generate in their wake. Here I take a different tack. I treat innovation as an act of translation in which those with power recognize others as innovative—or not. The conditions of these translations are power relations and political economy—the conditions in which some workers must become legible to powerful entities—whether those be states, design researchers, or even market consumers—as adding value, as innovative, and as authentic. I seek to provincialize innovation by revealing the specific historical, cultural, and geopolitical conditions that make innovation seem, to some, a universal good. I borrow this tack from the field of postcolonial studies. In *Provincializing Europe* (2000), historian Dipesh Chakrabarty examines how key categories of European social theory—identity, imagination, and nation, for example—cover over heterogeneous practices and conceptualizations. My argument is not that India, Hinduism, or concepts from vernacular Hindi contain an essentially different, separate domain of experience or understanding, leading to differences in how innovation is coded. Rather, I document everyday and historical practices of recognizing innovation or postulating alternatives in order to denaturalize innovation and to highlight the projects of power and accumulation that such translations serve.

I begin with a monument I encountered in New Delhi amid the tree-lined boulevards and estates near the Nehru Memorial Library, sited at the former home of India's first Prime Minister. A marble slab, taller than me, read: "Creation is the sign of life / Not repetition or imitation" (figure 7). Underneath, the monument attributed this quote to Jawaharlal Nehru, but residual layers of peeling paper posters obscured most of the first name. Above the quote, a halo of paper residue ringed a low-relief rose—evidence of past disrespect.

FIGURE 7. A marble block outside the Nehru Memorial Library, New Delhi, says "Creation is the sign of life / Not repetition and imitation / Jawaharlal Nehru." Dregs of sloughed-off poster scar its monumentality. (Photograph by author)

I snapped a photo of the monument, having felt the moral charge of "creation," "repetition, and "imitation" among celebrants of innovation. The words quoted were first published in 1934 in Nehru's book *Glimpses of World History* (1960 [1942], 47). Those words, I would learn, did not mean then what they would come to mean at the turn of the millennium.

Creativity, to Nehru, implied neither authorship nor expression. Rather, *Glimpses* defined "creativity" as the integration and adaptation of ideas from many places and people, including colonizers and invaders. "Imitation and repetition," by contrast, entailed refusing such infusions and changes; it was doing "what had been done." What was important about new ideas, for Nehru, was not where they had originated but rather the civilizational energy to selectively absorb them.[5] Civilization was the product of change via extension and transformation of what had come before, whereas imitation was "merely carrying on" as always (46–47).

This sense of creativity was manifest in the policies of the new nation as postcolonial leaders attempted to accelerate development, planning the economy and steering culture in the process. When India was newly independent, innovation meant not new technologies but rather new cultural movements or ways of life. The First Five Year Plan, for example, palpably grappled with a cataclysmic sense of social and technological change that would arrive with the adoption of science, technology, and new institutions. The problem was not that India would not innovate and rapidly change; rather, planners worried that India's masses could not adapt quickly enough. They called for programs to stimulate communities' "will to progress"—a willingness to adopt new forms of production—and their appetites for the forms of work, education, and social organization to come (Planning Commission 1951). In the Second through Tenth Five Year Plans that followed, innovation meant new ways of doing things. These innovations were not things but transformed practices of taxation, organization, or agriculture. These new practices were the substance of change in India, but they were not property. The Second FYP, for example, called new methods of accounting and administrative recruitment "innovation." Innovation in the Third FYP included "new ideas" developed and exchanged among managers of public enterprises, as well as farming techniques the state sought to urge upon agriculturalists.

By the 1980s the Sixth Five Year Plan did emphasize innovation as the adoption of technologies through research and development, but it also maintained that innovation could include new ways of organizing and administering development in the NGO, public sector, and private sectors. Through the early 2000s innovation remained a word that broadly referenced organizational novelty—something the state called for in the spirit of modernization. By the Eleventh FYP, however, following the negotiation of the Agreement on Trade-Related Intellectual Property Rights, Five Year Plans took up innovation as a source of wealth and form of property. The problem of innovation became not one of diffusion or bold new ideas but rather of producing recognizable authors of new products, services, and patents. The meaning of innovation thus shifted from a process of change to a source of value.

As a national task, innovation threw up political tensions. To some, it looked like Google, Apple, Twitter, Steve Jobs, and the Indian diaspora starting companies in Silicon Valley. To them, to build up the nation was to compete and win at capitalism in the name of the nation—high tech seemed a particularly promising domain for upper-caste Indians to do so (Subramanian 2015). To others, however, innovation had no meaning if it widened the chasm, both financial and cultural, between urban elites and the rural poor. TED Talks, news programs, and college pedagogies accommodated this tension by drawing high-tech CEOs, social entrepreneurs, and rural inventors into the same frame, collapsing the differences among them in the name of a popular innovation, driven by entrepreneurial citizenship, that all ought to be able to reach for.

In practice, middle-class professionals in India not only recognized the problem-solving practices of the rural poor but incorporated them in the name of human-centered design. Even as they incorporated the creativities of the poor, they also drew distinctions between their own problem-solving practices and those of poorer Indians. The "clean water" project in Andhra Pradesh (discussed in chapter 6) exposed the differential statuses of different practices of problem solving in the context of political economy and everyday life; it is therefore worth revisiting in more detail here.

Recall that in Andhra Pradesh, the designers went from village to village looking for people who might model future consumers of an inexpensive bacterial water filter. A global health NGO sought to develop a filter that could be marketed throughout Asia but commissioned DevDesign staff to specify filter mechanisms, shapes, and functions that would enroll people as consumers and users. The NGO, historically oriented toward public provision of health interventions, sought private, market-based provision as a way to achieve, in the words of their own documents, "innovation, responsiveness, efficiency, and sustainability." The work of the design studio was less about guiding mass cultural taste (Dutta 2009) than about incorporating mass taste into designs of development prophylactics that people would find desirable, usable, and affordable.

The designers spent days observing villagers; they filmed and noted how the villagers collected water from community taps, how they stored it in and around their homes, and how they filled bottles to send off with their kids to school. Many of those whom the designers met argued that they did not need bacterial filtration. They could boil their water if someone was elderly or ill, but largely they believed themselves to be acclimated to the locally available water. The design team worked to elicit a more desiring imagination from those they spoke with. They created a "magic box" activity, tasking people with imagining the functions of a magical box they would like to have. They designed exercises that asked people to create collages representing futures they might want.[6] One woman placed a picture of a building on the collage and, through the Telugu translator, explained that she wanted regular water service. Another said she wanted improvements to the local school. These desires were not the sort designers could act on. In English, Mukta, the lead design researcher, muttered to me, "The future looks like a bath every day. It's a five-year plan for these women." The "five-year plan" evoked the state's promises to bring development for the whole nation: *bijli, sadak, pani* (electricity, streets, water) and, before that, *roti, kapda, makaan* (food, clothing, house). These women cared about the future but not in a way that entrepreneurial citizens could address.

The designers had a dilemma. How could they drive the client's global-health agenda while appealing to people who were disinterested in bacteria? Moreover, people were vociferously asking for fluoride filtration. Fluorosis was endemic in the region. But fluorosis, even if it affected millions in India and China, seemed local by comparison. The immediate, present need for fluoride filters was perceived as a diversion from the global imaginary of development impact. To design for investors in search of a return, designers had to translate the embodied, the voiced, and the local into opportunities with reach, scale, and promise for partners. The refusal to tackle fluorosis turned the design team toward another challenge—sussing out latent desires that the design team could appeal to instead. These were the struggles and epistemic acrobatics I detailed in chapter 6.

If people did not want a bacterial water filter, what might they want? The designers observed material culture and people's everyday practice for hints, looking to people's homes, motorcycles, and clothing for clues as to what made a desirable arrangement of life. Their well-trained eyes picked out kitchen utensils tucked in the beams holding up thatched roofs, obviating the need for extra shelves (figure 8). They noted one of the younger men building an extension to his family home, purchasing concrete and adding his own labor as he was able to earn and save in small increments. All these helped the designers imagine a world and rhythm into which a water filter could be configured to fit.

One sweltering afternoon, designers spotted another crucial clue outside a family's home. A pair of vessels—a clay pot and a large plastic bottle—sat on the ground, wrapped in rough, wet cloth, each secured with some wire (figure 9). A woman named Kirti, who lived in the house, had soaked the cloth around the vessels, effectively creating an evaporative cooling device with items already available. The wire appeared carefully done; on the pot, it was crisscrossed across the wet cloth. Some of the materials—the cloth and the clay of the pot, for example—were inexpensive and widely available. The plastic bottle, by contrast, had come to the village through retail shops that sold privatized water; it found second life here as a storage device.

FIGURE 8. A sieve artfully tucked between a beam, made of tree branches, and a roof woven out of twigs and leaves is the sort of creativity that middle-class Indians usually recognized as jugaad. (Photograph by author)

FIGURE 9. During fieldwork, designers routinely photographed everyday creativity they found striking or inspirational, in addition to basic documentary photographs that established scenes, persons, and key practices for later reports. This photo depicts a lota and a reused plastic bottle wrapped in rough, wet cloth and secured by carefully wound wire ties.

A patent examiner would need schematic drawings to recognize exclusive rights to this invention. Prior examples of cloth-wrapped vessels would invalidate the claims to an originary design. But those questions seemed irrelevant to the work of going on with life; Kirti cooled water using available materials, without having to spend cash or take out a loan. This solution, however, failed to build the nation; it did not register as economic exchange, let alone figure into national economic metrics. It was made but not bought or sold. It was not proper innovation.

Designers saw Kirti's act of making not as a need fulfilled sustainably but as a "workaround" that signaled a need yet to be fulfilled by a properly designed product. In the weeks that followed, the designers and their sponsoring NGO seized on this as an opportunity. An American development consultant on the project read the cooling lota as a sign: "What [people] really want is cold water and consistent access." The designers described the cooling vessel as "inspiration" for their design efforts. By calling it inspiration, they invoked a social category that directs our attention to the rush of creativity in the one inspired, rather than to the labors of those that produced the inspiration. To see like an innovator was to see everyday creativity not as innovation but as a sign of where to add value through proper design.

The design professions frame encounters such as those between the Delhi designers and the villagers of Andhra Pradesh as participatory alternatives to modernist authoritarian planning without feedback (e.g., Scott 1998). Designers saw themselves as inviting subaltern knowledge so that they could humanize technology in turn. Kirti's jugaad became a resource out of which designers constructed opportunities in the overlap between people's existing practices, possible desires, and the goals and agendas of the designers' clients. In contrast to Kirti, however, designers could travel across sites, collecting stories and data about many people's practices. On returning to the studio, they could contemplate, synthesize, and posit a proposition for a form that addressed the needs of many, across wide spatial scales. Kirti's solution had no such aspirations; the form she created would move only if someone—a designer or another villager—thought the idea was worth recirculating through reenactment or documentation. Kirti's technological answer to the need for cool water was thus unrecognizable as innovation. It may have addressed local values, but it did not add value in the terms set out by the Five Year Plans that sought to make India a global player in the realms of intellectual property and entrepreneurial development.

"Bad or Not So Good Innovation"

The designers at DevDesign simultaneously saw creativity everywhere and yet consolidated their own status as innovating elites by distinguishing their practices from more everyday forms of creativity. They were not unique in this.

They borrowed from practices and categories that established hierarchies of creativity in public culture: the Hindi concept of jugaad, the design profession's expert category of "workaround," and Indian design scholars' concept of "people's solutions." I focus on each of these categories in turn.

Jugaad: Austere Innovation

To the expert designers from DevDesign, Kirti's cloth-wrapped vessels exemplified a Hindi social category of creativity called jugaad. Jugaad connotes a clever improvisation that achieves a goal in highly constrained situations. As the Indian press debated Indians' capacities to innovate, some marshalled jury-rigged devices, such as bullock carts propelled by diesel irrigation pumps, as evidence of a recognizably Indian form of innovation. If Silicon Valley or the West owned an image of innovation as gleaming equipment and expensive laboratories, some Indians thought that perhaps they could brand their expertise as jugaad—frugal, functional, and sustainable (see, for example, Radjou, Prabhu, and Ahuja 2010). Some elites even branded "jugaad innovation" as a uniquely sellable form of expertise and distinction in a global knowledge economy, rebranding weapons of the weak as natural national endowment to be sold as expertise in a global market (Kaur 2016; Birtchnell 2011; Philip, Irani, and Dourish 2012, 15–16). The search for value through branding generated contradictory forms of meaning.

Critics of jugaad countered that it stood for shoddy quality and short-term thinking that has hobbled India's development. In India's *BusinessLine*, a "strategy and innovation consultant" wrote that jugaad has no "design element or risk-taking. It is not born of research or from technical mastery—from identifying lacunae in customer needs or a eureka moment in a laboratory" (Chadha 2009). Critics painted jugaad as a form of situational reason—temporally and spatially particular, developed in the heat of the moment, and constrained by the rigors of necessity. One NID design professor explained jugaad to me as a form of *majboori*, translating the concept by way of explanation: "It's helplessness. The constraints are so high that you are pushed up in the corner. Do something with whatever is available!" IIM-Ahmedabad faculty Anil Gupta (2016, 338) similarly critiqued jugaad as "a transient suboptimal solution" that does not go "to the root of the problem." In these understandings, jugaad mostly reproduces the status quo while finding niches of survival within it. At a University of Pennsylvania conference called "India Innovation" (2014), Prime Minister Modi's then chief financial advisor and economics professor Arvind Subramanian called jugaad clever but also "bad or not so good innovation"—the sort of innovation that creates a disorderly and unstable India.

A Bollywood comedy titled *Jugaad* (Kumar et al. 2009) narrated how jugaad stymied entrepreneurship. In the film, an up-and-coming Delhi advertising consultant finds his office shut because of a legal mistake. As he pursues proper channels, he finds only lazy and corrupt bureaucrats; he spends his days pulling strings, chasing favors, and stepping outside the law to open the doors to his business again. The film illustrated that jugaad was central to Indian imaginations about transformational processes while failing to promise orderly progress, an end to corruption, rational planning, or the efficient conversion of Indians' energies into economic growth. In popular understanding, jugaad was what one figured out with one's back against the wall, reacting but without the freedom to deliberate or choose. Jugaad did not evidence the free will valued at the studio. It was not a liberal art. Nor did it register as value or recognizable order.

"Workarounds" and "Habits": Making Inventiveness Accidental

Categorizing inventiveness as jugaad implicitly ascribed a certain thoughtlessness to the solution finder. This rhetorical obfuscation of the thought that went into poor people's problem solving was a common theme in the world of professional design. For example, the multinational design firm IDEO published a book called *Thoughtless Acts?: Observations on Intuitive Design* (Suri and IDEO 2005). IDEO was a powerful force in crafting a global human-centered design discourse that was recognizable to multinational development, corporate, and philanthropic institutions. Its nonprofit arm received funding from the Gates Foundation, the Rockefeller Foundation, and the Ford Foundation to publish workbooks for NGOs, nonprofits, and social enterprises in human-centered design. *Thoughtless Acts* was a small volume that displayed the kind of professional vision for which IDEO prided itself.

The book depicts moments of human–environment interaction, suggesting lively beings pursuing immediate needs through whatever means possible. Much like Kirti's cooling vessel, the book presents these everyday solutions as inspiration as evidence of opportunity for designers. One photo shows a woman sitting on a staircase cooling her head on a soda can. Another shows a man lying in the park reading a newspaper, a backpack elevating and supporting his head. The front matter of the book sets the context: "Reacting? Responding? Co-opting?" Then the next page: "Exploiting? Adapting? Conforming? Signaling?" This front matter urges readers to think carefully about how the people pictured are interacting with their environments. Yet it implies that the people themselves are not putting much thought into their actions, saying "we interact automatically with objects and spaces that we encounter."

Through labeling everyday practices as thoughtless, even automatic, designers construct the acts as beyond intellect or reflexivity—the realm of habit, repetition, and reproduction. Such "thoughtless" acts apparently arise not from intention, planning, logic, or reason but from fleshly, wanting beings bumping about accidentally in the world. *Thoughtless Acts* encourages designers to "notice and document their habits, workarounds, and unspoken rules." To designers, these are the habits and accidents that social beings are made of—the very stuff of culture. *Thoughtless Acts* treats these practices as a kind of commons from which everyone is free to draw without obligation or responsibility. *Thoughtless Acts* illustrates how designers routinely learned to see the world in their training. This capacity for generative noticing was core to IDEO's own hiring practices, as well as to the practices of design research practiced by DevDesign.

"People's Solutions"

IDEO and other professional designers' practice of observing how everyday humans interacted with their lived environments was not novel; design faculty at the National Institute of Design had long articulated Indian material culture and "people's solutions" as a guide and resource for designers. They did so following the publication of *The India Report*, a document authored by famed American designers Ray and Charles Eames in 1958. The Ford Foundation sent the Eameses to India at Nehru's invitation, as part of a larger set of projects intended to develop small industries. Nehru worried that the organized sector, whether public works or private industries, could not create sufficient employment to enroll all Indians in development. "Idle hands" could generate instability in a nation already facing dissent (Lynch 2016; Staples 1992, 50–51). The Eameses spent five months in India (Mathur 2011). During the visit, they toured the worksites of shoemakers, potters, and other artisans to understand how these Indians could be made useful for development.[7] The outcome of the visit, *The India Report*, outlined recommendations for design education in India; it is still in circulation and hotly contested among Indian design theorists (Bir Kasturi 2002; see also Mathur 2011).

The India Report held up the lota as an exemplar of what India—as a culture, as a nation, and as an accumulation of history—could produce for its people (see also Balaram 2005, 14). The lotas were common vessels, carried on heads or on hips, used for storage and transport, and fashioned out of a range of materials, including brass and clay. (Today lotas come in plastic as well.) One of Kirti's cooling vessels was a lota, transformed through wet cloth and wire ties. The Eameses singled out the lota as "the greatest and most beautiful" object they encountered while in India. To the Eameses, the lota exemplified good design: an object culturally, aesthetically, and functionally optimal. They adoringly noted its size, its strength, its volume, the center of gravity both when full and empty. They celebrated "factor after factor": fit to palm, texture, heat transfer, cost, and even value as salvage (Eames and Eames 1958, 4).

While the Eameses singularized a form—"the lota"—that exemplified the material possibilities of an Indian good life, in reality there are only lotas, made by many hands, out of different materials, and transformed and varied in the process of production. The Eameses deemed the lota as designed but by many hands across time and space: "No one man designed the lota, but many men over many generations. Many individuals represented in their own way through something they may have added or may have removed or through some quality of which they were particularly aware" (7).

The craft production processes that produced the lota, the Eameses argued, were no longer appropriate. Postpartition migration, dam projects, new communication technologies, and heavy industries were producing massive displacements: geographic, cognitive, and in ways of life.[8] India was now undergoing "a change in *kind* not a change of degree" (7). Material culture would thus need to keep pace and, in Nehru's rush to industrialize, the people and social relations that generated forms like the lota over the long term would no longer suffice. *The India Report* largely echoed how governing elites understood the new nation's modernization challenges (Mathur 2011). Pupul Jayakar, a prominent handloom advocate, echoed the late 1950s conversations with her close friend Indira Gandhi (who would later become prime minister of India):

> We spoke of the need for a flexible mind that could hold the strength and beauty of heritage yet would participate in the technological revolution. Was that possible? But on other occasions we spoke of the hard realities of the weaver, the potter, the basket maker and the need for providing solutions to the problems of the rural poor, the skilled craftsmen; to find markets and services without which the way of life of rural India could wither away. (Jayakar 1992, 150)

It was Jayakar who had first met the Eameses at the Museum of Modern Art in New York and set off the events that brought them to India (Mathur 2011). Like the Eameses, Jayakar and Gandhi saw design as a provider of solutions *for* the rural poor rather than a transformation of heritage the poor themselves could lead (Bannerjee 1998; Jayakar 1983). "Flexible minds" would find new paths to guide the poor through "hard realities" and change.

Amid this urgency to industrialize, the Eameses proposed that designers should act as a "steering device" (1958, 2), whose flexible minds could bridge heritage with technological revolution. India and its people had produced the lota, but now, the Eameses advised, India needed a cadre of design experts to steer development, industrialization, and material culture. They proposed a design institute, the National Institute of Design, that would "hasten the production of the 'lotas' of our time" (6–9). The NID would mirror the IITs and IIMs as an institution to produce experts who could steer and administer Indian modernization for their others, a population defined by Nehru as superstitious, needy, and unscientific (S. Roy 2007). These others included artisans whose skill was taken as evidence that they were tradition-bound; among upper-caste elites and to the British before them, these artisans were seen as "corporeally productive" but "conceptually blind" (Dutta 2007, 140).

In a culture that changed slowly, the Eameses argued, craftspeople rarely needed to evaluate, decide, or analyze.[9] A modern India, conversely, required a "sober unit of informed concern," trained in "all the disciplines that have developed in our time," to judiciously shape modern science and technology into appropriate cultural forms (Eames and Eames 1958, 6–7).

Taking up this charge starting in 1961, the founding faculty of the NID built on pedagogical foundations of fabled German design schools Bauhaus and Ulm[10] but extended the curriculum over the twentieth century to fit design to the problems of Indian nation building. Like Ulm and Bauhaus, NID envisioned designers as avant-garde agents of material culture. Yet unlike their German counterparts, Indian designers could not work under the fiction of national homogeneity. Faculty attempted to train designers, typically from highly educated backgrounds, to turn toward villages, slums, and rural areas as a site of attention and problem solving "with a designer's sensibility" (Ranjan 2007, 6–7; Balaram 1992). This required remaking Indian students into synthesizers, connected to "real" India but able to imagine in the medium of mass production.

NID faculty also saw everyday material culture as a site of "people's solutions" (Balaram 1992, 17)—forms that designers needed to learn to recognize, borrow, and put into wider circulation through proper designs. Designers were to steer culture by selectively harvesting the creativity people produced in their lives, adapting it, and putting it into newly valuable circulations. Postcolonial design, then, offers one a prehistory of how powerful actors selectively "harvest" the creativity of other kinds of cultural producers and put it into circulation—a phenomenon some scholars misidentify as a feature of advanced capitalism or digital networks (Moulier-Boutang 2011).[11] "People's solutions" were the ground proper designers intervened from, but "people's solutions" were by definition unarticulated, unformalized, and thus immobile. As explained by longtime NID faculty member Singapalli Balaram (1992):

> Pressed by necessity, people often invent their own solutions which may be crude but are nevertheless genuine, indigenous and functional. Milk is supplied to two- and three-story flats with a simple rope and bucket. Old buckets are revealed to become no-cost stoves. Empty benzene stoves are converted to no-cost storage bins. The appropriateness of the solution lies in the fact that people know their own problems best even though they are not always in a position to articulate them. For design this could be an essential first resource.

Just as the Eameses had respect for the lota, Balaram advocated respect for the ingenuity, resourcefulness, and fit of "people's solutions" to daily life (see also Balaram 2011, 139). People's solutions were, like jugaad, creativity out of scarcity, evidence of where design, industry, and the state could address social need through products and environments. The proper designer was the one who could read people's solutions as a "first resource" but intervene with an articulated, formalized solution that could address wider populations of users.

In contrast with people's solutions, thoughtless acts, and jugaad, proper design was a form of creativity that could register as rationally planned and conceptualized, and in a liberalized economy, valorized as a contribution to development.[12] Proper design and innovation—that performed by designers and entrepreneurs—transformed moments of necessity into market opportunities and infrastructures by bringing research and inspiration to bear on "customer needs" and transforming them into sources of financial generativity. While designers might study and empathize with the constraints, compulsions, and necessities of everyday life, and may even have deadlines and other constraints imposed by their clients, designers are not "pushed up in the corner," to recall the NID professor's explanation of the problem with *majboori*. Design was the privilege to take the time and distance to "look into the future," in the professor's words, and construct opportunities. Crucially, they had the freedom to distance themselves and think from the perspective of masses of users and whole systems. The studio and the lab offered sites of distance, contemplation, and play, not unlike the philosopher's contemplative writing table (Ahmed 2006, 3) or the ethnographer's distance from the field (Clifford 1997). Design was thoughtful action constituted through the privilege of distance and support and infrastructure: salaries that offered livelihood, studio cleaners and cooks who maintained the milieu that gave designers creative freedom, as well as manufacturing workers who materialized design ideas as actual interventions into people's lives.

If jugaad made do with what was present to make solutions for now, designers worked at a distance and with a much larger imagined reach. Designers were experts in sensing, curating, and translating people's everyday lives into forms useful for the mass production of value. They spoke the language of investors. They drew up plans that could be put to use by engineers and manufacturers. They selectively translated the world of people into terms that could make people into customers. They translated the interests of investors and manufacturers into forms that spoke to customers. Design was not just mental generativity—the ideas that matter, as the mythmaking of TED goes. It crucially depended on designers' ability to move, gather, and translate in networks of production. It relied on the privilege to translate diverse forms of creativity into scalable stories about value and development.

"Grassroots Innovation": Translating Jugaad into Innovation

Mansukhbhai Prajapati, like Kirti, made cooling vessels. Prajapati was a Gujurati clayworker whose invention, the Mitticool, occupied a position between jugaad and high design.[13] His cooling device—a refrigerator that required no electricity—captivated journalists, designers, and policy makers who wanted Indian innovation to be an inclusive project. Like Kirti's cloth-wrapped vessels, his was a clay vessel that cooled through the evaporation of water; in Prajapati's, users poured the water into the top. His vessel, however, signified modernity: it was a cabinet with a hinged door, which placed this vessel in analogy to the refrigerators sold in stores. The vessel had a Mitticool logo embossed on top. Clayworkers reproduced the Mitticool according to specification—a singularity replicated on larger scales. While Kirti made cooling vessels for her home, Prajapati and the workers in his factory made vessels to sell to masses of consumers.

Unlike Kirti, Prajapati became a national icon. He met two presidents of India. He presented at TED Bangalore, speaking in his second language Hindi with the help of an English translator. Documentarians told his story. The central government awarded him a National Grassroots Innovation Award (National Innovation Foundation-India 2016). His work had become iconic of grassroots innovation. Quite literally. A trade business book entitled *Grassroots Innovation* included a rendering of the refrigerator on its cover (Gupta 2016). Designers-in-training heard about him as an example of what Indian idioms of innovation might look like; indeed, I first learned of Prajapati and the Mitticool through a design student.

Prajapati came from a long line of clayworkers—members of a Gujurati potter caste. Potters were often paid in grain rather than money, and he and his father had left the trade to attempt more profitable forms of employment. Prajapati's career had many phases. Working in construction, he sustained an injury that left one eye blind for five years. He ran a tea stall for several years—a low-prestige job he felt brought shame to his family. He eventually found waged work in a factory for several years but left; whether the factory closed or he left in dispute is unclear (Rajan 2012, 193, 194–95).

In 1988 Prajapati decided to reenter the production of clay cookware. He drew on a variety of material resources as he set up machinery, experimented with clays, and tweaked the form to achieve the desired function based on feedback from customers. He took out a loan from a local moneylender, backed by the son of the factory owner he had worked for, in a first attempt to develop the refrigerator at higher volumes of production. He saved money by enlisting the labor and reused bricks of family members (Rajan 2012, 196–98). He sought to produce in large numbers and market the product under his own brand. By implication, he forged himself as an entrepreneurial designer, hiring laborers—other potters from his community—to produce the controlled, branded, and recognizable form as he specified it. Labor, materials, advice, loans, and credit backing from his family, from the wider potter community, and from former employers formed the basis that allowed him to spend the time and energy to forge Mitticool into a proper innovation—something that translated local configuration to a reproducible, licensable concept or plan.

Eventually, Prajapati began a partnership with a government engineer who offered investment and marketing to scale up the production of the refrigerator. When the partnership fell apart, Prajapati was deep in debt and had to sell his home to support his family (Rajan 2012, 354–55). It was in the pits of debt that agents of the Indian state stepped in to help Prajapati's project survive. A representative of the NGO Grassroots Innovation Augmentation Network (GIAN) heard of Prajapati's project and visited him, encouraging him to continue the work (Rajan 2012, 201). The state government of Gujurat provided seed funding for GIAN in 1997 (Gupta 2003), setting it up as a charitable nonprofit that converted grassroots innovations into business enterprises. GIAN, in turn, was part of the Honeybee Network (HBN), an international network of policy makers, professors, citizens, and nonprofits coordinated by Professor Anil Gupta of IIM-Ahmedabad to disseminate and advocate for rural innovations. GIAN representatives set about establishing Mitticool as a legitimate invention: they conducted a prior art search to establish its novelty,[14] they tested it to scientifically validate its thermal properties, and they filed for a patent to officially recognize Prajapati as the author of a novel and useful object (Rajan 2012, 201). It took an institution to fully translate the Mitticool jugaad—an austere invention forged through necessity—to innovation.

The trajectory of the Honeybee Network was symptomatic of the changing status of innovation as an Indian state project. Professor Gupta of IIM-A founded the network to connect "agricultural scientists, NGOs, philosophers, and ruthless critics of this initiative" (Gupta 1990, 2). HBN volunteers attempted to document and intensify rural innovation: they conducted *yatras*,[15] walking from village to village to locate and document innovations and innovators; they circulated a newsletter in English and several other Indian languages; they produced databases of traditional knowledge; and they worked with NGOs like GIAN to mentor individual rural innovators. In 2000 the central government formally took an interest in Gupta's decades of effort; it formed the National Innovation Foundation (NIF) as a section of the Department of Science and Technology and named Gupta head. The 2002–2003 budget allocated forty million rupees to various NIF projects, to patent, incubate, and license indigenous knowledge and inventions (Gupta 2003). By 2004 Gupta had won a Padma Shri, the fourth highest civilian award in India.

Through TED Talks, film, and news coverage, the Honeybee Network granted visibility and status to rural inventions. By 2017 Gupta's TED Talk "India's Hidden Hotbeds of Innovation" had been viewed a half million times and translated into twenty-six languages. The blockbuster film *3 Idiots* (Chopra and Hirani 2009) featured two inventions documented by the network: a flour mill powered by a scooter engine, and a washing machine powered by bicycle (Gupta 2010). Yet HBN saw jugaad only as a starting point: the network existed to translate works from jugaad to "grassroots innovation" that might be scaled up and produce economic value (Gupta 2016). Case studies of HBN inventors highlighted the long-term commitment required of inventors developing and honing new things. HBN dedicated research staff to document the efficacy of innovations, find business partners for rural inventors, and advise them on legal matters.[16] With the support of HBN, rural inventors made use of locally available resources, often in the face of adversity, as in jugaad, but they devoted attention and thought over the long term, as in proper innovation.

Yet rural practices do not scale up and abstract without friction (Tsing 2005). Rural inventions emerge in a different moral economy than that of middle-class designers working with "bottom of the pyramid" users. HBN researchers found again and again that the rural inventors they worked with developed their inventions in close working relations with others who also made use of the inventions. These working relations generated feedback, ideas for improving inventions, and contributions of labor and tools (Rajan 2012, 266, 290). Organizational scholar Prashant Rajan interviewed and developed case studies of twelve HBN innovators, detailing and analyzing these innovation practices. In historical profiles of HBN-affiliated inventors, he describes how inventions emerged out of close collaborative and resource-sharing relationships between

HBN innovators and those around them. The rural inventors profiled by Rajan encouraged duplication or imitation as a way of developing these working relations and extending the value of their inventive activities in others' lives. Particularly for larger farming technologies, inventions did not emerge through separated processes of design, manufacture, and consumption. The distinction between designers and their users, with manufacturers and retail as mediators, often failed to hold.[17]

This mode of invention fit poorly with conventional Indian intellectual property policies. First, rural inventors encouraged imitation of their inventions as a way of sharing and developing knowledge among their relations. Second, rural inventors lacked the expertise to make legally defensible IP claims. In response, and in collaboration with rural inventors, HBN researchers developed a compromise: an intellectual property scheme called "Technology Commons" (TC). The scheme allowed the NIF to patent inventions as a way of preventing organized firms from exploiting the invention without compensating inventors. At the same time, it allowed individual people to freely and legally draw on the patented knowledge. The informal sector was free to imitate, but the organized sector would need to compensate inventors (Gupta 2008, 85). Through this compromise, HBN and NIF tried to make innovation count for development while adapting intellectual property to nonelite norms. Gupta's TED Talk described HBN's work patenting on behalf of rural inventors but left out the TC license, an omission that missed a chance to cast the politics of TRIPS into high relief.

The commitment to invention that HBN and NIF sought to render visible created an economy of glory for inventors who had otherwise been understood to be failures as workers and as providers for their families. The valorization of innovation, however, obscured the forms of precariousness this kind of work created for those surrounding the named inventors. In Rajan's studies, inventors relied on the support of families who contributed labor, took on debt, worked steady jobs, and released inventors from family responsibilities—all to create space and time for the labors of invention (2012, 308–10). These people who provided the necessary support constituted yet another group of innovators' others. They absorbed the uncertainty generated by entrepreneurial journeys while providing material support. One innovator profiled by Rajan study earned a stipend of three thousand rupees a month with no benefits, spending much of his time working on a stencil cutter for textile workers. His parents implored him to find steady work to earn more; the inventor argued that his parents did not understand him, showing Rajan newspaper clippings about his work to explain the validity his efforts in service of community and nation (255–56). Another inventor relied on his wife's steady teaching salary so he could give his uncompensated time to invention (308–9). Yet another wife complained that her husband's pursuits left her alone with her father-in-law to work the fields (307–8).

The labor of invention required the labor of also keeping life going. These were the labors written out of innovation awards, invention patents, and most histories of invention. These labors of reproducing the household primarily fell to women who were tasked with making ends meet and mouths fed. The inventors Rajan profiled were exclusively male; this was representative of the Honeybee Network as a whole, whose innovators were also almost exclusively male, even though women constituted the majority of the agricultural labor force (Gupta 2016, 130–32; Rajan, personal communication, December 2016). Entrepreneurial risk offers a masculine story of ambition, achievement, and calculation of possible futurities (Moodie 2013, 279–80). These risks, feminist anthropologist Megan Moodie argues, impose a form of peril on those who scramble, borrow, and adapt to live through the volatilities that risky practices presuppose and produce (Ananya Roy 2010). The risks taken by the innovators profiled by Rajan can intensify the peril of their families and communities making up for the loss of predictable wages of the organized sector or even the daily, informal income of the "need economy" (Sanyal 2007).

The work of HBN and NIF is a redistributional project when set against multinationals who prospect creativity and take those to scale as innovations (Birtchnell 2013, 84). In the process, however, other modes by which creativity might move through social life—through sharing among neighbors, observation, or simply ways of doing things that emerge in two places at once— become subject to questions of origin, authorship, and control. And in the shadows of innovators' struggles and glories, families and communities adjust to the strictures of invention, improvement, and development. Even though the state, via HBN, recognized and rewarded certain forms of "grassroots innovation," its processes still reinforced the divide between proper innovators and their others: those who wouldn't or couldn't afford the investments or risks to move beyond jugaad, and those who labored to support the efforts of the recognized innovators.

The Labors of Authenticity: "Nice Work, but It Doesn't Look Indian"

Recognizable intentionality and scale were two hallmarks of proper innovation. A third hallmark was recognizable authenticity. To be recognized as properly innovating was not enough. To win contracts, funding, and prestige, Indian entrepreneurs had to conform to expectations that NGOs, funders, and partners had of what "authentic" Indian aesthetic and creative expression ought to be.

"Nice work, but it doesn't look Indian." Kamal, a lauded graphic designer and partner of DevDesign, stood on stage at the British Council auditorium in Delhi. He was addressing an auditorium full of designers, entrepreneurs, activists, and development workers at the OpenLab Festival. The festival circulated around questions of what design, entrepreneurship, and activism ought to look like in India. Far from academic, the festival featured tales from the trenches like Kamal's. Kamal was recounting how he had stood before a design jury in Europe, having been invited to apply for admission to a prestigious international design association. In judging Kamal's portfolio, panelists examined the projects he had done for varied clients, including branding, graphic design, and type layout work. Across the varied commissions, they looked for evidence of consistent underlying skill and approach—what was called "point of view" in the design profession. It was in this moment of evaluation that one panelist had commented, "Nice work, but it doesn't look Indian."

The story was far from idiosyncratic. Groans and laughter erupted from the audience. A few people even tweeted the quip, offering no context, as none was needed owing to the familiarity of the situation. A Bangalore policy analyst with a global profile retweeted it with the simple caption, "LOL." Others retweeted without additional commentary; they expected readers that mattered to them to get it based on similar histories. Many of these people lived in a world where Europeans and Americans commonly read into Asia associations of piracy, copying, and certain images of tradition (Philip 2005). The quip summoned memories of misrecognition, judgment, and an extra burden of demonstrating authenticity as an "Indian" on an international stage.

In later conversations with me, Kamal unpacked the judge's complaint: "What it meant was very obvious. Some people just wanted [my designs] to match their image of a country." He recalled reactions, particularly by foreigners: "Ah, when I go to India, India is full of color! Why is this particular project so black and white?" Exasperated by his recollections, he threw his hands up, exclaiming, "In India, we don't have holi every day. I don't see tigers every day."

The subtext of these calls to look Indian was an implicit claim that modernity—the sparse, functional, scientific form of life (Galison 1990) indexed by "so black and white"—did not belong to Indians. It belonged to Europe. Europeans understood India through their own consumption of otherness—through tourism, textiles, and histories. Before Indian independence, British textile manufacturers worked with colonial administrators to appropriate ornamental forms—paisleys, floral patterns, and tie dyes—and sell them as Indian (Lowe 2014; Mathur 2007). These legacies of commodification continued to haunt practical evaluations of contemporary Indian designers' expertise.

Indian designers' failure to perform "authentic" Indianness was often implicitly interpreted as mimicry of forms that properly belonged to Europe. One of the worst accusations a designer could make of another designer was that of mimicry. Mimicry was a legal infraction under many trademark and patent regimes, but it was also a moral one—a failure to express individual freedom of thought and will prized by liberalisms (e.g. Chumley 2016, 151; Coleman 2013). The whiff of mimicry was also present in other designerly dismissals: cliché, derivative, and unoriginal, to name a few. Recall the Eameses' *India Report*, the only development report read and republished by generations of Indians. While the Eameses celebrated the lota as authentic, they assessed most Indian architecture students as producing "an assemblage of inappropriate clichés" (Eames and Eames 1958). A British designer working for the United Nations Industrial Development Organization similarly sought authenticity two decades later when assessing NID. His UN report noted: "It is sad that the first chair I saw [designed at NID] was of Scandinavian design in itself 'derived' from an American original" (cited in Clarke 2016). Kamal's story of the European jury was thus merely one instance of a long-standing pattern.

Accusations could also come from Indian designers themselves. Kamal told me about a "very senior" design professor who had critiqued some booklets he designed to summarize four years of sanitation research among the poor. The professor had commented only on the colors, saying they were not Indian. "My god," Kamal went on, "he's totally overlooked four years of work in slums. This guy just can't see beyond layout design. I could make his version of Indian design in a few hours by using some strange geometry and make it completely meaningless." The professor's dismissal was all the more disappointing to Kamal because this was a gatekeeper who was responsible for reproducing the design profession in India.

Kamal's problems revealed both the fiction and necessity of authenticity in advancing a career in design. He diagnosed the problem as one of "reference." His European design critic was attuned to reading certain forms—straight lines, pointy corners, simple colors—as modern. The cultural geometry (Murphy 2013) of modernism hogged all the attention, drowning out the subtle variations of contemporary Indian design efforts. He interpreted that form, in turn, as being of European provenance. Kamal wanted to undo these semiotic chains, resignifying those forms so they could belong to Indians too. Because Indian designers were not documenting their forms, he continued, "There's no reference left." "There are students practicing in India," he explained to me, "and they can't reference an Indian designer's work when talking to each other. We don't document." Students were left to reference European designers as they imagined and debated the possibilities of form in their own work in contemporary India.

So Kamal and his friends and collaborators sought to "document." Specifically, they spent four years producing a book.[18] The book anthologized interviews, case studies, and histories of "design in India." A labor of craft, love, and historical intervention, it venerated unsung design elders and inserted a range of modern Indian forms into the historical record. Crucially, the team scored a foreword by a famous New York design critic. They sent copies to and sought testimonials from internationally known graphic designers, including Stefan Sagmeister. Sagmeister, famous enough to have four TED Talks, filmed a clip reviewing the book. The book sought to make it less convenient for Europeans and Americans to read mimicry of modernism anywhere they saw straight lines, corners, or black. It also sought to expand Indian students' range of "reference" to forms linked to India as nation and territory.

Less intensive practices of "documentation" were routine among designers. The book was only an extreme example. Designers videotaped and photographed their work practices. The images and films formed an archive ready to deploy for websites, final reports, and project deliverables. The images and films of work process depicted brainstorming sessions, diagrams, previous prototypes, discarded sketches—scrap bins demonstrating intention, deliberation, and prudence that made a design not an accident but an achievement. The drawings, sketches, and sticky notes typical of such depictions demonstrated that designers arrived at their proposals through systematic, intense, and thoughtful processes. Documentation often accompanied presentations of final designs to bolster the intentionality, thoughtfulness, and rationality of the process. Documentation protected designers against accusations of mimicry, accident, or luck.[19] These were the practices by which innovators produced themselves as such, in contradistinction to their others—mimics, jugaadoos, and unsystematic makers.

The Burden of Authenticity: Brand as
Pehchaan, or Believable Identity

To be recognized as innovating, some people bear a higher burden of proof than others. Kamal and his colleagues—globally connected, highly literate, and well salaried—committed significant resources to undoing Europeans' exclusive claims to a modernist cultural geometry. They forced their histories to be heard. But very few had the kinds of networks, material resources, or authority to do this kind of authenticating labor. I found echoes of Kamal's challenges with European judges in a very different evaluative encounter—a Delhi workshop to train Indian villagers in the arts of marketable craft. Here too, the authenticity of creativity was called into question.

The central government's Ministry of Tourism, in partnership with the United Nations Development Program (UNDP), had hired the DevDesign studio to run the workshop. The workshop was for participants from villages that the state had identified for ecotourism development. These programs staged villages as an immersive experience exposing tourists to craft, culture, and sustainability while generating trade for rural Indians. The studio had previously worked on similar workshops with craft organizations. Akhil, the managing director of DevDesign, had met the ministry staffer, Smitha, through a referral from mutual acquaintances; I accompanied Akhil to his first meeting with her. As they chatted about their common backgrounds and interests in a posh South Delhi cafe, they found they each possessed a master's degree in business administration. Smitha complained about her boss as a "babuconcept"—I envisioned a bureaucrat working to protocol with tea breaks rather than solving problems—saying she wanted to move on to something more entrepreneurial. Akhil described the work he did with nonprofits and the private sector, bringing management knowledge to "capacity building"—a development term whose meaning had expanded from Freirean consciousness-raising projects to a catch-all for all kinds of training (Eade 2010). Smitha approvingly noted Akhil's use of "capacity building," interrupting him to note how impressed she was: "most design firms wouldn't know capacity building."

As they discussed craft, Akhil and Smitha rarely disagreed, quickly building on one another's characterizations of the problem. Smitha explained that craftspeople needed help figuring out "quality packaging" and "making goods more contemporary." Akhil extended her point: "Craftspeople are normally very good with their material. A brass vessel maker can make brass vessels with his eyes closed. But bringing craft to embellish another environment almost requires you to see like an interior designer." Craftspeople needed exposure, Smitha argued, to know what wealthy urban and international consumers wanted.

Smitha gave the studio the contract to run the workshop.

The Saturday of the workshop, the design staff and I crammed ourselves into cars and traveled to the center of Delhi. Smitha had provided a room in a government building. The room had a stage and a large floor area where we arranged tables for groups. We assigned each table to a group visiting from the village. The day was meant not for pedagogy of the individual, but for pedagogy of the group.

As people filed in, they arranged the craft goods they produced atop the tables. These were samples of what they sold tourists. The objects included woven shawls, wooden carvings of gods and goddesses, straw mats, and table ornaments—staples of Delhi craft emporiums catering to middle-class craft connoisseurs and clueless tourists alike. These objects seemed familiar cousins to those singled out as exemplars in museums and guidebooks.

The wares atop one table broke the mold. A pile of plush stuffed animals stood out from a distance in shiny white, fluorescent green, and bubblegum pinks. These were not the natural-seeming palettes of dark greens, browns, indigos, or saffron so customary in craft markets. Nor could the textiles possibly be handwoven. The animals were squishy, plush, and synthetically colored. Their textures left no fantasy of handlooms, natural dyes, or charkha spun thread; if that smooth, furry fabric had not come from machines, it would have to have come from an impossibly laser-precise virtuoso. The shiny machine-made bags protecting each object further broke the fantasy of rural India as sustainable, precapitalist, and preindustrial. The stuffed animals did not elicit appreciation as innovation or design, however much they broke with the mold of craft production.

In a postworkshop wrap-up meeting, Kamal pointed to them as evidence of rural and, in turn, national decline: "Their craft skills are deteriorating." To senses trained by a lifetime of nationalist-inflected material culture, these seemed an example of modernization's threat to national culture as articulated by Jayakar and the Eameses. Colonial and nationalist elites alike had held handcraft as a metonym for India (Venkatesan 2009; Mathur 2007): the British tried to "revive" craft skills (Venkatesan 2009; Dutta 2007), and Gandhi upheld craft and khadi as forms of production crucial to village India. Museums, craft emporiums, and books often mapped craft techniques to region, caste, and family (see, for example, Ranjan and Ranjan 2007). Craftspeople therefore bore the burden of representing the nation as an authentic whole, constituted by its fragments (Venkatesan 2009).[20]

Craft skills seemed to deteriorate for many reasons. Cultural change and economic mobility all threatened the authenticity of craftspeople. Families tired of doing handwork for poverty income sent their children to school and middle-class careers instead. Artisans failed to appeal to middle-class tastes to which they had no everyday social access; they depended on designers and elite craft NGO workers to teach such taste expertise. The Eameses had worried that craftspeople could not properly deliberate on the technological and cultural changes swirling around them. H. Kumar Vyas, an NID faculty member writing in 1984, warned that mass media threatened the sanctity of craft: "These master craftsmen are liable to be dazzled by so-called 'modern' forms, materials, and tools, images of which are constantly bombarded by the information media" (94). Designers were to act as a "bridge between tradition and modernity" (Balaram 2011; see also A. Chatterjee 1988; 2005, 5; Thapar 1974, 1), guiding cultural change and innovation into properly national forms. Workshops were one disciplinary technology by which NGOs, governments, and design professionals attempted to steer craftspeople in desirable directions (Varma 2015). The fluorescent stuffed animals seemed a threat of modernities run amok—the kind of "indiscriminate change" and aesthetic cultural disorder Vyas warned against.

The stuffed animals made plain the burden of authenticity. They could not be recognized as proper innovation by professionals, by the Cultural Ministry, or by material culture scholars. The rural craftspeople in Delhi were, for a moment, in a situation analogous to Kamal's before the European design judges. Their intentionality and authenticity were on trial. The question was whether this producer—marked by caste, regional, linguistic, and class differences—could have intended to produce this product. Design meant producing something different, but not so different as to seem random, thoughtless, or mimicking. ("Random" was in fact a complaint I had heard designers lodge at others' work.) Kamal or another pedigreed designer might have been able to wield their cultural capital and documentary labors to resignify such work as innovative. Among the craftspeople at the workshop, none waged such symbolic battles. None had the resources to do so.

The workshop pedagogy was organized around four concepts: branding, innovation, product packaging, and price. Each concept, they hoped, would train the sensibilities of the craftspeople who, in turn, would begin to adapt their practices to create more (financial) value. The stuffed animals revealed the contradiction between two of these concepts: innovation and branding.

In their lecture, studio staff began by introducing "innovation" to the auditorium full of rural craftspeople. They translated innovation as "nya soch, nya avishkar": new thought, new invention. And innovation, the slides went on to explain, required participants "to differentiate" themselves. Differentiated products were unique products, and unique products could charge a premium as they could not easily be acquired elsewhere, so the logic went. The team translated these principles into Hindi. "Sabse alag dikhna," they explained (translation: show yourself as different from everything else). This was the ethos of the studio—of "adding value," of finding their individual and collective "unique selling points"—now as a pedagogy for craft. Innovation called on these producers to "badalte zamaane ke saath chalna," or move with the changing times. (As we prepared the workshop, neither I nor the designers discussed how these producers had already been moving with changing times, not least through their involvement with this ecotourism initiative.) Through innovation, designers taught craftspeople to focus on how to produce themselves as recognizably different to the middle-class consumer. This model was not unique to this Delhi workshop. I had seen talks by and interviewed activists who conducted similar workshops with other workers in the informal economy, such as Bangalore scrap dealers learning to organize and streamline their shops around brands, and Delhi *jhoolewale* amusement workers learning to make their mobile playground rides more appealing to middle-class city dwellers.

Branding here, however, did not necessarily imply the forms of individuation noted by some analysts of neoliberal market subjectivities (Brown 2015; Marwick 2013; Feher 2009). At the Delhi workshop, participants were not individual subjects pitted in competition with each other. Rather, the workshop accommodated logics of community built into political systems since colonialism and, later, independence. Colonial administrators and, later, the postindependence state imagined the "Indian people" as "a series of discrete and well-bounded communities" of religion, caste, and custom (Hansen 1999, 60). Crafts catalogs, shops, and "geographical indicators" built on this much older recognition and valuation of difference by family, community, and region. The workshop drew on those differentiating formations, teaching people how to translate these differences to add value. Designers learned as they negotiated how to "add value" and articulate "unique selling points" (chapter 4) between their clients, patrons, and themselves. Competitors in the neoliberal marketplace, anthropologist Ilana Gershon notes, have to be "unique in the right way: a standardized way of being talented at some set of tasks . . . that companies value" (2016, 240). The invitation to innovate was an invitation to tweak symbolic forms and material cultures while remaining within elite understandings of community, culture, and authentic group difference. The stuffed animals made plain that not all differentiation and novelty registered as value.

Innovation and differentiation ultimately took form as "brand." In planning and executing the workshop, designers debated how to translate the concept of branding into the language and lifeworlds they imagined for craftspeople. Kamal and his team were experts on brand design. For corporate clients, they often ran workshops asking executives to articulate unique and believable values and commitments that could define their firm. Designers then worked to symbolize these values in logos, letterheads, marketing campaigns, and even product strategy. Designers were semiotic engineers who tried to make distant corporations seem predictable, coherent, and familiar to potential customers (Forty 1986). The workshop asked craftspeople to understand themselves and their collectives as small corporations, crafting a story to sell about their group and producing forms and symbols consistent with that story. The team spent an hour debating how to explain brand in familiar terms. "On one level, it's certification," a studio principal explained, "and on the other hand, it's storytelling." The director, Akhil, tried to bring him down to the practical: "It's just the very mechanical act of taking an identity and applying it to everything you sell." Kritika, a product designer, and Rahul, a graphic designer, picked up on Akhil's use of "identity" and came to it over and over in articulating the significance of brand in contemporary life.

AKHIL: Everything that has that identity has similarity of purpose or—
RAHUL: —a history which is attached to it—
KRITIKA: —a cultural story. *Pehchaan.*
KAMAL: Identity has to make sense. When you say your name is Singh and you're from this area, that's believable. But Singh from Kerala is not believable.
RAHUL: Identity is who you are, where you're from, what is your history. That is your story.
AKHIL: What is your identity and what it conveys.

They finally settled on the Hindi word *pehchaan*—first suggested by Kritika—as the central translation for brand. *Pehchaan* was a Hindi word meaning "recognition."[21] In the everyday, it could mean to become familiar or acquainted. It also had legal meaning as identification, as illustrated by the fact that government-issued "voter identification" cards were called *pehchaan patra*.

The correspondence that designers saw between "brand" and "identity" was, in one sense, obvious. Graphic designers commonly spoke of "corporate identity." The exchange above demonstrated how people understood brand recognition as analogous to processes of social and political recognition. Certain identity claims were not believable, at least from the standpoint of designers working out of the capital city. For example, Kamal asserted that "a Singh from Kerala is not believable." In Indian talk of "native places," people whose families have spent generations in major cities like Mumbai, Delhi, or Bangalore might still speak of a "native place"—a more rural place where family might have owned land or to which someone might express a sense of duty. Kamal's claim rests on this backdrop linking tradition to place and modernity to Western or global circulations (Lukose 2009, 78); people often interpret Singh as a north Indian name, regardless of the mediations of capital, or migration histories, or putative miscegenations that make such simplifications problematic. Names can also indicate caste, a hierarchical system by which more powerful Indians sanction or cut off mobility, access to resources like water, and jobs for people identified as lower caste. Kamal drew on surname as a metaphor for authenticity, making clear the ways authenticity does not come from one's inner expression alone. It must be authenticated in the practices of everyday life and even in infrastructures of government.

Designers illustrated brand as *pehchaan* using examples from nation, community, and region. The first example was the Indian flag, symbolizing the nation. Another example was the red logo and stamped mask icon of the Gujurati craft brand Gurjari. Next to it was an image of a Gujurati woman dancing in a mirrored and embroidered red dress. The juxtaposition was meant to show the similarity between the logo and iconic (as determined by Google Images algorithms) ethnic dress. A third logo example was Craftmark, which represented "hand made in India"—a mark of place and labor process. The "brand" symbols marked a similarity, or identity, among things. The Gurjari logo and the Indian flag signified product qualities by asserting similarities among people—here, Gujuratis and Indians as groups associated with symbols, aesthetics, and heritage.

Brand, and here identity, not only symbolized the qualities of products (and people). It also disciplined. Kamal and his colleagues, also graphic designers at DevDesign, debated how to explain brand to trainees:

SRIRUPA: How does it [brand or *pehchaan*] help?
KAMAL: It helps build the story. It builds authenticity.
RAHUL: It builds a stronger system rather than a leaf in the wind.
MIHIR: It builds pride.

Building on each other's statements with little disagreement, these designers understood authenticity as a crucial means of making change orderly. They valued "a stronger system" rather than "a leaf in the wind" flitting along changing currents. This discipline of orderly change is core to the symbolic techniques of corporations. Brand consultants are like corporate therapists, coaxing executives into agreements about ideals a company can publicly perform to over time. Brands are open ended (Nakassis 2012, 630) but not infinitely flexible. Brands are meant to signify qualities of the "authentic" products they mark; this semiotic promise can be upheld only if corporations act in ways that are "authentic" to their brands. When middle-class designers talked to poorer Indians about brand, then, they talked about the burden of authenticity to nation, region, and social position. This discipline of orderly change was an answer to postcolonial anxieties more broadly: it represented change with continuity, rather than chaos, and design in alignment with national identity, rather than dazzled distraction by foreign modernization.[22] The studio's designers promised that the performance of authenticity offered more than belonging; it could pay.

This is why the fluorescent stuffed animals could not be recognized as innovation. To middle-class evaluators, the animals broke expectations of what was authentic for a group of rural women from a Haryana village learning embroidery and tailoring through state-sponsored projects. Government training programs wanted them to innovate only so far as it improved the value of heritage and ecotourism goods. The call to innovate was not a call to manifest their own aspirations but rather to find, manage, and fill the gaps in government specification and implementation in commodity production. Middle-class evaluators—designer-trainers, state ministry workers—acted as proxies for middle-class consumer tastes. Trained on nationalist aesthetics, they (probably correctly) imagined that people seeking to buy vibrant India would never accept such goods as its authentic product. Without utility and market acceptance, this was not the kind of cultural change that generated value at scale. Those with money to spend—in India, 10 percent of Indians controlled 75 percent of the wealth in 2014 (Callimachi 2014), with inequality increasing in succeeding years (Chakravarty 2016)—could not recognize this creativity as valuable. It fell afoul of the practices valorized as "innovation."

For middle-class professionals, branding had become a technique of entrepreneurial citizenship—a technique for managing varying forms of knowledge, meaning, and community and their conversion into value. *Pehchaan*, however, seemed more adequate than brand to describe the way value is not simply a matter of production, skill, or form; it has to be recognized in exchange. The conditions of that recognition are social and historical. People could attempt to design with customers' frames of interpretation in mind. They could attempt to tweak the terms of recognition. But no matter how skilled the designer, innovator, or craftsperson, or how passionate their aspirations and visions, the terms of recognition were largely out of their hands. Few had the resources and authority that Kamal had as he aimed to redefine the history and cultural geometries (Murphy 2015) of Indian graphic design itself. As a professional, Kamal had a wide berth to perform cosmopolitanism and Indianness, with his accent, North Indian slang, and Camper shoes. Entrepreneurial citizens were meant to eke out new ways of making a living and building a nation in the near-to-medium term; they were meant to opt for financial value over resistance, struggle, or disturbance. As they did so, they had to perform authenticity in a world where the terms of recognition were out of their hands. To learn how to add value, people had to learn to channel their experiments, aspirations, and varied lifeworlds into the narrower band of difference recognizable as value. Existing interpretive patterns and symbolic infrastructures conditioned which claims, expressions, and desires could register as authentic and which would fall short in the development of value. In practice, people called on these histories of authenticity as they routinely drew the line between innovators and their others.

Conclusion

In 2009 the government of India declared a "Decade of Innovation" (Patil 2009). Then-president Pratibha Patil addressed the opening joint session of parliament, drawing postcolonial nationalism into terms recognizable as entrepreneurial citizenship:

My Government believes that in the knowledge society in which we live today, creativity, innovation and enterprise hold the key to people and nations realising their potential. The "dreary desert sand of dead habit" must be left behind. Our young people are tearing down the narrow domestic walls of religion, region, language, caste, and gender that confine them. The nation must invest in their hope. My Government will ensure that its policies for education and science and technology are imbued with a spirit of innovation so that the creativity of a billion people is unleashed.

The promise of central government and Indian business leadership was that India was a nation of a billion entrepreneurs (see Khanna 2007), "imbued with a spirit of innovation so that the creativity of a billion people is unleashed." Anthropologist Ravinder Kaur (2016, 315) argues that jugaad stories function as ideology; they renarrate the creativity of the poor as promises and hope and mobility despite inequality. This is certainly true. But jugaad as potential sits nested in a hierarchy of creativity still below design and proper innovation. The creative energy unleashed through jugaad and people's solutions endangered the project of development.

Recall that the "dead habit" of tradition and the "dazzle" of modernity both threatened the developmental project (Vyas 1984). Since the 1950s design had offered a set of practices by which middle classes could mediate culture, economy, and change, steering mass culture by bridging the past and the future. As elites called on private citizens to innovate the nation, design's importance grew as a practice of problematizing the present and its jugaads in search of opportunity. While champions of jugaad held up its potential, renarrating the nation as a vibrant laboratory of austerity, I rarely encountered anyone who celebrated jugaad without a note of melancholy. People routinely recognized jugaad as the clever, the resourceful, and the dynamic, but it usually marked a lack—a site of desire for development. Proper innovation would marshal the energies of jugaad into orderly transformation that added value.

The state, Patil promised, would "invest in [the] hope" of young people tearing down the constraints of "religion, region, language, caste, and gender." Like the Ahmedabad education reformers championing design thinking as civic pedagogy, Patil suggested that identities were a constraint to development. The creativity coming from within individuals, unleashed, could drive development. In practice, however, creativity is not unleashed from within. It is recognized from without. Everyone knows this; brand building is precisely the exercise of making such value recognizable. But this contradiction between rhetoric and practice reveals the limitations of entrepreneurial citizenship for those who do not have the power to remake others' interpretive categories. Elite designers, such as Kamal, had to literally rewrite history in order to challenge European monopoly claims on modern styles. Crafts producers, by contrast, are supported by the state precisely to produce a certain version of heritage; designers teach them to "innovate" and "brand" in ways to valorize their labor within a historically predetermined framework. Much of their novelty cannot be recognized as design or innovation but is rather seen as a threat to the national stage play. Those with symbolic resources can attempt an "authentic" creativity that aligns self, nation, and other identities while climbing a global value chain; those without the symbolic resources to forge "authentic" creativity can chase innovation but cannot make their living in this way. Though champions of entrepreneurial citizenship claim that all lives and knowledge potentially add value, the burdens and labors of sustaining a claim to value are unequally distributed.

8

Conclusion

THE CULTIVATION AND
SUBSUMPTION OF HOPE

Calling "Anyone" to "Change Everything"

The call to entrepreneurial citizenship is global. In transnational Delhi, the state and the middle classes elaborate its forms through histories of hope, development, and statecraft particular to place, class, region, and nation. But the call to render social transformation entrepreneurial can be heard well beyond India.

I spotted an ad for Rolex watches in the *Economist* in 2014. The *Economist* is the sort of global English magazine read by policy makers, professionals, investors, and those who aspire to ascend in their professions. It promised that "anyone can change everything." The anyones pictured in the ad (figure 10) were, crucially, people of color rather than the familiar white saviors. The ad honored "five young visionaries" for their "profound impact on the world; they were the "Young Laureates" who had won Rolex's Awards for Enterprise competition. The ad visually presented the laureates as nodes in a global network, placing them on a world map in South America, Cameroon, Rwanda, the Gulf States, and India. The portraits in the ad put a face on the networks that extended from the honorees' visionary work. Together, their networks—delineated in bright hues of orange, pink, blue, green, and yellow—added up to span the globe, but through their individual projects of visionary change.

Social enterprise promises a world without poles, where elites from the Global South can be presented as icons of grassroots, South-South achievement. Historically, colonial anthropologists worked for companies or states to produce knowledge about difference in service of governmentality and extraction (Philip 2004). Knowledge constructing tradition, caste, and tribe, for example, helped render "terra incognita" navigable, exploitable, and governable. Today, entrepreneurs appeal to a wider set of patrons—

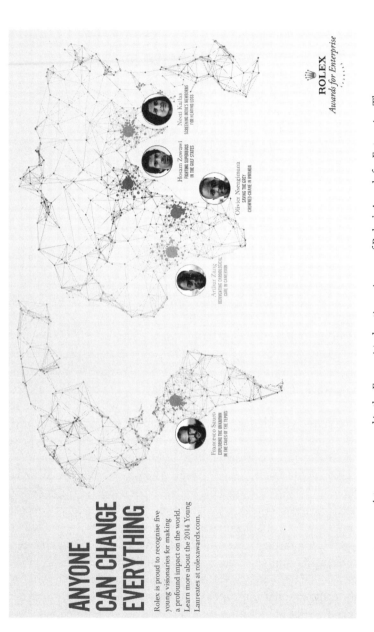

FIGURE 10. A two-page spread in the *Economist* advertises winners of Rolex's Awards for Enterprise. The ad pictures laureates' faces in different parts of the globe, connected to each other and others through abstracted, globe-spanning networks. (With special thanks to Rolex Awards for Enterprise)

financiers, philanthropies, government agencies, and companies. They too draw on applied anthropology and resource maps. But they also search themselves, their communities, and their resources to construct opportunity. Julia Elyachar argues that the idea of the "bottom of the pyramid" as a source of innovation, or "next practices," emerged in part out of critiques of development as a universal, top-down expertise. Entrepreneurs—in this case, the children of India's governing classes—appear as another postcolonial solution.

The networks depicted in the Rolex ad—globally spanning but differentiated in color—also represent former U.S. secretary of state Hillary Clinton's strategy of networked, entrepreneur-led development, in which potential threats would be transformed into generators of opportunity (Clinton 2010; see also Slaughter 2009). Anne-Marie Slaughter, a professor of political science at Princeton and ex-U.S. State Department official, described in policy journal *Foreign Affairs* a "networked century" where systems of command and control give way to supply chains and peer production "value webs." Community, collaboration, and self-organization take the place of hierarchy. Agents in the network are not individuals responsible for themselves but "manager-integrators" who link and sustain supply chains that produce value (Slaughter 2009, 97). These manager-integrators have included Indian software engineers and venture capitalists who move between India and the United States, welcomed by the government of India, to become agents of accumulation and development (Saxenian 2006; Bhatt, Murty, and Ramamurthy 2010). They have included professionals trained at Indian Institutes of Technology and Indian Institutes of Management who navigate corporate norms and Indian bureaucracy (Benjamin 2000). They have included IDEO designers who network across design scenes in Delhi, Singapore, Manchester, and Nairobi. These manager-integrators have been ideal citizens for global capital, putting postcolonial hybridity and difference to work for innovation (see Kraidy 2006; Dirlik 1997). They have learned how to add value amid turbulence and competition (chapter 4). They have translated across class, language, and expertise, drawing on skills of empathy (chapter 6) and the bias to action (chapter 5). And, crucially, these innovators have promised care for the other, not just themselves.

Absent entrepreneurship, policy makers and elites of the 2000s feared people's dissatisfied energies could become social disorder. Education reformers in Ahmedabad, we saw in chapter 2, promoted entrepreneurial citizenship as a liberalizing pedagogy in the wake of communal violence. The U.S. Department of State during the Obama administration promoted entrepreneurship as a soft power strategy to protect U.S. interests globally. Obama's speech in Cairo in 2009 announced entrepreneurship promotion, programs, and competitions as a key diplomacy and development strategy in Muslim-majority countries. A piece by then secretary of state Clinton in 2010 posited entrepreneurship as a way of producing a civilian "development community" abroad, inoculating people around the world against the temptations of terrorism by enlisting them in the promise of entrepreneurial growth (Clinton 2010). Prominent economist William Baumol argued in 1990 that all countries have some number of entrepreneurs, but those entrepreneurial people might allocate their energies to "productive activities such as innovation" or "largely unproductive activities such as rent seeking or organized crime." Cultivating and guiding the entrepreneurs, the logic went, would stabilize the networked global order.

In the Rolex ad, abstracted networks—as productively vague as a Nike swoosh—connect the depicted agents of change beyond their towns and nation-states. Are the bright, colorful lines and nodes meant to represent IT networks? Are they retail distribution chains? Are they self-help groups mobilized to sell or educate? Are they networks of friends and neighbors, mapped and organized by NGOs? All these could potentially put people and their social relationships within entrepreneurial reach. Entrepreneurial citizenship draws people's lives closer to the connective tissues of experiment, financial speculation, and accumulation—close enough to construct opportunities and experiment with enterprise. Anthropologist Julia Elyachar (2010) has shown how NGOs map Egyptian women's communicative channels—their "phatic labor"—as infrastructures for the microfinance industry. Jamie Cross (2013, 380), in his study of solar light bulbs in India, similarly found social entrepreneurs relying on NGOs as their distribution and retail infrastructure. Geographer Kasia Paprocki (2013) characterizes the ways microfinance transforms the social relations among Bangladeshi women, reshaping what social reproduction and production can look like. Projects of development appropriate and subsume social relations into projects of market development (Cross 2013, 380; Elyachar 2005, 2010, 2012).

Pedagogies of design and entrepreneurship train people to see such a world in which "everything is connected." This was true of the pedagogy of the National Institute of Design, of the Design in Education Conference, and of the workshops DevDesign taught. Seeing like an entrepreneur was to see the world as connected systems, complexity, and chaos. One TED conference in Delhi took the name "The Butterfly Effect," after the idea that a butterfly can flap its wings in one geographical location and dramatically transform weather systems around the globe. DevDesign taught students how to see at scales tiny and vast with the Eameses' film *Powers of Ten* (1968). They were "complex subjects" who oriented and acted on the world through a cosmology of complexity, systems, and connections (Maurer 1995). These pervasive imaginaries of connection were what made the Rolex ad, its networks, and its promise of networked world changing make sense.

In the assertion that "anyone can change everything," "change" is a wide-open signifier available to be filled in with myriad world-altering fantasies, from environmental activism to medical care. What matters is that, within the ethos of entrepreneurship, change is the product of a particular kind of historical agency; change comes about thanks to singular or small groups of visionaries, whose ideas circulate on the media that is other people's labor and infrastructure. Such a figure of change—the author of futures implemented by others—is prized in a post-TRIPS India. This is a world, as I showed in chapter 2, where monopolizable change—novel patents, products, and brands, for example—can be turned into money. This is the early 2000s class project of India's high-tech and pharmaceutical industries but asserted as "empowering" and "inclusive" for all (see also Varadarajan 2010). Historian Kavita Philip (2005) calls the ideal citizen of this moment in Indian political economy the "technological author"—a form of authorship celebrated and regulated in IT industries, in transnational piracy regulations, and in visions of software as freedom. This imagination of change erases and devalues the labor and infrastructures required to produce expression and culture. In this model, patents matter more than manufacture. The production of code matters more than the compilers, motherboards, or internet cables that are its conditions of efficacy (Irani 2015b; Starosielski 2015; Mackenzie 2006, 83). This model of change pervades more than just the world of digital production. I argue it has become a widespread model of change in a volatile, speculative economy that innovates and experiments in commodities and market formation.

Such a cultural imaginary makes sense of a global, capitalist way of organizing social relations and knowledge. In this world, the production of distinction promises value. Economists Derek Chen and Carl Dahlman (2005), contributors to several World Bank volumes on "knowledge economy" methodologies and innovation in India (Dutz 2007), describe the dynamics of innovation and other kinds of labor precisely in a paper on "the knowledge assessment methodology":

> Commodity production is usually allocated to lowest cost producers, but *intense competition resulting from globalization tends to drive profits from commodity production to nearly zero.* As such, it has become crucial to derive *additional value added from various means of product differentiation* via innovative designs, effective marketing, efficient distribution, reputable brand names, etc. (emphasis mine)

Even though the world will always require manufacture, competition squeezes its margins to zero. Economists, here, advise policy makers to pursue value through monopolizable difference—patents, designs, copyrights, and other defensible forms of distinction. This political economy emerges when capital can outrun rising wages in sites of production. It emerges when states allow people to earn less than it costs to live. It emerges when patents, as monopolies over form, become enforceable and tradable as objects. It emerges when information technologies make biological life a site of simulation, intensified experiment, and speculative investment (Sunder Rajan 2006). I argue that designers also make value out of life, but life here is not just biology but also culture. Designers in capitalist enterprise treat cultural processes as nature: an environment and life force to be managed and reconfigured as value.

In the knowledge economy, the production of same, similar, or natural— say, repetitive data processing (Roberts 2016), creative child care, or challenging repair work (Jackson, Pompe, and Krieshok 2011)—is a harder sell. The world requires these labors, but only innovation promises growth and market expansion. These are labors that do not produce discernable novelty, even if workers perform them differently every time (Suchman 1995, 59). On the contrary, doing these jobs well often means effacing oneself, remaining invisible, or restoring things to their taken-for-granted order (Roberts 2016; Dominguez Rubio forthcoming). By contrast, in her analysis of Silicon Valley research and development anthropologist Lucy Suchman (2011, 15) demonstrates how novelty is not a property of things but rather an account people establish: "an articulation that calls out differences from whatever is referenced as the thing that came before." New things always involve some imitation; imitations always have some difference. Yet while labors of care, maintenance, and manufacture claim small, certain returns, innovators promise the world.

The Subsumption of Hope

Global institutions promote entrepreneurialism as a way of filling the gaps left by state and industry, fueling growth and legitimating capitalism in turn. Civil society becomes an engine of enterprise, where resourceful individuals allegedly attend to the needs of the masses. As concrete practices, hackathons, user-centered design, and innovation competitions cultivate such resourceful, other-directed selves. Hackathons invite harsh critics of the state and reformist optimists to the table but leave only enough time to create minimum viable futures—the least common denominator people can agree on without resorting to a longer, slower mass politics. Design thinking invites children to imagine themselves as micro NGOs closing the last mile of state projects or reforming through affirmative persuasion rather than resistance.[1] Social enterprise competitions like Bir Sethi's Design for Change call on private citizens to turn their surroundings into laboratories of experimental development.

In the name of innovation, entrepreneurial citizenship asks people to organize and make value out of the lives of others.[2] Others might be consumers.

Others might be employees. Others might be those seen as surplus populations requiring management, uplift, and governing. Through conceptual sleight of hand and novel organizational forms, then, entrepreneurship converts surplus populations into economic potential.[3]

The practices of entrepreneurial citizenship attempt to render difference—cultural, gendered, political, whatever—generative rather than obliterate it. The political differences at the hackathon, for example, generated creative friction and were welcome so long as they did not stop the project. Intellectual property regimes structure regional differences in forms, patterns, crafts, and agriculture as geographical indicators—monopolizable difference that can be bought and sold. Entrepreneurial citizenship calls on citizens with varied needs, hopes, and histories to channel that difference into the nation-building project—the nation as accumulation—rather than allowing it to rend the nation apart.

Today, business schools promise that there is a fortune at the bottom of the pyramid, just as colonists and explorers promised fortunes in faraway lands. In pedagogies of entrepreneurialism, the fortunes at the bottom of the pyramid must be scouted, understood, and brought into connection with global capital—corporations like Grameen, Proctor and Gamble, and CitiBank. This is one reason why human-centered design was such a touchpoint for the entrepreneurs and middle-class professionals I observed working in India. It offered a vision of professional action as stewardship of innovators' others. This was a caring vision of capitalism that valorized empathy, travel, talking, listening, and mapping, processes that bring people into connection with "capitalist supply lines" (Tsing 2015, 301n2). Entrepreneurs cultivated lives of experiment, exploration, and curiosity—but directed toward problematizing the world as a site in need of innovation.

This process of problematization was not simply one of reducing everyday life to technical expertise; it was, I argue, a process of opening all aspects of life to the entrepreneurial ethos. Anthropological critiques of development have suggested that "rendering technical" is a key practice of development. Interpreting Foucault's writings on governmentality, Nikolas Rose describes rendering technical as a range of practices that represent a domain to be governed as a bounded, systematic field. Governing works by "defining boundaries, rendering that within them visible, assembling information about that which is included and devising techniques to mobilize the forces and entities thus revealed" (1999, 33). Rendering technical, then, is an assemblage of knowledge-making practices, instruments, theories, and concepts that translate the world into terms amenable to management and systematic intervention (Li 2007; Rose 1999; Ferguson 1994). Governing in the Foucauldian sense is not only the domain of states and formal governments; it is, rather, any effort to guide or steer the behavior of others. The work of steering might be done by artificially arranging things so that properly self-interested people will do what they ought to do (Scott 1995). Governmentality, then, is directed toward attaining a future state of affairs. Much "social impact," global health, and corporate social responsibility entrepreneurship attempts to guide the conduct of others. Though entrepreneurial citizens are not the state, the shrinking state relies on them to govern.

Rendering technical depoliticizes development interventions, legitimizing them to a population as rational and universal (Li 2007; Rose 1999; Ferguson 1994). While development rationality can take many forms, it has often removed deliberation from the realm of political contestation by appealing to putatively objective notions of welfare and progress. Generally, development discourses have constructed poverty in "developing countries" as a deficiency in technical means, know-how, and management strategies. Such reports and diagnoses circulate among development organizations, states, NGOs, philanthropies, and the media. These diagnoses systematically elide histories of exploitation, oppression, and uneven economic relations that account for conditions of poverty, instead suggesting that the poorer nations are at fault for their lack of proper health practices, private property arrangements, or market-structures (Li 2007; Ferguson 1994). Yet to call entrepreneurial citizenship a means of rendering technical would ignore the ways that its very promise is its inclusion of epistemic and cultural diversity, as well as affective ties, as potential resources for experiments in value.

The search for value is not only an epistemic exercise but also one that makes, draws on, and breaks social relations. In the mid-twentieth century, economist Joseph Schumpeter theorized the role of entrepreneurs as experimenters who drove the search for value, destroying some forms of life to make newly valuable forms of life possible. It was the entrepreneur, for Schumpeter, who assembled novel combinations of raw materials, others' labors, and machines to produce new commodities—new sources of value that would save capitalism from the falling rate of profit and imminent revolution that Marx predicted (see Foucault 2010, 231). Schumpeterian entrepreneurs do not only invest in themselves as human capital. They work to recognize life, social relations, and desire and draw them into sites of experimental production. This entrepreneur is far less individuated than those described by sociologists and cultural theorists of neoliberalism. This is not the atomized *homo economicus* theorists read out of Foucault—the one who invests in human capital, self-optimizes, and competes (Brown 2015; Freeman 2014; Feher 2009). Schumpeterian entrepreneurs see themselves as part of a larger social body: as interrelated with friends, family, coworkers, and fellow citizens. It is something more of the moral neoliberal that anthropologist Andrea Muehlebach (2012, 49–50) describes in Italy, the ethical citizen whose unpaid work replaces the social care of a withdrawing welfare state. But entrepreneurial citizenship economizes this sociality, translating these ties as partners, investors, customers, and supporters (see also Lindtner and Avle 2017). It asks people to reimagine these relations as resources for imagining and generating enterprise in the name of public welfare. In its obsession with proliferating investable novelty, Schumpeterian entrepreneurialism elides the contributions of those it depends on and the forms of life it seeks to displace in its cycles of expansion and destruction. This is not simply rendering technical. This is *rendering entrepreneurial*— the making of the world into a field legible as a site for improvement but in experimental forms directed by diverse capacities and knowledges of citizens. Venture capitalists and corporations stand at the ready to harvest the most successful of these experiments (see also Moulier-Boutang 2011). Like development projects, entrepreneurial projects almost always fail. But when those with capital to invest render entrepreneurial, they assume these failures as the costs of searching for value and externalize those costs to society.[4]

In this way, entrepreneurial citizenship subsumes the creativity of the social body while socializing failure. It subsumes hope. It subsumes critique, mutual aid, and desires for better, more just worlds. It disciplines hopes for the future into forms that fit existing institutional agendas through the language of "viability" and "sustainability." For Marx, subsumption was a process of absorbing life worlds into capitalist production. In his account of European production arrangements, subsumption could happen without a totalizing transformation of life, such as when a capitalist intensifies demands on guild workers but does not reorganize their production relations. In what Marx calls "real subsumption," however, capitalists take over and structure the organization of production completely, such as when they create a factory that destroys guild relationships. They create the factory that organizes bodies, machines, and time to generate and accumulate surplus value. The practices of entrepreneurial citizenship subsume in both senses: design researchers empathize with hopeful participation of Andhra villagers to generate opportunities for manufacturers without substantially reorganizing villagers' lives, but entrepreneurial citizens themselves substantially reorganize their friendships and scenes as they orient toward adding value and making their lives properly innovative.

Entrepreneurial citizenship also invites civil society to extend its reach and relations with poorer Indians, the nation's majority, as consumers. The informal economy is where the poor truck, barter, and labor to make ends meet. Indian economist Kalyan Sanyal (2007) documented how, over decades of anthropological advocacy and International Labor Organization studies, the informal economy became an object of knowledge and management. "The accumulation of capital," anthropologist Anna Tsing argues, "relies on translations in which peri-capitalist sites are brought into capitalist supply lines" (2015, 301n2). The peri-capitalist sites of the informal economy were of tremendous interest to global capital during the time of my fieldwork. Entrepreneurial citizens experimented with myriad ways to bring the vast informal economy in its diversity into connection with capitalist production, inviting the poor in as workers, as design research participants, as budding entrepreneurs, and as consumers. Entrepreneurial citizens imagined the nation as a community to be targeted for improvement, not only by the state or NGOs but by anyone who wanted to turn development into opportunity. The hope of these entrepreneurial citizens generated new experiments, ripe for corporate and financial investment. These experiments directed future-oriented hopes away from politics and into enterprises that added value.

Speculation as Politics and Resource

Scholars, not separate from the zeitgeists they study, have called for a reorientation toward futures—going beyond critique of what is toward speculation about what could be. In *Speculate This!* (2013), an anonymous collective called Uncertain Commons highlights the political import of speculation.[5] "Speculation," they write, "is essentially always about potentiality: a reach toward those futures that are already latent in the present, those possibilities that already exist embedded in the here and now, about human and nonhuman power, which is, in effect, the ability to become different from what is present." Insurance policies, risk indexes, and hedge funds work to quantify, manage, privatize, and individuate responsibility for the future. These are forms of "firmative speculation"—forms that attempt to stabilize, manage, and profit from uncertainties and futurities. The collective authors of Uncertain Commons point to "affirmative speculation" as an alternative—one that refuses "the foreclosure of potentialities" and understands aesthetic and political practices as collective, unfolding, and always more than one can recognize through cognition. Affirmative speculators refuse fixed descriptions and teleologies; they occupy themselves with futures that do not erase varied pasts.[6] Anthropologist Arjun Appadurai argues for speculation as a form of politics but maintains that speculative capacities are unevenly distributed among people. In an influential essay, "The Capacity to Aspire" (2004), he argues that the poor have less control over their day-to-day lives and thus get less practice in imagining futures and working toward them. He describes how the practices of an NGO in Mumbai cultivated this "capacity to aspire" among the poor. These practices look startlingly like the practices of entrepreneurial citizenship I have documented in this book. The NGO trained the poor in an ethos of "do first, talk later," designed prototypes of toilets they would like, and demanded those toilets of government officials in acts of political spectacle. The NGO practices are not reducible to entrepreneurial citizenship either—they make demands of the state and build collective political pressure. I caution, however, that aspiration and affirmative speculation alike can fuel value accumulation through innovation just as well as, or perhaps better than, they can subvert them.

This capacity to aspire—to desire, to intend, and eventually to *become*—is powerful. As an object of knowledge, it also becomes a resource for states, in collaboration with NGOs, to cultivate, manage, and make generative. Appadurai's "Capacity to Aspire" appeared in 2004 in *Culture and Public Action*, a collection edited by two World Bank economists who sought to demonstrate the importance of cultural processes in understanding social agency and the reproduction of inequality. The volume approached culture as symbolically mediated relationalities—meaningful relations negotiated among people in the practice of daily life (Rao and Walton 2004, 4). Ten years later, the concept of aspiration again seemed on the rise at the bank. An anthropologist (and physician), Jim Yong Kim, was at the helm. The *World Development Report* (World Bank 2015), a key artifact of the bank's epistemic agendas, was subtitled *Mind, Society, and Behavior* and acknowledged anthropologists and sociologists as contributors. But the report domesticated aspiration as a mental "scheme of meaning" (12) to be nudged and manipulated, rather than the substance of political action. The bank's job would be to manage aspiration by organizing institutions, pedagogies, and nudges so that targets of development would do as they ought.

Anthropologist Purnima Mankekar notes the dangers of rendering aspiration liberatory in her book *Unsettling India* (2015), arguing that neoliberalism in India operates precisely by cultivating aspiration along the lines of global value chains through films, work trainings, and the cultivation of consumption. Anthropologist Jamie Cross (2014) traces how managers and administrators of capitalist projects—a Special Economic Zone and a diamond factory, specifically—enlist participants by negotiating people's aspirations and anticipations: investors' expectations of returns, workers' hopes for mobility, and villagers' need for income. The contemporary moment makes virtue out of anticipation, displacing sciences of "the actual" with speculative forecast (Adams, Murphy, and Clarke 2009). Concrete devices like insurance policies, real estate investments, education exams, microloans, marriage, stock options, and design studios all form the devices that structure how people imagine sociality, opportunity, and possibility (Vora 2015; Patel 2006).

Economic theory too has theorized the need to structure people's speculative capacities. In 1990 economist William Baumol authored a paper, cited over five thousand times, entitled "Entrepreneurship: Productive, Unproductive, and Destructive." I came to the paper when a World Bank India specialist,

Mark Dutz, cited it in a talk in 2013 on "measuring innovation" given to experts in Jamaica. Dutz had himself edited a World Bank book called *Unleashing India's Innovation* (2007). Baumol, and Dutz with him, theorized entrepreneurship as the allocation of talent and energy. Baumol's paper (1990, 896) adopts Schumpeter's model of the entrepreneur as the one who introduces a new good, introduces a new method of production, opens up a new market, or manages "the conquest of a new source" of production inputs. To Schumpeter's account, Baumol adds technology transfer to explain why entrepreneurs make economies more productive. Entrepreneurship, in other words, can span invention, extraction, and empire. But not all entrepreneurs, Baumol warns, do this productively. Among those with entrepreneurial talent, he argues, some become criminals, some become rent seekers, and only some become productive innovators. The implication is that private enterprise has no bias to proper innovation; bias to transformation must be marshalled and directed. Dutz, the World Bank economist, elaborated the implications of Baumol's argument in his policy talk in 2013. "You know, most countries have entrepreneurs. Probably, you know, it's genetically determined. Some people are better at it than others. Some people are better at *not* being entrepreneurs," Dutz explained to the audience. In this extemporaneous aside, he revealed an assumption Baumol never wrote—that the difference between those with entrepreneurial talent and those without could be determined through biological inheritance; eugenic ideologies haunt the difference between innovators and their others. Though entrepreneurs *could* in principle lurk in any class or place, not everyone had entrepreneurial talent. The job of policy makers would be to set up policies so that those with talent would thrive and allocate their talents for the good of society. Policy makers would thus be tasked with structuring an environment that would direct, channel, and nudge the entrepreneurial and nonentrepreneurial alike into economically productive arrangements. For economists like Dutz, economic policy ought not to block entrepreneurial freedom but rather channel it to make it productive rather than destructive.

To a global system governed by postcolonial sensibilities, speculation and aspiration seem at once democratic and economically productive when they become entrepreneurial practice. Entrepreneurship appears to express popular desire while also channeling that desire for value. The entrepreneurial ethos harvests these desires, channeling ethical, cultural, and moral norms—empathy, uplift, and care—toward the production of innovation. As I observed, education reformers and hackathon organizers pushed people to notice what bothered them about the world and redress it through a "bias to action." Middle-class Indians picked up and evangelized methods like design thinking, hackathons, skill shares, and user testing, in dialogue with philanthropies and corporations whose techniques of organizing innovation were also taken up in Silicon Valley. Google, Ashoka, Acumen Fund, Facebook, and global media proliferated images of democratic participation that also looked like innovative work. In Delhi, Ahmedabad, Bangalore, and beyond, these venues of entrepreneurial citizenship taught people to translate the injustice around them into programs, products, and services by which the private sector could address public desire. They encouraged people to "problematize" in ways amenable to instruments partners had at hand (Sims 2017, 173; Li 2007). These projects proliferated opportunities for investment, rendering the world entrepreneurial.

Amid all the calls to innovate, my feminist tools for situating knowledge, proliferating voice, and enlisting participation seemed to fall short. Entrepreneurial citizenship accommodated and even benefited from these attempts to include. What gave me pause, rather, were the very ways civil society—in the form of design, hackathons, and workshops—organized participation to proliferate innovation rather than more demanding forms of inclusion, redistribution, or transformation. Entrepreneurial citizenship put civil society—including even its more critical voices—to work for experimental value generation. As it did so, it also served as what ethnographer Christo Sims (2017, 170) calls a "buffer zone" of politics. Writing about innovation in U.S. school reform, Sims argues that these buffer zones of techno-idealism help "absorb and fix volatile energies while leaving the source of those volatilities intact."

Venture capitalists, philanthropies, and nonprofits like Acumen Fund directly encouraged innovation and stood ready to selectively cultivate the most promising seeds from this entrepreneurial ferment. Design thinking pedagogies and practices encouraged people to locate their potential in what made them unique—where they "added value," as I detailed in chapter 3—rather than in what they shared in common with those whose lot they sought to improve. Design thinking certainly didn't encourage would-be entrepreneurs to see how they were complicit in the oppression or dispossession of others. Design thinking taught the skills of empathy, optimism, experimental openness, and complex systems analysis; it channeled those skills toward projects that generated novel lines of flight but occluded the possibility of solidarity building, oppositional politics, or even politics that destroy value.

Gatekeepers—investors, funders, and potential collaborators—subjected the designs of entrepreneurial citizens to tests of authenticity and innovation. To make futures, innovation had to be recognized by those who could invest projects with resources. Recall that Kamal, a graphic designer, met with critiques that his work seemed derivative because those evaluating the work arrived with expectations about which forms could authentically emerge from Indian places and bodies. Kamal and his colleagues at the design studio, as I showed in chapter 5, arrived with similar expectations when they interacted with poorer Indians, judging craft projects according to their fit with heritage.

Designers and investors marked some acts of making as innovation, constructing them not only as novel but also as appropriately authentic to the producers of the acts. The history of design, patents, and trademarks is a colonial and racialized history of labeling certain forms of creation as illegal, immoral, or mere repetition since time immemorial. "Innovation" smuggled this racial and colonial history of culture and knowledge into the conditions of valorization by which Indians could gain recognition and climb global value chains. This history and context undercuts the optimistic claim that "anyone" really can "change everything."

On this highly unequal terrain of future making, entrepreneurial citizenship has called on people to channel their energies and becomings only toward the production of value. Let us instead find ways to speculate collectively in ways that dismantle oppression as we imagine and build.

NOTES

Chapter 1. Introduction: Innovators and Their Others

1. I work in a long tradition of HCI that debates how computer systems design was implicated in reconfiguring power relations among workers, management, end-users, and designers. Informed by feminist and labor analyses, Lucy Suchman has persistently argued that HCI often represents managerial ideologies of personhood (1994, 2007; Suchman and Bishop 2000). Participatory design scholars collaborated with Swedish trade unions to support worker-centered technological change in the labor process (Bansler and Kraft 1994; Kensing and Blomberg 1998; Muller 2003). Another set of approaches, informed by philosophy and science studies, developed methods for making values explicit in the design process. Value sensitive design offers a method for identifying stakeholders affected by a technology project, identifying benefits and harms to stakeholders, mapping those tradeoffs to fundamental values (e.g., privacy or freedom), and making technology design decisions that support stakeholders' values (e.g., Friedman 1996). Values in design advocates argue that policy makers and citizens must evaluate emerging technologies on the basis of the values they manifest and intervene in design and policy according to explicit value commitments (Nissenbaum 2001; Knobel and Bowker 2011). Design scholars have argued for design processes linked to particular political theories, such as feminism (e.g., Bardzell 2010) or agonistic democracy (DiSalvo 2012).

2. Part of the Indian nationalist argument for independence from the British was mounted in cultural terms—that India had its own culture and languages (Chatterjee 1993). After independence, national elites debated how to create a way of life at once modern and distinctly national, attempting to unite the nation's many linguistic and cultural groups as India while decolonizing India from British influence (S. Roy 2007; Zachariah 2005). In the 1960s, for example, a group of cultural elites called for the development of a "design for living" suited to India and the newly decolonizing, nonaligned world (Prashad 2008). The group included architect Charles Correa, activist and friend of Indira Gandhi Pupul Jayakar, and Delhi publisher Romesh Thapar. This vision reached beyond economic integration, warning that India should not mimic Western industrialism, emulating its alienated labor and mechanical aesthetics. Instead, they called on educated and cosmopolitan Indians to develop a humanistic "standard of living"—a design of objects and environments in which the new person could flourish.

3. Rogers's model of diffusionism was key to modernization theory from the 1960s on; it proposes innovation as a process by which an invention moves through channels over time among members of a social system (Rogers 1983, 11; for a critique, see Philip, Irani, and Dourish

2012, 12). Diffusionism had earlier roots in the theories of French jurist Gabriel Tarde, writing at the turn of the twentieth century and taken up enthusiastically by Bruno Latour and others a century later (Latour and Lépinay 2010).

4. This analysis of entrepreneurialism as a relationship between innovators and their others emphasizes how entrepreneurialism is much more than an individuating project of the self. As a project of *the self*, entrepreneurialism can entail personal respectability (Freeman 2014), transnational capitalist mobility (Ong 1999), the bearing of risk (Moodie 2014; Neff 2012; A. Roy 2010; Adams, Murphy, and Clarke 2009), or appreciation of one's human capital (Feher 2009; Rose 1999). These studies often analyze the subjects produced by diverse and emergent neoliberal governmentalities (Foucault 1982, 1991, 2010). This reorganization of the self, I and others argue, also reorganizes myriad social relations—between self and varied social collectivities (Nguyen 2017; Avle and Lindtner 2016; W. Brown 2015; Lindtner 2014), gender relations (Yurchak 2003), and labor relations (Irani 2015a, 2015b).

5. Only in 2005 did the Citizenship Act expand diasporic eligibility to most countries (Varadarajan 2010, 138).

6. The nation's two bodies powerfully appear as economic statistics documenting the unevenness of its robust economic growth statistics; while the GDP has grown year after year, women, lower castes, and people in certain states have seen far less of the aggregate growth (Kannan 2007).

7. For poverty's threats to India's brand image, see member of parliament and diplomat Shashi Tharoor's "India Super Poor, Not Super Power," (2011). *Deccan Herald*, November 18, 2011, https://web.archive.org/web/20120119142058/http://www.deccanchronicle.com/channels/nation/south/india-super-poor-not-superpower-says-shashi-tharoor-244. At Davos 2012, diasporic venture capitalist Asha Jadeja (2012) argued that "I have this view of taking the poverty in India and lack of institutional structures as a huge plus."

8. Chatterjee (2004) theorizes the two Indias as civil society and political society: first, relatively elite members of *civil society*, that domain with the resources, literacies, and social status to substantively access the rights, protections, and political channels of the liberal democratic state, and second, *political society*, or the majority of Indians who fall outside of what bourgeois law can recognize. These masses become the targets of state projects of development, both in pedagogies of citizenship (see Sharma 2008; Cody 2009; Hull 2010) and through state attempts to restore limited means of livelihood to them. They work within, through, and around the categories of development to mobilize around their needs, whether food, water, education, access to space on the street.

9. Sanyal's argument directly responds to feminist economist J. K. Gibson-Graham's (2006) conceptions of alternative economies as forms of difference not subsumed by capitalism.

10. I take up modernity here as a cultural phenomenon—not as a universal but as something people interpret and pursue as real in varied ways from place to place (Ferguson 2003; Pigg 1996). People have long contested what counts as modern, but in the contesting they contend with ideas of modernity as, for example, located in Europe and the United States, as manifest in science and technology, or as secular (Gaonkar 2002; Pigg 1996, 163–65). The Indian nationalist movement argued for independence in part by claiming that nationalist elites, not the British, were the rightful stewards to usher India's masses into modernity (Zachariah 2005).

11. I assign pseudonyms throughout the book to protect the identities of those whom I observed and worked with in private settings.

12. During my fieldwork, government corruption protests broke out in Delhi, primarily among middle-class constituents (Khandekar and Reddy 2013). Studio members were moved by these protest call for political transformation but also tended to reject the movements' call for a powerful, singular arbiter of corruption and political morality.

13. Only 4 percent of Indians between the ages of eighteen and sixty-five spoke English fluently in 2005, and those fluent speakers were primarily members of the upper castes (Azam, Chin, and Prakash 2013).

Chapter 2. Remaking Development: From Responsibility to Opportunity

1. I join other scholars, including Ravinder Kaur, Paula Chakravartty, and Sreela Sarkar, who examine how entrepreneurship and innovation reimagine forms of community, work, and development in liberalizing India. The contribution of this chapter is not to repeat their work but to locate these developments through a history of legitimation and production practices among political elites, industrial elites, and experts so as to avoid collapsing these into a singular, pervasive imaginary.

2. The absence of interest in entrepreneurs among planners was not for lack of effort by American academics and foundations. In the 1950s and 1960s Harvard psychologists funded by Ford Foundation conducted studies to identify markers of "entrepreneurial" propensity and "achievement motivation" among peasants (McClelland 1961; see also Nandy 1972 for one critique). These studies seemed to have little impact on planning and policy making at the central government level.

3. In 2017 the Modi government announced that PIO status would be merged and superseded by OCI (S. Pal 2017).

4. Those with ancestors in Pakistan, Bangladesh, and a changing list of other countries are excluded from PIO and OCI.

5. I. da Costa Marques (2005) notes that Apple lobbied through the U.S. government to change Brazil's patent regime to guarantee a monopoly over Apple-compatible computers. This case shows how Apple disregarded distinctions in hardware-level design between Apple and Apple-compatible computers, instead declaring a monopoly over any compatible equivalents.

6. Extensive critiques of culture and knowledge as property were brushed aside in this move to make the poor authors of IP (see Philip 2006; Sunder 2006, 292). For critical accounts of the aftermath of IP in poorer countries, see Hayden (2010) for accounts of the politics of bioprospecting in Mexico, Boateng (2011) for the way IP distorted social relations among textile producers in Ghana, and Chan (2013) for the intensification of artisan exploitation with the rise of cultural property regimes in Peru.

7. See the work of business historian Jason Jackson (2013) for an examination of how state actors make moral distinctions among domestic, family firms, high-tech firms, and foreign capital along axes of "traditional/modern," and "productive/unproductive."

8. McKinsey & Company is a management consulting firm with strong ties with the Indian government as well as the World Bank. The state and central governments in India hire the firm to write policy prescriptions (see, e.g., Wyatt 2005; Mazzarella 2010a).

9. See also "CII Meet Focuses on IPR Issues" (2003); "India Should Implement IPR Laws" (2003); "Spread Quality Wave" (2003); and Our Bureau (2003b, 2003c).

10. Approved incubators are nonprofit but can take equity in the start-ups they incubate as part of their sustainability model. Corporate investors such as Mahindra not only make CSR grants to incubators but can, through the incubators, develop equity investment relations with start-ups (#startupindia n.d.; Hariharan 2015). Companies, public institutions, and entrepreneurs structure their organizational forms to manage and take advantage of different nonprofit and for-profit regulations (Gabriel, Engasser, and Bound 2016, 24).

Chapter 3. Teaching Citizenship, Liberalizing Community

1. Narendra Modi, when chief minister of Gujarat, responded to economic liberalization by branding Gujarat for foreign investment. In the wake of the 2002 riots, the state launched the Vibrant Gujarat Investors' Summit (Bobbio 2012).

2. For center and left examples of this position, see Bhan (2015) and Nussbaum and Chaudhury (2008). I met middle-class Modi voters who held this position as well.

3. Arundhati Roy, Booker Prize–winning author, alter-globalization activist, and prominent critic of Indian capitalism, was one such maverick designer. She began her career as a student at the School of Planning and Architecture. One of her early breakout films, *In Which Annie Gives It to Those Ones* (1989), narrates the optimism of wanting to bring about a better, different world and the disappointment at the strictures of existing design and planning work.

4. Joshi's disciplinary transition from engineering to the arts is also documented in Menon (2010).

5. Bir Sethi located her changemakers in a world where political scientists and policy experts saw networks cutting across nations. Hillary Clinton's foreign policy writings (2010) and USAID policy (2012) at the time called for a world that generated partnerships among citizens rather than stopping at aid relations or diplomacy across nations.

6. Intuition and the limits of rational logic have a long history in design theory. Lazslo Moholy-Nagy, a design professor of the Bauhaus and then Illinois Institute of Technology, articulated a theory of "organic functionalism" that called for designers to gather information about a design problem in diverse disciplinary terms and then reach syntheses by intuition. Intuition was required because the complexity of the design problem exceeded the possibilities of accountably rational, sequential logic (Findeli 1995).

7. The labor of action is a concept developed in conversation with Niloufar Salehi and others through engaged design work. See Salehi, Irani, and Bernstein (2015). McKinsey consultants Tom Peters and Robert Waterman, Jr., coined the term "champion" to describe that "pragmatic" individual who "bullheadedly pushes ideas to fruition" within organizations, driving innovation. In place of large research and development divisions, Peters and Waterman advised "armies of dedicated champions" and "small units with turned-on people" (1982, 207). Chapter 5 addresses the influence of these ideas on entrepreneurial subjectivities.

8. This conception of design goes back at least as far as 1940s to the models developed by László Moholy-Nagy, influenced by pragmatist John Dewey (Findeli 1995, 39–40) and the Bauhaus Foundation Course, which also provided a basis from which NID developed its Foundation Course.

9. I thank Akshay Roongta for help with this translation.

10. Author's interview with Ashish Rajpal, February 4, 2012.

11. Aurobindo's ideas also shaped Silicon Valley's own new age practices. The founder of the Esalen Institute, Michael Murphy, followed Aurobindo from Stanford to India and returned to Northern California to found a space to develop the techniques of the self-actualizing, democratic character (Kripal 2007, 151). At Esalen, yogis, encounter groups, and psychologists of creativity intersected to do the spiritual work of making Silicon Valley countercultures.

12. In *On Labour*, Gandhi wrote that "when labour comes to fully realize its strength, I know it can become more tyrannical than capital. The mill-owners will have to work, dictated by labour, if the latter could command the intelligence of the former. It is clear however that labour will never attain to that intelligence. If it does, labour will cease to be labour and become itself the master. The capitalists do not fight on the strength of money alone. They do possess intelligence and tact" (quoted in B. Chakrabarty 2011, 66).

Chapter 4. Learning to Add Value at the Studio

1. M. Alvesson (2001) explains this as a predicament of expert consulting work more generally. Firms often hire expert consultants precisely for knowledge they lack. Consultants who cannot demonstrate their expertise directly must rely on symbolic performances such clothing and shop talk.

2. Kalyan Sanyal (2007) argues that the Indian state works with an assemblage of international and civil society organizations to manage India's surplus populations and reverse the effects of primitive accumulation. These governance assemblages help legitimate the Indian state by blunting the worst effects of capitalism. Entrepreneurial citizenship, then, need not directly seek profit to participate in the work of development.

3. This shift from beauty to social management tracks a wider shift in design from aesthetic education to systems approaches. Architect and historian Arindam Dutta (2007) documents how liberal reformers saw aesthetic education as a way of uplifting workers and colonial subjects. These aesthetics were disinterested, objective, universal Western aesthetics. In later work, however, he traces a shift in 1960s architecture centered at MIT to a "technosocial" moment where designers seek to improve the performance of a social system by producing *relevant* expertise—expertise that is not universal but rather responsive to the environment. This is a prehistory of human-centered design, brainstorming, crowdsourcing, and hacking.

4. The celebration of scale and the disavowal of working with contractors implied a hierarchy borrowed from the corporate executive suite in an age of speculative investment. The foundation wanted to produce the promising strategy, but the time-intensive labors of maintaining political buy-in, digging sewer lines, and making an infrastructure that sits well with people was too much of a tangle. It made sense that the foundation, based in the United States, would not know how to manage the on-the-ground details. But it also refused to fund this work unless it would serve as a model replicable for development elsewhere.

5. In her study of American job seekers, Ilana Gershon (2016, 236) finds that employment coaches tell seekers to identify what makes them unique to impress potential employers. As Gershon points out, the thing that makes a person unique may not make him or her saleable. DevDesign staff members selectively cultivated and narrated aspects of themselves *and* the studio as "unique selling points" in specific reference to those they perceived as competitors.

6. The Hindi language includes grammatical constructs by which a subject can claim agency over the work of others. *Main banati hum* indicates "I build," while *Main banvati hum* indicates "I have it built."

7. Elsewhere (Irani 2015a, 2015b) I have argued that the necessity and disavowal of such labor makes systems of interfaced labor such as Amazon Mechanical Turk appealing to entrepreneurial high-tech workers.

8. Though American English speakers understand "peon" as an insulting designator, the word is used in professional contexts in India to refer to an employee who carries out odd jobs around the office. Storekeepers, for example, post signs in their windows notifying passersby that a peon position is vacant inside.

Chapter 5. Entrepreneurial Time and the Bounding of Politics

1. On a corporate webpage dedicated to women in computing, Google attributes the adage "It's better to ask forgiveness than permission" to early computing figure Grace Hopper. In the context of systematic underrepresentation of women, African Americans, and Latinos in the upper echelons of high-tech work, the adage celebrates minorities in high-tech as intrepid fighters, drawing attention away from systematic inequalities in hiring, merit evaluation, pay, and valuation of labor (Tiku 2017; Irani 2015b).

2. Ajit took inspiration from psychedelia and California counterculture, citing the 1969 Trips Festival as an inspiration. He saw LSD, music, conference talks, and condensed sociality equally as mediations for collectively transforming individual consciousness.

3. Occupy names a wide range of social movements that made global news and captured the public imagination in 2011 (see Schneider 2013). Occupiers took over public space in cities across the world to make a claim to it and to practice prefigurative forms of democracy that threw into question the legitimacy of financial capitalism and those who benefit from it.

4. Anthropologists have also taken up the question of prototyping as a practice particularly amenable to prefigurative politics (Corsín Jiménez 2014) and cosmopolitics (Wilkie 2014). Those conversations have emerged from a globally diffuse sense of dissatisfaction that similarly generated Occupy and calls for inclusive entrepreneurship. Though anthropologists and entrepreneurs have differing commitments to political theorizing, their commitments to the production of hope overlap. Chandra Mukerji argues that this hope that one might have agency over history—variously figured in different locations and times—defines what it is to be modern (2017).

5. Rosalind Gill and Andy Pratt (2008) note that post-Fordist workers often take pleasure in their work but criticize Marxist autonomists who see these pleasures as a sign of communist potential embedded in forms of affective and communicational labor. Instead, they call for pleasure to be theorized as a disciplinary technology in relation to the displeasures of work. Nick Dyer-Withford (2001) and others critique formulations of post-Fordist work that erase the work distanced in the supply chains and factories of the global South (and the global North, as Foxconn moves to the United States and eastern Europe [Sacchetto and Andrijasevic 2015]). This chapter traces how the pleasures of entrepreneurial work are tied precisely to the exclusion and erasure and distancing of those necessary but not likeminded others—manufacturing workers, those who produce the layers of code infrastructure, or those who might be called on to implement or maintain these systems. The creative pleasures of brainstorming and

imagining software were predicated precisely on the availability at a distance of those workers to whom we might outsource less pleasurable aspects of work. Pleasure was not only a technology to discipline the self but also a technology that predicated the making of other workers into infrastructure.

6. Despite India's global visibility as an English-language service exporter, English skills were rare. Only 4 percent of Indians between eighteen and sixty-five spoke English fluently in 2005, and those fluent speakers are primarily members of the upper castes (Azam, Chin, and Prakash 2013). The English language of this hackathon—that rare and casted skill in India—is the lingua franca of the international software "world of practice" (Takhteyev 2012).

7. Echoing Green Foundation, founded by a venture capitalist, runs annual competitions to identify, mentor, and network social entrepreneurs (Porter and Kramer 1999). Though based out of New York, it has global reach. Vivek from DevDesign, for example, went on to compete in Echoing Green.

8. Facebook rebranded its Internet.org initiative as Free Basics several years later. Free Basics offered Indian consumers free internet through their phones as long as they were accessing sites blessed by Facebook. A year after the launch, India's Telecom Regulatory Authority (TRAI) declared this violation of net neutrality illegal (Shahin 2017). The hackathon revealed the investments Indian civil society and high-tech entrepreneurs have in accessing India's poor without Facebook as the gatekeeper.

9. The history of design is more transnational than it might seem to those who ask whether design moves from Europe to the "rest of the world"—a question I once asked in graduate school as well (Irani et al. 2010). Historians Saloni Mathur (2007) and Arindam Dutta (2007) document the way design emerged as a form of knowledge about ornament and form in relation not only to industrial capitalism but also to colonial capitalism. The Eameses traveled to India in the 1950s to consult with the postindependence government in how to set up a school of design. NID was one product of this transnational circulation of postcolonial cultural politics and cold war expertise (Mathur 2011).

10. Peters and Waterman published the book as consultants at international management consulting firm McKinsey & Company. McKinsey acts as a key broker, publishing and dictating best practices for corporations and governments. McKinsey clients include major corporations and even the governments of Andhra Pradesh (J. Cross 2014) and West Bengal (S. Sarkar 2014).

11. This pragmatism is common in Silicon Valley sites of technology production as well. In his ethnography of a Silicon Valley virtual reality company, Thomas Malaby (2009) also identifies an organizational ideology that valorizes labor that moves projects forward as compared to labor that maintains and repairs existing projects.

12. The politics of the poor in India are often cast as being outside of proper liberal norms of democratic engagement, whether by exclusion, by cultural difference, or because of complex interactions between the material processes and histories of governmentality (Anand 2011; Hansen and Verkaaik 2009; Chatterjee 2004). These accounts often describe the politics of the poor animated through political patronage, protest, and legal informality. Vijayendra Rao and others counter that this image of the poor erases deliberative civic processes through institutions like self-help groups and *gram sabhas* (Rao and Sanyal 2010). Some scholars also point out that the Indian middle classes also acquire resources through informal and illegal means

(Truelove and Mawdsley 2011). My fieldwork does not intervene in this debate but rather analyzes middle-class figurations of popular politics and how those figurations undergird the practice of entrepreneurial civic action.

13. I am indebted to Karl Mendonca for pointing this out to me. Delhi-based artists and theorists Raqs Media Collective (2009) theorize biennales—ephemeral events repeated over the long term—acting like millions of earthworms mining, churning, and composting "cultural soil." As they churn and compost, they slowly transform the structures of cultural production. This transformation need not be innocent.

Chapter 6. Seeing Like an Entrepreneur, Feeling Out Opportunity

1. Grameen Bank, founded by Nobel laureate Muhammed Yunus, popularized the idea of the poor as borrowing investors to be served by microfinance (see A. Roy 2010, 23–25). According to economists Abhijit Banerjee and Esther Duflo (2011b, 207), Yunus, together with C. K. Prahalad, forged the idea of the entrepreneurial poor, "securing a space within the over-all anti-poverty discourse where big business and high-finance [felt] comfortable getting involved."

2. As a fair-skinned Iranian American, I benefited from being read as white in India as social practices in everyday life and in development practice were often subtly organized to privilege fairer-skinned persons (Redfield 2012). As a person of Iranian parentage, however, I was coded by the U.S. and Indian governments as a potential threat as I moved through visa acquisition and other travel checkpoints.

3. "With 58% Figures, India Tops in Open Defecation," *Times of India*, October 2, 2011, http://timesofindia.indiatimes.com/india/With-58-figures-India-tops-in-open-defecation /articleshow/10200781.cms.

4. "Bill Gates Meets Narendra Modi, Lauds Focus on Sanitation and Banking for Poor," *Economic Times*, September 14, 2014, https://web.archive.org/web/20140926010153/http:// articles.economictimes.indiatimes.com/2014-09-19/news/54108891_1_bill-gates-prime -minister-narendra-modi-swachh-bharat; Manu Balachandran, "Is Narendra Modi Losing the Battle of Toilets to Manmohan Singh?" *Quartz India*, January 13, 2015, http://qz.com/324877 /is-narendra-modi-losing-the-battle-of-toilets-to-manmohan-singh/.

5. BMGF calls this "catalytic philanthropy" (Social Research Unit 2011; Kramer 2009)—a model of philanthropy in which donors set agendas and coordinate funding and meetings to shepherd civil society, the private sector, and states in desired directions.

6. Anil Gupta, champion of rural innovation and founder of the Honeybee Network, implicitly acknowledges the fetish of scale when he criticizes it in his own work. Citing the "persistent fallacy of measuring the merit of every innovation on . . . scale," he wrote that "the long tail of innovation implies that not all innovations will achieve scale" (2016, 341). Gupta's organization still helps "scale up" inventions, but he eschews the maximal ambitions of financial investors and development experts.

7. HCD broadly names a set of practices and organizations that center anthropological and psychological understandings of people in design processes. HCD practitioners and debates often move through HCI, user experience, and design venues, drawing ideas, practices, and people across these divides. This chapter narrates shifts in design epistemology through HCI

because of the outsized influence of technology companies like Google, Microsoft, and Amazon on the labor market, in ideology production, and in other sectors, including development.

8. Scandinavian participatory design (PD) movements began as an exception to the trajectory of HCI from man-machine systems, to human information processing, to users practices as embodied and cultural. Scandinavian PD grew out of the concerns of workers and system designers that computerization deskilled and disempowered workers (Bjerknes and Bratteteig 1995). In response, PD called for worker empowerment at three levels: design, labor process, and the law (Kensing and Blomberg 1998). In the United States, "participation" became apolitical and turned into an interest in contextual meaning and practice in design (e.g., Holtzblatt and Jones 1993). Without institutional mandates to shape software decisions, U.S. worker participation provided management with information and enhanced buy-in but failed to radically reshape workplace systems agendas (Beck 2002; Kensing and Blomberg 1998; Bansler and Kraft 1994).

9. In an orientation binder at DevDesign, HealthWorks had included one business book that vividly illustrated this opportunity seeking as Blue Ocean Strategy (Kim and Mauborgne 2004). Red oceans were those where sharks had already hunted prey, bloodying the waters. Businesses, the book advised, ought to seek blue water opportunities where others were not hunting.

10. Faste Foundation, http://www.fastefoundation.org/about/zengineering.php.

11. See A Communications Primer" (Eames and Eames 1959), a film sponsored by IBM for an articulation of these ideas. The filmmakers credit eminent computer scientists and mathematicians of the day, including Norbert Weiner, John von Neumann, and Claude Shannon, for "ideas, direction, and material."

12. "A Changemakers' Guide to Storytelling," changemakers.com, https://www.changemakers .com/storytelling; "Storytelling," TED.com, https://www.ted.com/topics/storytelling; "The Art of Storytelling," Khanacademy.org, https://www.khanacademy.org/partner-content/pixar /storytelling; "5 Ways to Become a Better Storyteller," Ideou.com, https://www.ideou.com /blogs/inspiration/tagged/storytelling-for-influence.

13. U.S. Department of State, "Global Entrepreneurship Summits," India 2017, https://www .state.gov/e/eb/cba/entrepreneurship/ges/index.htm.

14. Consider the reproach "design by committee" for a way designers often formulate vision and the distribution of control as antagonistic.

Chapter 7. Can the Subaltern Innovate?

1. Benoit Godin (2015) traces the history of the word innovation in Europe and notes that during the Enlightenment, the word was a term of condemnation against novelties that threatened the church.

2. See Nguyen (2017), Dominguez Rubio (2016), Rosner (2014), M. Cohn (2013), Jackson, Pompe, and Krieshok (2011), Sandvig (2012), and Starosielski (2015) for works that question the pervasive focus on technological invention and emphasize a wide array of other practices that enliven technologies as part of social life. Nguyen's account of jailbreaking iPhones in Vietnam and Sandvig's account of residents on a Native American reservation building infrastructure to connect to the internet persuasively show how the production of newness erases

the value that (skillfully labored-for) connection to existing technologies and infrastructures holds for those pushed to the margins.

3. A forerunner to these concerns in technology studies were anthropologist Lucy Suchman and sociologist Susan Leigh Star, who called for attention to invisible "articulation work" alongside more heroic design work (see Suchman 1996).

4. David Stark (2009) also characterizes innovation as the search for value and as a process of recognition. His work, however, does not account for why the products of some labor do not count as new *value*. This requires an analysis of hierarchies of labor and the ways they are structured by racialized, gendered, classed, and caste processes.

5. Like with process patents described in chapter 2, this conception of creativity elevated the labor of adapting technologies from elsewhere.

6. The design team developed these techniques independently, but they aligned with wider explorations among global design researchers. See, for example, the "Bollywood Method" of design research (Chavan et al. 2009) and IDEO's human-centered design guide *Hear*, funded by the Bill and Melinda Gates Foundation (http://www.designkit.org).

7. The Ford Foundation invested in mitigating the negative effects of modernization through a range of experiments, research projects, and institution-building projects. They primarily did this by locating democracy not in redistributions of value but by investing in cultural and religious reforms that maintained difference with new forms of expression, interaction, and management (Turner 2013, 257; Hull 2010; McCarthy 1987, 107). The "idle hands" Nehru worried about in the countryside were part of a larger milieu of communist agitations among Indian peasants. The Ford Foundation saw India, on Maoist China's border, as a crucial front in the war against communism (McCarthy 1987). The foundation's investments in NID, IIM-A (Srinivas 2008), and IIT-Kanpur (Leslie and Kargon 2006) are a lasting legacy of this project of managing modernization and difference. Notably, the foundation's experiments included 1950s studies of entrepreneurship potential among peasants (McClelland 1961; see also Nandy 1972) and economic motivations among Indians (Pickren and Rutherford 2010, 249). Those experiments in entrepreneurship were not institutionalized, though they were picked up by champions of social entrepreneurship in the United States such as Bill Drayton (Bornstein 2007). One lasting impact of Ford's intervention was the arrival of John Bissell, a purchaser at Macy's in New York, to advise on how Indian textiles could be marketed for export. Bissell came as part of the same wave of work for which the Eameses came in the 1950s (Staples 1992). Bissell chose to stay in India and founded the export company FabIndia, now an international clothing chain. The history of design and sociotechnical relations of production are deeply entangled.

8. The Eameses noted that this process of breakneck change introduced by new technologies did not affect only India. They pointed out that the phenomenon of communication "affects a world not a country" (Eames and Eames 1958). Though they located Asia at a temporal delay in absorbing modern communication technologies, the transformative tremors of these technologies would be felt everywhere. The Eameses proposed design, then, as a mediator and "steering device" of change in all modern societies, not just ones labeled transitional within modernization frameworks.

9. The Eameses, following so many modernization theorists, characterized India as "a tradition-oriented society" (1958, 7). Tradition-oriented societies, according to modernization theorists, were those that valued social interdependence, filial piety, and "group orientation"

(Bronner 2008). The Eameses continued: "The decisions that are made in a tradition-oriented society are apt to be unconscious decisions—in that each situation or action automatically calls for a specified reaction. Behaviour patterns are pre-programmed, pre-set. It is in this climate that handicrafts flourish—changes take place by degrees—there are moments of violence but the security is in the status quo."

"Tradition-oriented" people in the Eameses' time and thoughtless late capitalist consumers whom IDEO's Fulton Suri wrote of seemed to have something in common. Anthropological knowledge underwrote these assumptions. For a century, anthropologists had produced synchronic accounts of culture as recurring, patterned, place-based social forms rather than as diachronic, dynamic systems (Fabian 1983). These anthropologies characterized the indigenous subject as unable to "symbolize" or "produce abstract representations" (Pandolfo 2000). The indigenous subject remained "trapped in the mimetic faculty, the prisoner of images from which it could not obtain a spectatorial distance" (Pandolfo 2000). Only the modern subject was thought to have the capacity to take a disembodied, abstracting perspective (D. Chakrabarty 2000).

10. The Bauhaus school was formed with the goal of creating an intuitive, constructive "new man" who could create "a new cultural equilibrium" for a Germany torn apart by World War I and in need of cultural reconstruction (Turner 2013; see also Findeli 1995). Bauhaus designers would combine form, elemental language, and reason into a new *Lebensordnung*, or form of life (Galison 1990, 716). Ulm extended much of the Bauhaus curriculum, adding education in society and politics. Design at Ulm was part of a project to make capitalism progressive while inoculating Germans against communism (Spitz 2002, 121).

11. Kavita Philip (2004) similarly identifies colonial scientists and explorers as learning local people's knowledge about plants and putting those plants into new circulation to accumulate value.

12. I thank Balaji Parthasarathy for clarifying this distinction between conceptualization and valorization.

13. My account of Mansukhbhai Prajapati in this chapter is heavily indebted to the excellent fieldwork, interviews, and case studies by organizational scholar Prashant Rajan, especially his dissertation, "Organizing Grassroots Innovations" (2012, 189–201).

14. Prior art names knowledge already known to the public. Prior art cannot be patented under many systems of patent law.

15. Hindus have made *yatra* into a ritual of community and participant transformation through pilgrimage (S. Roy 2007, 168). Indian politicians, beginning with Gandhi (Kothari 1994, 1592), and activists have also traveled as *yatris* (one who performs *yatra*) as journeys to meet and generate relationships in the work of political mobilization (see Singh and Nagar 2006).

16. While I rely heavily on others' writing about the Honeybee Network, I also spent over a week at the National Innovation Foundation's Festival of Innovation in 2017 where I interviewed staff from NIF and HBN.

17. For another example of the friction and exploitation of scaling up craft, see Anita Say Chan's (2013) analysis of elite-led projects to scale up local Peruvian pottery forms for an international market. The projects, initiated in the wake of Information Society and Cultural Economy policies, transformed the social relations in the village Chulcanas. Managerial elites

selected among rural artisans for their entrepreneurial attitudes, enforcing entrepreneurialism as an updated form of (colonial) civility (107).

18. To preserve the anonymity of Kamal and his colleagues, I do not include a citation to the book.

19. This was not the only function of documentation. Designers and other cultural entrepreneurs also produced documentation to demonstrate the use and impact of funds, or to make a project seem vibrant and active so others would want to join.

20. By some accounts, some are well aware of this burden and skillful in addressing the more powerful in the terms set by this discourse (Venkatesan 2009).

21. पहचान formally transliterates as pahachaan. However, government sites might spell it pehchaan or pehchan (e.g., "Mera Aadhaar, Meri Pehchan").

22. Kavita Philip (2012, 103–4) demonstrates the burden of authenticity in legal and political fights for affirmative action in India as well. Communities in India protesting for recognition under affirmative action regimes meet with challenges issued by prominent anthropologists and sociologists in India, who argue these tribes are too modern and inauthentic to claim social restitution.

Chapter 8. Conclusion: The Cultivation and Subsumption of Hope

1. Bill Drayton, the founder of Ashoka, a global nonprofit that promotes social entrepreneurship, cites Gandhi as a model empathic leader. Drayton, an ex-McKinsey consultant, cited Vinoba Bhave's *bhoodan* (land gift) movement as an example of how a brilliant organizer who knows others' hearts could persuade landowners to gift their land to their poorer neighbors without demanding structural change (Bornstein 2007, 48–61).

2. Entrepreneurial citizenship is only one approach—the gap-filling approach—to a patchwork of attempts by Indian state and civil society to make Indians into sources of value. For instance, anthropologist Michelle Friedner (2015, 117) identifies a similar but distinct process of making value out of deafness in postliberalization India.

3. The sleight of hand can at times be violent. In 2016 the government of India abruptly took the five-hundred-rupee and one-thousand-rupee note out of circulation, forcing millions of people into bank lines and onto digital payment platforms. Prime Minister Narendra Modi announced that this move would take "black money" out of circulation; by pulling millions of transactions and people onto digital platforms, he rendered a multitude of Indians infrastructurally accessible to digital India's financial technology entrepreneurs (Pham 2016; Venugopal 2016; Sharma 2016).

4. McKenzie Wark (2015), reviewing Yann Moulier-Boutang's *Cognitive Capitalism* (2011), articulates the entrepreneur thus: "The entrepreneur is a surfer who does not create the wave. Here, like Marx, Boutang understands value creation as taking place off-stage, and made invisible by a kind of market fetishism. These days it is not the commodity that is the fetish so much as the great man of business. As if the world just issued fully formed from Steve Jobs' brain. Cognitive capital is based on knowledge society, but is not the same thing." Moulier-Boutang (2011) characterizes the political economy of late capitalism as the anticipation of desire through invention-power, finance, and computationally networked knowledge. He argues that finance requires entrepreneurs to find the value in that which is external to the firm. His

NOTES TO CHAPTER 8   231

work is Eurocentric; he locates late capitalism in Euro-America and assumes that stored representations—in writing and in computation—are coextensive with knowledge. This book, in
contrast, demonstrates how entrepreneurial citizens produce unrecorded knowledge through
conversation, empathy, and experiment—encouraging mediated communicative action and
harvesting from it to produce value. The singular focus of Wark and Moulier-Boutang on digital and information knowledge misses the wider significance of entrepreneurial citizenship as a
machine for structuring social processes in the search for and production of value. Despite this,
the evidence presented in this book does support the formulation of the entrepreneur as one
who captures the value of externalities that social networks (or, I would say, relations) create.

5. These scholars work in conversation with feminist science studies scholars who have argued that neoliberalism, medical technologies, and insurance need to be understood for the
"regime of being in time" that they generate (Adams, Murphy, and Clarke 2009, 249).

6. Science studies scholars have also pointed to the importance of design and speculation as
the practice of politics. Fernando Dominguez Rubio and Uriel Fogué (2015) argue that through
design, people can make devices and infrastructures that make palpable a new cosmos of politics. Christopher Le Dantec and Carl DiSalvo (2013), drawing on Bruno Latour, agree that
infrastructures and design can form publics around issues. Carl DiSalvo et al. (2014), drawing
on Latour (2008), also argue that design can make matters of fact into matters of concern.

REFERENCES

Abbasi, K. 1999. "Under Fire." *BMJ* 318, no. 7189:1003–6.

Ablett, Jonathan, Aadarsh Baijal, Eric Beinhocker, Anupam Bose, Diana Farrell, Ulrich Gersch, Ezra Greenberg, Shishir Gupta, and Sumit Gupta. 2007. *The "Bird of Gold": The Rise of India's Consumer Market*. McKinsey Global Institute, May.

Abraham, Itty. 1998. *The Making of the Indian Atomic Bomb: Science, Secrecy and the Postcolonial State*. London: Zed Books.

———. 2006. "The Contradictory Spaces of Postcolonial Techno-Science." *Economic and Political Weekly* 41, no. 3:210–17.

Abraham, Itty, and Ashish Rajadhyaksha. 2015. "State Power and Technological Citizenship in India: From the Postcolonial to the Digital Age." *East Asian Science, Technology and Society* 9, no. 1:65–85. doi:10.1215/18752160–2863200.

Adams, Vincanne, Michelle Murphy, and Adele E. Clarke. 2009. "Anticipation: Technoscience, Life, Affect, Temporality." *Subjectivity* 28, no. 1:246–65.

Adas, M. 1989. *Machines as the Measure of Men*. Ithaca, NY: Cornell University Press.

Agrawal, Ajay, Devesh Kapur, John McHale, and Alexander Oettl. 2011. "Brain Drain or Brain Bank? The Impact of Skilled Emigration on Poor-Country Innovation." *Journal of Urban Economics* 69, no. 1:43–55.

Ahmed, Sara. 2004. *The Cultural Politics of Emotion*. Edinburgh: Edinburgh University Press.

———. 2006. *Queer Phenomenology: Objects, Orientations, Others*. Durham, NC: Duke University Press.

Akhtar, F., producer. 2011. *Zindagi Na Milegi Dobara*. Mumbai: Eros International. Film.

Akrich, Madeleine, Michel Callon, Bruno Latour, and Adrian Monaghan. 2002. "The Key to Success in Innovation Part I: The Art of Interessement." *International Journal of Innovation Management* 6, no. 2:187–206.

Albiez, Sean, and David Pattie. 2016. *Brian Eno: Oblique Music*. New York: Bloomsbury.

Alvesson, M. 2001. "Knowledge Work: Ambiguity, Image and Identity." *Human Relations* 54, no. 7:863.

American Jewish World Service. 2012. "Gagan Sethi on Empowerment and Identity in India." YouTube video. https://www.youtube.com/watch?v=BkkGzw3kkUw.

Amrute, Sarita. 2016. *Encoding Race, Encoding Class: Indian IT Workers in Berlin*. Durham, NC: Duke University Press.

Anand, N. 2011. "Pressure: The Politechnics of Water Supply in Mumbai." *Cultural Anthropology* 26, no. 4:542–64.

Anderson, B. 1991. *Imagined Communities: Reflections on the Origin and Spread of Nationalism.* New York: Verso.

Aneesh, A. 2006. *Virtual Migration: The Programming of Globalization.* Durham, NC: Duke University Press.

———. 2015. *Neutral Accent.* Durham, NC: Duke University Press.

Appadurai, Arjun. 1996. *Modernity at Large: Cultural Dimensions of Globalization.* Minneapolis: University of Minnesota Press.

———. 2004. "The Capacity to Aspire: Culture and the Terms of Recognition." In *Culture and Public Action*, edited by V. Rao and J. Walton, 59–84. Stanford, CA: Stanford University Press.

———. 2013. *The Future as Cultural Fact: Essays on the Global Condition.* London: Verso.

Arendt, Hannah. 1998 [1958]. *The Human Condition.* 2nd ed. Chicago: University of Chicago Press.

"Arvind Subramanian Keynote Address." 2013. Wharton San Francisco. November 14. YouTube video. https://www.youtube.com/watch?v=P_geC7UryLY&feature=youtube_gdata_player.

Ashoka. 2011. "The Brin Wojcicki Foundation Pledges $2 Million Honoring Ashoka's 30th Anniversary." *Journal of India.* May 24, 109.

Avle, Seyram, and Silvia Lindtner. 2016. "Design(ing) 'Here' and 'There': Tech Entrepreneurs, Global Markets, and Reflexivity in Design Processes." In *Proceedings of the 2016 CHI Conference on Human Factors in Computing Systems*, 2233–45. New York: ACM.

Azam, Mehtabul, Aimee Chin, and Nishith Prakash. 2013. "The Returns to English-Language Skills in India." *Economic Development and Cultural Change* 61, no. 2:335–67.

Baecker, R., J. Grudin, W. Buxton, and S. Greenberg, eds. 1995. "Human Information Processing." In *Readings in Human-Computer Interaction: Toward the Year 2000.* 2nd ed. San Francisco: Morgan Kaufmann.

Bahl, Ekta. 2014. "An Overview of CSR Rules under Companies Act, 2013." *Business Standard.* March 10. http://www.business-standard.com/article/companies/an-overview-of-csr-rules-under-companies-act-2013–114031000385_1.html.

Balaram, Singapalli. 1992. *The Impact of Government Policies on Design.* Ahmedabad: National Institute of Design.

———. 2005. "Design Pedagogy in India: A Perspective." *Design Issues* 21, no. 4 (2005): 11–22. https://doi.org/10.1162/074793605774597442.

———. 2011. *Thinking Design.* New Delhi: Sage.

Balch, Oliver. 2016. "Indian Law Requires Companies to Give 2% of Profits to Charity. Is It Working?" *Guardian.* April 5. https://www.theguardian.com/sustainable-business/2016/apr/05/india-csr-law-requires-companies-profits-to-charity-is-it-working.

Banerjee, A. V., R. H. Bates, A. Deaton, J. N. Bhagwati, A. H. Amsden, and N. Stern. 2007. *Making Aid Work.* Cambridge, MA: MIT Press.

Banerjee, A. V., and E. Duflo. 2011a. "More than 1 Billion People Are Hungry in the World." *Foreign Policy*, 66–72.

———. 2011b. *Poor Economics: A Radical Rethinking of the Way to Fight Global Poverty.* New York: PublicAffairs.

Banerji, Rishabh. 2016. "Meet Aravinda and Ravi, The Inspiration behind Shahrukh Khan's Movie 'Swades.'" *IndiaTimes.com.* January 9. http://www.indiatimes.com/lifestyle/self/meet-aravinda-and-ravi-the-inspiration-behind-shahrukh-khan-s-movie-swades-249108.html.

Bannerjee, R. K. 1998. "40 Years of NID." Unpublished ms., NID Publications.

Bansler, J. P., and P. Kraft. 1994. "Privilege and Invisibility in the New Work Order: A Reply to King." *Scandinavian Journal of Information Systems* 6, no. 1:97–106.

Barad, K. 2003. "Posthumanist Performativity: Toward an Understanding of How Matter Comes to Matter." *Signs* 28, no. 3:801–31.

Bardzell, Shaowen. 2010. "Feminist HCI: Taking Stock and Outlining an Agenda for Design." In *Proceedings of the SIGCHI Conference on Human Factors in Computing Systems*, 1301–10. April 10–15. New York: ACM. http://dl.acm.org/citation.cfm?id=1753521.

"Barefoot Evangelist Who Helps the Poor Pull Themselves Up by Their Own Bootstraps." 2006. *Times Higher Education*. April 26. https://www.timeshighereducation.com/features /barefoot-evangelist-who-helps-the-poor-pull-themselves-up-by-their-own-boot straps/202717.article.

Bartholomew, P. S. 2013. "Creativity Is Not Just for Decoration, It Has a Huge Potential for Income." *Hindustan Times*. Available from Factiva, accessed November 29, 2016.

Baruah, J. 2012. "Inclusive Growth under India's Neo-liberal Regime: Towards an Exposition." *Social Change and Development* 9, no. 1 (July).

Bauman, R. 2001. Verbal Art as Performance. In *Linguistic Anthropology: A Reader*, edited by A. Duranti. Malden, MA: Blackwell.

Baumer, E. P., and M. Silberman. 2011. "When the Implication Is Not to Design (Technology)." In *Proceedings of the SIGCHI Conference on Human Factors in Computing Systems*, 2271–74. May. New York: ACM.

Baumol, William J. 1990. "Entrepreneurship: Productive, Unproductive, and Destructive." *Journal of Political Economy* 98, no. 5:893–921.

Bavadam, Lyla. 2003. "The Bilgaon Model." *Frontline*. 20, no. 21 (October 11–24). http://www .frontline.in/static/html/fl2021/stories/20031024001208700.htm.

Baviskar, Amita. 1995. *In the Belly of the River: Tribal Conflicts over Development in the Narmada Valley*. Studies in Social Ecology and Environmental History. Delhi: Oxford University Press.

———. 2003. "Between Violence and Desire: Space, Power, and Identity in the Making of Metropolitan Delhi." *International Social Science Journal* 55, no. 175:89–98.

———. 2009. "Breaking Homes, Making Cities: Class and Gender in the Politics of Urban Displacement: Displaced by Development." In *Displaced by Development: Confronting Marginalisation and Gender Injustice*, edited by Lyla Mehta, 59–81. New Delhi: Sage.

Baviskar, A., S. Sinha, and K. Philip. 2006. "Rethinking Indian Environmentalism: Industrial Pollution in Delhi and Fisheries in Kerala. In *Forging Environmentalism: Justice, Livelihood, and Contested Environments*, edited by J. Bauer, 183–256. Armonk, NY: M. E. Sharpe.

Bayly, C. A. 1986. "The Origins of Swadeshi (Home Industry): Cloth and Indian Society, 1700–1930." In *The Social Life of Things: Commodities in Cultural Perspective*, edited by Arjun Appadurai, 285–322. Cambridge: Cambridge University Press.

Bear, Laura. 2015. *Navigating Austerity: Currents of Debt along a South Asian River*. Stanford, CA: Stanford University Press.

———. 2016. "Afterword: For a New Materialist Analytics of Time." *Cambridge Journal of Anthropology* 34, no. 1:125–29. doi:10.3167/ca.2016.340112.

Bear, Laura, Karen Ho, Anna Tsing, and Sylvia Yanagisako. 2015. "Gens: A Feminist Manifesto for the Study of Capitalism." *Cultural Anthropology* website. March 30. https://culanth.org /fieldsights/652-gens-a-feminist-manifesto-for-the-study-of-capitalism.

Beck, E. 2002. "P for Political: Participation Is Not Enough." *Scandinavian Journal of Information Systems* 14, no. 1. http://aisel.aisnet.org/sjis/vol14/iss1/1.

Becker, Howard S. 1978. "Arts and Crafts." *American Journal of Sociology* 83, no. 4 (January 1): 862–89. https://doi.org/10.1086/226635.

Behar, Yves, Tim Brown, and Peter Schwartz. 2013. "Design Thinking with Yves Behar and Tim Brown." *Commonwealth Club Inforum*. Podcast. http://audio.commonwealthclub.org/audio /podcast/cc_20130321_inforum_designthinking.

Bell, D. 1973. *The Coming of Post-industrial Society: A Venture in Social Forecasting.* New York: Basic Books.

Benegal, Shyam, director. 1976. *Manthan.* Film.

Benjamin, Solomon. 2000. "Governance, Economic Settings and Poverty in Bangalore." *Environment and Urbanization* 12, no. 1 (April 1): 35–56. https://doi.org/10.1177 /095624780001200104.

Bhan, Gautam. 2013. "In Search of a Liberal Education." *Kafila.* November 2.

Bhatt, Amy, Madhavi Murty, and Priti Ramamurthy. 2010. "Hegemonic Developments: The New Indian Middle Class, Gendered Subalterns, and Diasporic Returnees in the Event of Neoliberalism." *Signs* 36, no. 1:127–52.

Bholey, M. 2013. "Not Designed for Aam Aadmi." *Business Line (The Hindu).* June 14. https:// www.thehindubusinessline.com/opinion/not-designed-for-aam-aadmi/article22995546 .ece.

Bhowmick, Nilanjana. 2011. "The Women of India's Barefoot College Bring Light to Remote Villages." *Guardian.* June 24. http://www.theguardian.com/global-development/2011/jun/24 /india-barefoot-college-solar-power-training.

Birla, Ritu. 2009. *Stages of Capital: Law, Culture, and Market Governance in Late Colonial India.* Durham, NC: Duke University Press.

Birtchnell, Thomas. 2011. "Jugaad as Systemic Risk and Disruptive Innovation in India." *Contemporary South Asia* 19, no. 4:357–72.

———. 2013. *Indovation: Innovation and a Global Knowledge Economy in India.* Basingstoke, UK: Palgrave Macmillan.

Bjerknes, G., and T. Bratteteig. 1995. "User Participation and Democracy: A Discussion of Scandinavian Research on System Development." *Scandinavian Journal of Information Systems* 7, no. 1:73–98.

Blanchette, Jean-François. 2011. "A Material History of Bits." *Journal of the American Society for Information Science and Technology* 62, no. 6 (June 1): 1042–57. https://doi.org/10.1002 /asi.21542.

Boateng, Boatema. 2011. *The Copyright Thing Doesn't Work Here: Adinkra and Kente Cloth and Intellectual Property in Ghana.* Minneapolis: University of Minnesota Press.

Bobbio, Tomasso. 2012. "Making Gujarat Vibrant: Hindutva, Development, and the Rise of Subnationalism in India." *Third World Quarterly* 33, no. 4:657–72.

Bornstein, D. 2007. *How to Change the World: Social Entrepreneurs and the Power of New Ideas.* Updated ed. Oxford: Oxford University Press.

Borning, Alan, and Michael Muller. 2012. "Next Steps for Value Sensitive Design." In *Proceedings of the SIGCHI Conference on Human Factors in Computing Systems*, 1125–34. New York: ACM. https://doi.org/10.1145/2207676.2208560.

Bourdieu, Pierre. 1977. *Outline of a Theory of Practice*. Cambridge Studies in Social Anthropology 16. Cambridge: Cambridge University Press.

———. 1984. *Distinction*. Cambridge, MA: Harvard University Press.

———. 1993. *The Field of Cultural Production*. New York: Columbia University Press.

Bourdieu, Pierre, and L.J.D. Wacquant. 1992. *An Invitation to Reflexive Sociology*. Chicago: University of Chicago Press.

Bowker, Geoffrey C., and Susan Leigh Star. 1999. *Sorting Things Out: Classification and Its Consequences*. Cambridge, MA: MIT Press.

Boyer, Dominic. 2010. "Digital Expertise in Online Journalism (and Anthropology)." *Anthropological Quarterly* 83, no. 1:73–95.

Brand, Stewart. 2009. *Whole Earth Discipline: An Ecopragmatist Manifesto*. New York: Viking.

Bronner, S. 2008. "Tradition." In *International Encyclopedia of the Social Sciences*, vol. 8, ed. W. J. Darity Jr., 420–22. Farmington Hills, MI: Gale Group.

Brook, Daniel. 2014. "Slumming It: The Gospel of Wealth Comes for Dharavi." *Baffler* (March 1): 136–45. doi:10.1162/BFLR_a_00251.

Brown, S. L., and K. M. Eisenhardt. 1997. "The Art of Continuous Change: Linking Complexity Theory and Time-Paced Evolution in Relentlessly Shifting Organizations." *Administrative Science Quarterly* 42, no. 1:1–34.

Brown, T., and J. Wyatt. 2010. "Design Thinking for Social Innovation." *Stanford Social Innovation Review* (Winter). http://ssir.org/articles/entry/design_thinking_for_social_innovation.

Brown, Wendy. 2015. *Undoing the Demos*. Cambridge, MA: Zone Books.

Burroughs, Andrew. 2007. *Everyday Engineering: What Engineers See*. San Francisco: Chronicle Books.

Callimachi, R. 2014. "India's Staggering Wealth Gap in Five Charts—The Hindu." *Hindu*. December 8. http://www.thehindu.com/data/indias-staggering-wealth-gap-in-five-charts/article6672115.ece.

Callon, Michel, and John Law. 1982. "On Interests and Their Transformation: Enrolment and Counter-Enrolment." *Social Studies of Science* 12, no. 4:615–25.

Card, Stuart K., and Thomas P. Moran. 1995. "User Technology: From Pointing to Pondering." In *Readings in Human-Computer Interaction: Toward the Year 2000*, edited by Ronald M. Baecker, Jonathan Grudin, William A. S. Buxton, and Saul Greenberg. 2nd ed. San Francisco: Morgan Kaufmann.

Cartwright, L. 2008. *Moral Spectatorship: Technologies of Voice and Affect in Postwar Representations of the Child*. Durham, NC: Duke University Press.

Castells, M. 2000. *The Rise of the Network Society*. Sussex, UK: Wiley-Blackwell.

Chadha, Radhika. 2009. "The Limitations of 'Jugaad.'" *Hindu Business Line*. http://www.thehindubusinessline.com/todays-paper/tp-brandline/the-limitations-of-jugaad/article1083738.ece.

Chakrabarty, Bidyut. 2011. *Corporate Social Responsibility in India*. Oxford: Routledge.

Chakrabarty, Dipesh. 2000. *Provincializing Europe*. Princeton, NJ: Princeton University Press.

Chakravartty, Paula. 2001. "Flexible Citizens and the Internet: The Global Politics of Local High-Tech Development in India." *Emergences: Journal for the Study of Media & Composite Cultures* 11, no. 1:69–88.

———. 2004. "Telecom, National Development and the Indian State: A Postcolonial Critique." *Media, Culture & Society* 26, no. 2:227–49.

———. 2012. "Rebranding Development Communications in Emergent India." *Nordicom Review* 33: 65–76.

Chakravartty, Paula, and Sreela Sarkar. 2013. "Entrepreneurial Justice: The New Spirit of Capitalism in Emergent India." *Popular Communication* 11:58–75.

Chakravarty, M. 2016. "The Richest 1% of Indians Now Own 58.4% of Wealth." *Live Mint*. November 24. http://www.livemint.com/Money/MML9OZRwaACyEhLzUNImnO/The-richest-1-of-Indians-now-own-584-of-wealth.html.

Chakravorty, Pallabi. 1998. "Hegemony, Dance and Nation: The Construction of the Classical Dance in India." *South Asia: Journal of South Asian Studies* 21, no. 2:107–20.

Chan, Anita. 2013. *Networking Peripheries: Technological Futures and the Myth of Digital Universalism*. Cambridge, MA: MIT Press.

Chatterjee, Ashoke. 1988. "Design in India: A Challenge of Identity." Paper presented at the International Conference on Design & Development in South & South East Asia. Hong Kong University, December 5–8.

———. 2005. "Design in India: The Experience of Transition." *Design Issues* 21, no. 4:4–10.

Chatterjee, Partha. 1993. *The Nation and Its Fragments: Colonial and Postcolonial Histories*. Princeton, NJ: Princeton University Press.

———. 2004. *The Politics of the Governed: Reflections on Popular Politics in Most of the World*. New York: Columbia University Press.

Chaudhury, Shoma. 2007. "The IIT Mindset Feeds into the Fascist Nature of the Right." *Tehelka*. December 8. http://www.tehelka.com/story_main36.asp?filename=hub081207The_IIT.asp.

Chavan, A. L., D. Gorney, B. Prabhu, and S. Arora. 2009. "The Washing Machine That Ate My Sari—Mistakes in Cross-cultural Design. *Interactions* 16, no. 1:26–31.

Chen, Derek H. C., and Carl J. Dahlman. 2005. *The Knowledge Economy, the KAM Methodology and World Bank Operations*. SSRN Scholarly Paper ID 841625. Rochester, NY: Social Science Research Network. http://papers.ssrn.com/abstract=841625.

Chen, Katherine K. 2009. *Enabling Creative Chaos: The Organization behind the Burning Man Event*. Chicago: University of Chicago Press.

Chopra, Rohit. 2003. "Neoliberalism as Doxa: Bourdieu's Theory of the State and the Contemporary Indian Discourse on Globalization and Liberalization." *Cultural Studies* 17, no. 3–4 (May 1): 419–44. https://doi.org/10.1080/0950238032000083881.

Chopra, V. V., producer, and R. Hirani, director. 2009. *3 Idiots*. India: Reliance Big Pictures. Film.

Chumley, Lily. 2016. *Creativity Class: Art, School, and Culture Work in Postsocialist China*. Princeton, NJ: Princeton University Press.

Chun, W.H.K. 2005. "On Software, or the Persistence of Visual Knowledge. *Grey Room* 18:26–51.

"CII Meet Focuses on IPR Issues." 2003. *Business Standard*. October 17.

"CII Outlines Agenda for 8% Sustained Growth." 2004. *Hindustan Times*. July 31.

Citizenship (Amendment) Act, 2003. 2017. https://indiankanoon.org/doc/949775/.

Clarke, Alison J. 2016. "Design for Development, ICSID and UNIDO: The Anthropological Turn in 1970s Design." *Journal of Design History* 29, no. 1:43–57.

Clifford, James. 1997. "Spatial Practices: Fieldwork, Travel, and the Disciplining of Anthropology." In *Anthropological Locations: Boundaries and Grounds of a Field Science*, edited by Akhil Gupta and James Ferguson, 185–222. Berkeley: University of California Press.

Clinton, H. R. 2010. "Leading through Civilian Power: Redefining American diplomacy and Development." *Foreign Affairs* (November–December): 13–24.

Cody, F. 2009. "Inscribing Subjects to Citizenship: Petitions, Literacy Activism, and the Performativity of Signature in Rural Tamil India." *Cultural Anthropology* 24, no. 3:347–80.

Cohen, Lawrence. 1998. *No Aging in India: Alzheimer's, the Bad Family, and Other Modern Things.* Berkeley: University of California Press.

Cohen-Cole, J. 2014. *The Open Mind: Cold War Politics and the Sciences of Human Nature.* Chicago: University of Chicago Press.

Cohn, B. S. 1996. *Colonialism and Its Forms of Knowledge: The British in India.* Princeton, NJ: Princeton University Press.

Cohn, Marisa Leavitt. 2013. "Lifetimes and Legacies: Temporalities of Sociotechnical Change in a Long-Lived System." Ph.D. dissertation, University of California, Irvine.

Cohn, M. L., S. E. Sim, and P. Dourish. 2010. "Design Methods as Discourse on Practice." In *Proceedings of the 16th ACM International Conference on Supporting Group Work*, 45–54. November. New York: ACM.

Cohn, M. L., S. E. Sim, and C. P. Lee. 2009. "What Counts as Software Process? Negotiating the Boundary of Software Work through Artifacts and Conversation." *Computer Supported Cooperative Work* (*CSCW*) 18, nos. 5–6:401–43.

Coleman, Gabriella. 2013. *Coding Freedom: The Ethics and Aesthetics of Hacking.* Princeton, NJ: Princeton University Press.

Commonwealth Club. 2013. *Design Thinking with Yves Béhar and Tim Brown (Clip).* March 21, 2013. YouTube video. https://www.youtube.com/watch?v=PmKKdRzdAc4.

Corbridge, S., and J. Harriss. 2000. *Reinventing India: Liberalization, Hindu Nationalism and Popular Democracy.* Cambridge: Polity.

Cornwall, Andrea. 2000. *Beneficiary, Consumer, Citizen: Perspectives on Participation for Poverty Reduction.* Sida Studies, no. 2. Swedish International Development Corporation Agency.

Correa, C. M. 2012. *A Place in the Shade: The New Landscape and Other Essays.* Ostfildern: Hatje Cantz.

Corsin Jiménez, Alberto. 2014. "Introduction: The Prototype: More than Many and Less than One." *Journal of Cultural Economy* 7, no. 4 (October): 381–98. https://doi.org/10.1080/17 530350.2013.858059.

Cross, J. 2013. "The 100th Object: Solar Lighting Technology and Humanitarian Good." *Journal of Material Culture* 18, no. 4:367–87.

———. 2014. *Dream Zones: Anticipating Capitalism and Development.* London: Pluto Press.

Cross, Nigel. 1995. "Discovering Design Ability." In *Discovering Design: Explorations in Design Studies*, 105–19. Chicago: University of Chicago Press.

da Costa Marques, I. 2005. "Cloning Computers: From Rights of Possession to Rights of Creation." *Science as Culture* 14, no. 2:139.

Currid-Halkett, Elizabeth. 2007. *The Warhol Economy: How Fashion, Art, and Music Drive New York City*. Princeton, NJ: Princeton University Press.

Das, Gurcharan. 2001. *India Unbound*. New York: Knopf.

Das, KeshaB. 2003. "The Domestic Politics of TRIPs: Pharmaceutical Interests, Public Health, and NGO Influence in India." Paper prepared for Research Project on Linking the WTO to the Poverty-Reduction Agenda.

Das Gupta, Sanjukta. 2008. "Writing Histories of Adivasis of Central India." *Contemporary Perspectives* 2, no. 1:175–201.

Dasgupta, Simanti. 2008. "Success, Market, Ethics Information Technology and the Shifting Politics of Governance and Citizenship in the Indian Silicon Plateau." *Cultural Dynamics* 20, no. 3:213–44.

Dash, D.M.S. 2016. "One Person Company: A Critical Analysis." *Indian Journal of Applied Research* 5, no. 6.

Daston, Lorraine. 1995. "The Moral Economy of Science." *Osiris*, 2nd series, 10:3–24.

 Daston, L., and P. Galison. 2007. *Objectivity*. Boston: Zone Books.

Datta, D., and A. Sood. 2014. "Bihar Innovation Lab." http://www.impatientoptimists.org /Posts/2014/08/Bihar-Innovation-Lab#.VmXbwcpwKaA.

Datta Gupta, Sobhanlal. 2013. "Social Character of the Indian State: A Survey of Current Trends." In *Political Science*. Vol. 1: *The Indian State*, edited by Samir Kumar Das. New Delhi: Oxford University Press.

Davies, K. 2013. "Tired of Bad Products?" *NextBillion* (blog). July 4. http://nextbillion.net /blogpost.aspx?blogid=3384.

Deleule, Didier, and François Guéry. 2014. *The Productive Body*. N.p.: Zero Books.

Desai, Sonalde, and Amaresh Dubey. 2012. "Caste in 21st Century India: Competing Narratives." *Economic and Political Weekly* 46, no. 11:40.

Deshpande, Satish. 2003. *Contemporary India: A Sociological View*. Delhi: Viking.

Dirks, N. B. 2001. *Castes of Mind: Colonialism and the Making of Modern India*. Princeton, NJ: Princeton University Press.

Dirlik, A. 1997. *The Postcolonial Aura: Third World Criticism in the Age of Global Capitalism*. Boulder, CO: Westview Press.

DiSalvo, Carl. 2012. *Adversarial Design*. Cambridge, MA: MIT Press.

DiSalvo, Carl, Jonathan Lukens, Thomas Lodato, Tom Jenkins, and Tanyoung Kim. 2014. "Making Public Things: How HCI Design Can Express Matters of Concern." In *Proceedings of the 32nd Annual ACM Conference on Human Factors in Computing Systems*, 2397–2406. New York: ACM. http://dx.doi.org/10.1145/2556288.2557359.

Diwanji, A. K. 2004. "CII Hopes to Create the Swades Effect: CII-Indian American Council Will Assist NRIs Wanting to Help Their Home Towns." *India Abroad*. December 24.

Dominguez Rubio, Fernando. 2016. "On the Discrepancy between Objects and Things: An Ecological Approach." *Journal of Material Culture* 21, no. 1: 59–86.

———. Forthcoming. *MoMA and the Relentlessness of Things*. Chicago: University of Chicago Press.

Dominguez Rubio, Fernando, and Uriel Fogué. 2015. "Unfolding the Political Capacities of Design." In *What Is Cosmopolitical Design? Design, Nature and the Built Environment*, edited by Albena Yaneva and Alejandro Zaera. Burlington VT: Ashgate.

Dourish, Paul. 2004. *Where the Action Is: Foundations of Embodied Interaction*. Cambridge, MA: MIT Press.

Dourish, Paul, and Genevieve Bell. 2011. *Divining a Digital Future: Mess and Mythology in Ubiquitous Computing*. Cambridge, MA: MIT Press.

Drayton, Bill. 2006. "Everyone a Changemaker: Social Entrepreneurship's Ultimate Goal." *Innovations* 1, no. 1:80–96.

———. 2011. "Collaborative Entrepreneurship: How Social Entrepreneurs Can Tip the World by Working in Global Teams." *Innovations* 6, no. 2:35–38.

Dutta, Arindam. 2007. *The Bureaucracy of Beauty: Design in the Age of Its Global Reproducibility*. New York: Routledge.

———. 2009. "Design: On the Global (R) Uses of a Word." *Design and Culture* 1, no. 2:163–86.

———. 2013. "Linguistics, Not Grammatology: Architecture's a Prioris and Architecture's Priorities." In *A Second Modernism: MIT, Architecture, and the "Techno-Social" Moment*, edited by Michael Kubo, Stephanie Marie Tuerk, Irina Chernykova, and Arindam Dutta. Cambridge, MA: MIT Press.

Dutta, Soumitra. 2010. "Global Innovation Index and Report 2009–2010." *INSEAD and CII, India*.

———. 2017. Interview by Lilly Irani. October 25.

Dutz, Mark, ed. 2007. *Unleashing India's Innovation: Towards Sustainable and Inclusive Growth*. Washington, DC: World Bank.

———. 2013. *Measuring Innovation Capabilities for Competiveness and Growth*. Jamaica Productivity Center. YouTube video. https://www.youtube.com/watch?v=ewy-4hc0P2k.

Dyer-Witheford, Nick. 2001. "Empire, Immaterial Labor, the New Combinations, and the Global Worker." *Rethinking Marxism* 13, nos. 3–4:70–80.

Eade, Deborah. 2010. "Capacity Building: Who Builds Whose Capacity?" In *Deconstructing Development Discourse: Buzzwords and Fuzzwords*, edited by Andrea Cornwall and Deborah Eade, 203–14. Warwickshire, UK: Practical Action.

Eames, Charles, and Ray Eames. 1959. *A Communications Primer*. Classroom Film Distributors. Film.

———. 1968. *Powers of Ten*. Pyramid Films. Distributed by International Telefilm Enterprises. Film.

Eames, Ray, and Charles Eames. 1958. *The India Report*. Ahmedabad: National Institute of Design.

Easterly, William. 2006. *The White Man's Burden: Why the West's Efforts to Aid the Rest Have Done So Much Ill and So Little Good*. New York: Penguin.

Edgerton, David. 2007. *The Shock of the Old: Technology and Global History since 1900*. Oxford: Oxford University Press.

Edwards, Paul N. 1990. "The Army and the Microworld: Computers and the Politics of Gender Identity." *Signs* 16, no. 1:102–27.

Ehn, P. 1988. *Work-Oriented Design of Computer Artifacts*. Stockholm: Stockholm-Arbetslivscentrum.

Elyachar, J. 2005. *Markets of Dispossession: NGOs, Economic Development, and the State in Cairo*. Durham, NC: Duke University Press.

———. 2010. "Phatic Labor, Infrastructure, and the Question of Empowerment in Cairo." *American Ethnologist* 37, no. 3:452–64.

Elyachar, J. 2012a. "Next Practices: Knowledge, Infrastructure, and Public Goods at the Bottom of the Pyramid." *Public Culture* 24, no. 1 (66): 109–29.

———. 2012b. "Before (and After) Neoliberalism: Tacit Knowledge, Secrets of the Trade, and the Public Sector in Egypt." *Cultural Anthropology* 27, no. 1:76–96. doi:10.1111/j.1548–1360.2012.01127.x.

Erenhouse, R. 2014. "At the Intersection of Design and Financial Inclusion." Mastercard Center for Inclusive Growth. July 19. http://mastercardcenter.org/news/intersection -design-financial-inclusion/.

Erickson, T. 1995. "Notes on Design Practice: Stories and Prototypes as Catalysts for Communication." In *Scenario-Based Design: Envisioning Work and Technology in System Development*, edited by J. M. Carroll, 37–58. Hoboken, NJ: Wiley.

———. 1996. "Design as Storytelling." *Interactions* 3, no. 4:30–35.

Escobar, Arturo. 1991. "Anthropology and the Development Encounter: The Making and Marketing of Development Anthropology. *American Ethnologist* 18, no. 4:658–82.

———. 1995. *Encountering Development: The Making and Unmaking of the Third World*. Princeton, NJ: Princeton University Press.

———. 2018. *Designs for the Pluriverse: Radical Interdependence, Autonomy, and the Making of Worlds*. Durham, NC: Duke University Press.

Fabian, J. 1983. *Time and the Other: How Anthropology Makes Its Object*. New York: Columbia University Press.

Fabricant, R. 2014. "The Rapidly Disappearing Business of Design." *Wired*. December 29. http://www.wired.com/2014/12/disappearing-business-of-design/.

Fattal, A. 2012. "Facebook: Corporate Hackers, a Billion Users, and the Geo-Politics of the 'Social Graph.'" *Anthropological Quarterly* 85, no. 3:927–56.

Feher, M. 2009. "Self-appreciation; or, the Aspirations of Human Capital." *Public Culture* 21, 1:21–41.

Feldman, Allen. 1991. *Formations of Violence: The Narrative of the Body and Political Terror in Northern Ireland*. Chicago: University of Chicago Press.

Ferguson, James. 1994. *The Anti-Politics Machine: "Development," Depoliticization, and Bureaucratic Power in Lesotho*. Minneapolis: University of Minnesota Press.

———. 2003. "Stillborn Chrysalis: Reflections on the Fate of National Culture in Neoliberal Zambia." *Global Networks* 3, no. 3 (July): 271–97. https://doi.org/10.1111/1471 -0374.00062.

Ferguson, James, and Akhil Gupta. 2002. "Spatializing States: Toward an Ethnography of Neoliberal Governmentality." *American Ethnologist* 29, no. 4:981–1002.

Fernandes, Leela. 2004. "The Politics of Forgetting: Class Politics, State Power and the Restructuring of Urban Space in India." *Urban Studies* 41, no. 12:2415–30.

———. 2006. *India's New Middle Class Democratic Politics in an Era of Economic Reform*. Minneapolis: University of Minnesota Press.

Fernandes, Leela, and Patrick Heller. 2006. "Hegemonic Aspirations: New Middle Class Politics and India's Democracy in Comparative Perspective." *Critical Asian Studies* 38, no. 4:495–522.

Findeli, Alain. 1995. "Moholy-Nagy's Design Pedagogy in Chicago (1937–46)." In *The Idea of Design*, edited by Victor Margolin and Richard Buchanan, 29–43. Cambridge, MA: MIT Press.

First Post Staff. 2012. "Give Us Rs 200 Crore Says Ramesh to Gates." *Firstpost.* May 31. http://www.firstpost.com/india/help-with-sanitation-and-tribal-schemes-jairam-ramesh-tells-bill-gates-326969.html.

Fischer, M. M. 1999. "Emergent Forms of Life: Anthropologies of Late or Postmodernities." *Annual Review of Anthropology,* 455–78.

Fish, Allison. 2006. "The Commodification and Exchange of Knowledge in the Case of Transnational Commercial Yoga." *International Journal of Cultural Property* 13, no. 2:189–206.

Fisher, W. F. 1997. "Doing Good? The Politics and Antipolitics of NGO Practices." *Annual Review of Anthropology* 26, no. 1:439–64.

Florida, Richard. 2002. *The Rise of the Creative Class: And How It's Transforming Work, Leisure, Community and Everyday Life.* New York: Perseus Books Group.

Fortun, Kim, and Mike Fortun. 2005. "Scientific Imaginaries and Ethical Plateaus in Contemporary U.S. Toxicology." *American Anthropologist* 107, no. 1 (March 1): 43–54. https://doi.org/10.1525/aa.2005.107.1.043.

Forty, A. 1986. *Objects of Desie: Design and Society from Wedgewood to IBM.* New York: Pantheon.

Foucault, M. 1982. "The Subject and Power." *Critical Inquiry* 8, no. 4:777–95.

———. 1984. "What Is Enlightenment?" In *The Foucault Reader,* edited by P. Rabinow. New York: Random House.

———. 1991. "Governmentality." In *The Foucault Effect: Studies in Governmentality,* edited by Graham Burchell, Colin Gordon, and Peter Miller, 87–104. Chicago: University of Chicago Press.

———. 1995. *Discipline and Punish: The Birth of the Prison.* New York: Vintage.

———. 2010. *The Birth of Biopolitics: Lectures at the Collège de France, 1978–1979.* New York: Picador.

Fouché, Rayvon. 2006. "Say It Loud, I'm Black and I'm Proud: African Americans, American Artifactual Culture, and Black Vernacular Technological Creativity." *American Quarterly* 58, no. 3 (October 4): 639–61. https://doi.org/10.1353/aq.2006.0059.

Freeman, Carla. 2014. *Entrepreneurial Selves: Neoliberal Respectability and the Making of a Carribean Middle Class.* Durham, NC: Duke University Press.

Friedland, W. 1969. "A Sociological Approach to Modernization." In *Modernization by Design,* 35–84. Ithaca, NY: Cornell University Press.

Friedman, Batya. 1996. "Value-Sensitive Design." *Interactions* 3, no. 6:16–23.

Friedner, Michelle I. 2015. *Valuing Deaf Worlds in Urban India.* New Brunswick, NJ: Rutgers University Press.

Friends of River Narmada. 2002. "Invitation for Inauguration of Second Micro Hydel Project in Narmada Valley, January 14th 2003." Press release. Narmada.org. December 26. http://www.narmada.org/nba-press-releases/december-2002/bilgaon.html.

Fujimura, Joan H. 1988. "The Molecular Biological Bandwagon in Cancer Research: Where Social Worlds Meet." *Social Problems* 35, no. 3: 261–83.

Gabriel, Madeleine, Florence Engasser, and Kirsten Bound. 2016. *Good Incubation in India.* London: Nesta, Department for International Development, January. https://media.nesta.org.uk/documents/good_incubation_in_india_-_strategies_report.pdf.

Gajjala, Radhika and Dinah Tetteh. 2016. "Women Entrepreneurs, Global Microfinance, and Development 2.0." In *Oxford Encyclopedia of Communication.* Oxford: Oxford University Press.

Galison, P. 1990. Aufbau/Bauhaus: Logical positivism and architectural modernism. *Critical Inquiry* 16, 4:709–52.

Galloway, A. R. 2014. "The Cybernetic Hypothesis." *Differences* 25, no. 1 (January 1): 107–31. https://doi.org/10.1215/10407391-2420021.

Gandhi, M. K. 1921. "On Labour." *Hindu*. September 17.

Ganguli, Prabuddha. 1999. "Towards TRIPs Compliance in India: The Patents Amendment Act 1999 and Implications." *World Patent Information* 21, no. 4:279–87.

Ganti, Tejaswini. 2013. *Bollywood: A Guidebook to Popular Hindi Cinema*. 2nd ed. Hoboken, NJ: Taylor and Francis.

Gaonkar, D. P. 2002. "Toward New Imaginaries: An Introduction." *Public Culture* 14, no. 1:1–19.

Garfinkel, Harold. 1967. *Studies in Ethnomethodology*. Englewood Cliffs, NJ: Prentice-Hall.

Gates, Bill. 2007. "Remarks of Bill Gates, Harvard Commencement 2007." *Harvard Gazette*. June 7. https://news.harvard.edu/gazette/story/2007/06/remarks-of-bill-gates-harvard-commencement-2007/.

Gates, Bill, and Melinda Gates. 2014. "Text of the 2014 Commencement Address by Bill and Melinda Gates." *Stanford Report*. http://news.stanford.edu/news/2014/june/gates-commencement-remarks-061514.html.

Gates, Melinda. 2011. "Making a Difference One Life at a Time." *Huffington Post*. April 19. http://www.huffingtonpost.com/melinda-gates/making-a-difference-one-l_b_851027.html.

Gershon, Ilana. 2016. "'I'm Not a Businessman, I'm a Business, Man': Typing the Neoliberal Self into a Branded Existence." *HAU: Journal of Ethnographic Theory* 6, no. 3 (December 1): 223–46. https://doi.org/10.14318/hau6.3.017.

Ghose, Aurobindo. 1921a. *A System of National Education*. Madras: Tagore.

———. 1921b. "A Preface on National Education." In *On Education*, edited by Sri Aurobindo Ashram. Pondicherry: Sri Aurobindo Ashram Press.

———. 1997 [1922]. *Essays on the Gita*. Pondicherry: Sri Aurobindo Ashram Press.

Ghose, A., and P. P. Khetan. 2003. *The Bhagavad Gita: With Text, Translation, and Commentary in the Words of Sri Aurobindo*. Jhunjhunu, Rajasthan: Sri Aurobindo Divine Life Trust.

Gibson-Graham, J. K. 2006. *A Postcapitalist Politics*. Minneapolis: University of Minnesota Press.

Gidwani, Vinay, and Rajyashree N. Reddy. 2011. "The Afterlives of 'Waste': Notes from India for a Minor History of Capitalist Surplus." *Antipode* 43, no. 5:1625–58.

Gill, Rosalind, and Andy Pratt. 2008. "In the Social Factory? Immaterial Labour, Precariousness and Cultural Work." *Theory, Culture & Society* 25, nos. 7–8:1–30.

Giridharadas, Anand. 2008. "36 Hours in Mumbai." *New York Times*. June 22. http://www.nytimes.com/2008/06/22/travel/22hours.html.

Godechot, Olivier. 2008. "'Hold-up' in Finance: The Conditions of Possibility for High Bonuses in the Financial Industry." *Revue Française de Sociologie* 49, no. 5:95–123.

Godin, Benoît. 2015. *Innovation Contested: The Idea of Innovation Over the Centuries*. New York: Routledge.

Goh, D.P.S. 2006. "States of Ethnography: Colonialism, Resistance, and Cultural Transcription in Malaya and the Philippines, 1890s–1930s." *Comparative Studies in Society and History* 49, no. 1:109–42.

Goldman, M. 2006. *Imperial Nature: The World Bank and Struggles for Social Justice in the Age of Globalization*. New Haven, CT: Yale University Press.

Goodman, E., E. Stolterman, and R. Wakkary. 2011. "Understanding Interaction Design Practices." In *Proceedings of the SIGCHI Conference on Human Factors in Computing Systems*, 1061–70. New York: ACM. http://doi.org/10.1145/1978942.1979100.

Goodwin, C. 1994. "Professional Vision." *American Anthropologist* 96, no. 3:606–33.

Google. "Women—Google." Google.com. https://www.google.com/diversity/women/our-inspiration/index.html.

Gowariker, Ashutosh, director. 2004. *Swades*. Film.

Gramsci, Antonio, Quintin Hoare, and Geoffrey Nowell-Smith. *Selections from the Prison Notebooks of Antonio Gramsci*. New York: International Publishers, 1971.

Grameen Foundation. 2013. "Human Centered Design." YouTube video. http://www.youtube.com/watch?v=6mcZKWhjr9o&feature=youtube_gdata_player.

Granovetter, M. S. 1973. "The Strength of Weak Ties." *American Journal of Sociology*, 78, no. 6:1360–80.

Grant, Adam. 2013. "Economics Is Making Us Greedier." *Quartz* (blog). October 21. http://qz.com/137754/economics-is-making-us-greedier/.

Gregg, Melissa. 2015. "FCJ-186 Hack for Good: Speculative Labour, App Development and the Burden of Austerity." *Fibreculture Journal*, no. 25. http://twentyfive.fibreculturejournal.org/fcj-186-hack-for-good-speculative-labour-app-development-and-the-burden-of-austerity/.

Gregg, Melissa, and Carl DiSalvo. 2013. "The Trouble with White Hats." *New Inquiry*. November 21. http://thenewinquiry.com/essays/the-trouble-with-white-hats/.

Grudin, Jonathan. 2005. "Three Faces of Human-Computer Interaction." *IEEE Annals of the History of Computing*, no. 4:46–62.

Guha, Ranajit. 1991. *A Disciplinary Aspect of Indian Nationalism*. Santa Cruz, CA: Merrill College.

Gupta, Akhil, and Aradhana Sharma. 2006. "Globalization and Postcolonial States." *Current Anthropology* 47, no. 2: 277–307.

Gupta, Anil. 1990. "To: The Members of Informal Network on Farmers' Innovations and Local Technical Knowledge." *Honey Bee*. May.

———. 2003. *Learning from Green Grassroots Innovators: How Does a Tail Wag the Dog?* Ash Institute for Democratic Governance and Innovation, John F. Kennedy School of Government, Harvard University. http://anilg.sristi.org/wp-content/Papers/Learning%20from%20green%20grassroots%20innovators,%20harvard.pdf.

———. 2006. "From Sink to Source: The Honey Bee Network Documents Indigenous Knowledge and Innovations in India." *Innovations*. Summer.

———. 2008. "Emerging IPR Consciousness in India: Strengthening IP and Open Source Systems of Technological Innovations." *VIKALPA* 33, no. 2:71.

———. 2009. *India's Hidden Hotbeds of Invention*. https://www.ted.com/talks/anil_gupta_india_s_hidden_hotbeds_of_invention.

———. 2010. "Innovator Network Plans Giant Leap on the Back of 3 Idiots." *anil k gupta* (blog). January 4. http://anilg.sristi.org/innovator-network-plans-giant-leap-on-the-back-of-3-idiots/.

———. 2016. *Grassroots Innovation: Minds on the Margin Are Not Marginal Minds*. Delhi: Random House India.

Guyer, Jane I. 2007. "Prophecy and the Near Future: Thoughts on Macroeconomic, Evangelical, and Punctuated Time." *American Ethnologist* 34, no. 3:409–21.

Hansen, Thomas Blom. 1999. *The Saffron Wave: Democracy and Hindu Nationalism in Modern India*. Princeton, NJ: Princeton University Press.

Hansen, Thomas Blom, and Oskar Verkaaik. 2009. "Introduction—Urban Charisma: On Everyday Mythologies in the City." *Critique of Anthropology* 29, no. 1 (March 1): 5–26. https://doi.org/10.1177/0308275X08101029.

Haraway, Donna. 1985. "A Manifesto for Cyborgs: Science, Technology, and Socialist-Feminism in the 1980s." *Socialist Review* 80:65–108.

———. 1988. "The Science Question in Feminism and the Privilege of Partial Perspective." *Feminist Studies* 14, no. 3:575–99.

———. 1991. Simians, Cyborgs, and Women: The Reinvention of Nature. New York: Routledge.

———. 2008. *When Species Meet*. Minneapolis: University of Minnesota Press.

Hardt, Michael. 1994. *Labor of Dionysus: A Critique of State-Form Ate-Form*. Minneapolis: University of Minnesota Press.

Hariharan, Sindhu. 2015. "CSR Serves as Startup Capital—Times of India." *Times of India*. April 30. https://timesofindia.indiatimes.com/business/india-business/CSR-serves-as-startup-capital/articleshow/47102517.cms.

Harrison, S., P. Sengers, and D. Tatar. 2011. "Making Epistemological Trouble: Third-Paradigm HCI as Successor Science." *Interacting with Computers* 23, no. 5:385–92.

Harvey, David. 2005. *A Brief History of Neoliberalism*. Oxford: Oxford University Press.

Hayden, Cori. 2003. *When Nature Goes Public*. Princeton, NJ: Princeton University Press.

———. 2010. "The Proper Copy." *Journal of Cultural Economy* 3, no. 1:85–102. doi:10.1080/17530351003617602.

Helmreich, S. 2000. *Silicon Second Nature: Culturing Artificial Life in a Digital World*. Berkeley: University of California Press.

Hesmondhalgh, David. 2005. "Subcultures, Scenes or Tribes? None of the Above." *Journal of Youth Studies* 8, no. 1:21–40.

Hickey, Sam, and Giles Mohan. 2005. "Relocating Participation within a Radical Politics of Development." *Development and Change* 36, no. 2 (March 1): 237–62. https://doi.org/10.1111/j.0012-155X.2005.00410.x.

High Level Committee on the Indian Diaspora. 2001. *Report of the High Level Committee on Indian Diaspora*. Delhi: Ministry of External Affairs.

Hill, Charles, and Gareth Jones. 2007. *Strategic Management: An Integrated Approach*. Boston: Cengage Learning.

Holtzblatt, Karen, and Sandra Jones. 1993. "Contextual Inquiry: A Participatory Technique for System Design." In *Participatory Design: Principles and Practices*, edited by Douglas Schuler and Aki Namioka, 177–210. Hillsdale, NJ: Erlbaum.

Hull, Matthew S. 2003. "The File: Agency, Authority, and Autography in an Islamabad Bureaucracy." *Language & Communication* 23, nos. 3–4:287–314. https://doi.org/10.1016/S0271-5309(03)00019-3.

———. 2010. "Democratic Technologies of Speech: From WWII America to Postcolonial Delhi." *Journal of Linguistic Anthropology* 20, no. 2:257–82.

Hutchins, Edwin. 1995. *Cognition in the Wild*. Cambridge, MA: MIT Press.

Huxley, J. 1948. "Dr. Huxley's Suggestions for the Advance of World Civilization." *UNESCO Courier* 1, no. 10 (November): 1–6.

Hyysalo, Sampsa. 2006. "Representations of Use and Practice-Bound Imaginaries in Automating the Safety of the Elderly." *Social Studies of Science* 36, no. 4:599–626.

IDEO. 2009. "Design Kit: The Human-Centered Design Tool" (blog). https://www.ideo.com /post/design-kit.

"Importing Efficiency: Can Lessons from Mumbai's Dabbawalas Help Its Taxi Drivers?" 2011. *Knowledge@Wharton*. October 12. http://knowledge.wharton.upenn.edu/article /importing-efficiency-can-lessons-from-mumbais-dabbawalas-help-its-taxi-drivers/.

"In the Spirit of Ashoka." 2002. *Business Standard*. January 28. New Delhi.

"India@Davos: Batting for Inclusive Growth." 2011. *NDTV*. January 29. Video. https://www .ndtv.com/video/news/the-big-fight/india-davos-batting-for-inclusive-growth-189493.

India Chartbook of Economic Inequality. 2017. Website. http://www.chartbookofeconomicinequality .com/inequality-by-country/india/.

"India Has Exam System, Not Education System: CN Rao." 2011. *India Education Review*. April 14. http://www.indiaeducationreview.com/news/india-has-exam-system-not -education-system-cn-rao.

"India Must Now Start Delivering World-Class Products: ET Jury." 2011. *Economic Times*. October 6. http://articles.economictimes.indiatimes.com/2011-10-06/news /30250498_1_innovation-unilever-coo-harish-manwani.

"India Needs 115 Million Non-Farm Jobs over Next Decade: President Pranab Mukherjee." 2016. *Economic Times*. March 13. http://economictimes.indiatimes.com/industry/jobs /india-needs-115-million-non-farm-jobs-over-next-decade-president-pranab-mukherjee /articleshow/51381899.cms.

"India Placed at 43rd among 45 Nations in Global Innovation Index." 2017. *Hindustan Times*. February 8. http://www.hindustantimes.com/india-news/india-placed-at-43rd-among -45-nations-in-global-innovation-index/story-4gtIA7cWoUnaJklPe95BfJ.html.

"India Should Implement IPR Laws to Become Dominant." 2003. *Economic Times*. November 20. https://economictimes.indiatimes.com/news/economy/policy/india-should-implement -ipr-laws-to-become-dominant/articleshow/292293.cms.

"Indialogues: Conversations with the World." 2012. Davos. http://www.indialogues.in /InDialogues@Davos.pdf.

"The Indian Diaspora." 2015. Indiandiaspora.nic.in website. March 30. New Delhi: Ministry of External Affairs. https://web.archive.org/web/20150330050718/http://indiandiaspora .nic.in/DUALCITIZENSHIP.htm.

"Indian Industry Should Evolve New Paradigm." 2003. *Hindu Business Line*. April 29. https:// www.thehindubusinessline.com/2003/04/29/stories/2003042901930400.htm.

"India's Biggest Asset Is 'Soft Power.'" 2011. *Hindu*. Oct 31. http://www.thehindu.com/news /national/tamil-nadu/article2583279.ece.

Ingold, T. 2009. "Against Space: Place, Movement, Knowledge." In *Boundless Worlds: An Anthropological Approach to Movement*, edited by P. W. Kirby, 29–43. New York: Berghahn.

Irani, Lilly. 2015a. "Difference and Dependence among Digital Workers: The Case of Amazon Mechanical Turk." *South Atlantic Quarterly* 114, no. 1:225–34.

———. 2015b. "The Cultural Work of Microwork." *New Media & Society* 17, no. 5:720–39.

Irani, Lilly. 2018. "'Design Thinking': Defending Silicon Valley at the Apex of Global Labor Hierarchies." *Catalyst: Feminism, Theory, Technoscience* 4, no. 1.

Irani, Lilly, Janet Vertesi, Paul Dourish, Kavita Philip, and Rebecca E. Grinter. 2010. "Postcolonial Computing: A Lens on Design and Development." In *Proceedings of the SIGCHI Conference on Human Factors in Computing Systems*, 1311–20. New York: ACM. http://doi.acm.org/10.1145/1753326.1753522.

Irwin, John. 1977. *Scenes*. City & Society, vol. 1. Beverly Hills: Sage.

Isaacson, Walter. 2014. *The Innovators: How a Group of Inventors, Hackers, Geniuses and Geeks Created the Digital Revolution*. New York: Simon and Schuster.

Jackson, Jason. 2013. "The Political Economy of Foreign Investment: Constructing Cultural Categories of Capitalist Legitimacy in India." Ph.D. dissertation, Massachusetts Institute of Technology.

Jackson, S. J., A. Pompe, and G. Krieshok. 2011. "Things Fall Apart: Maintenance, Repair, and Technology for Education Initiatives in Rural Namibia." In *Proceedings of the 2011 iConference*, 83–90. New York: ACM.

Jadeja, Asha. 2012. Opening remarks presented at the World Economic Forum, Davos, Switzerland. January 26. http://www.indialogues.in/Dspeakers_AshaJadeja.htm.

Jain, Sara S. Lochlann. 2006. *Injury: The Politics of Product Design and Safety Law in the United States*. Princeton, NJ: Princeton University Press.

Jayakar, Pupul. 1983. "The Design of History." *Times of India (1861–Current)*. November 20, sec. Editorial Letters.

———. 1992. *Indira Gandhi: An Intimate Biography*. New York: Pantheon Books.

Jayal, Niraja Gopal. 2013. *Citizenship and Its Discontents*. Cambridge, MA: Harvard University Press.

Jeffrey, Craig. 2010. *Timepass: Youth, Class, and the Politics of Waiting in India*. Stanford, CA: Stanford University Press.

Jenkins, Robert. 2004. "Labor Policy and the Second Generation of Economic Reform in India." *India Review* 3, no. 4:333–63. doi:10.1080/14736480490895660.

Jiménez, Alberto Corsín. 2014. "Introduction: The Prototype: More than Many and Less than One." *Journal of Cultural Economy* 7, no. 4 (October 2): 381–98. https://doi.org/10.1080/17530350.2013.858059.

Jodhka, Surinder S. 2002. "Nation and Village: Images of Rural India in Gandhi, Nehru and Ambedkar." *Economic and Political Weekly*, 3343–53.

Jodhka, Surinder S., and Katherine Newman. 2007. "In the Name of Globalisation: Meritocracy, Productivity and the Hidden Language of Caste." *Economic and Political Weekly* 42, no. 41:4125–32.

Jones, Graham M., Beth Semel, and Audrey Le. 2015. "'There's No Rules. It's Hackathon': Negotiating Commitment in a Context of Volatile Sociality." *Journal of Linguistic Anthropology* 25, no. 3 (December 1): 322–45. https://doi.org/10.1111/jola.12104.

Jones, S., and N. Greene. 2013. Crossfire: Can "Admitting Failure" Help the WASH Sector Learn and Improve Its Work?" *Waterlines* 32, no. 2:100–105. http://doi.org/10.3362/1756–3488.2013.011.

Jose, A., A. Ghimray, M. Kadu, S. R. Tudu, and R. Rajeevan. 2007. *Unni: The Plight of a Kid and Many Others*. Ahmedabad. Film. https://vimeo.com/24413579.

Kannan, K. P. 2007. "Interrogating Inclusive Growth: Some Reflections on Exclusionary Growth and Prospects for Inclusive Development in India." *Indian Journal of Labour Economics* 50, no. 1:17–46.

Karim, F. S. 2011. "Modernity Transfers: The MOMA in Postcolonial India." In *Third World Modernism: Architecture, Development, and Identity*, edited by Duanfang Lu. New York: Routledge.

Karim, L. 2011. *Microfinance and Its Discontents: Women in Debt in Bangladesh*. Minneapolis: University of Minnesota Press.

Kasturi, Poonam Bir. 2002. *The India Report Revisited*. https://web.archive.org/web/20140821140520/https://innovstrategy.files.wordpress.com/2007/05/the_india_report_revisited.pdf.

———. 2005. "Designing Freedom." *Design Issues* 21, no. 4:68–77.

Kaur, Ravinder. 2012. "Nation's Two Bodies: Rethinking the Idea of 'New' India and Its Other." *Third World Quarterly* 33, no. 4:603–21. doi:10.1080/01436597.2012.657420.

———. 2016. "The Innovative Indian: Common Man and the Politics of Jugaad Culture." *Contemporary South Asia* 24, no. 3:313–27.

Kelty, Christopher M. 2008. *Two Bits: The Cultural Significance of Free Software*. Durham, NC: Duke University Press.

Kensing, F., and J. Blomberg. 1998. "Participatory Design: Issues and Concerns." *Computer Supported Cooperative Work (CSCW)* 7:167–85.

Kesavan, Mukul. 2016. "Purging the Poor." *Telegraph India*. November 21. https://www.telegraphindia.com/1161121/jsp/opinion/story_120304.jsp#.WLFK5oEzqRs.

Kestenbaum, D. 2010. "India's China Envy." NPR.org. May 20. http://www.npr.org/templates/story/story.php?storyId=127014493.

Khandekar, Aalok, and Deepa S. Reddy. 2013. "An Indian Summer: Corruption, Class, and the Lokpal Protests." *Journal of Consumer Culture*. August. https://doi.org/10.1177/1469540513498614.

Khanna, Tarun. 2007. *Billions of Entrepreneurs: How China and India Are Reshaping Their Futures—and Yours*. Boston: Harvard Business School Press.

Kiely, R. 1998. "Neo Liberalism Revised? A Critical Account of World Bank Concepts of Good Governance and Market Friendly Intervention." *Capital & Class*, 22, no. 1:63–88.

Kienzie, L. 2014. "Best of 2013: Product Development for the Poor: A Crash Course in Human-Centered Design." *NextBillion* (blog). January 2. http://nextbillion.net/blogpost.aspx?blogid=3384.

Kim, W. Chan, and Renée Mauborgne. 2004. *Blue Ocean Strategy: How To Create Uncontested Market Space And Make The Competition Irrelevant*. Boston: Harvard Business Review Press.

Kimbell, Lucy. 2011. "Rethinking Design Thinking: Part I." *Design and Culture* 3, no. 3 (November 1): 285–306. https://doi.org/10.2752/175470811X13071166525216.

Kini, Ashvin R. 2014. "Diasporic Relationalities: Queer Affiliations in Shani Mootoo's 'Out on Main Street.'" *South Asian Review* 35, no. 3. http://www.academia.edu/download/36288452/Kini_Diasporic_Relationalities.pdf.

Kloos, Stephan. 2016. "The Recognition of Sowa Rigpa in India: How Tibetan Medicine Became an Indian Medical System." *Issues* 3, no. 3.

Knobel, Cory, and Geoffrey C. Bowker. 2011. "Values in Design." *Communications of the ACM* 54, no. 7:26–28.

Kochanek, Stanley A. 1995. "The Transformation of Interest Politics in India." *Pacific Affairs* 68, no. 4:529–50. doi:10.2307/2761275.

Kogut, Bruce. 1985. "Designing Global Strategies: Comparative and Competitive Value-Added Chains." *MIT Sloan Management Review* 26, no. 4 (Summer): 15–28.

Kohli, Atul. 2006a. "Politics of Economic Growth in India, 1980–2005: Part I: The 1980s." *Economic and Political Weekly* 41, no. 13:1251–59.

———. 2006b. "Politics of Economic Growth in India, 1980–2005: Part II: The 1990s and Beyond." *Economic and Political Weekly* 41, no. 14:1361–70.

———. 2012. *Poverty amid Plenty in the New India*. Cambridge: Cambridge University Press.

Kothari, Rajni. 1994. "Rise of the Dalits and the Renewed Debate on Caste." *Economic and Political Weekly* 29, no. 26:1589–94.

Kothari, Rita, and Rupert Snell. 2011. *Chutnefying English: The Phenomenon of Hinglish*. Delhi: Penguin India.

Kraidy, M., 2006. *Hybridity, or the Cultural Logic of Globalization*. Philadelphia: Temple University Press.

Kramer, Mark R. 2009. "Catalytic Philanthropy." *Stanford Social Innovation Review* 7, no. :30–35.

Kreiss, D., M. Finn, and F. Turner. 2011. "The Limits of Peer Production: Some Reminders from Max Weber for the Network Society." *New Media & Society* 13, no. 2:243–59.

Kripal, Jeffery. 2007. *Esalen: America and the Religion of No Religion*. Chicago: University of Chicago Press.

Krishen, Pradip, director. 1989. *In Which Annie Gives It Those Ones*. Film.

Krueger, Norris F., Jr. 2003. "The Cognitive Psychology of Entrepreneurship." In *Handbook of Entrepreneurship Research*, edited by Zoltan J. Acs and David B. Audretsch, 105–40. International Handbook Series on Entrepreneurship 1. New York: Springer.

Kudva, Neema. 2005. "Strong States, Strong NGOs." In *Social Movements in India: Poverty, Power, and Politics*, edited by Raka Ray and Mary Fainsod Katzenstein, 233–66. New York: Rowan and Littlefield.

Kumar, Nagesh. 2003. "Intellectual Property Rights, Technology and Economic Development: Experiences of Asian Countries." *Economic and Political Weekly* 38, no. 3:209–15, 217–26.

Kumar, R. Anand, Sandiip Kapur, Priya Kapur, Manoj Bajpai, Vijay Raaz, Hrishita Bhatt, Sanjay Mishra, and Mushtaq Khan. 2009. *Jugaad*. Mumbai: Madhu Entertainment & Media. Film.

Kumarappa, J. C. 1958. *Economy of Permanence: A Quest for a Social Order Based on Non-violence*. 4th ed. Rajghat: Akhil Bharat Sarva-Seva-Sangh.

Kunda, Gideon. 2006. *Engineering Culture: Control and Commitment in a High-Tech Corporation*. Rev. ed. Philadelphia: Temple University Press.

Latour, Bruno. 2008. "A Cautious Prometheus? A Few Steps toward a Philosophy of Design (with Special Attention to Peter Sloterdijk)." In *Networks of Design: Proceedings of the 2008 Annual International Conference of the Design History Society*, ed. Jonathan Glynne, Fiona Hackney, and Viv Minton, 2–10. Boca Raton, FL: Universal Publishers.

Latour, Bruno, and Vincent Antonin Lépinay. 2010. *The Science of Passionate Interests: An Introduction to Gabriel Tarde's Economic Anthropology*. Chicago: Prickly Paradigm Press.

Lave, Jean, and Etienne Wenger. 1991. *Situated Learning: Legitimate Peripheral Participation.* Cambridge: Cambridge University Press.

Lazzarato, Maurizio. 2002. "From Biopower to Biopolitics by Maurizio Lazzarato." generation -online.org. http://www.generation-online.org/c/fcbiopolitics.htm.

Le Dantec, Christopher A., and Carl DiSalvo. 2013. "Infrastructuring and the Formation of Publics in Participatory Design." *Social Studies of Science* 43, no. 2:241–64.

Leslie, Stuart W., and Robert Kargon. 2006. "Exporting MIT: Science, Technology, and Nation-Building in India and Iran." *Osiris* 21, no. 1:110–30. doi:10.1086/507138.

Li, Tania Murray. 2007. *The Will to Improve: Governmentality, Development, and the Practice of Politics.* Durham, NC: Duke University Press.

Lindtner, Silvia. 2014. "Hackerspaces and the Internet of Things in China: How Makers Are Reinventing Industrial Production, Innovation, and the Self." *China Information* 28, no. 2:145–67.

Lindtner, S., K. Anderson, and P. Dourish. 2012. "Cultural Appropriation: Information Technologies as Sites of Transnational Imagination." In *Proceedings of the ACM 2012 Conference on Computer Supported Cooperative Work,* 77–86. February. New York: ACM.

Lindtner, S., and S. Avle. 2017. "Tinkering with Governance: Technopolitics and the Economization of Citizenship." *Proceedings of the ACM on Human-Computer Interaction,* vol. 1, issue CSCW. November. New York: ACM. doi:10.1145/3134705.

Lok Sabha, India. 2010. "The Companies Bill, 2009." Standing Committee on Finance, Twenty-First Report.

Lowe, Lisa. 2014. *The Intimacies of Four Continents.* Durham, NC: Duke University Press.

Lu, Duanfang. 2010. *Third World Modernism: Architecture, Development, and Identity.* New York: Routledge.

Lucchi, M. 2015. "Poonam Bir Kasturi Honoured as India's 2015 Social Entrepreneurs of the Year." *World Economic Forum.* November. https://www.weforum.org/press/2015/11 /poonam-bir-kasturi-honoured-as-indias-2015-social-entrepreneurs-of-the-year/.

Ludden, David. 2005. "Development Regimes in South Asia: History and the Governance Conundrum." *Economic and Political Weekly* 40, no. 37:4042–51.

Lukose, Ritty. 2009. *Liberalization's Children: Gender, Youth, and Consumer Citizenship in Globalizing India.* Durham, NC: Duke University Press.

Lynch, Jane. 2016. "The Good of Cloth: Bringing Ethics to Market in India's Handloom Textile Industry." Ph.D. dissertation, University of Michigan, https://deepblue.lib.umich.edu /handle/2027.42/135934.

Mackenzie, A. 2006. *Cutting Code: Software and Sociality.* Bern: Peter Lang.

Madhok. Ruchita. 2013. "5 Reasons Why We Need Design Histories in India." *Perch.* September 21. http://perchontheweb.com/design-history-india/.

Mahindra, Anand, and Tarun Khanna. 2004. "Building 100 Indian MNCs." *India Today.* March 29.

Maira, Arun. 2009. "An Effective Governance Model." *Economic Times.* December 4. https:// economictimes.indiatimes.com/opinion/et-commentary/an-effective-governance-model /articleshow/5298319.cms.

———. 2015. "Will India Muddle along, Fall Apart or Will the Flotilla Advance?" *Founding Fuel* (blog). November 10. http://www.foundingfuel.com/article/will-india-muddle-along -fall-apart-or-will-the-flotilla-advance/.

Maiti, D., and K. Sen. 2010. "The Informal Sector in India: A Means of Exploitation or Accumulation?" *Journal of South Asian Development* 5, no. 1:1–13.

Makri, Anita. 2017. "India Prompts Rethink for Global Innovation Index." *SciDev.net*. March 15. http://www.scidev.net/global/innovation/multimedia/india-global-innovation-index-gurry.html.

Malaby, Thomas. 2009. *The Making of Virtual Worlds: Linden Lab and Second Life*. Ithaca, NY: Cornell University Press.

Mamdani, M. 1996. *Citizen and Subject: Contemporary Africa and the Legacy of Late Colonialism.* Princeton, NJ: Princeton University Press.

Mani, B., and L. Varadarajan. 2005. "The Largest Gathering of the Global Indian Family: Neoliberalism, Nationalism, and Diaspora at Pravasi Bharatiya Divas." *Diaspora: A Journal of Transnational Studies* 14, no. 1:45–74.

Mankekar, Purnima. 2015. *Unsettling India: Affect, Temporality, Transnationality*. Durham, NC: Duke University Press.

Mansuri, Ghazala, Vijayendra Rao, and World Bank. *Localizing Development: Does Participation Work?* Washington, DC: World Bank, 2013. http://public.eblib.com/choice/publicfullrecord.aspx?p=1076074.

Marcus, George E. 1995. "Ethnography in/of the World System: The Emergence of Multi-Sited Ethnography." *Annual Review of Anthropology* 2, no. 24:95–117.

Marwick, A. E., 2013. *Status Update: Celebrity, Publicity, and Branding in the Social Media Age*. New Haven, CT: Yale University Press.

Marx, Karl. 1978. "The German Ideology." In *The Marx-Engels Reader*, edited by Robert C Tucker, 146–200. New York: Norton.

Mathur, Saloni. 2007. *India by Design: Colonial History and Cultural Display*. Berkeley: University of California Press.

———. 2011. "Charles and Ray Eames in India." *Art Journal* 70, no. 1 (Spring): 34–53.

Maurer, W. M. 1995. "Complex Subjects: Offshore Finance, Complexity Theory, and the Dispersion of the Modern." *Socialist Review* 25, nos. 3 and 4. http://escholarship.org/uc/item/3pr7f1d4.pdf.

———. 2012a. "Mobile Money: Communication, Consumption and Change in the Payments Space." *Journal of Development Studies* 48, no. 5:589–604.

———. 2012b. "Payment: Forms and Functions of Value Transfer in Contemporary Society." *Cambridge Journal of Anthropology* 30, no. 2:15–35.

Mavhunga, Clapperton Chakanetsa. 2014. *Transient Workspaces: Technologies of Everyday Innovation in Zimbabwe*. Cambridge, MA: MIT Press.

Mazer, R. 2009. "Should Irrationality Be Incorporated into Product Design?" *CGAP* (Microfinance blog). November 6. https://web.archive.org/web/20091122030346/http://microfinance.cgap.org/.

Mazzarella, William. 2002. "Cindy at the Taj: Cultural Enclosure and Corporate Potentateship in an Era of Globalization." *Ms.* http://www.academia.edu/757359/Cindy_at_the_Taj_cultural_enclosure_and_corporate_potentateship_in_an_era_of_globalization.

———. 2003. *Shoveling Smoke: Advertising and Globalization in Contemporary India*. Durham, NC: Duke University Press.

———. 2004. "Culture, Globalization, Mediation." *Annual Review of Anthropology* 33 (January): 345–67.

———. 2005. "Middle Class." *Keywords in South Asian Studies*, edited by R. Dwyer. SOAS, University of London. https://www.soas.ac.uk/south-asia-institute/keywords/.

———. 2009. "Affect: What Is It Good for?" In *Enchantments of Modernity: Empire, Nation, Globalization*, edited by S. Dube, 291–309. New Delhi: Routledge.

———. 2010a. "Beautiful Balloon: The Digital Divide and the Charisma of New Media in India." *American Ethnologist* 37, no. 4:783–804.

———. 2010b. "Branding the Mahatma: The Untimely Provocation of Gandhian Publicity." *Cultural Anthropology* 25, no. 1:1–39.

Mazzucato, Mariana. 2013. *The Entrepreneurial State: Debunking Public vs. Private Sector Myths.* New York: Anthem Press.

McCarthy, Kathleen D. 1987. "From Cold War to Cultural Development: The International Cultural Activities of the Ford Foundation, 1950–1980." *Daedalus* 116, no. 1:93–117

McClelland, David C. 1961. *The Achieving Society.* New York: Irvington.

McGoey, L. 2015. *No Such Thing as a Free Gift: the Gates Foundation and the Price of Philanthropy.* London: Verso.

Mehrotra, N. N. 1987. "Indian Patents Act, Paris Convention and Self-Reliance." *Economic and Political Weekly* 22, no. 34:1461–65.

Menon, Lekha. 2010. "Abhijat: Why Should Joy Vanish from Studies?" *Times of India.* January 17. http://articles.timesofindia.indiatimes.com/2010-01-17/news-interviews /28130686_1_raju-hirani-idiots-success-story.

Menon, N., and A. Nigam. 2007. *Power and Contestation: India since 1989.* Halifax, NS: Fernwood.

Merchant, Carolyn. 2003. *Reinventing Eden: The Fate of Nature in Western Culture.* New York: Routledge.

Mialet, H. 2012. *Hawking Incorporated: Stephen Hawking and the Anthropology of the Knowing Subject.* Chicago: University of Chicago Press.

Ministry of Corporate Affairs, Government of India. 2013. *The Companies Act 2013.* http://www .mca.gov.in/MinistryV2/companiesact2013.html.

Ministry of Science and Technology, Government of India. 2003. "Science and Technology Policy—India." http://dst.gov.in/stsysindia/stp2003.htm.

Modi, Sanjay. 2017. "The Elephant in the Room —Our Population." *Hindu Business Line.* June 18. http://www.thehindubusinessline.com/opinion/indias-demographic-dividend-is-a-myth /article9729947.ece.

Mol, A. 2002. *The Body Multiple: Ontology in Medical Practice.* Durham, NC: Duke University Press.

Moodie, M. 2013. "Microfinance and the Gender of Risk: The Case of Kiva.org." *Signs* 38, no. 2:279–302.

Moore, Karl. 2011. "The Best Way to Innovation?—An Important Lesson from India." *Forbes.* May 24. http://www.forbes.com/sites/karlmoore/2011/05/24/the-best-way-to -innovation-an-important-lesson-from-india/.

Morgan, L. H. 1877. *Ancient Society; or, Researches in the Lines of Human Progress from Savagery, through Barbarism to Civilization.* New York: Holt.

Morozov, Evgeny. 2013. *To Save Everything, Click Here: The Folly of Technological Solutionism.* New York: PublicAffairs.

Morse, Chandler. 1969. *Modernization by Design; Social Change in the Twentieth Century.* Ithaca, NY: Cornell University Press.

Moyo, Dambisa. 2010. *Dead Aid: Why Aid Is Not Working and How There Is a Better Way for Africa.* New York: Farrar, Straus, and Giroux.

Mosse, David. 2011. "Social Analysis as Corporate Product: Non-economists/Anthropologists at Work in the World Bank in Washington DC." In *Adventures in Aidland: The Anthropology of Professionals in International Development,* edited by David Mosse, 81–102. Oxford: Berghahn.

———. 2013. "The Anthropology of International Development." *Annual Review of Anthropology* 42, no. 1:227–46. doi:10.1146/annurev-anthro-092412–155553.

 Moulier-Boutang, Yann. 2011. *Cognitive Capitalism.* New York: Polity.

Muehlebach, A. 2012. *The Moral Neoliberal: Welfare and Citizenship in Italy.* Chicago: University of Chicago Press.

Mukerji, Chandra. 2009. *Impossible Engineering: Technology and Territoriality on the Canal du Midi.* Princeton, NJ: Princeton University Press.

———. 2017. *Modernity Reimagined: An Analytic Guide.* New York: Routledge.

Muller, M. J. 2003. "Participatory Design: The Third Space in HCI." *Handbook of HCI.* Mahway, NJ: Erlbaum.

Murphy, Keith. 2005. "Collaborative Imagining: The Interactive Use of Gestures, Talk, and Graphic Representations in Architectural Practice." *Semiotica* 1, no. 4:113–45.

———. 2013. "A Cultural Geometry: Designing Political Things in Sweden." *American Ethnologist* 40, no. 1:118–31.

———. 2015. *Swedish Design: An Ethnography.* Ithaca, NY: Cornell University Press.

 Murphy, Michelle. 2006. *Sick Building Syndrome and the Problem of Uncertainty: Environmental Politics, Technoscience, and Women Workers.* Durham, NC: Duke University Press.

 ———. 2012. *Seizing the Means of Reproduction.* Durham, NC: Duke University Press.

———. 2017. *Economization of Life.* Durham, NC: Duke University Press.

Nadeem, Shehzad. 2013. *Dead Ringers: How Outsourcing Is Changing the Way Indians Understand Themselves.* Princeton, NJ: Princeton University Press.

Nakassis, C. V. 2012. "Brand, Citationality, Performativity." *American Anthropologist* 114, 4:624–38.

Nandy, Ashis. 1972. "Motivating Economic Achievement. David C. McClelland, David G. Winter." *Economic Development and Cultural Change* 20, no. 3:575–81. doi:10.1086/450577.

National Innovation Council, Government of India. 2011. *Report to the People: First Year.* November. https://static1.squarespace.com/static/5356af05e4b095ff0fea9e11/t/5398b142e4b02d32b20de300/1402515778055/Report+to+the+People+2013+-+National+Innovation+Council+%28English%29.pdf.

National Innovation Foundation-India, Government of India. 2016. "Earthen Kitchen Products." http://nif.org.in/innovation/earthen_kitchen/8.

National Knowledge Commission. 2008. *Entrepreneurship in India: A Study by the National Knowledge Commission.* New Delhi.

Nee, E. 2009. "Q & A: Judith Rodin (SSIR)." *Stanford Social Innovation Review*, 13–15.

Neff, Gina. 2012. *Venture Labor: Work and the Burden of Risk in Innovative Industries*. Cambridge, MA: MIT Press.

Nehru, Jawaharlal. 1960 [1942]. *Glimpses of World History*. New York: John Day.

Nelson, Harold G., and Erik Stolterman. 2012. *The Design Way: Intentional Change in an Unpredictable World*. 2nd ed. Cambridge, MA: MIT Press.

Neveling, P. 2014. "Structural Contingencies and Untimely Coincidences in the Making of Neoliberal India: The Kandla Free Trade Zone, 1965–91." *Contributions to Indian Sociology* 48, no. 1:17–43.

Nguyen, Lilly Uyen. 2013. "Networks at Their Limits: Software, Similarity, and Continuity in Vietnam." Ph.D. dissertation, University of California Los Angeles. http://escholarship.org/uc/item/2m98s62z.

———. 2017. "Ethnic Platforms and the Failure of Techno-Futurity." *Journal of Asian American Studies* 20, no. 1: 51–68. doi:10.1353/jaas.2017.0004.

Nigam, A. 2004. "Imagining the Global Nation: Time and Hegemony." *Economic and Political Weekly* 39, no. 1:72–79.

———. 2011. *Desire Named Development*. Delhi: Penguin India.

Nilekani, Nandan. 2009. *Imagining India: The Idea of a Renewed Nation*. New York: Penguin.

Nissenbaum, Helen. 2001. "How Computer Systems Embody Values." *Computer* 34, no. 3 (March): 120, 118–19.

Noble, D. F. 1979. *America by Design: Science, Technology, and the Rise of Corporate Capitalism*. New York: Oxford University Press.

Nussbaum, Martha, and Shoma Chaudhury. 2008. "IIT Feeds into the Fascist Nature of the Right." *Tehelka*. December 8.

Obama, Barack. 2009. "President Obama's Speech in Cairo: A New Beginning." http://www.state.gov/p/nea/rls/rm/2009/124342.htm.

Oldenziel, Ruth. 1999. *Making Technology Masculine: Men, Women and Modern Machines in America, 1870–1945*. Amsterdam: University of Amsterdam Press.

Olson, J. R., and G. Olson. 1995. "The Growth of Cognitive Modeling in Human-Computer Interaction since GOMS." In *Readings in Human-Computer Interaction: Toward the Year 2000*, edited by Ronald M. Baecker, Jonathan Grudin, William A. S. Buxton, and Saul Greenberg. 2nd ed. San Francisco: Morgan Kaufmann.

"On New Year, Modi Brings in NITI Aayog to Replace Planning Commission." 2015. *India Today*. January 1. https://www.indiatoday.in/india/story/narendra-modi-brings-niti-aayog-replace-planning-commission-233705-2015-01-01.

Ong, Aihwa. 1998. *Flexible Citizenship: The Cultural Logics of Transnationality*. Durham, NC: Duke University Press.

Ong, A., and S. J. Collier. 2005. *Global Assemblages: Technology, Politics, and Ethics as Anthropological Problems*. Malden, MA: Wiley-Blackwell.

Orta, Andrew. 2013. "Managing the Margins: MBA Training, International Business, and 'the Value Chain of Culture.'" *American Ethnologist* 40, no. 4 (November 1): 689–703. https://doi.org/10.1111/amet.12048.

Our Bureau. 2003a. "Indian Industry Should Evolve New Paradigm." *Hindu Business Line*. April 29. https://www.thehindubusinessline.com/2003/04/29/stories/2003042901930400.htm.

Our Bureau. 2003b. "By 2020, Quality Should Be—Every Indian's Birth Right." *Hindu Business Line*. November 5. https://www.thehindubusinessline.com/2003/11/05/stories /2003110502290400.htm.

———. 2003c. "It's All about Services." *Hindu Business Line*. November 7. https://www .thehindubusinessline.com/2003/11/07/stories/2003110701500700.htm.

"Out of India." 2011. *Economist*. March 3. http://www.economist.com/node/18285497.

Pal, Sanchari. 2017. "Why Are NRIs Being Asked to Change from PIO to OCI? Here's Everything You Need to Know." *Better India*. January 9. http://www.thebetterindia.com/81394 /nri-pio-oci-pravasi-bharatiya-diwas-india/.

Pal, Yash. 2009. "Report of the Committee to Advise on Renovation and Rejuvenation of Higher Education" (Yash Pal Committee Report). https://web.archive.org/web/20170911094527 /http://mhrd.gov.in/sites/upload_files/mhrd/files/document-reports/YPC-Report_0 .pdf.

Pandolfo, S. 2000. "The Thin Line of Modernity: Some Moroccan Debates on Subjectivity." In *Questions of Modernity*, edited by T. Mitchell. Minneapolis: University of Minnesota Press.

Paprocki, Kasia. 2013. "'Selling Our Own Skin': Microcredit, Depeasantization and Social Dispossession in Rural Bangladesh." *Geoforum* 74:29–38.

Parliamentary Research Services. 2013. "Standing Committee Report Summary: The National Institute of Design Bill 2013." August 27. http://www.prsindia.org/uploads/media/NID /SCR%20summary-NID%20Bill.pdf.

Patel, Geeta. 2006. "Risky Subjects: Insurance, Sexuality, and Capital." *Social Text* 24, no. 4:25–65.

———. 2015. "Seeding Debt: Alchemy, Death, and the Precarious Farming of Life-Finance in the Global South." *Cultural Critique* 89:1–37.

Patil, Pratibha. 2009. "Pratibha Patil Address to Joint Session." *eGov* 5, no. 7:6–9. https://issuu .com/egov_magazine/docs/egov_july_2009_issue.

Patnaik, Dev, and Peter Mortensen. 2009. *Wired to Care: How Companies Prosper When They Create Widespread Empathy*. Upper Saddle River, NJ: FT Press.

Pedersen, Jørgen Dige. 2000. "Explaining Economic Liberalization in India: State and Society Perspectives." *World Development* 28, no. 2:265–82. doi:10.1016/S0305-750X(99)00132-1.

Peters, Tom, and Robert Waterman, Jr. 1982. *In Search of Excellence: Lessons from America's Best-Run Companies*. New York: Harper Collins.

Pham, Jessica. 2017. "Fintech Investment in India Picks Up after Demonetization Move—Crowdfund Insider." *Crowdfund Insider*. January 3. https://www.crowdfundinsider .com/2017/01/94208-fintech-investment-india-picks-demonetization-move/.

Philip, Kavita. 2004. *Civilizing Natures: Race, Resources, and Modernity in Colonial South India*. New Brunswick, NJ: Rutgers University Press.

———. 2005. "What Is a Technological Author? The Pirate Function and Intellectual Property." *Postcolonial Studies* 8, no. 2:199–218.

———. 2008. "Producing Transnational Knowledge, Neoliberal Identities, and Technoscientific Practice in India." In *Tactical Biopolitics: Art, Activism, and Technoscience*, edited by Beatriz Da Costa and Kavita Philip, 243–68. Cambridge, MA: MIT Press.

———. 2012. "¿Tecnologías para pobres o tecnologías pobres? Poscolonialismo, desarrollo y tecnología en India." *Nómadas* 36:91–108.

————. 2016. "Telling Histories of the Future: The Imaginaries of Indian Technoscience." *Identities* 23, no. 3:276–93.

Philip, K., L. Irani, and P. Dourish. 2012. "Postcolonial Computing: A Tactical Survey." *Science, Technology & Human Values* 37, no. 1:3–29.

Pickren, Wade, and Alexandra Rutherford. 2010. *A History of Modern Psychology in Context.* Hoboken, NJ: Wiley.

Pigg, S. L. 1996. "The Credible and the Credulous: The Question of 'Villagers' Beliefs' in Nepal." *Cultural Anthropology* 11, no. 2:160–201.

Pinney, C. 2008. "The Prosthetic Eye: Photography as Cure and Poison." *Journal of the Royal Anthropological Institute* 14:S33–S46.

Planning Commission, Government of India. 1951. "First Five Year Plan." Delhi.

————. 1962. "Third Five Year Plan." Delhi.

————. 1970. "Fourth Five Year Plan." Delhi.

————. 1976. "Fifth Five Year Plan." Delhi.

————. 1980. "Sixth Five Year Plan." Delhi.

————. 1985a. "Seventh Five Year Plan v1." Delhi.

————. 1985b. "Seventh Five Year Plan v2." Delhi.

————. 1992a. "Eighth Five Year Plan v1." Delhi.

————. 1992b. "Eighth Five Year Plan v2." Delhi.

————. 2002a. "Tenth Five Year Plan v1." Delhi.

————. 2002b. "Tenth Five Year Plan v2." Delhi.

————. 2002c. "Tenth Five Year Plan v3." Delhi.

————. 2006. "Report of the Committee on Technology Innovation and Venture Capital." Delhi. http://planningcommission.gov.in/reports/genrep/rep_vcr.pdf.

————. 2007a. "Eleventh Five Year Plan v1." Delhi.

————. 2007b. "Eleventh Five Year Plan v2." Delhi.

————. 2007c. "Eleventh Five Year Plan v3." Delhi.

————. 2012a. "Twelfth Five Year Plan v1." Delhi.

————. 2012b. "Twelfth Five Year Plan v2." Delhi.

————. 2012c. "Twelfth Five Year Plan v3." Delhi.

————. 2012d. "Creating a Vibrant Entrepreneurial Ecosystem." June. http://planningcommission.nic.in/reports/genrep/rep_eco2708.pdf.

————. 2013. "Scenarios: Shaping India's Future." http://planningcommission.nic.in/reports/genrep/rep_sce2307.pdf.

Pollock, Anne, and Banu Subramaniam. 2016. "Resisting Power, Retooling Justice: Promises of Feminist Postcolonial Technosciences." *Science, Technology & Human Values* 41, no. 6:951–66. doi:10.1177/0162243916657879.

Porter, Michael E., and Mark R. Kramer. 1999. "Philanthropy's New Agenda: Creating Value." *Harvard Business Review* 77:121–31.

Poster, W. 2013. "Subversions of Techno-masculinity: Indian ICT Professionals in the Global Economy." In *Rethinking Transnational Men: Beyond, between and within Nations*, edited by J. Hearn, M. Blagojevic, and K. Harrison, 123–35. New York: Routledge.

Prahalad, C. K. 2005. *The Fortune at the Bottom of the Pyramid: Eradicating Poverty through Profits.* Philadelphia: Wharton School.

Prakash, Gyan, 1999. *Another Reason: Science and the Imagination of Modern India*. Princeton, NJ: Princeton University Press.

Prashad, Vijay. 2007. *The Darker Nations: A People's History of the Third World*. New York: New Press.

———. 2012. *The Poorer Nations: A Possible History of the Global South*. New York: Verso.

Prayag, Anjali. 2007. "Indian Retail and Biyanispeak." *Hindu Business Line*. http://www .thehindubusinessline.com/todays-paper/tp-new-manager/indian-retail-and-biyanispeak /article1687363.ece.

Press Information Bureau, Government of India. 2007. "National Design Policy." Delhi: Government of India. http://pib.nic.in/newsite/mbErel.aspx?relid=124039.

———. 2015. "Government Establishes NITI Aayog (National Institution for Transforming India) to Replace Planning Commission." January 1. https://perma.cc/RXX2-4U5A.

Prime Minister's Office, Government of India. 2004. "National Common Minimum Programme of the Government of India." https://web.archive.org/web/20130418073521/ http://pmindia.nic.in/cmp.pdf.

Punathambekar, A. 2005. "Bollywood in the Indian-American Diaspora: Mediating a Transitive Logic of Cultural Citizenship." *International Journal of Cultural Studies* 8, no. 2:151–73.

Radhakrishnan, Smitha. 2007. "Rethinking Knowledge for Development: Transnational Knowledge Professionals and the 'New' India." *Theory and Society* 36, no. 2:141–59.

Radjou, Navi, Jaideep Prabhu, and Simone Ahuja. 2010. "Jugaad: A New Growth Formula for Corporate America." *Harvard Business Review*. January 25. https://hbr.org/2010/01 /jugaad-a-new-growth-formula-fo.

Rai, Saritha. 2016. "Nilekani: Nandan Nilekani Joins Battle to Map India's Post-Cash Future." *Economic Times*. December 8. http://economictimes.indiatimes.com/news/economy /policy/nandan-nilekani-joins-battle-to-map-indias-post-cash-future/articleshow /55871177.cms.

Rajadhyaksha, M. 2013. "You Have to Teach Empathy Like Literacy: Bill Drayton, Ashoka Foundation." *Economic Times*. July 8. https://economictimes.indiatimes.com/opinion /interviews/You-have-to-teach-empathy-like-literacy-Bill-Drayton-Ashoka-Foundation /articleshow/20952746.cms.

Rajadyaksha, Niranjan. 2011. "What the Poor Really Want." *Hindustan Times*.

Rajagopal, Arvind. 2001. *Politics after Television: Religious Nationalism and the Reshaping of the Indian Public*. New York: Cambridge University Press.

———. 2002. "Violence of Commodity Aesthetics: Hawkers, Demolition Raids and a New Regime of Consumption Author(s): Arvind Rajagopal Reviewed Work(s)." *Economic and Political Weekly* 37, no. 1:65–67, 69–76.

———. 2006. "Art for Whose Sake? Artistic Citizenship as an Uncertain Thing." In *Artistic Citizenship: A Public Voice for the Arts*, edited by Mary Schmidt Campbell and Randy Martin, 137–50. New York: Routledge.

———. 2011. "The Emergency as Prehistory of the New Indian Middle Class." *Modern Asian Studies* 45, no. 5:1003–49. doi:10.1017/S0026749X10000314.

Rajan, Prashant. 2012. "Organizing Grassroots Innovations: Examining Knowledge Creation and Sharing Practices for Technological Innovation at the Grassroots." Ph.D. dissertation, Purdue University. http://search.proquest.com/docview/1328167526.

Raje, Aparna Piramal. 2011. "Using Design Principles for Good Governance." Livemint.com. March 24. http://www.livemint.com/Industry/0T6edJX62RaisWOSxuYzQN/Using-design-principles-for-good-governance.html.

Rajpal, A. 2008. *Ashish Rajpal on Multiple Intelligences-2*. April 13. YouTube video. http://www.youtube.com/watch?v=psAANUqHUbw.

Ramamurthy, Priti. 2004. "Why Is Buying a 'Madras' Cotton Shirt a Political Act? A Feminist Commodity Chain Analysis." *Feminist Studies* 30, no. 3:734–69. doi:10.2307/20458998.

———. 2014. "Why Are Men Doing Floral Sex Work? Gender, Cultural Reproduction, and the Feminization of Agriculture." *Signs* 40, no. 1.

Ramanna, Anitha. 2002. "Policy Implications of India's Patent Reforms: Patent Applications in the Post-1995 Era." *Economic and Political Weekly* 37, no. 21:2065–75.

Ramesh, Randeep. 2004. "Shock Defeat for India's Hindu Nationalists." *Guardian*. May 14. https://www.theguardian.com/world/2004/may/14/india.randeepramesh.

Ranjan, Aditi, and M. P. Ranjan. 2007. *Handmade in India: Crafts of India*. New Delhi: Council of Handicraft Development Corporations.

Ranjan, M. P. 2007. "Lessons from Bauhaus, Ulm and NID: Role of Basic Design in Post-Graduate Education." In *Design Education: Tradition & Modernity*, edited by Vijay Singh Katiyar and Shashank Mehta. Ahmedabad: National Institute of Design.

Rao, C. H. Hanumantha. 2009. "Inclusive Growth: Recent Experience and Challenges Ahead." *Economic and Political Weekly* 44, no. 13:16–21.

Rao, Veena. 2004. "The Real Swadesis." *NRI Pulse*. https://perma.cc/4LNP-E77A.

Rao, Vijayendra, and Michael Walton. 2004. *Culture and Public Action*. Stanford, CA: Stanford University Press.

Rao, Vijayendra, and Paromita Sanyal. 2010. "Dignity through Discourse: Poverty and the Culture of Deliberation in Indian Village Democracies." *Annals of the American Academy of Political and Social Science* 629, no. 1 (May 1): 146–72. https://doi.org/10.1177/0002716209357402.

Raqs Media Collective. 2009. "Earthworms Dancing: Notes for a Biennial in Slow Motion—Journal #7 June-August 2009—e-Flux." *E-Flux*, no. 7 (June). http://www.e-flux.com/journal/07/61387/earthworms-dancing-notes-for-a-biennial-in-slow-motion/.

Ray, Debraj. 2006. "Aspirations, Poverty, and Economic Change." In *Understanding Poverty*, edited by A. V. Banerjee, R. Benabou, and D. Mookherjee, 409–21. Oxford: Oxford University Press.

Ray, Raka, and Mary Fainsod Katzenstein, eds. 2005. *Social Movements in India: Poverty, Power, and Politics*. Asia/Pacific/Perspectives. Lanham, MD: Rowman & Littlefield.

Ray, Raka, and Seemin Quyum. 2009. *Cultures of Servitude*. Stanford, CA: Stanford University Press.

Raymond, Eric S. 2001. *The Cathedral & the Bazaar: Musings on Linux and Open Source by an Accidental Revolutionary*. Sebastopol, CA: O'Reilly Media.

Redfield, Peter. 2012. "The Unbearable Lightness of Expats." *Cultural Anthropology* 27, no. 2:358–82.

———. 2015. "Fluid Technologies: The Bush Pump, the LifeStraw® and Microworlds of Humanitarian Design." *Social Studies of Science*. December 31. https://doi.org/10.1177/0306312715620061.

Rice, A. K. 1958. *Productivity and Social Organization, the Ahmedabad Experiment: Technical Innovation, Work Organization and Management*. London: Tavistock.

Roberts, Sarah. 2016. "Commercial Content Moderation: Digital Laborers' Dirty Work." In *The Intersectional Internet: Race, Sex, Class and Culture Online*, edited by S. U. Noble & B. Tynes. Bern: Peter Lang.

Rofel, L. 1992. "Rethinking Modernity: Space and Factory Discipline in China." *Cultural Anthropology* 7, 1:93–114.

Rogers, Everett. 1973. *Communication Strategies for Family Planning*, New York: Free Press.

———. 1983. *Diffusion of Innovations*. 3rd ed. New York: Free Press.

———. 2003. *Diffusion of Innovations*. 5th ed. New York: Free Press.

Rogers, E. M., and W. Herzog. 1966. "Functional Literacy among Colombian Peasants." *Economic Development and Cultural Change* 14, no. 2:190–203.

Roper, C. 2013. "The Human Element: Melinda Gates and Paul Farmer on Designing Global Health." *Wired* 21, no. 12 (November 12). http://www.wired.com/2013/11/2112gatefarmers/.

Rose, Nikolas S. 1999. *Powers of Freedom: Reframing Political Thought*. Cambridge: Cambridge University Press.

Rosenberg, E. 2013. "Zuckerberg Latest to Aim for Universal Internet Access." *US News and World Report*. August 21. http://www.usnews.com/news/articles/2013/08/21/zuckerberg-latest-to-aim-for-universal-internet-access-facebook-founders-internetorg-initiative-partners-with-tech-giants-to-extend-access-to-5-billion-people.

Rosner, Daniela K. 2014. "Making Citizens, Reassembling Devices: On Gender and the Development of Contemporary Public Sites of Repair in Northern California." *Public Culture* 26, no. 1 (72): 51–77.

———. 2018. *Critical Fabulations Reworking the Methods and Margins of Design*. Cambridge, MA: MIT Press.

Rostow, W. W. 1960. *The Stages of Economic Growth: A Non-Communist Manifesto*. Cambridge: Cambridge University Press.

Roy, Ananya. 2010. *Poverty Capital: Microfinance and the Making of Development*. New York: Routledge.

———. 2014. "Slum-Free Cities of the Asian Century: Postcolonial Government and the Project of Inclusive Growth." *Singapore Journal of Tropical Geography* 35, no. 1:136–50.

Roy, Arundhati. 2014. *Capitalism: A Ghost Story*. Chicago: Haymarket Books.

Roy, B., and J. Hartigan. 2008. "Empowering the Rural Poor to Develop Themselves: The Barefoot Approach (Innovations Case Narrative: Barefoot College of Tilonia)." *Innovations: Technology, Governance, Globalization* 3, no. 2:67–93.

Roy, C., and A. Celestine. 2009. *Legislative Brief: The Companies Bill, 2009*. Parliamentary Research Services. http://www.prsindia.org/uploads/media/Company/Legislative%20Brief--companies%20bill%202009.pdf.

Roy, Srila. 2011. "Politics, Passion and Professionalization in Contemporary Indian Feminism." *Sociology* 45, no. 4:587–602.

Roy, Srirupa. 2007. *Beyond Belief: India and the Politics of Postcolonial Nationalism*. Politics, History, and Culture. Durham, NC: Duke University Press.

Roy Chowdhury, Supriya. 2013. "Political Economy of India: A Selected Review of Literature." In *Political Science*, 1:79–110. ICSSR Research Surveys and Explorations. New Delhi: Oxford University Press.

Russell, Andrew, and Lee Vinsel. 2016. "Hail the Maintainers: Capitalism Excels at Innovation but Is Failing at Maintenance, and for Most Lives It Is Maintenance That Matters More." *Aeon* (blog). April 15. https://aeon.co/essays/innovation-is-overvalued-maintenance-often-matters-more.

Sacchetto, Devi, and Rutvica Andrijasevic. 2015. "Beyond China: Foxconn's Assembly Plants in Europe." *South Atlantic Quarterly* 114, no. 1 (January 1): 215–24. https://doi.org/10.1215/00382876-2831654.

Said, Edward. 1974. *Orientalism.* New York: Vintage.

Sainath, P. 1996. *Everybody Loves a Good Drought: Stories from India's Poorest Districts.* Delhi: Penguin India.

Salehi, Niloufar, Lilly C. Irani, and Michael S. Bernstein. 2015. "We Are Dynamo: Overcoming Stalling and Friction in Collective Action for Crowd Workers." In *Proceedings of the 33rd Annual ACM Conference on Human Factors in Computing Systems,* 1621–30. New York: ACM. http://www.kristymilland.com/papers/Salehi.2015.We.Are.Dynamo.pdf.

Salvador, T., G. Bell, and K. Anderson. 1999. "Design Ethnography." *Design Management Journal* 10, no. 4:35–41.

Saltzman, Jason. 2015. "Drop Entrepreneurs, Not Bombs." *CNN.com.* http://money.cnn.com/2015/04/10/technology/kuwait-entrepreneurs/index.html.

Sandvig, Christian. 2012. "Connection at Ewiiaapaayp Mountain." In *Race after the Internet,* edited by Lisa Nakamura and Peter Chow White. New York: Routledge.

Sanyal, Kalyan. 2007. *Rethinking Capitalist Development: Primitive Accumulation, Governmentality, and Postcolonial Capitalism.* New Delhi: Routledge.

Sanyal, Kalyan, and Rajesh Bhattacharyya. 2009. "Beyond the Factory: Globalisation, Informalisation of Production and the New Locations of Labour." *Economic and Political Weekly* 44, no. 22 (May 30–June 5): 35–44.

Sarkar, Jadunath. 1917. *Economics of British India.* 4th ed. Calcutta: M. C. Sarkar & Sons. http://www.archive.org/stream/economicsofbriti00sarkrich#page/50/mode/2up.

Sarkar, Sreela. 2017. "Passionate Producers: Corporate Interventions in Expanding the Promise of the Information Society." *Communication, Culture & Critique* 10, no. 2 (June): 241–60. https://doi.org/101111/cccr.12159.

Sarkar, Swagato. 2014. "Contract Farming and McKinsey's Plan for Transforming Agriculture into Agribusiness in West Bengal." *Journal of South Asian Development* 9, no. 3 (December 1): 235–51. https://doi.org/10.1177/0973174114549100.

Satchell, C., and P. Dourish. 2009. "Beyond the User: Use and Non-Use in HCI." In *Proceedings of OzCHI 2007.* Melbourne.

Saxenian, Annalee. 1996. *Regional Advantage: Culture and Competition in Silicon Valley and Route 128.* Cambridge, MA: Harvard University Press.

———. 2006. *The New Argonauts.* Cambridge, MA: Harvard University Press.

Schindler, Seth. 2014. "Producing and Contesting the Formal/Informal Divide: Regulating Street Hawking in Delhi, India." *Urban Studies* 51, no. 12: 2596–2612.

Schneider, Nathan. 2013. *Thank You, Anarchy: Notes from the Occupy Apocalypse.* Berkeley: University of California Press.

Schumacher, E. F. 1973. *Small Is Beautiful: Economics as If People Mattered.* New York: Harper & Row.

Schumpeter, Joseph A. 1934. *The Theory of Economic Development: An Inquiry into Profits, Capital, Credit, Interest, and the Business Cycle*. New Brunswick, NJ: Transaction Books.

———. 1947. "The Creative Response in Economic History." *Journal of Economic History* 7, no. 2:149–59.

Schwittay, Anke. 2008. "'A Living Lab' Corporate Delivery of ICTs in Rural India." *Science, Technology & Society* 13, no. 2:175–209.

Scott, David. 1995. "Colonial Governmentality." *Social Text*, no. 43:191–220. https://doi .org/10.2307/466631.

 Scott, James C. 1998. *Seeing like a State: How Certain Schemes to Improve the Human Condition Have Failed*. New Haven, CT: Yale University Press.

Scott, Mark. 2015. "What Uber Can Learn from Airbnb's Global Expansion." *New York Times*. July 7. https://www.nytimes.com/2015/07/08/technology/what-uber-can-learn-from -airbnbs-global-expansion.html.

Segal, L. D., and J. F. Suri. 1997. "The Empathic Practitioner: Measurement and Interpretation of User Experience." In *Proceedings of the Human Factors and Ergonomics Society Annual Meeting*, 1:451. Human Factors and Ergonomics Society. http://search.proquest.com/openview/b70 abb11b9072b3d5623a5888104305a/1?pq-origsite=gscholar.

Selvaratnam, V. 1988. "Higher Education Co-Operation and Western Dominance of Knowledge Creation and Flows in Third World Countries." *Higher Education* 17, no. 1.

Sen, A. 1999. "The Possibility of Social Choice on JSTOR." *American Economic Review* 89, no. 3 (June): 349–78.

———. 2000a. "A Decade of Human Development." *Journal of Human Development* 1, no. 1:17–23.

———. 2000b. *Development as Freedom*. New York: Anchor Books.

Sengers, P., K. Boehner, S. David, and J. J. Kaye. 2005. "Reflective Design." In *Proceedings of the 4th Decennial Conference on Critical Computing: Between Sense and Sensibility*, 49–58. New York: ACM.

Sengupta, D. 2012. "India Achieves a 10.2% Internet Penetration Rate." *Economic Times of India*. April 12. http://articles.economictimes.indiatimes.com/2012-04-10/news /31318824_1_internet-users-penetration-number-of-facebook-users.

Sengupta, Mitu. 2015. "Modi Planning: What the NITI Aayog Suggests about the Aspirations and Practices of the Modi Government." *South Asia: Journal of South Asian Studies* 38, no. 4:791–806.

Sennett, Richard. 2006. *The Culture of the New Capitalism*. New Haven: Yale University Press.

Sethi, Kiran Bir. 2008. "The Man behind the Mahatma." *Gandhi-King Community*. September 17. http://gandhiking.ning.com/forum/topics/2043530:Topic:3348.

———. 2009. "Kiran Bir Sethi Teaches Kids to Take Charge." *TEDIndia*. November. TED Talk video. http://www.ted.com/talks/kiran_bir_sethi_teaches_kids_to_take_charge.html.

Shah, H. 2011. *The Production of Modernization: Daniel Lerner, Mass Media, and the Passing of Traditional Society*. Philadelphia: Temple University Press.

Shah, P. 2013. "India CSR Bill Creates Ripples in the Social Sector." *Acumen* (blog). March 12. http:// acumen.org/blog/our-world/new-bill-means-big-funding-for-indias-social-enterprises/.

Shahin, Saif. 2017. "Facing up to Facebook: How Digital Activism, Independent Regulation, and Mass Media Foiled a Neoliberal Threat to Net Neutrality." *Information, Communication & Society* (June 26): 1–17. https://doi.org/10.1080/1369118X.2017.1340494.

Sharma, Anita. 2014. "Design Manifesto (for a Design Enabled Technical Education)." Ministry of Human Resource Development, Government of India. https://web.archive.org/web/20171215092734/http://design.iith.ac.in/pdfs/DesignManifesto.pdf.

———. 2015. "Harnessing Heritage." *Financial Chronicle.* http://archives.mydigitalfc.com/indian-knowledge-series/harnessing-heritage-543.

Sharma, Anuradha. 2016. "If India's Demonetization Was All about Going Digital, Then Why the Rush?" *Diplomat.* December 1. http://thediplomat.com/2016/12/if-indias-demonetization-was-all-about-going-digital-then-why-the-rush/.

Sharma, Sarah. 2014. *In the Meantime: Temporality and Cultural Politics.* Durham, NC: Duke University Press.

Sherman, Erik. 2010. "Google Struggles with Its 'Do First, Ask Forgiveness Later' Strategy." *CBS News.* March 12. https://www.cbsnews.com/news/google-struggles-with-its-do-first-ask-forgiveness-later-strategy/.

Shinn, Larry. 1984. "Auroville: Visionary Images and Social Consequences in a South Indian Utopian Community." *Religious Studies* 20, no. 2:239–53.

Shiva, Vandana. 1993. "The Greening of the Global Reach." In *Global Visions: Beyond the New World Order,* edited by Jeremy Brecher, John Brown Childs, and Jill Cutler, 53–60. Boston: South End Press.

———. 1999. "Ecological Balance in an Era of Globalization." In *Global Ethics and Environment,* edited by Nicholas Low, 47–69. London: Routledge.

———. 2001. *Protect Or Plunder? Understanding Intellectual Property Rights.* London: Zed Books.

Silverstein, M. 2003. *Talking Politics: The Substance of Style from Abe to "W."* Cambridge: Prickly Paradigm Press.

Singh, Richa, and Richa Nagar. 2006. "In the Aftermath of Critique : The Journey after Sangtin Yatra." In *Colonial and Post-Colonial Geographies of India,* edited by Saraswati Raju, M. Satish Kumar, and Stuart Corbridge. New Delhi: Sage India.

Simon, Herbert A. 1981. *The Sciences of the Artificial.* Vol. 136. Cambride, MA: MIT Press.

Sims, Christo. 2017. *Disruptive Fixation: School Reform and the Pitfalls of Techno-Idealism.* Princeton, NJ: Princeton University Press.

Singh, Manmohan. 1991. General Budget 1991–91, Lok Sabha Debates. July 24.

Singh, Shubha. 2010. "What an Idea!" *India Now* 1, no. 5 (December–January): 20–23.

Slaughter, Anne-Marie. 2009. "America's Edge: Power in the Networked Century." *Foreign Affairs* 88, no. 1:94–113.

Snow, D. A., et al. 1986. "Frame Alignment Processes, Micromobilization, and Movement Participation." *American Sociological Review,* 464–81.

Social Research Unit, Bill and Melinda Gates Foundation. 2011. "Achieving Lasting Impact at Scale: Behavior Change Innovations in Low-Income Countries." November 1–2.

Special Correspondent. 2010. "New 5,000-Crore Fund Proposed to Promote Innovation." *Hindu.* http://www.thehindu.com/todays-paper/tp-national/tp-newdelhi/New-5000-crore-fund-proposed-to-promote-innovation/article15910813.ece.

Spitz, R. 2002. *HfG Ulm: The View Behind the Foreground: The Political History.* Stuttgart: Edition Axel Menges.

Spivak, Gayatri. 1996. "Scattered Speculations on the Question of Value." In *The Spivak Reader,* edited by Donna Landry and Gerald MacLean. New York: Routledge.

"Spread Quality Wave—CII Chief." 2003. *Business Standard*. November 6.

Srinivas, Nidhi. 2008. "Mimicry and Revival: The Transfer and Transformation of Management Knowledge to India, 1959–1990." *International Studies of Management & Organization* 38, no. 4:38–57.

Srinivasan, Janaki, and Jenna Burrell. 2013. "Revisiting the Fishers of Kerala, India." In *Proceedings of the Sixth International Conference on Information and Communication Technologies and Development: Full Papers*, vol. 1, 56–66. New York: ACM. https://doi.org/10.1145/2516604.2516618.

Srinivasan, Radhika. 1997. "Export Processing Zones in the Context of Trade Liberalization: The Salience of Casualized Labor in India." Ph.D. dissertation, Cornell University.

Srivastava, Sanjay. 1998. *Constructing Post-Colonial India: National Character and the Doon School*. Culture and Communication in Asia. London: Routledge.

Stangler, D., and J. Konczal. 2013. "Give Me Your Entrepreneurs, Your Innovators: Estimating Employment Impact of a Startup Visa." SSRN Scholarly Paper no. 2226454. Ewing Marion Kauffman Foundation. February. http://papers.ssrn.com/abstract=2226454.

Staples, Eugene S. 1992. *40 Years: A Learning Curve: The Ford Foundation in India 1952–1992*. New York: Ford Foundation.

Star, S. L., and A. Strauss. 1999. "Layers of Silence, Arenas of Voice: The Ecology of Visible and Invisible Work." *Computer Supported Cooperative Work* 8:9–30.

Stark, David. 2009. *The Sense of Dissonance: Accounts of Worth in Economic Life*. Princeton, NJ: Princeton University Press.

Starosielski, N. 2015. *The Undersea Network*. Durham, NC: Duke University Press.

#startupindia. N.d. "Guidelines for Corporates to Set Up Incubators." Ministry of Commerce and Industry, Government of India. https://startupindia.gov.in/pdffile.php?title=Guidelines for Corporates to set up Incubators&type=information&content_type=&q=guidelines_for_corporates_to_set_up_incubators.pdf.

Stiglitz, J. E. 2002. *Globalization and Its discontents*. New York: Norton.

———. 2007. *Making Globalization Work*. New York: Norton.

Stolberg, Sheryl Gay, and Jim Yardley. 2010. "Countering China, Obama Backs India for U.N. Council." *New York Times*. November 8. http://www.nytimes.com/2010/11/09/world/asia/09prexy.html?_r=0.

Straw, Will. 2001. "Scenes and Sensibilities." *Public*, no. 22–23.

Subramanian, Ajantha. 2015. "Making Merit: The Indian Institutes of Technology and the Social Life of Caste." *Comparative Studies in Society and History* 57, no. 2:291–322. doi:10.1017/S0010417515000043.

Subramanian, Arvind. 2013. "Arvind Subramanian Keynote." India Innovation Conference. PennGlobal. Youtube video. https://www.youtube.com/watch?v=zmI0jW5SvHQ.

Subramanian, Samanth. 2011. "Where Is India's Steve Jobs?" *New York Times: India Ink* (blog). October 10. http://india.blogs.nytimes.com/2011/10/10/where-is-indias-steve-jobs/?_r=0.

Suchman, L. 1994. "Do Categories Have Politics?" *Computer Supported Cooperative Work (CSCW)* 2, no. 3:177–90.

———. 1995. "Making Work Visible." *Communications of the ACM* 38, no. 9:56–64.

———. 1996. "Supporting Articulation Work." *Computerization and Controversy: Value Conflicts and Social Choices* 2:407–23.

———. 2002. "Practice-Based Design of Information Systems: Notes from the Hyperdeveloped World." *Information Society* 18, no. 2:139. https://doi.org/10.1080/01972240290075066.

———. 2007. *Human-Machine Reconfigurations: Plans and Situated Actions.* Cambridge: Cambridge University Press.

———. 2008. "Striking Likeness to Difference." Paper presented at 4S/EASST, Rotterdam, August 23. http://www.sand14.com/archive/relocatinginnovation/download/suchman_4S2008.pdf.

———. 2011. "Anthropological Relocations and the Limits of Design." *Annual Review of Anthropology* 40, no. 1:1–18. http://doi.org/10.1146/annurev.anthro.041608.105640.

Suchman, L., and Libby Bishop. 2000. "Problematizing Innovation as a Critical Project." *Technology Analysis and Management* 12, no. 3:327–33.

Sundaram, Ravi. 2010. *Pirate Modernity: Delhi's Media Urbanism.* New York: Routledge.

Sunder, Madhavi. 2006. "IP^3." *Stanford Law Review* 59, no. 2:257–332.

———. 2007. "The Invention of Traditional Knowledge." *Law and Contemporary Problems* 70, no. 2:97–124.

Sunder Rajan, Kaushik. 2005. "Subjects of Speculation: Emergent Life Sciences and Market Logics in the United States and India." *American Anthropologist* 107, no. 1 (March 1): 19–30. https://doi.org/10.1525/aa.2005.107.1.019.

———. 2006. *Biocapital: The Constitution of Postgenomic Life.* Durham, NC: Duke University Press.

Suri, Jane Fulton. 2001. "The Next 50 Years: Future Challenges and Opportunities for Empathy in Our Science." *Ergonomics* 44, no. 14:1278–89.

Suri, Jane Fulton, and IDEO. 2005. *Thoughtless Acts? Observations on Intuitive Design.* San Francisco: Chronicle Books.

Surie, Gita. 2014. "The University as a Catalyst of Innovation, Entrepreneurship, and New Markets in the Indian System of Innovation." In *Innovation in India: Combining Economic Growth with Inclusive Development,* edited by Shyama Ramani. Cambridge: Cambridge University Press.

Suzuki, S., and T. Dixon. 1970. *Zen Mind, Beginner's Mind.* New York: Walker/Weatherhill.

Takhteyev, Yuri. 2012. *Coding Places: Software Practice in a South American City.* Cambridge, MA: MIT Press.

Tanaka, S. 2006. *New Times in Modern Japan.* Princeton, NJ: Princeton University Press

Taylor, A. S. 2011. "Out There." In *Proceedings of the SIGCHI Conference on Human Factors in Computing Systems,* 685–94. New York: ACM.

Tejaswi, M. J. and S. John. 2012. "What May Spur Internet Penetration in India." *Times of India.* September 4. http://timesofindia.indiatimes.com/tech/enterprise-it/infrastructure/What-may-spur-internet-penetration-in-India/articleshow/16249083.cms?referral=PM.

Thaler, R. H., and Cass R. Sunstein. 2009. *Nudge: Improving Decisions about Health, Wealth, and Happiness.* New York: Penguin.

Thapar, R. 1974. "Report of Review of Committee on National Institute of Design." Ministry of Industrial Development, Government of India. Delhi.

Thomas, Pradip Ninan. 2012. *Digital India: Understanding Information, Communication and Social Change.* Delhi: Sage India.

Thomke, Stefan, and Mona Sinha. 2013. "The Dabbawala System: On-Time Delivery, Everytime." 610059–PDF–ENG. Harvard Business School. January 22.

Thompson, Edward P. 1971. "The Moral Economy of the English Crowd in the Eighteenth Century." *Past & Present*, no. 50:76–136.

Thrift, N. 1997. "The Rise of Soft Capitalism." *Journal for Cultural Research* 1, no. 1:29–57.

———. 2008. *Non-Representation Theory: Space, Politics, Affect*. Oxford: Routledge.

Tiku, Nitasha. 2017. "Google Deliberately Confuses Its Employees, Fed Says." *Wired*. July 25. https://www.wired.com/story/google-department-of-labor-gender-pay-lawsuit/.

Townsend, John Converse. 2014. "Ready for the Real World: How India's Riverside School Graduates Changemakers." *Ashoka Changemakers* (blog). May 13. https://www.changemakers.com/play2learn/blog/ready-real-world-how-indias-riverside-school-graduates.

Traweek, S. 1988. *Beamtimes and Life Times. The World of High Energy Physicists*. Cambridge, MA: Harvard University Press.

Trouillot, Michel Rolph. 2002. "The Otherwise Modern: Caribbean Lessons from the Savage Slot." In *Critically Modern: Alternatives, Alterities, Anthropologies*, 220–37. Bloomington: Indiana University Press.

Truelove, Y., and E. Mawdsley. 2011. "Discourses of Citizenship and Criminality in Clean, Green Delhi." In *A Companion to the Anthropology of India*, edited by Isabelle Clark-Deces, 407–425. Oxford: Blackwell.

Tsing, Anna Lowenhaupt. 2005. *Friction: An Ethnography of Global Connection*. Princeton, NJ: Princeton University Press.

———. 2008. "The Global Situation." In *The Anthropology of Globalization*, edited by J. X. Inda and R. Rosaldo. 2nd ed. Oxford: Blackwell.

———. 2009. "Supply Chains and the Human Condition." *Rethinking Marxism* 21, no. 2:148–76. doi:10.1080/08935690902743088.

———. 2015a. "Salvage Accumulation, or the Structural Effects of Capitalist Generativity." *Cultural Anthropology* website. March 30. https://culanth.org/fieldsights/656-salvage-accumulation-or-the-structural-effects-of-capitalist-generativity.

———. 2015b. *The Mushroom at the End of the World: On the Possibility of Life in Capitalist Ruins*. Princeton, NJ: Princeton University Press.

Turnbull, D. 2000. *Masons, Tricksters and Cartographers: Comparative Studies in the Sociology of Scientific and Indigenous Knowledge*. London: Routledge.

Turner, Fred. 2006. *From Counterculture to Cyberculture: Stewart Brand, the Whole Earth Network*. Chicago: University of Chicago Press.

———. 2009. "Burning Man at Google: A Cultural Infrastructure for New Media Production." *New Media & Society* 11, no. 1–2:73.

———. 2013. *The Democratic Surround: Multimedia and American Liberalism from World War II to the Psychedelic Sixties*. Chicago: University of Chicago Press.

United Nations Development Programme (UNDP). 2017. "India Human Development Reports." http://hdr.undp.org/en/countries/profiles/IND.

United States Senate. 2010. "Building on Success: New Directions in Global Health." Hearing before the Committee on Foreign Relations, United States Senate, 111th Congress. March 10. http://purl.fdlp.gov/GPO/gpo423.

Upadhya, Carol. 2009. "Imagining India: Software and the Ideology of Liberalisation." *South African Review of Sociology* 40, no. 1:76–93.

Upadhya, Carol, and A. R. Vasavi. 2006. *Work, Culture and Sociality in the Indian Information Technology (IT) Industry: A Sociological Study*. Bangalore: National Institute of Advanced Studies. http://eprints.nias.res.in/107/.

———, eds. 2008. *In an Outpost of a Global Economy: Work and Workers in India's Technology Industry*. Abingdon, UK: Routledge.

Upadhyaya, Venus. 2014. "Startup Village in India Shows Path for Indian Innovation." *Epoch Times*. July 24. http://www.theepochtimes.com/n3/811603-startup-village-in-india-shows-path-for-indian-innovation/.

Uncertain Commons, ed. 2013. *Speculate This!* Durham, NC: Duke University Press.

USAID. 2012. "USAID/India Country Development Cooperation Strategy: 2012–2016." https://www.usaid.gov/sites/default/files/documents/1861/India_CDCS.pdf.

Vaidya, A. P. 2014. "The Origin of the Forest, Private Property, and the State: The Political Life of India's Forest Rights Act." PhD. dissertation, Harvard University.

Van Der Veer, Peter. 2005. "Virtual India: Indian IT Labor and the Nation-State." In *Sovereign Bodies: Citizens, Migrants, and States in the Postcolonial World*, edited by Thomas Blom Hansen and Finn Stepputat, 276–90. Princeton, NJ: Princeton University Press.

Varadarajan, Latha. 2010. *The Domestic Abroad: Diasporas in International Relations*. New York: Oxford University Press.

Varma, Meher. 2015. "Making Designs on Fashion: Producing Contemporary Indian Aesthetics." Ph.D. dissertation, University of California Los Angeles.

Vatsal, A. B. 1970. "Managerial Ideology in India." *Economic and Political Weekly*, M2–M18.

Venkatesan, Soumhya. 2009. "Rethinking Agency: Persons and Things in the Heterotopia of 'Traditional Indian Craft.'" *Journal of the Royal Anthropological Institute* 15, no. 1 (March 1): 78–95. https://doi.org/10.1111/j.1467-9655.2008.01531.x.

Venugopal, Vasudha. 2016. "Demonetisation in a booming economy is like shooting at the tyres of a racing car: Jean Drèze." November 22.

Vidyasagar, N. 2004. "Design—Next BPO Frontier for India." *Times of India*. March 2. https://timesofindia.indiatimes.com/business/india-business/Design-Next-BPO-frontier-for-India/articleshow/527729.cms.

Viswanathan, Vijayalakshmi. 2011. "Globalising India and Inclusive Growth." *RITES Journal*. January. http://demo.indiaenvironmentportal.org.in/files/globalising%20India.pdf.

Vora, Kalindi. 2015. *Life Support: Biocapital and the New History of Outsourced Labor*. Minneapolis: University of Minnesota Press.

Vyas, H. Kumar. 1984. "Design: Art and Craft as a United Concept." *India International Centre Quarterly* 11, no. 4:91–94.

Vyas, P. 2009. "Tete a tete: Conjuring Change." *DSigned* 1, no. 1:3–7.

Wadhwa, V. 2011. "TechCrunch: Finally, a Startup Visa Bill That Works." *Wadhwa.com*. March 14. http://wadhwa.com/2011/03/14/finally-a-startup-visa-bill-that-works/.

Waring, Marilyn. 2003. "Counting for Something! Recognising Women's Contribution to the Global Economy through Alternative Accounting Systems." *Gender and Development* 11, no. 1:35–43.

Wark, McKenzie. 2009. *A Hacker Manifesto*. Cambridge, MA: Harvard University Press.

———. 2015. "Cognitive Capitalism." *Public Seminar*. February 19. http://www.publicseminar.org/2015/02/cog-cap/.

"Why We're Here: WaterAid Global." 2018. January 19.

Wertz, B. 2013. "The 'Startup Visa': Why Canada Made It a Priority & Why the U.S. Should Too." *VentureBeat.com.* April 19. http://venturebeat.com/2013/04/19/the-startup-visa-why-canada-made-it-a-priority-why-the-u-s-should-too/.

Wigley, Mark. 2001. "Network Fever." *Grey Room,* no. 4 (July): 83–122.

Wilkie, Alex.2014. "Prototyping as Event: Designing the Future of Obesity." *Journal of Cultural Economy* 7, no. 4 (October 2): 476–92. https://doi.org/10.1080/17530350.2013.859631.

Williams, Rebecca. 2014. "The Production of India as a Laboratory for Population Control." Paper presented at Spaces of Technoscience Workshop. July 21–22. National University Singapore.

Wilson, Dominic, and Roopa Purushothaman. 2003. "Dreaming with BRICs: The Path to 2050." *Global Economics Paper* no. 99:1.

Winograd, T. 1996. *Bringing Design to Software.* New York: ACM Press; Menlo Park, CA: Addison-Wesley.

Winograd, T., and F. Flores. 1986. *Understanding Computers and Cognition: A New Foundation for Design.* Menlo Park, CA: Addison-Wesley.

Wisnioski, Matthew H. 2012. *Engineers for Change: Competing Visions of Technology in 1960s America.* Cambridge, MA: MIT Press.

Wood, S. J. 1989. "Review Article: New Wave Management?" *Work, Employment & Society* 3, no. 3:379–402.

World Bank. 2004. *World Development Report 2004: Making Services Work for Poor People.* Washington, DC: World Bank. https://openknowledge.worldbank.org/handle/10986/5986.

———. 2015. *World Development Report 2015: Mind, Society, and Behavior.* Washington, DC: World Bank. http://www.worldbank.org/en/publication/wdr2015.

World Bank Institute. 2008. *Measuring Knowledge in the World's Economies.* Washington, DC: World Bank.

Wright, P., and J. McCarthy. 2008. "Empathy and Experience in HCI." In *Proceeding of the Twenty-Sixth Annual SIGCHI Conference on Human Factors in Computing Systems,* 637–46. Florence, Italy: ACM. http://doi.org/10.1145/1357054.1357156.

Wyatt, A. 2005. "Building the Temples of Postmodern India: Economic Constructions of National Identity." *Contemporary South Asia* 14, no. 4:465–80.

Xiang, Biao. 2007. *Global "Body Shopping": An Indian Labor System in the Information Technology Industry.* Princeton, NJ: Princeton University Press.

Yurchak, Alexei. 2002. "Entrepreneurial Governmentality in Postsocialist Russia." In *The New Entrepreneurs of Europe and Asia: Patterns of Business Development in Russia, Eastern Europe, and China,* edited by Victoria E. Bonnell and Thomas B. Gold, 278–324. New York: M. E. Sharpe.

———. 2003. "Russian Neoliberal: The Entrepreneurial Ethic and the Spirit of 'True Careerism.'" *Russian Review* 62, no. 1:72–90. doi:10.1111/1467-9434.00264.

Zachariah, Benjamin. 2004. *Nehru.* New York: Routledge.

———. 2005. *Developing India: An Intellectual and Social History.* New Delhi: Oxford University Press.

Zakus, D., O. Bhattacharyya, and X. Wei. 2014. "Health Systems, Management, and Organization in Global Health." In *Understanding Global Health*, edited by W. H. Markle, M. A. Fisher, and R. A. Smego. 2nd ed. New York: McGraw-Hill Education.

Zaloom, Caitlin. 2006. *Out of the Pits: Traders and Technology from Chicago to London*. Chicago: University of Chicago Press.

Zuboff, Shoshana. 1988. *In The Age of the Smart Machine: The Future of Work and Power*. New York: Basic Books.

Zukin, Sharon. 1996. *The Cultures of Cities*. Hoboken, NJ: Wiley-Blackwell.

INDEX

access, 2, 8, 29, 62, 122–123, 197; in intellectual property, 36
Acumen Fund, 145, 216–217
adding value, 2, 22, 83, 90, 96, 99–100, 107, 140, 175, 198–199, 202, 213; contention over, 98–99; to the nation, 84
affect, 4, 32, 64, 67, 71–72, 84–85, 139, 143, 152–153, 161–168, 170–171
agency, 66, 75, 119–122, 127–128, 137, 160, 173–174, 209, 215
agent of change, 1
Ahmed, Sara, 170–171
Ahmedabad, 53, 56, 64, 68, 79,
alienation, 58, 77, 118; and children, 56
alternative futures, 160
analysis paralysis, 129, 158
antipolitical, 66, 137, 139, 212
Appadurai, Arjun, 3, 214
Apple. *See* Jobs, Steve
Arab Spring, 26
artificial intelligence (AI), 160–161
Ashoka, 17, 76, 116, 145, 164, 216–217
aspiration, 3, 32, 46, 60–61, 76, 86–87, 107, 109, 132, 160, 162, 174, 201, 215
Aurobindo, Sri, 73–75
Auroville, 75, 91
authenticity, 3, 65, 67, 69–73, 76–77, 83, 91–92, 96, 98, 107, 192–202, 217–218; as group identity, 195–202; as individual identity, 55–78, 89–92; as input to production, 89–92
authoritarianism, 24, 69, 79, 109, 143, 181

balanced growth, 9, 26
Balaram, Singapalli, 186–187
Banerjee, Abhijit, 42

Barefoot College, 50–51
Bauhaus, 67, 186
Baumol, William, 208, 215–216
Bear, Laura, 35, 138–139
beginners, 17, 159–160. *See also* naïveté
bias to action, 22, 65, 69, 110–112, 116–117, 124–140, 158, 216
Bir Kasturi, Poonam, 50–51
Bir Sethi, Kiran, 55–56, 60–83, 86, 90, 116, 210
BJP (Bharatiya Janata Party), 8–9, 38, 44
bottom of the pyramid, 43, 47, 52, 85, 97, 110, 151, 190, 207, 211
Bowker, Geoffrey, 124, 137
brain drain, 31, 60–61
brainstorming, 14, 65, 88, 101–103, 112, 116–117, 121–122, 129, 142, 195
brand, 11, 41, 44, 83–84, 87, 89, 107, 175, 182, 189, 198–204
BRICs, 43
bureaucrats, 29, 183, 196

capacity building, 69, 196
capacity to aspire, 214–215
caste: and citizenship, 8; and education, 59, 72; erasure of, 79–82; and the global Indian, 5–6, 39; haunting by, 67–68; and liberal community, 69; and privilege, 62
Chakrabarty, Dipesh, 134, 175
Chakravartty, Paula, 38
channelizing, 68
Chatterjee, Partha, 29, 46,
children, 25, 47–50, 56–67, 72, 79–80, 210
China, as an authoritarian model for India, 24, 69, 109
choiceless identities, 68

A NOTE ON THE TYPE

This book has been composed in Arno, an Old-style serif typeface in the
classic Venetian tradition, designed by Robert Slimbach at Adobe.